STRESS
and COPING
in Time of War

Generalizations from the
Israeli Experience

Brunner/Mazel Psychosocial Stress Series
Charles R. Figley, Ph.D., Series Editor

1. Stress Disorders Among Vietnam Veterans
   Edited by Charles R. Figley, Ph.D.
2. Stress and the Family Vol. 1: Coping with Normative Transitions
   Edited by Hamilton I. McCubbin, Ph.D., and Charles R. Figley, Ph.D.
3. Stress and the Family Vol. 2: Coping with Catastrophe
   Edited by Charles R. Figley, Ph.D., and Hamilton I. McCubbin, Ph.D.
4. Trauma and Its Wake: The Study and Treatment of Post-Traumatic Stress Disorder
   Edited by Charles R. Figley, Ph.D.
5. Post-Traumatic Stress Disorder and the War Veteran Patient
   Edited by William E. Kelly, M.D.
6. The Crime Victim's Book, Second Edition
   By Morton Bard, Ph.D., and Dawn Sangrey
7. Stress and Coping in Time of War: Generalizations from the Israeli Experience
   Edited by Norman A. Milgram, Ph.D.

BRUNNER/MAZEL PSYCHOSOCIAL STRESS SERIES No. 7

STRESS and COPING in Time of War

Generalizations from the Israeli Experience

Edited by

Norman A. Milgram

BRUNNER/MAZEL Publishers • New York

Library of Congress Cataloging-in-Publication Data

Stress and coping in time of war.

(Brunner/Mazel psychosocial stress series; no. 7)
"All chapters, with one exception, were presented
at the Third International Conference on Psychological
Stress and Adjustment in Time of War and Peace
(Tel-Aviv, January 1983) . . . [and] extensively
rewritten for publication"—Pref.
Bibliography: p. 353
Includes indexes.
1. Stress (Psychology)—Congresses. 2. War—Psychological aspects—Congresses. 3. Post-traumatic stress
disorder—Congresses. 4. Adjustment (Psychology)—
Congresses. 5. Lebanon—History—Israeli intervention,
1982—Psychological aspects—Congresses. I. Milgram,
Norman A. II. International Conference on Psychological
Stress and Adjustment in Time of War and Peace (3rd:
1983: Tel-Aviv, Israel). III. Series. [DNLM:
1. Adaptation, Psychological. 2. Combat Disorders.
3. Stress—psychology. 4. Stress Disorders, Post-
Traumatic. 5. War. W1 BR 917TB / WM 184 S914]
BF575.S75S772 1986   155.9   86-9715
ISBN 0-87630-430-7

Copyright © 1986 by Norman A. Milgram

Published by
BRUNNER/MAZEL, INC.
19 Union Square
New York, New York 10003

MANUFACTURED IN THE UNITED STATES OF AMERICA

This volume is dedicated to the important women in my life

Mother Ann

Wife Roberta

Daughters Shoshana and Wendy

and Granddaughters Rachel, Tali, and Jenny

Editorial Note

Stress and Coping in Time of War is the seventh book in the Psychosocial Stress Book Series. The purpose of the Series is to develop and publish books that in some way make a significant contribution to the understanding and management of the psychosocial stress reaction paradigm. The books are designed to advance the work of clinicians, researchers, and other professionals involved in the varied aspects of human services. The primary readership of this Series includes those practitioners, scholars, and their students who are committed to this purpose.

The quality and significance of the Series are guided by a nationally and internationally respected group of scholars who compose the Editorial Board. The Board must review and approve each book that is published in the Series. Like the readership, the Board represents the fields of general medicine, pediatrics, psychiatry, nursing, psychology, sociology, social work, family therapy, political science, and anthropology.

Books in the Series focus on the stress associated with a wide variety of psychosocial stressors. Similar to this present volume, the first volume in the Series (*Stress Disorders Among Vietnam Veterans*), published in 1978, focused on the immediate and long-term effects of war. It alerted the nation to the difficulties of coping with one's war experiences long after the war was over. It provided a state-of-the art source book for scholars and practitioners working in the area of war-related stress reactions and disorders. With the publication of that book and other resources, mental health professionals and policy makers began to recognize the complexity of the postwar readjustment of Vietnam veterans. Soon a national outreach program emerged within the Veterans Administration with storefront Vet Centers in every major city in the country and inpatient treatment programs in many VA Medical Centers across the country to focus on these problems. As a result, thousands of professionals have since become aware of the special circumstances of war veterans.

The next two volumes in the Series, *Stress and the Family, Volume I: Coping With Normative Transitions* and *Stress and the Family, Volume II: Coping with Catastrophe*, provide a comprehensive summary of the available information about how families cope with psychosocial stress. The former volume attends to the typical and predictable stressors of family life, whereas the latter volume focuses on how families cope with extraordinary and unpredictable stressors. Each chapter follows the same outline, which first introduces the stressor, then identifies the functional and dysfunctional ways families and family members cope.

Volume #4 in the Series is *Trauma and Its Wake: The Study and Treatment of Post-Traumatic Stress Disorder.* It is the first attempt to generalize research and clinical findings among a wide variety of traumatic or catastrophic events towards a generalized view of traumatic and post-traumatic stress reactions. Chapters focus on the immediate and long-term psychosocial consequences of exposure to many types of catastrophic events: war, rape, natural disasters, incest. Other chapters focus on effective methods of treating or preventing stress reactions or disorders. It is the first in a series of books that will review the latest innovations in theory, research, and treatment of this disorder, caused by a wide variety of stressful life events.

The fifth volume in the Series, *Post-Traumatic Stress Disorder and the War Veteran Patient,* again focuses on war veterans in general, and Vietnam war veterans in particular. Building upon the most important contributions of the past, this volume provides a specific blueprint for conceptualizing and treating war-related post-traumatic stress disorders. In many ways, it serves as an excellent introduction for the volume that follows this editorial note. Both are concerned about the direct aftermath of war on those who fought it, though focusing on significantly different conflicts.

Volume #6, *The Crime Victim's Book,* presents yet another context in which individuals struggle to manage their violent life experiences. This beautifully written book is intended as a primer for those interested in working with victims of crime, particularly violent crime, although the authors hoped that victims themselves would read it. It provides summaries of two important recent task force reports: one produced by the President's Task Force on Victims of Crime and the other by the American Psychological Association Task Force on Victims of Crime and Violence, which was chaired by the book's senior author, Morton Bard.

Together with this most recent Volume #7, all these books form a new orientation for thinking about human behavior under extraordinary conditions. They provide an integrated set of source books for scholars and practitioners interested in how and why some individuals and social systems thrive under stressful situations, while others do not.

Stress and Coping in Time of War is the first in the Series to focus on an international issue: the special psychosocial stress of war upon not only those who fight, but also the nations, communities, and social systems directly affected. Although the volume focuses on the special circumstances faced by one country, Israel, its content has far-reaching implications for any nation that must commit its resources to an all-out national defense. Indeed, considerable attention is focused on the Vietnam war, contrasting both the war and the response to it in the U.S. with Israel's most recent wars. In contrast to the other books published in this Series and elsewhere, *Stress and Coping in Time of War* focuses on the *context* of war and its multilevel impact. It is the first to focus on war-related stress and coping at the levels of the individual, the group, and the nation-state.

Norman Milgram, professor of psychology at Tel-Aviv University, is an internationally respected scholar and editor. He has been instrumental in the organization of several international conferences on the topic of this book. Indeed, most of the chapters were presented at the most recent conference in Israel in 1983 on the impact of war.

As editor, Milgram has performed an important service for his readers by writing a general introduction to the 22 chapters, integrative introductions for each of the five subdivisions of the book, and a closing chapter (in collaboration with Stevan Hobfoll) that reviews major concepts, applies them in a variety of stressful situations, and presents specific recommendations for research and practice. Each introduction provides a theoretical and factual context for the chapters with which it deals and offers elucidation of concepts where necessary.

Dr. Milgram's introduction provides not only an overview of the volume, but also important directions to conceptualization in the new and quickly emerging field of traumatic stress. He is especially insightful, for example, in noting the unique context of war as a stressor which can be generalized to other contexts only with great caution. Moreover, his introduction is extremely timely. In illustrating the impact of various national, warlike crises on government policy, he discusses the 1985 TWA hostage crisis in Beirut. He notes that prevailing assumptions about terrorism held by Western societies (i.e., the problem can be resolved and the government is responsible) exacerbate the problem.

Stress and Coping in Time of War, containing 22 chapters, is written by 34 scholars, representing six scientific disciplines and collaborating to provide new theoretical insights, scientific findings, and clinical treatment innovations. I am certain that it will be viewed as the most comprehensive review of the topic available for many years to come.

In the final chapter, in collaboration with Stevan Hobfoll, Milgram selectively reviews certain concepts and findings presented in the volume. They provide an integrative perspective which leads to specific recommendations for research, theory building, assessment/diagnosis, and therapeutic intervention in the area of war-related stress and coping. They attempt in the closing chapter—as did authors in many other chapters in the book—to derive generalizations from Israeli-based data that are applicable to non-war stressors and to other societies. Thus, for example, they apply the Salmon treatment principles (1919)—proximity, immediacy, expectancy, and community—to intervention in a recent major accident in which 19 children and 3 adults died in a school bus-train collision. They also propose an innovative treatment program for veterans with longstanding post-traumatic stress disorder refractory to conventional treatments. This basic retraining program, currently being used in Israel, may well be of value to Vietnam veterans.

To scholars and practitioners devoted to preventing and ameliorating human stress disorders and their causes, a book about war may seem inappropriate at best and antithetical to the goals of our profession at worst. It is argued at the close of the final chapter, however, that war is an inevitable reality of humankind, though all of us hope that some day this will no longer be so.

> In the meantime, societies have an obligation to care for their physically and emotionally wounded. Soldiers and civilians need to be treated by the best state-of-the-art techniques that psychology and psychiatry can provide. . . . We may also make efforts to enhance the quality of life in people affected by life stressors in general and by war-related stress in particular. (p. 352)

This volume is an eloquent and bold effort towards these goals and a valuable new addition to the Psychosocial Stress Book Series.

Charles R. Figley, Ph.D.
Purdue University
Series Editor

Contents

Editorial Note by Charles R. Figley vii

Contributors xv

Preface xix

General Introduction to the Field of War-Related Stress xxiii

SECTION I: THE ROLE OF ATTRIBUTION IN STRESS AND COPING

Introduction to Section I 3

1. An Attributional Analysis of War-Related Stress: Modes of Coping and Helping 9
   Norman Milgram

2. The Precipitating Event in Crisis Theory: Calamity or Opportunity 26
   Adrienne Chambon

3. The Masada Syndrome: A Case of Central Belief 32
   Daniel Bar-Tal

4. Pathogenesis and Salutogenesis in War and Other Crises: Who Studies the Successful Coper? 52
   Aaron Antonovsky and Judith Bernstein

SECTION II: RISK FACTORS IN COMBAT STRESS REACTIONS AND POST-TRAUMATIC STRESS DISORDERS (PTSD)

Introduction to Section II 67

5. Battle and Military Unit Characteristics and the Prevalence of Psychiatric Casualties 73
   Shabtai Noy, Chen Nardi, and Zahava Solomon

6. Who Is at High Risk for a Combat Stress Reaction Syndrome? 78
   Zahava Solomon, Shabtai Noy, and Reuven Bar-On

7. Subsequent Military Adjustment of Combat Stress Reaction
   Casualties: A Nine-Year Follow-Up Study 84
      Zahava Solomon, Bruce Oppenheimer, and Shabtai Noy
8. Risk Factors, Premorbid Adjustment, and Personality
   Characteristics of Soldiers with Refractory Combat Stress
   Reactions 91
      Ruben Segal and Chaim Margalit

SECTION III: TREATMENT OF COMBAT STRESS REACTIONS AND POST-TRAUMATIC STRESS DISORDERS IN THE WAR IN LEBANON

Introduction to Section III 97
9. The Clinical Picture of Combat Stress Reactions in the 1982 War
   in Lebanon: Cross-War Comparisons 103
      *Reuven Bar-On, Zahava Solomon, Shabtai Noy, and Chen
      Nardi*
10. The Forward Treatment of Combat Stress Reactions: A Test
    Case in the 1982 Conflict in Lebanon 110
      Shabtai Noy, Zahava Solomon, and Rami Benbenishti
11. A Therapeutic Community in a Forward Army Field Hospital:
    Treatment, Education, and Expectancy 117
      Yosef Toubiana, Norman Milgram, and Shabtai Noy
12A. The Combat Fitness Retraining Unit 129
      *Chaim Margalit, Yochanan Wozner, Chen Nardi, Ruben
      Segal, Yair Goren, and Yosef Triest*
12B. Behavioral Milieu of the Combat Fitness Retraining Unit 136
      *Yochanan Wozner, Chen Nardi, Chaim Margalit, and Ruben
      Segal*
12C. Behavioral Group Treatment 142
      Chen Nardi, Yochanan Wozner, and Chaim Margalit
12D. Dynamic Group Psychotherapy 147
      Yair Goren, Yosef Triest, and Chaim Margalit
12E. Individual Psychotherapy 155
      Chaim Margalit, Ruben Segal, and Yair Goren
12F. Physical Activities in Rehabilitation 168
      Chaim Margalit, Yochanan Wozner, and Ruben Segal
12G. A Multidimensional Model for Treatment of Post-Traumatic
     Stress Disorders: Summary Statement 172
      Yochanan Wozner and Chaim Margalit

SECTION IV: PERFORMANCE IN HIGHLY STRESSFUL SITUATIONS

Introduction to Section IV 177

13. Confidence Expectancy as a Predictor of Military Performance Under Stress 183
    Giora Keinan
14. Stress and Motivation During Maximal Physical Performance ... 197
    Ema Geron and Omri Inbar
15. The Effects of a Coacting Setting and Competitive Motivation on Performance Under Heat Stress 205
    Dan Zakay, Yoram Epstein, and Yair Shapiro
16. Componentiality as a Survival Strategy in a Total Institution: Case Study of a POW in Solitary Confinement in a Syrian Prison 216
    Ori Shachak
17. Coherence of Cognitive Appraisal and Coping in a Stressful Military Task: Parachute Jumping 230
    Benjamin Shalit, Leif Carlstedt, Berit Stahlberg Carlstedt, and Inga-Lill Taljedal Shalit

SECTION V: THE EFFECT OF WAR ON CIVILIAN POPULATIONS

Introduction to Section V 237

18. The Psychological Impact of Terrorism on Society: A Two-Edged Sword 243
    Nehemia Friedland and Ariel Merari
19. Survivors of Terrorist Victimization: A Follow-Up Study 257
    Ofra Ayalon and David Soskis
20. The Stress and Coping of Uprooted Settlers: The Yamit Experience 275
    Yosef Toubiana, Norman Milgram, and Herzl Falach
21. Civilian Adjustment to War-Related Stress 294
    Stevan Hobfoll

* * *

22. Generalizations from Theory and Practice in War-Related Stress 316
    Norman Milgram and Stevan Hobfoll

References 353
Author Index 373
Subject Index 381

Contributors

Aaron Antonovsky
Department of the Sociology of Health, Ben-Gurion University of the Negev, Beersheba

Ofra Ayalon
School of Education, Haifa University

Reuven Bar-On
Department of Mental Health, Israel Defense Forces

Daniel Bar-Tal
School of Education, Tel-Aviv University

Rami Benbenishti
Department of Mental Health, Israel Defense Forces and School of Social Work, The Hebrew University, Jerusalem

Judith Bernstein
Department of the Sociology of Health, Ben-Gurion University of the Negev, Beersheba

Berit Stahlberg Carlstedt
National Institute for Defense Research, Division of the Behavioral Sciences, Karlstad, Sweden

Leif Carlstedt
National Institute for Defense Research, Division of the Behavioral Sciences, Karlstad, Sweden

Adrienne Chambon
School of Social Work, Haifa University

Yoram Epstein
Heller Research Institute of Environmental Influences on Behavior, Tel-Aviv University

Herzl Falach
Tel Hashomer Hospital and Department of Psychology, Tel-Aviv University

Nehemia Friedland
Department of Psychology, Tel-Aviv University

Ema Geron
Department of Sports Psychology, Wingate Institute for Physical Education and Sport

Yair Goren
Arsuf Psychotherapy Clinic and Department of Psychotherapy, Sackler School of Medicine, Tel-Aviv University

Stevan Hobfoll
Department of Psychology, Tel-Aviv University

Omri Inbar
Mor Institute, Bnei Brak

Giora Keinan
Department of Psychology, Tel-Aviv University and Center for Research on Psychological Stress, Haifa University

Chaim Margalit
Department of Mental Health, Israel Defense Forces and Department of Psychology, Tel-Aviv University

Ariel Merari
Department of Psychology, Tel-Aviv University

Norman Milgram
Department of Psychology, Tel-Aviv University

Chen Nardi
Department of Mental Health, Israel Defense Forces

Shabtai Noy
Department of Mental Health, Israel Defense Forces

Bruce Oppenheimer
School of Education, The Hebrew University, Jerusalem

Ruben Segal
Kibbutz Child and Family Clinic, Tel-Aviv

Ori Shachak
Social Studies Center, The Jacob Blaustein Institute for Desert Research, Ben-Gurion University of the Negev, Sde Boqer Campus

Benjamin Shalit
National Institute for Defense Research, Division of the Behavioral Sciences, Karlstad, Sweden

Inga-Lill Taljedal Shalit
National Institute for Defense Research, Division of the Behavioral Sciences, Karlstad, Sweden

Yair Shapiro
Heller Research Institute of Environmental Influences on Behavior, Tel-Aviv University

Zahava Solomon
Research Section in Mental Health, Israel Defense Forces

David Soskis
Institute of the Pennsylvania Hospital, Philadelphia

Yosef Toubiana
Youth Guidance Clinic, Petach Tiqwa and Department of Psychology, Tel-Aviv University

Yosef Triest
Arsuf Psychotherapy Clinic and Department of Psychology, Tel-Aviv University

Yochanan Wozner
   Bob Shapell School of Social Work, Tel-Aviv University

Dan Zakay
   Department of Psychology, Tel-Aviv University

Preface

This volume contains 22 papers dealing with the personal and situational factors affecting coping effectiveness, breakdown, and recovery in war and other stress situations. It is divided into five sections with the number of chapters indicated in parentheses:

I. The Role of Attribution in Stress and Coping (4).
II. Risk Factors in Combat Stress Reactions and Post-traumatic Stress Disorders (4).
III. Treatment of Combat Stress Reactions and the Post-traumatic Stress Disorders in the War in Lebanon (4).
IV. Performance in Highly Stressful Situations (5).
V. The Effect of War on Civilian Populations (4).

All chapters, with one exception (Chapter 18), were presented at the Third International Conference on Psychological Stress and Adjustment in Time of War and Peace (Tel-Aviv, January 1983), organized by the editor. The chapters were selected from 160 papers given at that conference and were extensively rewritten for publication. Many were revised when follow-up data were obtained and were incorporated in the final draft.

All chapters but one (Chapter 17) were written by Israeli investigators, and most deal with coping with war in Israel by individuals, groups, and society as a whole. Many chapters are wholly theoretical and offer broad implications for theory and practice in stress and coping. Other chapters are empirical and offer generalizations for dealing with war-related stressors and with large-scale crises other than war. The central core of the book deals with combat stress reaction and its treatment in front- and rear-echelon settings. The relevant chapters provide sufficient detail to constitute a training manual for the organization of similar programs in other countries for the treatment of traumatic and post-traumatic stress conditions.

All empirical data presented in Sections Two and Three are percentages rather than actual frequencies. The Israel Defense Forces were generous in opening their files to research during and soon after the actual events. They stipulated, however, that frequencies are not to appear for reasons of military security. Since Israel is in a state of war with many neighboring Arab countries, this restriction is understandable. The percentages are compelling because they are based on very large numbers. Statistical tests are cited whenever they do not readily translate into the natural frequencies on which they are based.

An effort was made by the editor to (a) generalize theories and findings to other societies and (b) integrate all chapters into the section to which they are assigned. This effort may be noted in the General Introduction, in the introductions to each of the five sections, and in the closing chapter (Chapter 22). The latter was written by the editor in collaboration with Stevan Hobfoll.

The book is designed to be of interest to several kinds of readers.

First, to professional workers, research scientists, and policy makers in the areas of military psychology and psychiatry.

Second, to workers and researchers in the fields of mental health and the social and behavioral sciences who are concerned (a) with the effect of war-related stressors on civilian populations or (b) with large-scale and long-term crises and disasters other than war. The treatment approaches used with traumatic and post-traumatic combat stress conditions are models for the treatment of other acute stress reactions, e.g., soldiers released from POW captivity, civilians released from harrowing hostage episodes, members of communities whose homes and/or livelihoods were wiped out by natural disasters or economic crises, and survivors of school bus traffic accidents and their classmates.

Third, to people interested in the State of Israel and the manner in which its citizens, as members of a citizens' army or as civilians, have coped with the stressors of war since its inception in 1948.

Few, if any, books deal with the diversified efforts of a society to cope with the stressors of war. A companion volume for the present one is Volume 8 of the Spielberger and Sarason Series on *Stress and Anxiety* (1982, New York: Hemisphere Publishing Corporation). The latter book was edited by me and consists of 47 papers from the first and second international conference on war-related stress (Tel-Aviv, January 1975; Jerusalem, June 1978; see Milgram, 1978).

I wish to acknowledge with gratitude the encouragement and guidance of Charles Figley in judicious pruning of chapters and in bringing this volume to publication in an appropriate context, his Psychosocial Stress Series; the permission by *Political Psychology* to publish Chapter 18, which appeared in Volume 6, 1986; the permission by *Military Med-*

icine to publish Chapter 7, which appeared in Volume 152, 1986; and the permission by *Israel Annals of Psychiatry* to publish Chapter 6, which appeared in Volume 23, 1986. Appreciation is expressed to Dr. Roberta Milgram for her sage comments and constructive criticisms in reading the introductions. I completed work on the book while on sabbatical leave from Tel-Aviv University in 1985–1986 as Visiting Professor at Radford University and at Virginia Polytechnic Institute and State University. I wish to express my thanks to Dr. Alistair Harris and Dr. Joseph Sgro, heads of the respective departments of psychology, for their assistance.

A single, comprehensive reference list was compiled from the references cited in the texts of all chapters and introductions. An author index and a subject index are also presented at the end of the book.

General Introduction to the Field of War-Related Stress

NORMAN MILGRAM

War has been a scourge of humankind since the days of Cain. There have been many *scholarly* efforts by historians, philosophers, and social, behavioral, and political scientists to comprehend the nature and nurture of human aggression and its ultimate expression in war. There have been many *diplomatic* efforts to create organizations, institutions, and negotiation strategies to reduce the necessity for and to prevent the occurrence of war. Finally, there have been many *rehabilitative* efforts to bind the physical wounds of war and, in recent years, some efforts to bind the psychic and behavioral wounds of war.

There have been far fewer efforts, however, on the part of behavioral and social scientists (1) to study war and the threat of war as a major source of stress in modern society; (2) to systematically organize the field of war-related stress into a coherent, logical scheme; (3) to conduct basic and applied research in a programmatic manner to reduce the toll of psychic suffering associated with war; and (4) to apply the generalizations derived from research on war-related stress to the theory and treatment of stress phenomena in general.

The orientation implicit in these goals is that the threat and conduct of war are endemic to the human condition, constitute a human catastrophe that afflicts nations and people from time to time, and are a proper object of scientific inquiry. This orientation runs counter to a commonly held view that since war is an abomination and is, therefore, unthinkable, all effort should be channeled toward its elimination rather than toward its investigation or toward making its occurrence or its aftermath more tolerable. This book and a previous volume on war-related stress edited by this writer (Spielberger, Sarason, & Milgram, 1982) were complied as a modest beginning to address some of these issues.

This introductory paper attempts first to explain why war has been a minor topic in the overall field of stress research. Second, it delineates the field of war-related stress, listing research in the field in general and commenting on the research presented in this book in particular. Third, it makes recommendations to expedite new research in the field and to initiate practice in new areas.*

THE LEGITIMACY OF BEHAVIORAL AND SOCIAL SCIENCE RESEARCH ON WAR-RELATED STRESS

The relative paucity of research by behavioral and social scientists on war-related stress is not a consequence of the lack of empirical data or of suitable subject populations. There have been many wars in this century and millions of people have been affected and afflicted. There is no lack of research questions or of opportunities to answer these questions. There is only a lack of scientific interest and motivation on the part of scientists in the universities and in the nonmilitary sector to raise the questions and to search for answers.**

This lack of interest and the reluctance to sustain initial interest over time appear to be culturally transmitted avoidant responses that have developed for several reasons.

1. In studying war-related stress, we must expose ourselves to human suffering of enormous proportions that is entirely of man's own making. This exposure can be a disturbing experience. In so doing, we become aware of the enormity of the evil perpetuated by human beings against one another in all centuries and in all parts of the world and, thereby, become susceptible to depression and despair about the human condition and man's fate. This sense of despair may be heightened by the pessimistic belief that we are powerless to intervene in human history and to arrest the course of these cataclysmic events.

---

*This paper is based in part on an earlier paper, entitled "War-Related Stress: Review of Research and Recommendations," prepared by me at the request of the Division of Mental Health and Behavioral Medicine, Institute of Medicine, National Academy of Sciences, Washington, DC, 1982.

**There has been considerable social, behavioral, and organizational stress research *within* the military establishment since the end of World War II, much of which was performed in response to specific requests by the military establishment. In recent years conclusions drawn from military research on stress have come into the broader literature (e.g., family adjustment and mobility, victimology, sensory isolation, and extended confinement, to cite a few).

2. When we regard war-related stress as a legitimate field of interest, we bestow on war itself a kind of legitimacy. When we engage in research and/or treatment to alleviate the pain and suffering of war, we may be perceived as aiding the current war effort by making it more tolerable. In so doing, we also make future wars more conceivable.

3. There is the concern that scientific and technological advances in research and treatment of war-related stress will be exploited by the leaders of some nation-states to manipulate their people for militaristic purposes.

Despite these reservations that are voiced by many people, war-related stress is a proper area of scientific and professional interest. We should concern ourselves with the price paid by society in the conduct of war, and even as we make all aware of this price, we should search for ways to reduce the price.

STRESS PHENOMENA AND THEIR CONTEXT

Some investigators may allay their ethical and emotional qualms about studying these phenomena by subsuming them under nonwar rubrica—coping with natural disasters, crisis intervention, mourning, rehabilitation—and by glossing over the specific context of war. It is proper to attempt to generalize from nonwar stress situations to war-related and the reverse, but it is poor science and poor treatment to ignore the unique context of war as a source of human stress. We should, therefore, resist the understandable temptation to study war-related phenomena out of context.

The meanings that people attach to the human tragedies they encounter determine to a large extent the nature of their coping efforts and the probable consequences of these efforts (Frankl, 1955; Lazarus, 1966). There are important differences between coping with the loss of a son-brother-husband-father who died in war and with the loss of the same man in a traffic or work accident or in illness. These differences are crucial to an understanding of the relevant stressors, the cognitive appraisals, and the coping mechanisms used by the afflicted parties, and to the selection of effective interventions to further their rehabilitation.

Evidence of the effect of these differences in context may be found in the biased evaluations that modern society applies to damage to limb and loss of life, designating some contexts as intolerable and requiring immediate concern, and other contexts as of passing interest only. When 50,000 people lose their life annually in traffic accidents in the United States, for example, no special provisions are made to commemorate, dignify, or otherwise acknowledge the senseless and needless carnage on the roads. Apart from occasional outbursts of anger and sorrow and spasmodic efforts to reduce this toll, people calmly drive to work or play each day with the confident expectation that they and their loved ones will not contribute to the daily mortality statistics by the end of the day. When it comes to traffic deaths, we appear to believe and to behave as if the price were worth the return of intra- and intercity transport as we know it.

Contrast this accepting attitude with that engendered by far fewer casualties in war. The loss of life in the Vietnam War was also 50,000 spread over a number of years, but it was perceived in a very different light from the like number of traffic deaths in a single year. Even supporters of the war came to regard the loss of life in the Vietnam War as a terrible waste because the return to the society for this investment of lives and suffering was not commensurate. The same kind of accounting took place in Israel with regard to the rising casualties of the conflict in Lebanon since 1983.

The human costs of war are judged by a more demanding standard than the human costs of transportation, work accidents, and inadequate, improper use of medical technology, to mention a few of the institutions in society that have exacted a far greater toll than war in the last 40 years. Why war merits this higher standard is discussed in this writer's chapter on attributional analysis of war-related stress elsewhere in this volume (Chapter 1).

Understandably it makes a great deal of difference to the way people evaluate the sacrifices made by some in war if there is a national consensus favoring the war. But war is *sui generis*, and the loss of life in war continues to generate a different set of attitudes and frames of reference than loss of life by natural disasters, illness, or man-made calamities other than war. We conclude that war-related stress should not be investigated or treated in a manner that divorces it from the unique context of war in general or of a specific war in particular.

A SCHEME OF WAR-RELATED STRESSORS AND THEIR CONSEQUENCES

Thus far, we have been discussing war-related stress without defining the range of phenomena subsumed under that heading. In this section a list of substantive entities that are adversely affected by war is proposed. Some of the more obvious entities at risk in war are:

1. *Life and Limb.* Our own lives and limbs and those of others for whom we care are threatened by a state of war.
2. *Enforced Privation.* War exacts a heavy price in depleting the supply of the necessities of life: food, shelter, clothing, personal property, sleep, and the other amenities that we take for granted during peacetime.
3. *Damage to the Physical Terrain.* Modern bombs, rockets, and missiles cause enormous destruction to man-made entities (buildings, roads, electric lines) and to natural resources (forests, streams).

It is important to include as stressors not only the impact of the actual destruction of these entities, but also the threat of their destruction. The former is far more stressful than the latter, but we should not minimize the deleterious effects of living in a state of intermittent or constant threat to entities that one holds precious.

War threatens or actually damages not only the material entities cited above, but also several less material entities. These include the following:

1. *The territorial integrity and sovereignty of the nation-state.* There is a significant diminution of this feature of national life in the event of defeat, occupation, annexation, forced migration, or other outcomes short of outright annihilation. This feature is defined both in physical and in psychological terms, but the relationship between these definitions is highly variable. A geographical area in dispute between two nations may be small, e.g., a few square miles, yet the passion unleashed on both sides of the border as to its "true" ownership would appear to imply that vast territories are involved.

Consider the controversy over the ownership of Taba, less than a square mile of territory on the border of Israel and the Sinai. Its size is insignificant, both in absolute terms and in relative terms. The Sinai Peninsula, 25,000 square miles, was returned to Egypt as part of a comprehensive peace settlement between Israel and Egypt, but the level of rhetoric over this postage-stamp-size area in current dispute dwarfs the magnitude of the earlier concession by Israel.

2. *The threat to or destruction of the cherished values and institutions of the society.* Values and institutions are at risk as a consequence of a protracted war or the outcome of the war. This is true not only for the society that loses the war, but also for the society that wins it. The victorious society suffers during the war and after the war, as a consequence of the changes mandated in the society by having to wage war and subsequently by

having won it. These consequences for victims and vanquished may include the entities described below.

3. *Drastic curtailment of voluntary peacetime activities*. Curtailment occurs not only when one lives under military occupation or foreign domination, or when one is a prisoner of war or a hostage, but also when one lives in the victorious society and accepts regimentation as a soldier or civilian during the war, suffers the suspension of civil and property rights for the duration, and accepts the imposition of a new form of government brought to power to handle the consequences of the great victory.

4. *The threat or damage to one's sense of physical and psychological invulnerability and integrity*. People lose their innocence and question the assumptions "It can't happen to me" or "It can't happen here." People in war become aware that life and limb are fragile entities that are easily destroyed and that our beliefs in the permanence of our cherished possessions are illusions all too easily shattered.

5. *The threat to one's sense of the familiar, the predictable, and the controllable*. People come to realize that their ability to control events in their environment and even to control their own behavior is more limited and situationally determined than they had once believed.

RELATIONSHIP OF MATERIAL AND NONMATERIAL ENTITIES AT RISK IN WAR

Destruction of the first three categories of entities may be assessed objectively, e.g., the area leveled by bombing, the number of people dead or injured, the food and water ration. The magnitude of the threat or the destruction of the more subtle entities in the second list is more difficult to assess objectively, but it can be assessed by obtaining self-report of individuals and groups and by assessing the behavioral consequences of exposure to threat or damage.

The relationships between the more material and the less material entities at risk are complex. In general, the greater the degree of death, destruction, and privation in war, the greater the psychological victimization and the impaired functioning of people directly and indirectly exposed to the physical stressors (Janis, 1971). Conversely, the greater the threat to the nonmaterial entities and especially to the belief that, individually and collectively, members of the nation-state can control their own destiny and protect the entities at risk, the greater the resulting victimization and inability to defend the state against destruction. So-called psychological warfare is premised on the assumption that if one destroys the enemy psychologically, physical destruction is easier to achieve or becomes unnecessary since the victor can now achieve his purposes without engaging in physical destruction.

Whether threats or actual destruction achieve their purpose in disrupting the functioning of the military and civilian populations in a society depends more on the *interpersonal context* of the war and the *nonmaterial resources* of the society than on the size of the army, the quantity and quality of the various weapons systems, and other material indices of military strength. By *interpersonal context*, we refer to such questions as: Is there a national consensus about the legitimacy of the war and its conduct? Is this consensus shared by both the military and the civilian population? Does this consensus cut across the ethnic and class barriers that divide all modern societies? Do individual members of the society and of the military justify their personal participation in the war? Do they perceive vital and legitimate interests of the state to be at stake? Are they willing to take the necessary risks and to make the necessary sacrifices to wage the war effectively?

Given a just cause and a motivated society, are the *human resources* within the society sufficient for the task at hand? What is the state of military and civilian preparedness? What were the prior experiences of civilians and soldiers in war? What is the current physical and mental health of the society to handle any major national crisis, much less to wage the war in question?

If the answers to these questions are affirmative, then, all other things being equal, the society will wage war and cope more effectively with the course of the war and its consequences than an internally fragmented society, an irresolute and confused society, or an exhausted one.

FORMS OF COPING WITH STRESS

Coping at the level of the individual, the group, or the nation-state takes two major forms:

1. *Problem solving*: Coping with the external stressors so as to solve the problem that they pose and seeing the crisis through to a satisfactory outcome.
2. *Palliation*: Coping with internal, potentially maladaptive stress

reactions (e.g., panic, depression, exhaustion) that threaten to disrupt efforts to deal effectively with the crisis (Lazarus, 1966). If palliation is not effective, then in any protracted crisis, the copers will become increasingly unable to deal with the demands of the crisis situation.

The contribution of the social, behavioral, and medical sciences and their corresponding professional groups to palliative coping during a crisis and to rehabilitation and restoration of optimal function after the crisis is well recognized. From the prescribing of tranquilizers to the aesthetic and emotionally gratifying arrangements for the burial of a fallen soldier, these sciences and helping professions provide strategies, rituals, and substances that facilitate coping during and after a protracted crisis.

Their contribution to problem solving or decision making and following through in the optimal conduct of society at war and in the ensuing negotiations for its cessation is less well recognized, but no less important (Janis & Mann, 1977). Recently Weisz, Rothbaum, and Blackburn (1984a, 1984b) drew a distinction between primary and secondary control in coping with a stressful situation. The former refers to efforts to solve, resolve, or eliminate an existing reality by one's direct actions. The latter refers to efforts at compromise by accommodating to existing reality, maximizing satisfaction, and minimizing dissatisfaction with things as they are.

Secondary control differs from palliation in several respects. Palliation assumes that the cause is just and is worth suffering for until victory is achieved. Palliation itself is achieved when people at risk for adverse stress reactions utilize cognitive and behavior mechanisms to conserve their energies and minimize the toll exacted by persisting in primary control. By contrast, secondary control makes no flat assertions about the justice of one's cause. It may even assume that the opposite is true, namely, that our cause is not just, and that when we cognitively reappraise the problem situation, we will arrive at an interpretation that alters our conception of the problem and our subsequent behavior. Secondary control falls within the theoretical framework of conflict resolution as practiced between antagonists and is, therefore, an important form of coping in war-related crises. It also has other implications for action as discussed below in an analysis of one much publicized war-related stressor, *the phenomenon of terrorist hostage taking.*

THE APPLICATION OF THE FORMS OF
COPING ON GOVERNMENT'S POLICY ON
FORMS OF MODERN TERRORISM

Let us consider the implications of beliefs about primary and secondary control when dealing with this highly dramatic act of terrorism against persons. A small number of individuals seize a civilian aircraft and hold its passengers as hostages under penalty of death until demands for release of prisoners or other political concessions are met by the government (whose citizens are being held hostage) or by other friendly governments.

This phenomenon is discussed at length for two reasons. First, because it ranks high in the concerns of Western nations in recent years. Second, because this introduction was being written as the drama of the American hostages in the TWA plane in Beirut was drawing to its conclusion. It was evident that the solution of freeing the hostages by freeing prisoners in another country would advance the major goals of the Shiite militiamen. It is equally clear that this is a poor tradeoff that bodes ill for a stable world community. The pool of potential hostages in future terrorist operations is practically unlimited and certainly far greater than the number of successful hijackings necessary for fanatical groups to shape events for their own benefit and to the disadvantage of the hostage nations. This phenomenon and its relationship to beliefs about primary and second controls lie at the heart of the terrorist phenomenon in our time.

Terrorism achieves its major effects because of two assumptions widely held by people in Western societies: First, that the problem is soluble—either one prevents acts of terrorism (e.g., the hijacking and taking of hostages) from happening, or one takes rapid, decisive action to rescue hostages and neutralize their captors, or one accedes to the demands of the terrorists to secure the release of the hostages. Second, that it is the proper responsibility of government to deal with all aspects of terrorism, and if the government fails in any aspect, it is culpable and accountable to its own people and to world opinion.

Because of these assumptions, Western government officials are under enormous pressure to achieve optimal solutions with minimal loss of life, property, and electoral support. As a consequence, these governments may behave in any of a number of irresponsible ways, by applying force without discretion, distinction, or proportion, or by acceding to excessive demands of the terrorists. The consequences of either course of action may be disastrous in the short term or the long run. A government may be fully aware of these dire consequences even as it elects to follow a particular course of action, but believes that it has no other viable option. This avoidance-avoidance conflict is brought about by the strength of the above assumptions.

Consider how the nature of the conflict is resolved, if and when people no longer hold these assumptions. We come to regard occasional acts of terrorism and the death or injury of hostages as inevitable, as one of the risks of living in modern society. This is a form of *secondary control*, adapting ourselves to an unpleasant reality, because reliance on primary control alone leads to a more unpleasant scenario. According to the view proposed here, we should engage in all feasible precautions to prevent the hijacking or kidnapping from happening. If it takes place, the government is considered no more responsible than it is for the far more frequent traffic or work accidents that occur daily in our society. By the same token, the government is now free to consider many options in resolving the situation. It no longer operates under the gun of public accountability for outcomes, because *it too is regarded as a victim*. There remains only one villain in the new scenario, the terrorists who created the political and ethical predicament and who hope to capitalize on it by applying their own rules of the game.

Since the government is no longer culpable or accountable for the possible loss of life of the innocent victims, it can wait the terrorists out, it can negotiate confidently and offer minimal concessions or none whatsoever, or it can end the predicament by attacking the site and capturing or killing the terrorists. Under these new rules of the game, terrorism would not achieve its desired effects. The society would not be cowed and the government would not be goaded into indiscriminate violent reaction or concession. Terrorist activity, like other unreinforced behaviors, would then extinguish over time.

This new scenario requires a different conception of coping, secondary control, in which people come to accept an uncertain fate if they become victims of terrorist kidnapping, but they are spared the far more noxious consequences to all of society of espousing only primary control: the deterioration of confidence in government, the freeing of murderers, the appeasement of violent acts by small numbers of fanatical people, etc.

In summary, a recommended program for dealing with hostage crises is (1) primary control to prevent these crises from occurring; (2) secondary control as the major emphasis of a public educational program on terrorism; (3) refusal to accede to terrorist demands, when an actual situation arises; (4) primary control in bringing the crisis to a conclusion and in treating the hostages and others affected by its occurrence; and (5) palliation as a form of coping with the internal strain on hostages, decision makers, policy executors, and the general public throughout the ordeal.

THE FIELD OF WAR-RELATED STRESS

Some of the major topics subsumed under the heading of war-related stress and coping include the following:

Stress in the armed forces during peacetime: Basic training, other training courses in one's military service, geographical mobility in military service, and family disturbances associated with a parent or spouse serving in the military.

Stress in the armed forces during wartime and in its aftermath: Combat stress, the extreme stress of being a prison of war, rehabilitation following physical or psychic injury, adjustment of the family to injury or death of soldier, and reentry into civilian life after discharge.

Stress of civilians in wartime: Coping with the stressors associated with the outbreak and the conduct of war, e.g., privation, wartime regulations, anxiety and apprehension about potential harm to family and friends in dangerous situations; becoming hostages or victims of terrorism in or outside one's own country.

The stress of growing up in a society at war: The effects of war, acts of terrorism, or violence on children and youth growing up in the society.

This list is incomplete and a moment's reflection will induce the reader to propose additions to the list. The present volume deals with the following topics in the order of their appearance: First, the belief systems and attribution styles that bolster or weaken the individual, the group, and the society as a whole in times of crisis. Second, traumatic combat stress reaction and post-traumatic combat stress disorder, etiology, precipitating and inoculating circumstances, control, and treatment. Third, front-echelon treatment of combat stress reaction and rear-echelon treatment of potentially chronic post-traumatic combat stress disorder. Fourth, the physiological and psychological stressors that affect optimal performance in exhausting and dangerous tasks. Fifth, the effect of terrorism and other war-related stressors on civilians—children, youth, and adults—in the society. Introductions are provided by the editor for each of the five sections of the book.

MAJOR CONCEPTS IN THE CHAPTERS

The major conception of the majority of chapters in the book is that behavior is a function of the interaction of situational circumstances and trait and state expectancies and appraisals. The latter variables are drawn from social learning theory, cognitive expectancy, self-efficacy, and social facilitation (Bandura & Walters, 1963; Bandura, 1977), learned helplessness and attribution process (Seligman, 1975), cognitive behavioral modification and learned resourcefulness (Rosenbaum, 1983), and the threat to the validity of one's beliefs and the response to that threat (Kruglanski, 1980; Lerner, 1970).

GENERALIZABILITY OF FINDINGS AND PRACTICES

These concepts were derived from and are applied extensively to phenomena in everyday life. The direction of generalization and application is from the civilian sector to the military. Are there any examples of the reverse, generalizations and applications from the military to the civilian? There have been a few. These are the exceptions that prove the rule. In the aftermath of World War I, a neurologist, Kurt Goldstein (1939), noted that veterans with head injuries had become impaired in abstract ability and displayed a "catastrophic reaction" when this impairment placed them in danger of manifest failure evident to others or to themselves. This work entered the mainstream of personality and cognition in the form of organismic theory, theories about minimal and maximal brain damage, and theories about perceptual learning disability and remediation. By contrast, a psychiatrist, Thomas Salmon (1919), observed posttraumatic stress reactions in soldiers during or after combat in World War I and evolved a form of treatment based on the expectancy of rapid recovery and return to one's unit and on environmental supports that confirm this expectancy. The treatment was highly successful, but its features and the theoretical implications of this work were ignored even in the military domain a quarter of a century later in World War II, and have been applied to the more general phenomena of stress and coping and victimization only in recent years.

This writer proposes that social and behavioral scientists and mental health practitioners have been reluctant to generalize from war phenomena to peacetime. Physics, biology, engineering, and other technologies have not been encumbered, however, by these qualms and have achieved maximum utility for peacetime use of the knowledge and techniques developed with weaponry and communications in wartime. The former situation can be changed, however, i.e., the scrapping of swords for plowshares, if deeply engrained prejudices about war can be relaxed for these specific purposes.

GENERALIZATIONS FROM THE ISRAELI EXPERIENCE

As noted in the Preface, most contributors to this volume are Israelis, and with one exception all empirical studies are based on Israeli samples. One may ask why there is an exclusive focus on Israeli investigators and the Israeli experience in war. This focus or bias is based on the unique geopolitical situation in which Israel finds itself. Other nations have been in a state of intermittent wars or a single, protracted war with intermittent battles (e.g., Vietnam, Korea, Northern Ireland), but the character of these societies and the distribution of human resources in each have precluded extensive research or mental health treatment at primary, secondary, or tertiary levels.

Israel has been unfortunate in having to wage wars and combat terrorist attack for over 30 years since its inception as a state. Jewish inhabitants in pre-Israel were also subject to attack and death in the 70 years that preceded the establishment of the Jewish State. It has been fortunate in that the extent of physical damage, destruction, and death has been limited (when compared with the devastation afflicted on the countries cited above), while the manpower available for research and treatment has been ample. Israel has been able to accumulate considerable data on some aspects of war-related stress. Given its Western character, one can argue for the generalization or applicability of these findings to other Western societies. An effort is made to emphasize these generalizations throughout the book.

HOW TO ADVANCE AND APPLY BASIC AND
APPLIED RESEARCH ON WAR-RELATED STRESS

If we agree that the topics of war-related stress can profit from nonwar sources of knowledge and professional practice *and especially the reverse*, then we should give serious consideration to the means by which these goals are to be achieved.

First, by reducing the culturally avoidant reactions toward the field of war-related stress that are so prevalent in many societies, including the United States and Western Europe. This can be done by organizing scientific and professional conferences on these topics and publicizing the content and the conclusions of these meetings in the mass media.

Second, by using national forums to encourage researchers and practitioners in these fields to summarize and share their conclusions with others; by establishing a new journal or journals in the field; by publishing a series of edited volumes on war-related stress with invited contributions.

Third, by encouraging closer cooperation between researchers in the universities and research centers and their counterparts in the armed forces.

Fourth, by encouraging collaboration between the researchers of various countries through international meetings, and international forums for publication, etc.

SECTION I

The Role of Attribution in Stress and Coping

The theme that runs through the four chapters in Section One is the effect of cognitive appraisals on one's coping behavior in stressful situations. This theme is reflected in the following topics that are dealt with in one or more of the chapters:

1. Cognitive appraisals of the threat of war (Chapter 1)
2. The power and the vulnerability of positive beliefs about control (Chapters 1 and 2)
3. The effect of attribution of accountability-responsibility for the occurrence and resolution of crisis on coping behavior (Chapters 1 and 2)
4. Historical consciousness and current and future appraisals of threats in individuals and in nations (Chapter 3)
5. The bias in stress research and practice to deal with pathology rather than health (Chapter 4)

WAR AS A UNIQUE STRESSOR

In Chapter 1, Milgram analyzes the unique character of war-related stress and asserts that the horror with which war is regarded is derived from several sources. Apart from enormous destructiveness and loss of life, war poses an unusual threat with respect to target and to source.

3

It threatens the permanence of cherished entities (people, property, pursuits, institutions, and values) and by implication, it threatens the fundamental belief in our ability to control our destinies and to control ourselves. Its source, unlike the threat of natural disasters (earthquakes, floods, hurricanes), is goal-directed behavior by human beings acting in concert to destroy other human beings. War, moreover, gives its sanction and even its blessing to people to commit immoral and destructive acts that are forbidden by law to individual citizens.

One form of war, *psychological warfare*, attempts to undermine one's beliefs about personal control so as to render him ineffectual and willing to surrender or, at least, not to resist the designs of the other side to further their interest. If the belief system is undermined, one becomes incapable of defending one's interests even though no shots may have been fired and there is no physical damage to the person, his property, etc. This argument applies to nations as well as to individuals.

ATTRIBUTIONS MAKE A DIFFERENCE FOR COPERS AND FOR HELPERS

In Chapter 1, Milgram also discusses the different appraisals that people make of the predicaments in which they find themselves and how they hope to extricate themselves. Attributions affect how one reacts to adverse experiences and to the problems and consequences that they generate. Attributions also affect how one proceeds to extricate oneself from the predicaments at hand. Individuals coping with the vicissitudes of life may differ in these kinds of attribution from one another, from their families and friends, and from professional helpers. Consensus about attribution models of coping and helping selected in a given situation, or the absence of consensus, exercises powerful effects on the course of personal coping and utilizing the help of significant others.

Brickman and his associates (Brickman et al., 1982) propose four models of coping and helping derived from the four combinations of internal/external attribution of responsibility (a) for personal problems occurring in stressful life situations, and (b) for coping with these problems and resolving them or learning to adjust to them. The authors of Chapters 1 and 2 differ in their recommendation of the optimal attribution model of coping in stressful situations.

Milgram argues that the preferred model is *mastery of adversity* in which one attributes responsibility for the initial problem or crisis to external events beyond one's control, and responsibility for solving or resolving the crisis to internal events, i.e., one's personal responsibility. His analysis of the treatment of combat-related stress conditions supports this view. Other models, especially the medical model, characterized by external responsibility for the problem and its solution, may be injurious to the soldier and impede recovery. Milgram asserts that the mastery-of-adversity model is preferable for dealing with *civilian stress reactions* as well, e.g., working with families whose fathers or sons, and occasionally daughters, died in war.

In Chapter 2, Chambon proposes what may be termed the *moral model* of attribution, internal attribution of responsibility both for the crisis and for its resolution. She adopts an existential-humanist orientation toward crisis intervention and identifies the event that precipitated the crisis and the breakdown in coping as invariably holding personal meaning for the individual. She regards the precipitating event as attesting to the necessity for making a highly personal transition from one's precrisis developmental phase to a higher postcrisis one. The crisis is not regarded as a calamity, but rather as an opportunity for utilizing an unfortunate, fortuitous circumstance to achieve personal growth as an existentially free individual.

This view recommends itself in life crises in the world of family and occupation where there is continuity between past, present, and future and where crises largely evolve from changes within the system. These crises include stressful life events such as divorce, discord between parents and children, and even the suicide of an adolescent child.

Some life crises arise because of the unforseen intrusion of foreign elements from outside the system or the operation of events that are random with respect to their victims. These crises may be the occasion for a search for new meaning in life, because the old meanings were invalidated by the crisis. The *possibility* of becoming stronger and more mature exists, but the *probability* of growth is low. The problem often is how to restrict the diminution of self that results from a severe combat stress disorder, violent sexual assault, or loss of limb or life caused by a hit-and-run drunken driver. For this latter category of crises, this writer prefers to absolve the victim of responsibility for being in the crisis situation and to emphasize the victim's responsibility for coping with and resolving the crisis.

THE EFFECT OF HISTORICAL CONSCIOUSNESS
ON PRESENT AND FUTURE APPRAISALS OF
THREAT IN INDIVIDUALS AND NATIONS

The appraisals that individuals, groups, and entire nations make about the threat to them from others are based not only on current features of the geopolitical and psychological fields, but also on historical referents. These are events that either occurred in their own lives or that exist in the historical consciousness of the people and their leaders, although the events themselves actually occurred centuries ago.

In Chapter 3, Bar-Tal uses the major historical incident of the fall of Masada in the year 72 C.E.* to illustrate this phenomenon. The struggle of the Jewish defenders of the besieged stronghold and their decision to commit suicide rather than to surrender to the Roman invaders has become a symbol of heroism as well as the source of the term Masada complex or syndrome. This term refers to the central belief that the entire world either bears hostile intentions toward the Jewish people or at best is indifferent to their fate. This belief has been reinforced on numerous occasions from 72 C.E. to the present, with the supreme confirmation coming during World War II. In the eyes of Jewish observers, the Western world either colluded with the Nazis to destroy the Jewish people or remained silent throughout the Nazi effort to achieve the Final Solution.

The author makes two major arguments: First, that *this belief is not unique to the Jewish people*. Other nations and groups have formulated the same beliefs at different periods in their own history. He cites the isolation of Albania, South Africa, Japan before World War II, and the Soviet Union during the foreign interference in the civil war between 1918 and 1920. Second, that *this central belief may distort perceptions in planning for the future*, even when justified by the past and confirmed by the present.

He cites several dire consequences of holding to the Masada syndrome:

1. Believers develop negative attitudes not only toward groups who openly voice hostile intentions toward them, but also toward groups who may bear them no animosity. One may come to mistrust and hate everyone, a conclusion not justified by the evidence.

---

*C.E. (Common Era) equivalent to A.D.

2. Believers develop hypersensitivity to cues indicating hostile intentions. They may misinterpret the behavior of others or may selectively attend to those features of the behavior of others that validate their own central belief.
3. Believers prepare themselves for the worst possible scenario by emphasizing unity and conformity from within to answer the threat from without. This demand for conformity may not be in the best interests of the beleaguered group.
4. Believers may take drastic action when they believe their basic interests are in jeopardy. In so doing they may engage in activities that are unacceptable to many of their own members as well as to neutral or potentially friendly groups. These actions may serve an immediate need, but their consequences may prove counterproductive in the long run.

Bar-Tal suggests two strategies to reduce blind adherence to central beliefs and thereby reduce the deleterious consequences that follow from such adherence: First, to provide information and the opportunity for experiences that modify, qualify, or otherwise correct the belief. Second, to point out the dangerous consequences that follow from blind adherence to the belief. Presumably when people realize how costly are the consequences of accepting a given belief and following a drastic path of action, they may consider other beliefs or more conservative actions.

THE CONSEQUENCES OF THE PATHOGENIC BIAS IN STRESS RESEARCH

In the fourth, and closing, chapter in the section, Antonovsky and Bernstein demonstrate that the bulk of research in stress and coping is dominated by a *pathogenic* paradigm: to investigate the factors that effect physical and psychological breakdown. They examine 31 studies drawn from recent research literature in several journals and conclude that a bias to investigate pathology rather than health exists and leads to a number of negative consequences:

1. The dependent variable in these studies is the presence or absence of a specific disease. If we bear in mind that health is not simply the absence of disease, but a more fortunate condition, then we might suggest that using health measures as dependent variables would yield different answers than illness measures.

2. In focusing on a specific disease as dependent variable, we fail to consider other diseases that may occur as a consequence of the stress situation under investigation.
3. If the dependent variable is disease, then the independent variables are also seen as pathogenic in nature, i.e., undesirable features of the person or the stressful situation that affect the person adversely. We learn little, if anything, about those features of the person or the situation that sustain successful coping and health in the coper.
4. The pathogenic orientation does not investigate the person who seeks out stressful situations and regards them as challenge and opportunity. It ignores the salutary aspect of stress as challenge in all human beings.

1

An Attributional Analysis of War-Related Stress: Modes of Coping and Helping

NORMAN MILGRAM

This paper discusses two sets of questions about war-related stress and coping. The first set of questions refers to a taxonomy of war-related stressors and coping mechanisms:

1. What is threatened, damaged, or destroyed in war?
2. What kinds of coping mechanisms are used by people *directly and indirectly involved* in war to cope with these stressors?

For the purposes of this paper, *indirectly involved* people experience war-related stress situations secondhand by watching, hearing, reading, or talking to *directly involved* people. Parents whose son was wounded in combat in Vietnam or in Lebanon are directly involved; their friends whose son was not in a similar situation are indirectly involved. This distinction is not all-or-none, and people may be distributed on a continuum with respect to involvement.

The second set of questions refers to the identification and application of efficacious attributions and expectancies in coping with war-related stressors and in helping others to cope.

9

1. Who is to be held responsible for the incapacitated condition of one who can no longer cope with a given war-related stress situation?
2. Once a person has become incapacitated, who is to be held responsible for helping that person to recover?

Responsibility in the first instance refers to the locus of those variables that were instrumental in bringing about the breakdown in coping behavior, and in the second instance to those variables likely to bring about a solution to the problem—the person's recovery and resumption of coping with present and future stressors.

In this chapter, we make a formal distinction between *copers* and *helpers*. People who struggle to function appropriately under conditions of severe stress are called copers without regard to the success or failure of their efforts. People who attempt to assist copers are called helpers, without regard to their status (professional or lay) or the success or failure of their efforts. In most long-term stress situations, helpers also need help in order to continue functioning in their various activities. Similarly, some copers find themselves helping others in the course of their own coping efforts. The distinction between coper and helper refers to a formal role or a formal emphasis in behavior at a particular point in time.

WHAT IS THREATENED BY WAR?

War is regarded by most people as the greatest stress situation encountered in human experience, more intensive and extensive in its effects than other large-scale catastrophes such as famine, flood, fire, or disease. Indeed, war often contributes in no small measure to these other catastrophes and goes beyond them in horror and human tragedy. The effects of war follow from the mere threat of war, from the outbreak and conduct of a state of war, from the aftermath of war, or from any and all of these (see Blank, 1982, for an excellent summary of these stressors).

The entities at risk in war include:

1. *Human beings*: The lives and limbs of copers and of their loved ones.
2. *Property*: Personal and collective property of people as individ-

uals and as members of society. The term includes both man-
made property and natural resources.
3. *Pursuits*: Their work, family and leisure activities, and other
   activities reflecting the privileges and responsibilities associated
   with their status in society.
4. *Institutions*: The social, political, cultural, and religious organizations and institutions that operate in the society.
5. *Values*: Those personal and collective standards that determine
   the value of any and all of the above entities at risk and their
   hierarchy of importance.

The Threat to Control of Events and to Control of Oneself

A second category of entities at risk in war or in any other severe crisis
is the ability to comprehend, predict, and control events. Comprehension and prediction are both necessary for control and are forms of
control in their own right (Seligman, 1975). Understanding a given phenomenon and its antecedent contingencies permits one to predict when
and under what circumstances the phenomenon will occur. Comprehension and prediction in turn facilitate one's behaving so as to bring
about the phenomenon at a time and place of one's choosing to minimize
its adverse consequences. The term "control" is used in the present
discussion to refer to comprehension and prediction as well as to behavior directly affecting the phenomenon itself. Control over external
events may be exercised by the individual acting alone or in concert with
significant others to influence outcomes affecting others, one's group,
or oneself.

Control abilities are essential for the protection, maintenance, and
enjoyment of the entities cited earlier. What satisfaction can we derive
from our lives, property, pursuits, institutions, and value systems if we
cannot be reasonably sure that we can protect them against encroach-
ment or attack? If we cannot control external events, we can possess and
enjoy nothing.

In addition to control over external events, there is control over internal events. Threatening external events constitute a challenge not
only to our problem-solving ability, but also to our ability to control
ourselves, to maintain an optimal emotional balance, and not give way
to anxiety, anger, depression, or other emotional reactions to the stressful events. Control over oneself is essential if one is to persist in problem
solving and to function in an appropriate and efficient manner over a

long period of time. Without control over self, control over events invariably deteriorates.

The Unique Threat Posed by War: Goal-Directed Destructiveness of Humans Against Other Humans

War poses a unique threat both to the various entities at risk cited earlier and to one's cherished ability to control events and their consequences. Unlike tornadoes, hurricanes, floods, volcanoes, and droughts, which appear to occur capriciously or are variously attributed to divine powers or to nonhuman forces in nature, war is conducted by humans with deliberation and dispatch. War presents a far greater potential threat to all five categories at risk than natural catastrophes, since the enemy may systematically endeavor to destroy all human life and property and succeed far better than natural disasters whose consequences are without malice or cognitive calculation.

The deliberate and calculated intention characterizing the war-making behavior of the enemy (and most human behavior, for that matter) poses an unparalleled threat not only to our persons, property, pursuits, institutions, and values, but also to the various forms of control that we have painstakingly acquired during childhood and adolescence and zealously maintain in our adult lives. The intention or purpose of the "enemy" is to destroy us or to weaken or destroy our power to control our own destinies as we see it. The enemy engages in two kinds of warfare: physical warfare to destroy people and property, and psychological warfare to impair our ability to control events, external and internal, and thereby achieve his or her goals.

The Preservation of Beliefs and the Conservation of Entities

Assuming that the control abilities are essential for the protection and enjoyment of our prized possessions (life and limb, property, institutions, etc.), how can we be reasonably sure that they will be available and as effective in the routines and in the crises of tomorrow as they were in those of yesterday? No matter how many times we have confirmed the hypothesis that our control systems are in good working order, there is always the possibility that in the next or in subsequent crises, these abilities will fail us.

What sustains us from day to day is (1) a set of beliefs about the constancy and efficacy of our control systems, and (2) a corresponding set of beliefs about the constancy and predictability of the laws of nature and of human behavior that determine the external world in which our control systems function. We enjoy life, liberty, and property because we *believe* that they are ours by right, that we can protect them against predators, or that there are no predators to concern us. If the belief in the control abilities of the individual or of society is undermined, then long before the property is stolen or destroyed, the pleasure in its possession has disappeared.

The Effect of Threat on Beliefs

War is an external stressor *par excellence* because more than any other catastrophe, it threatens these sets of beliefs and thereby undermines the basis for our existence and any enjoyment we might derive from our lives. It is in the character of threats, that they achieve their primary adverse effect on the *belief* system demoralizing the individual, the group, or the nation, even though the entities at risk may still be intact (Janis, 1971).

The effect of threats and even of actual damage or destruction is a function of the resilience and content of these belief systems. For the true believer, considerable evidence is required before he disconfirms his beliefs, if at all. For the person of little faith, even minor evidence is sufficient to topple the belief edifice and to disrupt that person's functioning. The same generalization applies to the content of the belief system. If what is destroyed is regarded as essential and irreplaceable, its loss is cataclysmic. If what is lost is regarded as of less consequence than what survives, the effect of the destruction is more tolerable.

The effect on copers of damage or destruction to specific entities is also a function of the breadth of the generalizations made. If one generalizes broadly from a particular instance of death or destruction to large-scale death and destruction, the effect is more devastating than if the generalization is more circumscribed and circumspect. Generalizations from the particular to the general are especially powerful with respect to the belief systems about control. Each of us possesses highly personal beliefs about cosmic, collective, and individual control of external events and about personal control of internal events. Evidence of impairment of control, collective or individual, even in a matter of minor consequence may be taken as indicating that impairment of control in major matters is imminent or likely, and the effect of this generalization can be devastating.

In summary, the relationship between damage and destruction to entities and the undermining of control beliefs is direct, but complex.

The greater the threat, or the actual damage or destruction of the above-mentioned entities, the greater the threat to and the impairment of the validity of one's beliefs about control with reference to these entities. Belief systems are highly idiosyncratic, however, differing in content, susceptibility to confirmation or disconfirmation, adaptability, and generalizability.

Control Over Events and Control Over Self

The belief systems about control over external events and control over self or internal events are also imperfectly correlated. Generally, the greater the extent to which the former is undermined, the greater the adverse effect on the latter. Nevertheless, some people may maintain equanimity despite enormous adversity, while others break down completely because of what appear to be minor privations. The reverse relationship is the more disruptive of the two: When self-control breaks down, there can be no control over external events at all.

An illustration of the interdependence of external and internal control may be found in occupational therapy of a psychiatrically disturbed patient. The importance of occupational therapy lies in its influence on these belief systems. That one can control external events of apparent minor consequence is evidence that one possesses a modicum of control over self and events and, by inference, may be able to control external events and achieve internal control of far greater consequence. Enhancement or restoration of the belief in one's control abilities is not a matter of minor consequence and has a direct effect on rehabilitation because of the importance of these control abilities to a person.

War and the Moral Issue

The conduct of war introduces another powerful stressor in the undermining of our conventional moral behavior and moral beliefs. War threatens to undermine the validity of our moral assumptions and moral postures in a way that natural disasters do not. We may transgress moral conventions in the course of coping with a natural disaster and even justify our immoral behavior before, during, or after the fact, but we generally do so on an individual basis. Our stress-related immorality is a private matter. By contrast, war sanctions, and even rewards, behaviors that we would regard as criminal and abhorrent during peacetime: lying, theft, espionage, sabotage, and homicide. During the commission of these acts and long afterward, we mull over their implications for our personal character and national character, the moral rectitude of our nation's leaders, and the moral stature of the society in which we live. Evidence of this powerful effect is the persistent moral debate and assessment on the community level that follow a war and the agonizing appraisal in which the individual engages in his own private hell (Hendin et al., 1985; Marrs, 1985; Shatan, 1985; Silver, 1985).

Specificity of War-Related Stressors

We regard the threat to entities and their corresponding belief systems as *specific*, differing from person to person and from society to society in a specific war and differing from war to war for people in a specific society. Some wars are more terrible than others. The threat to territory or natural resources, for example, is different from the threat to the very existence of the society and the nation-state.

Similarly, the death of an elderly man in wartime has a different effect on the survivors than the death of his middle-aged son or his young-adult grandson. The first event is less likely to invalidate our beliefs in a just world than the second, and the second less than the third: People are expected to pass away with good grace in their 70s, but men are not supposed to outlive their sons, much less their grandsons (Lerner, 1980). Hence, the threats to entities and to their corresponding belief systems are highly differentiated. They may vary from culture to culture and differ even with a given culture.

Relationships of Outer- and Inner-Directed Control

Lazarus speaks of two kinds of coping behavior, outer-directed to solve the pressing external problem at hand, and inner-directed so as to sustain oneself during the lengthy coping period (1966). These coping behaviors correspond, in turn, to the two kinds of control cited above: control over events and control over oneself.

The relationship between the two kinds of control and the relationship between threat to entities and threat to the corresponding belief systems introduce complexity in evaluating the effectiveness of the outer-directed and inner-directed coping behaviors in a given stress situation. Criteria for evaluating the effectiveness of outer-directed coping behavior are generally regarded as objective and well defined. They refer to expenditure of human and material resources over time to achieve a given consequence. We generally prefer the most efficient behaviors because they are also the most effective, but there are many exceptions. Certain problem-solving behaviors may be less effective in getting the job done, but they are more efficient for that individual or group. The less efficient behaviors may be more available, less fatiguing, and, in the long run, more effective.

There are, however, other criteria for evaluating the effectiveness of outer-directed coping behaviors: whether they contribute to an enhancement of the belief that one is in control of events, and by implication in control of oneself. However inconsequential or ineffective certain behaviors may be in fact, they may be effective at least for the short haul in permitting the individual to function and sustain a sense of perceived control of the problem and of oneself, until more effective options become available. Gal and Lazarus (1975) have shown that any activity regarded as problem-oriented reduces the deleterious effects of a chronic stress situation.

If we require a number of perspectives for evaluating the effectiveness of outer-directed behaviors, we also require many perspectives for evaluating the effectiveness of inner-directed palliative behaviors. Society provides a highly diverse and rich menu of activities that enable people to carry on in stressful situations: sleep and sleep-inducing substances; cigarettes, alcohol, coffee, and other psychoaffective substances; sports, exercise, hobbies; prayer, meditation, walks in nature; contact with loved ones and with symbolic reminders of the good life that preceded and that will follow the current crisis. A palliative activity that enhances the inner- and outer-coping ability of one person may have the opposite effect on another. It is necessary to consider the various sources of data (the observed effectiveness of given inner-directed activities, self-report, and physiological measures, and their consequences for subsequent coping behavior) and then weigh the gain against the loss exacted by these activities.

ATTRIBUTION OF RESPONSIBILITY FOR EVENTS AND THEIR CONSEQUENCES

In all crisis situations people invariably engage in responsibility attribution: Who is responsible for the crisis situation? Who is responsible for the individual's personal failure to function effectively in the crisis situation? And who is responsible for the person's recovery and resuming of adequate functioning in the continuing crisis or in the aftermath of the crisis? A man-made crisis like war provides a field day for spec-

ulations about the causal factors, villains, and fools to be held accountable for the catastrophe and its consequences. Could the war have been
averted, World War I or II, for example, or the 1967 Arab-Israeli War?
Would the number of casualties have been reduced if the armed forces
had been alerted and mobilized before the actual attack by the enemy
at Pearl Harbor in 1941, or the Egyptian attack across the Suez Canal at
the start of the Yom Kippur War in 1973? Would the consequences of
the war have been less devastating if it had been conducted with clearly
defined and limited objectives? McArthur's conduct of the Korean War
in 1950 and Israel's Lebanon War in 1982 are cases in point.

These questions and the answers given affect the behavior of all involved parties, even as the copers bind the wounds of war or reminisce
about the war years later. These issues enter into the appraisal that
helpers make about the circumstances leading to the breakdown of a
soldier or a civilian and about the help to be provided to restore functioning. Helpers are known to be less helpful in unpopular wars. Elsewhere in this volume (Chapter 20) evidence is presented for the failure
of the mental health profession in Israel to appreciate the coping difficulties of the Yamit settlers who were evicted from their former homes
in order to return the entire Sinai Peninsula to Egypt. Evidence is also
cited of the initial failure of the mental health professions in the United
States to appreciate the plight of the returning Vietnam veterans.

The attribution of responsibility for the outbreak of war and its conduct
is an important question, but is not dealt with in this chapter. For the
purposes of the present discussion, we accept the crisis as given and
ask why people are differently affected by it and how they are to be
helped to recover.

Combat Stress Reactions: An Instance of Attribution Model Confusion

When a soldier breaks down in combat and another does not, how
do we explain to ourselves and to both soldiers why this happened?
Was it the fault of the first soldier himself, or of the training he received,
the behavior of his commanding officers in the field, or the failure of
social institutions (the schools, the home, the church) to inculcate in
him the proper manly and martial virtues and values? These are complex
questions, but their complexity does not deter most people, professional
and lay, from offering highly simplistic answers. People are typically
unsatisfied with highly complex answers or with generalities such as it
is everybody's fault or it is nobody's fault. They generate their own

hypotheses and validate them to their own satisfaction, because of an inveterate need to identify the locus of responsibility for important events.

Scientists are also susceptible to this need for structure. Suppose we rephrase the above-mentioned attribution questions a little differently: What is the relationship of the intensity of combat stress reaction and its sequelae to certain premorbid personal and characterological varia- bles? What is their relationship to parent-child rearing practices? To the accumulation of highly stressful life experiences immediately prior to the combat experience? To indecisive, ineffective leadership on the bat- tlefield? Or to the failure of the combat unit to achieve the necessary group cohesiveness before entering combat?

Whatever answer we offer or accept for this question, the soldier is currently incapacitated and his impaired status raises the question of attribution of responsibility for recovery: Who or what can contribute the most to his recovery and his return to his military unit or to civilian life? The soldier himself, his comrades-in-arms, his parents, his wife and children, his friends, others who recovered from similar stress reactions, or members of the various helping professions?

Let us take as a second example a *civilian stress reaction*: A family is griefstricken because of the death in combat of a man who was at one and the same time a son, a brother, a husband, and a father. Who or what is responsible for the stress reaction of the family members? Who should assume responsibility for their resuming their ordinary routines at home and in the workplace, and for eventually restoring some sem- blance of meaning, purpose and pleasure in their lives? The family mem- bers themselves, relatives and friends, or professional helpers who actively intervene?

Brickman's Model of Coping and Helping

Brickman (Brickman et al., 1982) described four classical models of coping and helping. In any given model, responsibility for current in- capacity of the coper is attributed either to the coper himself (internal attribution) or to helpers or circumstances beyond the coper's control (external attribution). Similarly, responsibility for the coper's recovery may also be attributed to the coper himself or to helpers and helping institutions. Each model is reinterpreted here and assigned a name ac- cording to the philosophical and evaluative assumptions of this writer about the loci of responsibility.

The best-known models are the wholly consistent ones, internal-internal and external-external, respectively. The former is called the *moralistic model*. In this model the coper is held responsible for his reactions and his initiatives. The soldier is responsible for the combat stress reaction that he experiences because of personal inadequacies and is also responsible for shaping up. The model does not preclude the soldier asking for and receiving help from individuals or agencies, but the initiative, the sustaining effort, and the ultimate success or failure of the helping process depend on the soldier himself.

The diametrically opposed model is the *medical model*. It is named after the typical doctor-patient relationship in which the latter is not held responsible for his illness or for his recovery. The patient's motivation to cooperate with the medical regime is very important, but he is not responsible for the helping process—the doctor is. Surgery, medication, medical knowledge, medical directives, and patient compliance—these are the necessary, although not the sufficient, conditions for whatever recovery is possible. In using the term "medical model," this writer is not unaware of recent trends toward health-oriented medical practice and community health practices. In these new approaches the patient may be held responsible for his illness because of substance abuse or improper life-style. More important, he may be permitted, encouraged, or required to assume responsibility for his own recovery. These approaches are still the exception, however, rather than the rule.

A third coping and helping model may be labeled the *incompetent muddler model*. Here the individual gets into an unfortunate predicament because of personal incompetence in some areas of life functioning, but can only extricate himself with the help and direction of others. This is undoubtedly the working model of some professional mental health workers with regard to acute or chronic combat stress reactions.

The fourth model is *mastery of adversity*. In the mastery model the coper is not held responsible for the adverse situation in which he finds himself or for his current incapacity. Forces beyond his control and ken have brought about the current incapacity. On the other hand, only the coper can resolve his or her current predicament by selecting the direction and initiating the steps to recovery with the judicious use of helpers on one's own terms.

Attribution Models and Combat Stress Reactions

It is patently obvious that lack of consensus is the rule when copers and helpers apply their own personal models of coping and helping to a particular class of war-related stress reactions or to a specific instance

of the class. Consider the implications for treatment of this lack of consensus about attribution model in the case of a soldier without physical
injury who is the only one in his combat unit to demonstrate a severe
combat stress reaction.

He may regard himself as having fallen apart because of forces beyond
his control and expect that others will put him back together again. His
comrades may see him as cowardly and lacking moral fiber, or as emotionally unstable. They may assume that he will not return to his former
self in the near future, if ever, even with professional help. In the nearby
treatment center to which he is evacuated, he is again confronted with
diverse attribution models of coping and helping. The psychiatrist may
apply the medical model, the medical orderly the moralistic model, and
still others, that of the incompetent muddler. When he is later evacuated
to a more remote treatment center, his former commanding officer may
visit him, exhort him to be a man, and in exasperation strike him in the
face. I am referring to a famous incident in World War II when General
George S. Patton did exactly that. The soldier is also visited by members
of his own family, who blame everybody except the soldier for what
happened and expect others to cure him since they are responsible, after
all, for his condition. The inconsistency in attributional behavior and the
confusing signals that it generates benefit no one, certainly not the incapacitated soldier.

Is there one model that is more appropriate than the others for war-
related stress situations? Or are all four models efficacious, depending
on the characteristics of the situation, the copers, the helpers, and other
variables not yet cited in this discussion? In the opinion of this partici-
pant-observer of Israel in times of war and peace, two models recommend themselves more than the others. These are the mastery and the
medical models. They share in common external attribution of responsibility for the individual's predicament and thereby absolve him of
blame, shame, guilt, and inferiority feelings by emphasizing the exten-
uating circumstances of the stress situation. It is efficacious for the soldier
with combat stress reaction to put responsibility for his current incapacity
on forces beyond his control, and to put the responsibility for his recovery on himself. A given soldier may also recover rapidly, however,
if he follows the counsel and guidance of the authorities, especially if
they are attempting to restore his autonomous functioning.

The classical treatment, described at length elsewhere in this volume,
is based on Salmon's three principles of proximity, immediacy, and
expectancy and assumes that the soldier will resume his former military
role and return to his former combat unit within a few days at most

(1919). If he is unable to do so, he is referred to a second military rehabilitation center where he engages in a variety of military and psychological activities for several days or weeks before returning to his original unit or to another military support unit. The initiative that the soldier demonstrates during the recovery period and the corresponding orientation of the helpers will determine whether the operating model is the mastery or the medical one. The former model emphasizes the assumption of an active role by the soldier and his taking the initiative. The medical model emphasizes soldier compliance to authority figures, but may be successful in this context because the soldier must engage in demanding activities in the course of which he regains mastery over self and over his behavior in previously upsetting situations.

Why not propose the moralistic model, the most heroic of them all, to the soldier at war? First, the *prima facie* case for internal attribution of responsibility for breakdown in war is weak. After all, the soldier functioned in a competent manner in civilian life and during his basic training and subsequent military duties until the current situation. Second, internal attribution reinforces a perception of personal inadequacy, self-castigation, and possibly acknowledging in oneself an element of malingering. Nothing is gained from reinforcing any of these perceptions or insights and giving them credence or publicity. It is more efficacious to dwell on the importance of the long-term struggle to recover and to return to one's unit, and later to resume normal civilian life with innumerable opportunities for rehabilitation and restitution rather than dwelling in an obsessive-compulsive manner on the moral opprobrium of a single, short-term episode.

In summary, this researcher favors the mastery model, but also recommends the medical model in those circumstances when desirable consequences for rehabilitation result from the willingness and ability of the individual to follow firm and clearly defined directions from a respected authority figure. Under these circumstances the soldier resumes active engagement with his former activities and comrades and maintains them afterward without the active ministrations of the authority figure and other helpers.

Attribution Models and Bereaved Parents

The same arguments and the same models apply to bereaved parents whose son died in war. Blaming themselves for the son's death is not condoned by society and is rejected out of hand by all potential helpers and most copers. It is also unacceptable to most bereaved parents as a viable option for subsequent behavior. The only exception is an unpopular war, in which a national consensus is lacking for its initiation or conduct. In this case, the parents may berate themselves for having passively complied with government policy instead of resisting and changing that policy before their son went into combat and died.

This exception aside, society regards the son's death and the parents' suffering as a tragedy for which they bear no responsibility and, therefore, gives considerable latitude in the initial stages of mourning for a wide range of behaviors by the bereaved parties. There is, however, a limit to society's tolerance of upsetting public behaviors by bereaved parents, and the range of acceptable behaviors begins to narrow as the socially defined period of intense mourning draws to a close.

Just as society does not tolerate bereaved parents assuming internal responsibility for their predicament, it strongly reinforces internal responsibility by bereaved parents for their recovery and resumption of normal activities. It selectively highlights heroic, altruistic, and patriotic statements and behaviors by these parents. For those parents who cannot rise to the occasion and conduct themselves in a heroic fashion, society recommends the medical model and the intervention of professional helpers.

In these distinctions and recommendations society has been in agreement with the mental health professions. Conventional wisdom and professional thinking until very recently were characterized by the above-mentioned stereotypes about the normal course of grief work and recovery. Recent reviews of the empirical data on these phenomena have shown, however, that there is no "normal" course and that bereaved parties vary widely in the pace and manner of resuming so-called "normal" activities (Silver & Wortman, 1980). These researchers and other professional workers (Caplan, 1974) strongly urge us not to dictate to bereaved parties how they should behave, but serve as consultant-observers encouraging them to determine the pace and nature of their recovery and the kind of help that they want and will accept from others. Such an approach emphasizes the intervention of lay rather than professional helpers and the utilization of the indigenous support systems familiar to the bereaved family, with an emphasis on the mastery model over the medical.

Social Consensus as a Support System in War

One factor affecting the recovery of a soldier from a severe combat stress reaction or the recovery of bereaved family members following the death of their loved one is whether the damage or the loss was incurred in the service of the greater good of the society as a whole. National consensus that a given war is legitimate and that sacrifices made in the conduct of the war are appreciated by society is a major source of support for people attempting to cope with their loss. It is very difficult for them to cope with an irretrievable loss that is unappreciated or even castigated. Bereaved parents ask, "What did our soldier son die for?" and society's answer can be reassuring or demoralizing. The effect of the erosion of national consensus on the grief and coping behavior of bereaved parents is examined in the two recent wars fought by the United States and Israel.

The response of American society to those affected by the Vietnam War was hostile and demeaning at its worst and ambiguous at its best. Only recently has an effort been made to redress the balance and to express the nation's appreciation to victimized copers. Appreciation and castigation are not abstract concepts, but are attitudes that become manifest in concrete behaviors: statements and personal anecdotes presented in the mass media, in popular novels and movies written about the war, in periodic memorial ceremonies, and in other rituals.

A civil war without weapons was fought in Israel over the purposes and the goals of the conflict in Lebanon and about the meaning of the resulting loss of life, limb, and peace of mind. Many political leaders (primarily from the party then out of power) and many citizens interpreted the war as an Israeli Vietnam and as a gross miscalculation by certain political and military leaders pursuing personal aggrandizement and policies at variance with the national interest. These interpretations undermined the time-honored belief in Israel that the casualties of war represented acts of heroism and were not in vain. Many bereaved parents and other affected parties became enraged by efforts to undermine their belief that the sacrifice was called for in good faith and made to a good purpose. This reaction was so strong that in the recent national elections (July 1984), the party that had been out of power deliberately avoided the issue of the conflict in Lebanon so as not to antagonize large segments of the population. Since coming to power, this same party has assiduously avoided this issue as it gradually reduces Israel's presence and involvement in Lebanon.

Generalizations About Crises in Daily Life

Several recommendations about coping and helping in civilian crises follow from this discussion of war-related stress: first, that professional helpers clarify in advance their own implicit coping and helping models as they approach afflicted people; second, that they determine the models being used or requested by these people; third, that they develop intervention strategies that take into consideration discrepancies in attributional models that inevitably appear between copers and helpers and among helpers; fourth, that helpers not interpret the behavior of copers exclusively in terms of their own norms for "normal" or constructive behavior; fifth, that helpers treat with respect the interpretations that people make about their personal tragedies and their efforts to transcend them.

For example, some bereaved parents in Israel visit the gravesite of their departed son once a week for years after his death. Many people, professional and lay, regard this behavior as a morbid preoccupation and an obsessive-compulsive ritual detrimental to the resumption of normal functioning. Yet research has shown that the frequency of visits to the cemetery is correlated *positively* and not *negatively* with a variety of adjustment indicators in these parents (Gay, 1982). This behavior may go against the conventional wisdom of disengagement from the irreversibly lost love object, yet this self-initiated behavior may be regarded as constructive from several points of view.

First, the parents are visiting a cemetery after all, and the visit indicates acceptance that the son is, indeed, dead and will not magically return. Second, personal grief and mourning can be restricted to a time and place considered appropriate for grief, and not appear in the privacy of the home where they may become unrestrained and perseverative, or in public settings where their occurrence would be strongly censured. Third, even if the parents address their son aloud on these weekly visits and persist in the belief that he exists in some manner, at least for them, this belief may be efficacious for them, especially since it is manifested outdoors in the light of day and possibly in the company of mourners visiting other graves.

Since the behavior of people coping with tragedy is open to many, different interpretations, one concludes that professional helpers should look, listen, and learn from copers about the nature of their belief systems: about that which was damaged or destroyed, about control over events and over self, about the permanence of entities and control systems. Professional helpers tend to impose automatically their own implicit belief systems and give insufficient attention to the belief systems of their clients.

Some helpers, especially professional psychotherapists, regard belief systems as a matter of values that have no place in conventional psychotherapy. Yet, as Bergin (1980) has argued, values invariably appear in the work of all therapists. We must raise our own consciousness about our own belief systems and sharpen our scrutiny about the belief systems of others. If values are relevant to the treatment of neurotic clients who are struggling with the discrepancy between so-called objective and psychodynamic reality, they are certainly relevant to the existential struggle of people coping with genuine tragedies of life, illness, irreversible injury, and death.

2

The Precipitating Event in Crisis Theory: Calamity or Opportunity

ADRIENNE CHAMBON

A major concept in crisis theory is that of the precipitating event (PE). This term has been variously defined as a catalyst of new or wholly novel behavior or as a release mechanism for the emergence of such behavior, with analogies drawn from the chemistry of liquid suspensions and/or the physics of release mechanisms. The use of these analogies in crisis theory is illustrative of the influence of the neopositivist tradition and representative of the linear, additive, and predictable nature of phenomena in the physical sciences (Kuhn, 1962).

This chapter proposes that the use of these analogies is both restricting and misleading in dealing with human experience. The chapter elaborates critically on the features and functions of the precipitating event in crisis theory, offers alternative interpretations, and develops implications for alternative intervention strategies. The viewpoint elaborated here relies heavily on an experiential mode of understanding, with the meaning of events based on the phenomenological observations of the individual.

BASIC ISSUES IN CRISIS THEORY

Crisis theory conceives of the crisis process as a linear unfolding of stages initiated by a "hazardous event" (whether of internal or external origin), followed by a "vulnerable state" that is characterized by increasing difficulty in coping with the demands of the situation, and by progressive loss of control. The state of tension builds until a "turning point" or PE occurs in which the accumulated tension is released and the individual is propelled into a state of "active crisis" characterized by loss of control over the situation and over oneself. The crisis is resolved when the individual renews his efforts to cope and reestablishes control over situation and self (Golan, 1978).

There are three issues in crisis theory relevant to our discussion. The first is the controversy between the static and dynamic models of interpretation of the crisis. According to the static model, the crisis is an upset in a steady state (Rapaport, 1970), whereas in the dynamic model, it is a developmental phenomenon associated with transitional stages of personal growth. The treatment goal in the first instance is restoration of the previous equilibrium, and in the second, establishment of a new equilibrium.

A second issue is whether to regard the crisis situation as rising from an unfortunate failure in habitual coping mechanisms on the part of the victim or as representing a welcomed opportunity for utilizing therapeutic intervention and a readiness for change on the part of the coper.

A third issue refers to the characterization of the PE. It has been described as an accident of negligible importance from an objective point of view, and without direct significance to the core conflict of the individual in the crisis situation. It is merely the straw that breaks the camel's back. This chapter questions these assertions and argues the reverse, that the PE is internal rather than external in origin, that it is highly significant to the individual, although perhaps not to the objective observer, and that its role is highly important in the unfolding of the stages of crisis disorganization and reorganization.

These issues are resolved by phenomenologists by reference to the personal meaning that the individual gives to events transpiring in one's life prior to and during the crisis. Personal meaning can be best exemplified with reference to three major categories of the existential-phenomenological approach—time, space and its material contents, and causality.

TIME IN CRISIS INTERVENTION

Time is a crucial concept both in understanding the crisis process and in undertaking effective crisis intervention. With respect to the first, crisis is a developmental phenomenon with successive stages following one another in a time-bound and orderly fashion (Caplan, 1964). With respect to the second, timing is based on two therapeutic considerations: (1) offering immediate and intensive first aid for a major behavioral and psychological disruption and (2) exploiting the "time-limited opportunity" for openness to change that occurs during the stage of active crisis (Golan, 1978).

In crisis situations there is both objective time and subjective or "lived time." The latter is the subjective perception of the movement, flow, and direction of time as reflected in such personalized metaphors as "time eating away" versus "time as a soaring bird or arrow." The diversity of personal meanings attributed to time is related to the state of mind and existential situation of the individual with reference to the world at a particular moment and is, in turn, blended with associated meanings from past experiences, such as remorse and regret over the past, as well as wishes and expectations about the future (Ellenberger, 1958).

The effect of psychopathology on time perception has been well documented. Minkowski (1958) describes depressed patients as experiencing an arrest in the flow of time, stagnation and immobilization in the present, and a block in the movement toward the future. In the stage of vulnerability that precedes the active crisis, the individual may find himself in a similar situation, locked up in repetitive and increasingly painful attempts to cope and experiencing a growing sense of the futility of such efforts. We assume that this futility stems from efforts to maintain a *present* equilibrium by using coping skills from one's *past* repertoire, in the absence of *future* expectations and hope.

In the existential-phenomenological view, the time orientation changes dramatically and therapeutically in the breakdown that ushers in the active crisis. This breakdown may be regarded as an active choice behavior brought about by the individual to break out of the no-win situation rather than as a victimizing event for which one bears no responsibility. The PE is used as the occasion for redefining the problem and for regaining a sense of hope and urgency to find a solution now. The urgency mandates action now and implies that it is not only possible, but will be crowned with success.

SPACE AND MATERIAL

Space, like time, has a subjective dimension, "attuned space" analogous to "lived time." This subjective definition of space and its significant contents is reflected in the unique significance of the PE to the individual. A person in treatment identified "the accidental breaking of an object" as the PE introducing an active crisis, explaining that it meant all of the following: (1) "Another negative, depressive thing has happened to me"; (2) "I deserve to have such things happen to me"; (3) "I feel that the situation is breaking down and I am breaking down"; and (4) "There is no way that I can restore the wholeness in life that used to be." The contrast between the objectively trivial nature of this PE and the richly condensed meanings that it represents for this client is highly instructive.

In and of itself, the PE is nothing—an empty vessel, a blank screen—but given its symbolic content in the eyes of the experiencing individual, it is highly significant and as a condensed metaphor becomes an active way of proceeding from the *known* to the *unknown* (Breznitz & Eshel, 1983; Turner, 1974).

CAUSALITY

Causality as a phenomenological category is distinct from the other two cited above, but links them in clarifying the nature of the relationship between the individual and the crisis situation. In existential thought, the individual is presumed to make a free choice between innumerable behavioral alternatives and to fulfill his own personal intention. Although we live in a world full of externally induced factors and consequences, the authentic individual accepts complete responsibility for his choices despite the existential anguish of being in a world one cannot control. By contrast, psychiatric patients tend to adopt highly subjective and nonauthentic perceptions of causality, the paranoiac believing in the omnipotence of personal intentions, the manic in the overriding importance of benign fate, and the depressed patient in determinism (Ellenberger, 1958).

Symbolic interactionists have formulated the concept of *accounts*, a form of interpersonal communication by which one communicates to others why certain consequences follow certain circumstances in one's life (Scott & Lyman, 1968). These accounts adopt consensual vocabularies of motives and follow socially conventional rules.

A prime example is "the appeal to accident." This account relieves one of personal responsibility for an unfortunate consequence and is especially important in modern Western society, which places a high premium on personal achievement and control over the environment. By appealing to accident, one protects oneself against the accusation of incompetence or malpractice and gains the further advantage of being considered a victim of the accident. This type of account is very compelling for a person in a crisis situation because he avoids, at least temporarily, the social stigma of having failed to cope and/or of suffering a nervous breakdown and can now turn legitimately to extraordinary sources for help with the expectation that his request will be answered immediately.

The contrast between the internal attribution of responsibility for behavior and its consequences in conventional psychodynamic psychotherapy and the external attributions or accounts that are honored in crisis situations is instructive. Therapists typically indict defense mechanisms and other internal processes in accounting for the symptomatology of their clients, but not when there is a widespread cataclysmic event recorded in the mass media, e.g., a flood, fire, tornado. The violent event transforms their client into a victim and they themselves may adopt a new, but comfortable, role of savior. The crisis situation permits the intrusion into a rationalistic, internally oriented culture of a dramatic/fatalistic element that justifies the appeal to accident and the formal status of victim. However tempting this account may be for the individual, existentially oriented crisis intervention strongly urges the adopting of an authentic internal account as explained below.

IMPLICATIONS FOR TREATMENT

Existential crisis intervention is short-term, focuses on the here and now, emphasizes the use of existing cognitive and other problem-solving skills and the acquisition of new skills, and attempts to help the individual regain control over oneself and one's life situation.

The PE is the most recent event that affected the client before coming for treatment and is the motivation or occasion for treatment itself. Typically the PE is the answer to the opening ploy in therapy: What brings you here now? In giving immediate attention to the PE in initiating treatment, the therapist can both offer emergency first aid and at the same time gain access to "the real problem," since the PE is a precipitant of the major symbolic meanings of the objective event to the client.

Much more can be achieved if the PE is recognized for what it is, a bridge between the ineffectual coping behaviors of the past and the efficacious new behaviors of the future, and if it is utilized in pursuing that goal. The role of the PE as key element in a transitional stage between precrisis and crisis resolution is better understood against the framework of rites of passage in cultural anthropology. In the latter, Van Gennep (1908) speaks of separation from the old stage of obligations and duties and entry into a new stage of limbo, a protected environment where he is trained for his new role and responsibilities in a directive, highly supportive environment, prior to assuming his new role in the society. These three stages in cultural transition correspond to the three stages in crisis theory and highlight the importance of the roles adopted by client and therapist in the second, transitional and therapeutic, stage.

Classical crisis theory has tended to emphasize, and even to foster, the dependent relationship of the victim-client on the savior-therapist. This approach is inherently contradictory to the manifest goal of crisis theory: the fostering of autonomy in the client. Existential crisis intervention begins with a different premise, that the individual's "falling apart" is his or her own responsibility and that recovery will come from this recognition and appropriately autonomous learning and problem solving, and not from an acceptance of one's weakness in the face of malevolent fate. This view is consistent with that of Argyris (1968), who emphasizes the active role of the client in determining the nature and course of treatment, and with that of Oxley (1971), who assigns the client the major responsibility for identifying the causes of one's distress and for attempting to change one's behavior.

In the view presented here the client is both the stage director and the actor in the drama to which he or she is a witness and at the same time participates. In answer to the question "What brought you here today?" the client should be helped to understand that he brought himself. The PE did not bring the client to the door, but rather the client's symbolic transformation of the PE into a crisis catalyst and into an opportunity for moving from an earlier to a new equilibrium. Not infrequently the very decision to come for help and the recognition that help is more from within than without may be sufficient to initiate a series of coping and problem-solving behaviors without further contact with the therapist. This view challenges the homeostatic conception of crisis resolution as merely restoring the previous equilibrium. Its developmental corollary implies that there will be further crises on the horizon with recurring demands and opportunities for adaptation and change (Stretch, 1967).

3

The Masada Syndrome:
A Case of Central Belief

DANIEL BAR-TAL

This chapter attempts to bridge two worlds—scientific analysis of human behavior and real-life problems—by using a social psychological framework to analyze a political phenomenon. To accomplish this, one must begin with several psychological assumptions.

Knowledge within human beings consists of numerous beliefs. Some beliefs are unique to specific individuals, while others are common to members of a group or even to a number of groups. In principle, individuals' knowledge determines their reactions since individuals act on the world that they believe to exist. This assumption serves as a basis for the present chapter.

Not all beliefs have equal importance (centrality) in a given time and situation. Among the beliefs that an individual has, some are central, while others are less central. Moreover, individuals may differ with regard to the importance they attach to the same belief. Thus, the order of centrality of beliefs differs from one individual to another. Also, the order may change with time for the same individual. The degree of a belief's centrality is expressed by the frequency in which the belief is available in the cognitive system and the extent to which it is relevant for a wide range of evaluations. That is, central beliefs are often available

The author would like to thank Anat Raviv for providing bibliographic help, Nehemia Geva, Arie Kruglanski, Amiram Raviv, and Leonard Saxe for comments on the earlier draft of this paper, and Jonathan Frenkel, Charles Liebman, Irad Malkin, and Ben Ami Shiloni for advice with regard to examples used.

in the cognitive system (i.e., we often think about them) and they are frequently taken into consideration when individuals evaluate other issues including decisions to perform various behaviors.

The present chapter focuses on one belief that becomes very important in understanding group behavior, if it becomes central for the group's members. It is proposed that when group members believe in it, they are in a certain psychological state, which has important consequences for the group's life. These consequences usually go together and can be viewed as symptoms of the described psychological state. Therefore, I will refer to this state as a syndrome.* Specifically, in this chapter, I intend to describe origins and consequences of a syndrome to be called the Masada syndrome. Also, in order to support several propositions suggested in this chapter, an attempt will be made to use examples from the experiences of different groups. Special attention will be directed to the experience of Israeli Jews.

The expression "Masada syndrome" or "Masada complex" has been widely used by journalists and social scientists in Israel and other countries to describe a political-psychological situation (see, for example, Alsop, 1971, 1973; Alter, 1973; Kedar, 1973; Lewis, 1975; Shweitzer, 1982). However, the term has never been formally defined, to my knowledge. On the assumption that definitions cannot be wrong as long as they formulate the conditions that are both necessary and sufficient for the applicability of the terms defined (Kaplan, 1964), the present chapter attempts to define and analyze the term. Although the syndrome is based on a specific historical event that occurred approximately 2,000 years ago, the phenomenon may appear *at any time in any human group.*

DEFINITION

The term Masada syndrome has meaning in relation to one of the most dramatic historical events, which took place in Israel in the first century of the common era (C.E.). In the year 66 C.E., while the land of Israel was occupied by the Romans, the Jews began a revolt to regain freedom and sovereignty. The Romans crushed the rebellion, and in the year 72 C.E. Flavius Selva, the Roman governor, decided to conquer the last outpost of Jewish resistance—Masada, a fortified mountaintop over-

---

*The term "syndrome" was selected over the term "complex" since while the latter implies pathological reactions, the first implies a pattern of symptoms that characterize a particular social condition.

looking the Dead Sea.* In Masada, a group of Jewish zealots, determined to continue their battle against the Romans, prepared themselves for defense. The siege lasted for months, during which the outnumbered Jewish zealots fought bravely against the Roman Legion. They knew that the world (as they perceived it) was conquered by the Roman Empire and no help could reach them. In the end, as the Romans were close to conquering the fortress, the defenders realized that only two alternatives were open to them: surrender or death. They chose the second and took their lives with their own hands. The events at Masada have become a symbol. "Masada shall not fall again" has become a slogan that characterizes the spirit of the present generations of Israeli Jews.

The study of Masada has many elements with political-psychological meanings that have been emphasized by different historians and publicists (e.g., Lewis, 1975; Yadin, 1966). The present chapter draws from the Masada story one element that has very important implications for understanding a group's behavior in certain political-psychological situations: namely, when group members believe, as Masada's defenders did, that they are surrounded by a hostile world that wants to harm them. In his last speech Elazar, the commander of the defenders, referred to this perception implying that the fate of Jews in this world is hopeless. He described the events in Caesarea, Scythopolis, Syria, and Egypt where Jews were murdered by hostile crowds, although they had not revolted against Rome. The implication was that in this hostile world there is no place where Jews can live peacefully—the world has negative intentions toward them (Flavius, 1928).

This emphasis leads me to the following definition of the Masada syndrome: *The Masada syndrome is a state in which members of a group hold a central belief that the rest of the world has highly negative behavioral intentions toward that group.* As a central belief held by group members, it is not a disposition or stable trait, but a temporary state of mind that can last for either a short or long period of time—as long as the belief is central. This state is aroused when the belief becomes central in the cognitive repertoire of the group's members. But, with a change in the conditions or circumstances, the belief may become less central. Over time, it may even disappear from the repertoire, depending on the group's experiences. The conditions that arouse this belief will be described in the next section.

The Masada syndrome may characterize a part or a whole group in

---

*In Hebrew Masada is pronounced "Matzadah."

a society. It is not necessary that all members of the group hold the belief. The syndrome occurs within a group when a significant part of the group, who are not marginal, hold it. The strength of the syndrome is related (positively) to the number and the influence of the group's members who believe in the negative intentions of the world. The larger and more influential the group, the stronger the consequences of the syndrome.

The essence of the Masada syndrome is a belief in a specific content. A belief is defined as a proposition of any possible content in which an individual has a meaningful degree of confidence that it is true. The content of the discussed belief refers to the negative behavioral intentions that the rest of the world has toward the group. Negative intentions refer to the tendency to do wrong or to inflict harm. In general, they imply threat to a group's welfare. Thus, it is probable to assume that the belief in the negative intentions of the world is associated with other beliefs, such as that they are alone in the world, that there is a threat to their existence, and that they cannot expect help from anyone in time of need.

The crucial component of the definition refers to the subject of the belief—the rest of the world. This element is unique to the belief, since each group probably believes that at least one other group has negative intentions toward it. But, with the Masada syndrome, the situation is far more extreme. Members of the group believe not only that the group is surrounded by hostile neighbors, but that all other groups are hostile toward them. This belief indicates a very tragic perception, comparable to one held by Masada defenders, that the group is alone in a hostile world. It should be noted, however, that the subject of the belief does not have to include *all* the groups in the world. It refers to those groups that are relevant to the belief holders, those groups in the world that function as reference groups—either because of the desire to have positive relations with them or because they have influence on the welfare of the group. Clearly, the number and importance of these reference groups may change with time depending on political, social, and economic conditions.

The proposed definition implies that the Masada syndrome is a psychologically subjective state. Members of a group *believe* that other groups have negative intentions toward them and as a consequence may feel a threat to their existence. It is not important whether other groups actually have such intentions. The phenomenon is determined by the fact that the negative intentions are believed to exist. The objectivity of this belief cannot be determined since if this reality exists for certain people, it is difficult to convince them that the subjective reality of other people is more objective. As psychologists have pointed out:

> Man acts upon his ideas. His irrational acts no less than his rational acts are guided by what he thinks, what he believes, what he anticipates. However bizarre the behavior of men, tribes, or nations may appear to an outsider, to the men, to the tribes, to the nations, their behavior makes sense in terms of their own world views. (Krech, Crutchfield, & Ballachey, 1962, p. 17)

Individuals hold their beliefs with various degrees of confidence. Highly confident beliefs are considered as facts, while beliefs held with low confidence are considered as hypotheses. Facts and hypotheses are beliefs, however, since beliefs considered to be facts have often been found to be erroneous. This position, that all our knowledge is ultimately conjectural and uncertain, is maintained by the influential nonjustificationist philosophers of knowledge such as Karl Popper, Thomas Kuhn, Imre Lakatos, and Paul Feyerabend. Recently, Kruglanski and his colleagues (Kruglanski, 1980; Kruglanski & Ajzen, 1983; Kruglanski, Baldwin, & Towson, 1986) have applied this approach to an analysis of various psychological contents. Kruglanski has suggested that the contents of beliefs cover an infinite number of topics, which differ with regard to the confidence with which they are held. All of these beliefs, however, are formed via the same epistemic process.

In this framework, called lay epistemology, the belief in negative intentions of other groups is not an exception and, therefore, it may be held by different individuals with different degrees of confidence. Individuals interpret differently the same information, and while some members may see danger creeping up, other members may not notice any threat. Moreover, members of other groups may not themselves believe that they have negative intentions toward a specific group. Robert Jervis (1976), in his highly acclaimed book *Perception and Misperception in International Politics*, provides numerous examples of erroneous beliefs held by nations with regard to their relations with other nations. Nevertheless, it should be emphasized that this position does not claim that the experiences of the group may not be true. The experiences are the reality of the given group, considered by them as facts. This believed reality determines the behavior of the group members, including their intergroup relations (de Rivera, 1968; Holsti, 1977; Shapiro & Bonham, 1973; Stagner, 1967).

EXAMPLES

In the history of the human race there are quite a few examples of the Masada syndrome. There were and still are groups that believed and/or believe that the rest of the world has negative intentions toward them. A few examples follow taken mainly from modern history.

One example is the Albanian situation for the last two decades. Following a change in Soviet leader Khrushchev's policy toward Yugoslavia, relations between the Eastern block and Albania started to deteriorate until in October 1961 relations broke off completely. These events isolated Albania entirely in the world because it had not had relations with the West since the end of World War II. Following these events, Albanian leaders, believing that they were surrounded by a hostile world, refused any type of relations offered by Western countries and used the political and economic boycott to strengthen Albanian socialistic patriotism and isolationism. For years, Albanians have continued to believe in a "capitalist-revisionist blockade and encirclement." The isolation of this country continues until today and foreigners are treated with suspicion (Marmullaku, 1975; Pollo & Puto, 1981).

Another example of the Masada syndrome is South Africa. Especially since the expulsion of South Africa from the British Commonwealth in 1961, following a violent incident in Sharpeville, South Africans perceive themselves as a nation driven with its back to the wall by a hostile world (see for example Barber, 1974; Brown, 1966; Johnson, 1977). Legum and Legum (1964) have cited numerous expressions of South African political leadership that demonstrate this perception:

The world is against us. But we have stood before—belied, slandered and spied upon. (Dr. Hertzog, Minister of Post and Telegraphs, *The Star*, December 16, 1960)

Or

The world is driving South Africa with apartheid into a corner where the matter will have to be fought out, back against the wall—that is unless the present government abdicates in the name of the black man which by implication is unthinkable. (President Swart, *Die Oosterlig*, December 8, 1961)

Also in Japan, in the 1930s, there was a widespread belief that the world had negative intentions toward it. The immediate event that increased the availability and centrality of this belief was the vote of the League of Nations in 1933, which approved almost unanimously an anti-Japanese resolution. This vote followed Japanese military action in Manchuria. As a result, Japan withdrew from the League of Nations. The feeling among the Japanese leadership was that the world was hostile toward them (see Crowley, 1966; Morley, 1974). Hashimoto Kingoro, a prominent army leader of an extremist group, expressed this belief in the following way:

At the time of the Manchurian incident, the entire world joined in criticism of Japan. They said that Japan was an untrustworthy nation. (Tsunoda, de Barry, & Kenne, 1958, p. 797)

And in another place he complained that

. . . emigration has been barred to us by the anti-Japanese immigration policies of other countries. . . . the advance into world markets is being pushed shut by tariff barriers and the abrogation of commercial treaties. (p. 796)

The Masada syndrome was observed among the Bolsheviks during the foreign intervention in the civil war between 1918 and 1920. Various countries (the Russians claim 14) intervened by sending military units to fight in the civil war and by imposing economic sanctions (see Fischer, 1951; Kennan, 1960). Russia perceived these actions as a capitalistic conspiracy to crush the emerging state (e.g., Ponomaryov, Gromyko, & Uhvostov, 1969). The following description exemplifies this belief:

The imperialists had no intention of allowing the new socialist system to exist and went to all ends to destroy it by armed force. (Ponomaryov, Gromyko, & Uhvostov, 1969, p. 141)

Lenin and other Soviet leaders expressed this belief frequently on different occasions. In the closing speech at the eighth party congress on March 23, 1919, Lenin said:

The time at which we have met is exceptionally difficult because international imperialism, and of this there is absolutely no doubt, is making a last and very strenuous effort to crush the Soviet Republic. (Lenin, 1943, p. 45)

On November 7, 1918, Lenin said:

The capitalists of the whole world in terror and hatred hurried to rally together for the revolution's suppression. And the Socialist Soviet Republic of Russia is a particular thorn in their side. The combined imperialists of the world are prepared to attack us, to involve us in more battles, and to impose more sacrifice on us. (Lenin, 1965, p. 167)

Similarly, Stalin on Feb. 22, 1919, in describing the events, suggested that imperialism "was rattling the sabre and treatening to overrun Russia with its armed hordes" (Franklin, 1973, p. 86).

The State of Israel provides a final example of the Masada syndrome in this discussion. The proposition that the world has negative intentions toward them has been believed by Jews in Israel for years, although the centrality of this belief has changed from time to time depending on specific events. Here are a few recent examples of situations when the belief became central.

After the Arab oil embargo in 1973 that followed the Yom Kippur War, Amnon Rubinstein, a leading Israeli publicist, wrote:

The entire world is in hysteria. With the Arab oil weapon aimed at their heads, the governments of the world are standing with a stop-watch and urge us to withdraw, to concede, to yield. (*Haaretz*, December 12, 1973)

Abba Eban, the Foreign Minister at that time, said:

The October war brought us face to face with the crisis of our human vulnerability. Anyone who reads or writes about Jewish history comes up against this preoccupation again and again. The special pathos of Jewish History lies in the immense place occupied by the problem of being Jewish yet staying alive. (*Jerusalem Post*, December 4, 1973)

Following the adoption by the General Assembly of the United Nations on November 10, 1975 of a resolution defining Zionism as a form of racism and racial discrimination, the belief in the negative intentions of the world toward Israel again became central. The Israeli government issued a statement on November 11, 1975 stating that

The resolution adapted tonight by the General Assembly of the United Nations denigrating Zionism is aimed at the entire Jewish people since anti-Zionism is simply anti-Semitism. . . . this resolution has roots in Hitler's teachings. (*Ma'ariv*, November 11, 1975)

Yitzhak Rabin, then Israel's Prime Minister, said,

> The Assembly has reached its nadir in adapting two resolutions
> whose meaning is the denial of the State of Israel's right to exist.
> (*Ma'ariv*, November 11, 1975)

The last example is the most recent. Following the massacre of Palestinian Arabs in the Sabra and Shatila refugee camps by Lebanese
Christian Phalangists between the 16th and 18th of September, 1982, the
media as well as many world leaders vociferously denounced the Jewish
State government as being responsible for the events. In turn, many
Israelis believed the criticism was not justified and that world reaction
reflected negative intentions against Israelis and, more generally, Jews.
This belief is expressed in the statement by the Israeli government issued
on September 20, 1982, which said, "At the New Year a blood libel was
hurled at the Jewish State and at the Israel Defense Forces" (*Yedioth
Ahronoth*, September 20, 1982). Ariel Sharon, the Defense Minister, in
a television interview on September 25, 1982 said: "We live in a hostile
world of anti-Semitism and political plans it tries to enforce on us"
(*Yedioth Ahronoth*, September 26, 1982). Itzhak Shamir, the Foreign Minister, said in New York on September 27, 1982 that: "We must push
back the murky flood of terrible lies disseminated in the world aimed
at denigrating our name and letting our blood" (*Yedioth Ahronoth*, September 28, 1982). On September 25, 1982, the Chief of Staff of the Israel
Defense Forces, Rafael Eitan, issued a letter to soldiers in which he said:
"Throughout our long history we were the victims of pogroms, and
massacres in which the blood of innocent people was spilled. . . . The
nations of the world now express pain at what happened in Beirut. Their
anguish is not genuine anguish. They are cynically settling accounts
with us while exploiting the tragedy for their political needs" (*Haaretz*,
September 26, 1982). Finally, the President, Yitzhak Navon, said on
September 30, 1982, in reaction to the British Labour Party's recognition
of the PLO, that "Labour's decision is a further libel in the framework
of the defamation campaign taking place throughout the world against
Israel because of the massacre in Beirut" (*Ma'ariv*, October 1, 1982).

ORIGINS

This section will focus on three possible origins of the Masada syndrome: (a) past experience, (b) present perceived intentions, and (c)

group needs. Each of the origins will be discussed separately, although they are not mutually exclusive.

Past Experience

Human history is, unfortunately, full of wars and hostility. Through-out history, many groups experienced persecutions, pogroms, and hatred by other groups. Understandably they believed they were sur-rounded by hostility. Such experience may result in a persistence of the Masada syndrome years after the events took place. Even when the circumstances change drastically, the belief may still persist. Traumatic experiences leave their mark for generations, even centuries (Krystal, 1968). New generations are socialized on the basis of the past experience and they continue to hold the belief that causes the Masada syndrome. As a result, even when the political circumstances and conditions change, the beliefs may continue to persist. Members of the group may continue to search and/or to find evidence that validates the belief. As long as cultural mechanisms such as literature, art, and educational materials maintain this belief, it will persist.

Jewish history is one of the most tragic examples of past hostile ex-periences. The hatred of Jews can be traced from the Roman period through the Dark Ages, the Crusades, the Inquisition, the Reformation, and the Industrial Revolution until our day (Poliakov, 1974). In the twentieth century the Holocaust, the climax of anti-Semitism, took place and served as "the final solution to the Jewish problem." The book by Grosser and Halperin (1979) catalogs and lists hundreds of anti-Semitic incidents from the Roman period to present times in Western civilization, as well as in Islamic countries. According to their catalog, these incidents took the form of anti-Semitic writings, libel, requirements for distinctive dress, special taxes, restrictions of all kinds—social, religious, civil, res-idential, and economic—and forced conversions, expulsions, violent attacks, and mass murder.

The belief that the world is anti-Semitic has become part of the cog-nitive repertoire of Jews throughout the world (e.g., Liebman, 1978; Stein, 1978). Liebman (1978) suggested that:

> Jewish tradition finds Antisemitism to be the norm, the natural response of the non-Jew. . . . The term "Esau hates Jacob" sym-bolizes the world which Jews experience. It is deeply embedded in the Jewish folk tradition. (p. 45)

Results of an opinion poll taken in Israel on September 24–26, 1978, following the broadcasting of the TV series "Holocaust" (Levinson, 1979), provide evidence for this proposition. In this poll, 533 adults and 540 adolescents were interviewed in the four Israeli cities (Jerusalem, Tel-Aviv, Haifa, and Beersheba). The results showed that 41% of the adults and 39% of the adolescents believed that "what happened then, can happen again." Among respondents, 72% of the adults and 67% of the adolescents believed that there still is a hatred of Jews in the world. It is therefore proposed that if one is to understand Israeli Jewish reactions, one has to take into consideration the effects of the belief in the hostility of the world toward them (Brecher, 1975; Liebman & Don-Yehiya, 1986).

Golda Meir, Israeli Prime Minister from 1969 to 1974, expressed this belief directly, saying, "We do have a Masada complex. We have a pogrom complex. We have a Hitler complex" (Alsop, S., *Newsweek*, March 19, 1973). The late Finance Minister, Pinhas Sapir, said in the Knesset:

> We have a Warsaw Ghetto complex, a complex of the hatred of the Jewish People, just as we are filled with a Masada complex. . . . From the fighters of the Warsaw Ghetto, from the fighters in the ghettoes, in the forests and from the other camps we inherited the justified feeling with our backs to the wall. This feeling guided us in our various struggles and wars. . . . (*Haaretz*, April 29, 1973)

The effect of past experiences on maintenance of the Masada syndrome is not unique to the Israelis. A number of political scientists and historians suggested that in part the reactions of the Soviet leadership, such as the secretiveness, suspicion, hostility, and lack of frankness, can be understood in light of the Allied intervention during the Civil War between 1918 and 1920 (e.g., Bronfenbrenner, 1964; Kennan, 1947, 1960; Warth, 1963). The belief that the aims of the capitalistic world are antagonistic to the Soviet regime are based, at least partially, on the past experiences and:

> The cultivation of the semi-myth of implacable foreign hostility, has gone far to shape the actual machinery of Soviet power as we know it today. (Kennan, 1947, p. 571)

In this vein, Stalin defended organs of suppression several years after the war ended on the grounds that:

> As long as there is a capitalist encirclement there will be danger

of intervention with all the consequences that flow from that danger. (in Kennan, 1947)

Present Perceived Intentions

The Masada syndrome may also originate as a result of present perceived intentions. Even without past traumatic experiences, members of a group may perceive negative intentions by the rest of the world toward them in a specific situation. The belief may originate as a consequence of explicit cues such as verbal threats, hostile declarations, and even an actual attack or as a consequence of implicit cues such as criticism or armament. In this vein, Pruitt (1965) has suggested that the definition of the situation is determined in part by actions of other nations that serve as a major source of information about intentions. However, although some actions are unambiguous, others are obscure and are open to various interpretations. Members of the group may interpret the cues as indicating negative intentions. If the belief did not exist before in the cognitive repertoire of the group, the perceived intentions bring it out.

Group Needs

The Masada syndrome may also originate as a result of the needs of the members of a group. In this case, the belief may be relevant to the needs of the individuals and/or the group, but be unrelated to the group's relations with others. In other words, the belief that other groups have negative intentions may not be based on past experience or a present perceived threat, but may originate within the group, independently of the information coming from other groups. In this case, channels of communication within the group may provide information indicating that other groups have negative intentions toward this group. The provided information may be absorbed and become a belief widely shared by group members. The causes for acceptance of the information and formation of the belief are based on the proposition that the discussed belief may be functional for group members as individuals and/or for the group as a whole.

From the individual's perspective, much has been written about the functions of personal hostility and paranoia toward other groups (e.g., Adorno, Frenkel-Brunswik, Levinson, & Sanford, 1950; Allport, 1954). But I would like to focus only on three functions that do not necessarily refer to pathological reactions. First, such a belief permits us to define the world in relatively simple terms. It provides a simple structure to organize the individual's world and allows one to respond in well-defined ways. The belief that other groups have negative intentions allows group members to evaluate the world in terms of "we" and "they" (Hornstein, 1976). The "we" versus "they" distinction allows for a clear definition of group boundaries. As Coser (1956) pointed out,

> . . . group boundaries are established through conflict with the outside, so that a group defines itself by struggling with other groups. (p. 87)

Frenkel-Brunswik (1949) proposed that some people find it difficult to tolerate or manage cognitive ambiguities. These people tend to dichotomize the world. Things, people, groups are seen as all good or all bad.

> They tend to resort to black-white solutions, to arrive at premature closure as to valuative aspects often at the neglect of reality and to seek for unqualified and unambiguous over-all acceptance and rejection of other people. (Frenkel-Brunswik, 1949, p. 115)

The black and white picture of "good guy and bad guy" reduces effort, since there is no need to make lengthy judgments or decisions in the face of ambiguous information, but merely to categorize the information as "we" and "they."

Recently Kruglanski and Ajzen (1983) sharpened this idea by proposing that individuals may have a need for structure in a certain situation. According to them, the need for structure is the desire to have some guiding knowledge on a given topic as opposed to confusion and ambiguity. This desire may heighten the tendency to seek cognitive closure and to refrain from critical probing. The need for structure intensifies every time an individual is under pressure to form a clear opinion or reach a definite decision. The categorization "we" against "they" satisfies the described desire since it provides structure and enables one to make quick judgments.

Second, the belief prepares individuals for the worst in their life. Disappointment in this case is impossible; only an unexpected surprise can occur. Individuals have a need to live in a world in which the future can be predicted. Unpredictable events may cause serious negative reactions, especially if the events are harmful. Individuals prefer to be surprised for the good, but not for the bad. Expectations of negative events prevent disappointment, when they occur. Therefore, some individuals may prefer to form negative expectations rather than to experience disappointments. The belief in the negative intentions of other groups does not allow disappointment and unpredictable negative acts. Liebman (1978), in discussing the acceptance of the anti-Semitic norm by religious Jews, similarly points out that:

> . . . it provides some protection against the trauma of anti-Semitism since it prepares the traditionally religious Jew, at least psychologically, for this phenomenon. (p. 45)

The late Finance Minister Pinchas Sapir expressed this idea directly when he said:

> If we don't believe [that our backs are against the wall], if we don't take into account the worst possibility, we will bring upon ourselves a Holocaust because of our short sightedness. (*Haaretz*, April 29, 1973)

Third, the belief in the negative intentions of the other groups may enable the belief holders to act freely. Individuals often think that since the world is against them, they are less restricted by considerations that usually limit alternatives for reactions. Considerations that usually guide intergroup relations do not apply to the situation when the members of a certain group feel a real threat from the negative intention of other groups. The social pressure of other groups is rejected. In this case, they can reject the social pressure of these other groups and can freely decide what course of action to take in order to avert the danger.

From the group perspective, Coser (1956), in his classic book about group conflicts, describes the functionality of an intergroup conflict. He suggests two principal functions: (1) outside conflict heightens morale within the group, and (2) conflict with other groups "leads to mobilization of the energies of group members and hence to increased cohesion of the group" (p. 95). It is, thus, not surprising that various elements within a group may use the belief to increase unity, personal sacrifice, or cohesiveness, or to facilitate achievement of desired objectives. Such use has been known through history especially during times of civil conflict, economic hardship, or political failure. Simmel (1955) wrote 30 years ago that:

> Within certain groups, it may even be a piece of political wisdom

to see to it that there be some enemies in order for the unity of the members to remain effective and for the group to remain conscious of this unity as its vital interest. (p. 98)

In this vein, Collins (1973), who analyzed the relationship between foreign conflicts and domestic disorders in African countries, noted that:

In times of extreme domestic tension, among elites, a policy of uniting a badly divided nation against some real or alleged outside threat frequently seems useful to a ruling group. Elites fearful of losing their position in the nation as a result of sharp ideological and group conflict, . . . attempt to displace the attention of the disaffected portion of the nation from its grievance and toward some outside target. (p. 62)

CONSEQUENCES

The Masada syndrome may have various consequences, of which four will be discussed. First, it is suggested that the threatened group develops negative attitudes toward other groups. Second, the threatened group becomes sensitive to cues emitted by other groups that may indicate negative intentions. Third, the threatened group develops internal mechanisms to cope with the threat by increasing pressures among group members toward conformity and unity. Finally, the group, in view of the perceived threat, uses all necessary means toward other groups for self-defense.

Development of Negative Attitudes

Members of a group who believe that other groups have negative intentions toward them develop negative attitudes toward those groups. This reaction can be predicted on the basis of a number of psychological theories. Balance theory predicts that individuals tend to dislike those who dislike them (Heider, 1958). Exchange theory predicts that individuals reciprocate with harm to perceived negative intentions (Blau, 1964). Theorists of aggression suggest that individuals react aggressively when they perceive an intention to harm them (Baron, 1977; Berkowitz, 1969). This reaction is not unique to interpersonal relations, but is also observed in intergroup relations as well (e.g., Lieberman, 1964; Phillips, 1973). Negative actions of one group are met with negative reactions of the other group. The belief that other groups have negative intentions causes them to be disliked. The threatened group develops hostility toward other groups. Moreover, members of the group who have negative attitudes toward other groups may also develop lack of trust and suspiciousness toward these groups. This framework contributes to the understanding of possible causes of suspicion and mistrust that Soviet and Albanian governments exhibit in dealing with Western countries (Kennan, 1947; Pollo & Puto, 1981).

Development of Sensitivity

Members of a group who feel threatened by other groups develop sensitivity to cues emitted by those groups that may indicate their negative intentions. Since the group's members do not want to be surprised by the negative actions of the other groups, they search for information that may indicate their expected intentions. This sensitivity may lead to motivation for a specific conclusion (Kruglanski & Ajzen, 1983) that denotes the desire to uphold a belief in a particular content. Individuals who have this motivation refrain from replacing the held belief by being less sensitive to evidence and ideas that are inconsistent with the belief and by being more disposed to accept the evidence or ideas that support the given belief. In our case, members of the group may search for information to validate their belief in the negative intentions of other groups and disregard information inconsistent with this belief. Thus, from the incoming information they will select especially those cues which show the negative intentions of other groups. Also, ambiguous information may be interpreted as validating the belief. In this situation, any criticism, disapproval, blame, or condemnation, even in the most constructive and friendly way, may be perceived as a demonstration of negative intentions. Finally, members of the group may even unintentionally distort information in order to validate their belief. In this context of special interest is George Kennan's proposition that:

> It is an undeniable privilege of every man to prove himself in the right of the thesis that the world is his enemy; for if he reiterates it frequently enough and makes it the background of his conduct, he is bound eventually to be right. (Kennan, 1947, p. 569)

Psychologists have long recognized the possibility of selective sensitization and distortion. Numerous studies show that cognitive sets may sensitize individuals to lower their threshold for recognizing and attending to certain information (e.g., Dearborn & Simon, 1958; Postman & Brown, 1952). Also, studies have demonstrated that individuals may distort the incoming information so that it fits cognitive sets (e.g., Hastorf & Cantril, 1954; Pepitone, 1950).

Pressure Toward Conformity

At times when members of the group believe that the other groups have negative intentions toward them, they prepare themselves for the worst possible coming actions. At these times, cohesiveness and unity are important conditions to withstand the possible threat. In order to achieve these objectives, members who most strongly hold the belief exert pressure on others toward conformity and unity. This pressure can take various forms, among them calls for unity and calls for concealment of disagreement within the group, as well as exerting negative sanctions against those who disagree within the group. Coser (1956) suggested that:

> Groups engaged in continued struggle with the outside tend to be intolerant within. They are unlikely to tolerate more than limited departures from the group unity. (p. 103)

In another place, Coser continued this idea even further by suggesting that:

> Not only does such a group define an actual dissent as "enemy activity," but it tends to "invent" both inside and outside enemies in order to strengthen its inner solidarity. (p. 102)

Examples of calls for unity can be found in the speeches by leaders who believe in the negative intentions of the rest of the world toward their group. During the Civil War, Lenin called the workers to:

> close their ranks more firmly than ever and set an example of organisation and discipline in this struggle. (Lenin, 1965, p. 33)

Yitzhak Rabin, the Prime Minister during the time of the UN resolution against Zionism, proposed that:

> Israel and the entire Jewish people must learn a lesson from the latest resolutions by the General Assembly. The lesson is that we

must all fight as one man for the aims we believe in for the sake of the Jewish people and the State of Israel. (*Maariv*, November 11, 1975)

Also, following Sabra and Shatila in September 1982, an editorial in *Maariv* on October 1, 1982 stated:

Many of us would like to see during these terrible times a sign of national reconciliation after everything that we have gone through, especially after the anti-Israeli and anti-Jewish pogrom atmosphere in Europe and also partly in the United States.

Self-Defense

In a situation in which members of a group believe that other groups have negative intentions toward them, they may take drastic measures in order to prevent possible danger. Their actions may not be within the range of accepted norms of intergroup behavior. A group that feels danger may decide that the goal to survive is so important that all means can be used and therefore may decide to take courses of action considered extreme and unacceptable by the international community. In this situation, group members may disregard any unfavorable reactions from these other suspect groups and continue to behave in a way they believe will repulse possible dangers to the group's existence. It is, thus, not surprising that Pruitt and Snyder (1963) suggested that a perceived threat is one of the causes for wars, and Lieberman (1964) noted that militant actions are strengthened under external threat. For example, in Israel voices are heard that call for the disregard of possible reactions by the international community in making political decisions. In a statement issued by the Israeli government following the Beirut massacre there is a sentence saying: "Nobody will preach to us on ethics and dignity of human life" (*Yediot Ahronoth*, September 20, 1982). Minister of Energy Yitzhak Berman, who resigned following the massacre, said in an interview: "The belief is held by several ministers that 'the people shall dwell alone' which in practice means that Israel does not have to take into consideration the reactions of other countries . . ." (*Yediot Ahronoth*, September 24, 1982).

The disregard of accepted norms applies not only to intergroup relations, but also to intragroup processes. When group members are threatened by other groups, they may use means within the group that are not accepted at other times. In times of danger, the group members may take action to ensure unity, to mobilize the group members for struggle, and to facilitate acts that eliminate the threat beyond the accepted norms. The repulsion of the perceived threat in such times is considered more important than norms that guide intragroup and intergroup relations.

It is in this perspective that Lenin's justification for the use of terror after the Allied intervention should be seen. On July 15, 1918 Lenin said:

> Everyone must give his life if necessary to defend Soviet power, to defend the interests of the working people, the exploited, the poor, to defend socialism. . . . we shall fully and wholeheartedly support and carry out the ruthless punishment of the traitors. (Lenin, 1965, p. 541)

Later, on December 5, 1919, Lenin explained that:

> The terror was forced on us by the terrorism of the Entente and by the terrorism of all powerful Capitalism. (pp. 66–67)

CONCLUSIONS

The basic assumption of this chapter is that the beliefs about the world that people have determine their reactions. Central beliefs are of special importance in determining behavior. They are available in the cognitive repertoire of individuals and are frequently considered when individuals decide how to react.

This chapter described one belief, namely, that the world has negative intentions toward one's own group. Group members who have this belief may take courses of action that they would not take otherwise.

This chapter describes the nature of the belief, its origins and consequences, but does not intend to imply any valuative evaluation. The belief can be part of a group member's reality, and no one has a monopoly on objectivity to judge whether the belief is valid. What can be seen as an ambiguous cue for one person can be viewed as validated evidence for another. History is full of examples of minorities who perceived certain cues as predicting events that later occurred and of majorities who predicted certain events that never took place. In the same way, the belief in the world's negative intentions is real for a group suffering persecutions or pogroms. *The thesis of this chapter does not deny the experiences of the group, but emphasizes their subjective nature.*

Nevertheless, I would like to point out one aspect of the presented analysis that has implications for the stability and centrality of the belief—namely, the type of epistemic motivation that guides group members in collecting information regarding the intentions of other groups. The type of epistemic motivation that group members have determines the extent to which they are open to various types of information. If group members are motivated by a need for a specific conclusion, that is, to maintain the belief in the negative intentions of the world, then the belief is "frozen," the individuals no longer evaluate it against competing alternatives and/or inconsistent bits of information. With the freezing, the belief is held with greater confidence. Group members are open only to information that validates the belief and disregard contradictory information. Moreover, group members may actively search for information that validates the belief and may even distort inconsistent evidence.

The question at this point is whether it is possible to unfreeze such beliefs. According to Kruglanski and Ajzen (1983), it is possible to unfreeze a belief either by changing the individual's cognitive capacity or by evoking the fear of the invalidity, which is another epistemic motivation. With regard to changing the capacity, the authors propose to enhance group members' stored knowledge via learning or education, in order to improve their capacity to recognize various bits of evidence and to entertain alternative hypotheses. New information may enhance cognitive availability of new ideas and unfreeze the belief. The second method, to evoke fear of invalidity, stems from the need to avoid costly mistakes. In situations in which group members fear invalidity they are reluctant to commit themselves to a given hypothesis. Instead, they search for information that raises competing alternatives to the presently entertained hypothesis.

The primary question of the present analysis is whether group members have the capacity and motivation to collect information that may contradict the belief that other groups have negative intentions toward them. If they do not, it should be understood that the consequences of the belief have serious effects on the group's life.

4

Pathogenesis and Salutogenesis in War and Other Crises: Who Studies the Successful Coper?

AARON ANTONOVSKY and JUDITH BERNSTEIN

The first formulation of the idea of salutogenesis appeared in a study of concentration camp survivors (Antonovsky, Maoz, Dowty, & Wijsenbeek, 1971):

> Out data are very consistent in showing that middle-aged Israeli women of central European origin who were concentration camp survivors are, as a group, more poorly adapted . . . than are the women in a control group. . . . What is, however, of greater fascination and of human and scientific import . . . is the fact that a not-inconsiderable number of concentration camp survivors were found to be well-adapted. . . . What, we must ask, has given these women the strength, despite their experience, to maintain what would seem to be the capacity not only to function well, but even to be happy. (p. 190)

PATHOGENESIS AND SALUTOGENESIS

The bulk of stress research is dominated by a pathogenic paradigm. The central question asked is: How do stressors eventuate in undesirable illness outcomes? The Holmes-Rahe Schedule of Recent Experiences is a prototypical example of this approach. A vast amount of work has been invested in studies of the stressor-illness paradigm. When paradigms fail to explain data, they are tinkered with, but not necessarily rejected. Mediating or coping variables are introduced as buffers. They add increased validity to the paradigm, but the outcome variable remains illness.

In contrast, the salutogenic orientation (Antonovsky, 1979) makes three radically different proposals. First, studies should be designed to test hypotheses explaining successful, i.e., healthy, outcomes. Second, in data analysis and discussion, thought should be given to the deviant case, i.e., the always substantial number of people who, even when the pathogenic hypothesis is supported, do well even though they are in the high stressor category. And third, our thinking should be open to the possibility that stressors may have salutary consequences.

Let us give a few examples of the predominance of the pathogenic orientation. First, in the concentration camp survivor study mentioned above, it did not occur to the researchers to obtain data that might help explain why some survivors were well adapted. Second, we are all familiar with the type A behavior pattern and its relation to coronary heart disease. Do we know anything about type B's other than that they are non-type A? Why don't they get heart disease? Third, in the November 1982 APA *Monitor* appeared a report of a study of schizophrenia in Israel, which compared kibbutz and city children of schizophrenic mothers. Different percentages of each group of children in the follow-up study exhibited schizophrenia or suffered from an affective illness. There was no mention, however, of those who, despite growing up with a schizophrenic mother, did not merit a DSM-III diagnosis. Is not this an equally crucial question?

METHOD

Is the salutogenic orientation really as rare as we suggest? Of greater import, what are the consequences of adopting a pathogenic versus a salutogenic orientation? To begin answering these questions, we decided to review a manageable number of published papers. A set of six papers deal with war-related stress, chiefly in Israel. A second set of 25 papers are analyzed, which appeared in three selected journals: *Journal of Health and Social Behavior, Psychosomatic Medicine,* and the *International Journal of Psychiatry in Medicine.* To obtain this set of papers, we reviewed all the original articles published in the most recent issues available to us. In all, we covered 20 issues, which included 138 papers. Of these, 25 met our criteria for consideration: first, that the study provided some original data; second, that it referred to some outcome variable that could be ranked on a desirable-undesirable continuum in health-illness terms (not only disease or mortality, but symptoms, pain, smoking, and the like); and third, that there was some implicit or explicit reference to stressors. The journals are not, of course, representative of all the scientific work that deals with the stressor-health/illness relationship. We think, however, that we have not obtained a distorted picture. We did not examine journals directed specifically to psychologists in the hope that psychologists will be stimulated to examine their own journals with a fresh eye.

We do not think it particularly important that of the 31 papers reviewed, 19 had a fairly clear pathogenic orientation, 10 were salutogenic, and two had elements of both approaches—although we were pleasantly surprised that the array was less lopsided than we had anticipated. Our concern, rather, in analyzing these papers is to illustrate the two different modes of thinking in research, and, in particular, to suggest the power of salutogenic research.

RESULTS

War and Stress Studies

Six papers analyzed are studies of war-related stress. Four deal with mental breakdown during the Yom Kippur War; the fifth is a study of psychiatric hospitalization of Israeli soldiers during peacetime; and the sixth relates to the outcome of stressors of the war in Vietnam.

Jaffe and Rosenfeld (1982) compared men who had broken down in combat to a volunteer control group. Their concern was to test hypotheses relating three personality attributes—field dependence, intropunitiveness, and impaired sexual differentiation—to the likelihood of war neurosis. Despite some consideration in their introductory remarks about how reactive hostility may be functional and protective in a war situation, their overwhelming concern, which becomes their exclusive concern in the discussion of the data that support their hypotheses, is with breakdown. We learn that the combat stress reaction group was characterized by guilt, shame, and the inhibition of aggression and frustration. We learn nothing from this pathogenically oriented paper about those who did not break down.

Dasberg (1982), dealing with the same problem, takes one step in this direction. He presents, in contrast to loneliness, the idea of "belonging, which is based on a feeling of secure identity" (p. 143) and speaks of the "acceptance of the army unit as a substitute family" (p. 144). But Dasberg, a pathogenically oriented clinician, emphasizes the factors that promote battle breakdown. His case examples and his detailed analysis are oriented to delineating factors interfering with group belonging. Are we to conclude that the factors that enhance group belonging are so well understood as to obviate all consideration?

Steiner and Neumann's (1982) comparison of 74 men with post-traumatic combat reactions to 100 elite paratroopers without breakdown, on the other hand, is clearly salutogenic. Their data focused on trust in commanding officers, self-confidence, perception of high group morale, and fighting the entire war in one's own outfit. Particularly noteworthy is the fact that those in the control group had had significantly more difficult combat experiences—being cut off, heavy losses in their units, exhaustion, etc.—yet they did not break down. This is the real mystery to be explained.

Levav, Greenfeld, and Baruch's (1979) epidemiologic study of psychiatric combat reactions of Israeli soldiers during the Yom Kippur War compares soldiers who were physical casualties with those who were psychiatric casualties on a variety of demographic and sociopsychological characteristics. Since these investigators were not concerned with soldiers who stayed on the "ease" end of the continuum, they did not include a control group of noncasualties in their study. The only treatment outcome for the psychiatric patients was change in military-psychiatric profile evaluation. Fifty-five percent of the soldiers who had psychiatric combat reactions received poorer evaluations at the end of the war than they had at its outset, and the status of these soldiers tended to worsen during an 18-month follow-up. We learn a great deal about those with pathological outcomes. We learn nothing about the "deviant" 45% whose psychiatric profiles remained unchanged or improved.

By contrast, a salutogenic orientation guides the study of Keren, Mester, Asphormas, & Lerner (1983), who were interested in determining the characteristics of Israeli soldiers who had a successful outcome of psychiatric hospitalization from 1977 to 1980. The outcome measures were behavioral: return to duty, completing military service, and no rehospitalization within six months after discharge from the hospital. Of the 69% of the soldiers who returned to duty, 76% completed their army service without rehospitalization. These soldiers were older, had higher army ranks and military occupations and more education than soldiers with unsuccessful outcomes, and were less likely to have been AWOL or detained in military prison.

Laufer, Gallops, and Frey-Wouters (1984) investigated the relationship between three types of war stressors (combat experience, witnessing abusive violence, and participating in abusive violence) and two measures of psychiatric symptomatology (Boulanger's Stress Scale and the Psychiatric Epidemiology Research Instrument [PERI]). Their data were based on responses to telephone interviews conducted in 1977 and 1979 with 350 Vietnam veterans who were asked whether they had these symptoms at any of several points in time since their Vietnam service. Using hierarchical regression analysis to test the relationships between the independent and dependent variables, the authors found that each of the three stressors was differentially related to symptomatology and that the relationships differed among black and white veterans. They report, for example, that black soldiers who participated in abusive violence had higher PERI scores than their white counterparts.

Because of the statistical methods they employed, and because they were interested in maladjustment, the investigators do not report whether any of the respondents who had been exposed to the stressors were free of psychiatric symptoms at any time since their war experience. Had they used a salutogenic orientation, they would have designed their study to allow for the probability that some veterans coped well. To explain the unexpected low symptom score of white veterans who participated in abusive violence, the authors suggest that these soldiers lacked empathy. Their pathogenic orientation forced them to ignore the question that we have been reluctant to face since World War II: How could Nazi soldiers who bayoneted babies and pregnant women sleep well at night?

Other Health-Illness Studies

In organizing the 25 papers from the *Journal of Health and Social Behavior*, *Psychosomatic Medicine*, and the *International Journal of Psychiatry*, our first finding emerged. Of the eight papers dealing with illness as the dependent variable, only one has a partly salutogenic approach. Of the 11 papers focusing on symptoms, four are salutogenic. Of the six that deal with behaviors—defined as desirable-undesirable for health—only one is clearly pathogenic. Selection of the problem, then, clearly influences the adoption of a particular orientation. If one chooses to study an illness or symptom outcome, it is most likely that one will examine the bad stressors and the absence of coping strengths. The study of behaviors, on the other hand, predisposes one to look at the presence of coping strengths. But we must go one step further and ask: Why is it that, with one partial exception, there are no studies of health and well-being in this sample of journal papers? Why do only a minority of the symptom studies focus on the absence of symptoms? Let us now turn to the individual papers.

Illness studies. Two of the studies are large-scale epidemiological investigations of hypertension. Zimmerman and Hartley (1982) identify the 14% of women employed in four companies who had high blood pressure and, using discriminant function analysis, analyze the predictive power of 40 variables. Gentry, Chesney, Gary, Hall, and Harburg (1982) studied the effect of a low level of expression of anger on hypertension and found that black males living in areas of high socioecological stress and who did not express anger were at highest risk. In neither study is there any attempt to understand normotensiveness, though we get a tantalizing hint in the former, when it is reported that only 6% of the workers in unionized companies were hypertensive compared to 25% of those in the nonunionized company. Why, with respect to the latter study, is "anger out" salutary? What are the characteristics of black males living in stress areas who are normotensive?

Please note: We do not suggest that it is not worthwhile to learn that working in a nonunionized plant, living alone, or being black is conducive to hypertension. But the question remains: How does one come to be normotensive under these circumstances?

The study by Shekelle et al. (1981) is a classic pathogenic paper. The hypothesis tested is that depression, as measured by the MMPI, is predictive of cancer mortality. After a 17-year follow-up study, it was found that the subjects who had been classified as depressed were more than twice as likely to die of cancer as the nondepressed. But we are talking of 7.1 and 3.4%. Of the 379 men defined as depressed, the great majority did not die of cancer or other causes. What protected them? What were the MMPI profiles of the survivors as distinguished from those who died?

In very much the same vein, Kornitzer, Kittel, DeBacker, and Dramaix

(1981) found that Belgian coronary patients more often exhibit type A behavior than healthy controls. We learn nothing of type B as a presumably protective behavior, and nothing of noncoronary type A's. Though the subject matter is quite different, precisely the same model is followed by Ackerman, Manaker, and Cohen (1981). A group of 24 adolescent peptic ulcer patients are compared to matched appendectomy patients. The former, as predicted, are retrospectively found to have had a much higher rate of separation or loss in the previous year. Healthy adolescents are not of interest.

In the above studies, the dependent variables were diseases. Studies of patient recovery or improvement might seem to lend themselves more to focusing on the successful coper. But the understandably human concern for helping those at high risk for unfavorable outcome inhibits such a focus. Winefield and Martin (1981) studied a cluster of outcome measures among 28 post-MI patients. They found that poor outcome is predicted by high-trait anxiety, manual occupation, dissatisfaction with work, and few confiding relationships.

A likewise pathogenically oriented study considers what happened to severe chronic asthma patients who had been hospitalized and discharged (Dirks, Schraa, & Robinson, 1982). Testing a hypothesis linking panic-fear responses on the MMPI, symptom mislabeling, and rehospitalization, they found that 32% of 587 patients were rehospitalized. The 15 other papers published by this research team and referenced in the paper also appear to be oriented toward the maladaptive result. But had the researchers asked the additional question—Why are 68% of this severely ill population able to avoid rehospitalization—they might have sought instruments that identify strengths, not only clinical pathology.

The final study to be considered in this section is the one which, at least in part, begins to ask salutogenic questions. Graves and Thomas (1981) administered the Rorschach test to a large group of medical students. Responses were scored on a scale measuring what they called "youthful relationship potential." Six patterns of interaction were identified. Years later, subjects were identified who had cancer, mental disorder, and cardiovascular disease, and a healthy comparison group was selected. The heart disease and healthy groups were found to be characterized by "well-balanced," i.e., flexible or conformist, interaction patterns; avoidance responses were associated with cancer; and ambivalence, with cancer and mental disorder. Here there is an attempt to predict those who will stay healthy.

Symptom studies. Three studies are concerned primarily with pain.

Pilowsky, Basett, Begg, and Thomas (1982) tested the hypothesis that hospitalization in childhood and adolescence stimulated a "tendency to utilize illness behavior as a coping strategy, albeit maladaptive." They compared the early hospitalization experiences of 114 adult pain clinic patients who were free of somatic disease to those of patients in a rheumatology clinic and of depressives in a psychiatric clinic. A salutogenic approach would have led to quite a different study: Who does not report pain when there is a somatic basis for expecting pain? But we do not set up nonpain clinics and don't study the good copers.

Wolcott, Wellisch, Robertson, and Arthur's (1981) study of ulcer patients is similarly pathogenic. They investigated the effects of anxiety, depression, life change units, and perception of family environment on severe pain and serum-fasting gastrin level. Their data hint at a salutogenic finding: Gastrin level is positively correlated with two subscales on the Moos family environment scale; independence and expressiveness. But this finding is noted in passing, because of the concern of the investigators with maladaptation.

One of the implications of the salutogenic orientation is that health-illness is a continuum, not a dichotomy. One can then ask: What factors contribute to the movement of people, wherever they are located on the continuum, toward the more desirable pole? An excellent example of this approach is found in Nehemkis, Charter, Stampp, and Gerber's (1982) study of perceived pain in cancer patients. Their concern was to test hypotheses related to the use of mechanisms to lower the levels of perceived pain and discomfort. They hypothesized that by reattributing the source of pain and discomfort from the disease itself to therapy procedures or to benign sources, a cancer patient would tend to perceive less pain. Furthermore, they proposed that such functional reattribution would be more common among those with a high internal locus of control orientation. These hypotheses were tested in a sample of 25 cancer patients with a mean time of diagnosis 29 months earlier.

It seems reasonable, in this population, most of whom showed metastatic involvement, to see the perception of less pain as indicative of successful coping. Thus their question is salutogenic *par excellence*. They wanted to test the power of attribution theory, as an intervention strategy. If we can find out, they were saying, who copes successfully with pain, perhaps we can help those who don't.

Their hypotheses were rejected. Cognitive reappraisal through reattribution does not diminish pain intensity; moreover, the patients with an external locus of control orientation tend to perceive less severe pain. Nevertheless we have learned something important. Their discussion,

albeit *post hoc*, explores the possibility that reattribution may be functional only in earlier stages of the disease, while at later stages denial
is more functional. Could a pathogenic orientation have been as fruitful?

Four of the symptom studies deal with emotional symptomatology.
Schwartz and Schwartz (1982) reviewed the records of 46 patients with
Crohn's disease (ileitis and colitis) referred to them for psychiatric consultation. They found a very high incidence of traumatic childhood experiences (33 of 46) in this population. It did not occur to them to
investigate Crohn patients who were not referred for psychiatric problems. Clinicians, even more than researchers, are concerned with weaknesses, not strengths.

The paper by Schmale et al. (1982) provides an excellent example of
a study that begs for a salutogenic analysis but, given the practical
orientation of clinicians, forgoes the opportunity, despite a passing salutogenic reference. They attempted to identify radiation oncology patients who would be most likely to have problems during treatment and,
hence, for whom intervention is indicated. They conducted a clinical
interview with 60 consecutive patients about to start radiation treatment,
classifying 17 as high risk, 35 as low risk, and 8 as belonging to neither
category. At 1, 3, 6, and 18-24 months follow-up, each patient was given
a composite, psychological-social-illness behavior problem score. At the
first two follow-ups, high-risk patients had significantly higher problem
scores, but these differences disappeared at the 6 and 18-24 months
follow-up.

The brief theoretical exposition underlying the risk classification is
focused entirely on the characteristics of high-risk patients, with no
thought given to low risk except by elimination. As in the type A studies,
one is only low risk if one manifests no high-risk characteristics. In the
discussion, attention is focused on the misclassified cases. They are
concerned primarily with the patients incorrectly judged at low risk.
Those incorrectly judged at high risk are viewed as minimizers; although
they scored low on problems, they really do have problems.

It is true that the authors close their discussion by considering the
importance of "engagement-involvement," which represents an individual's psychic integration. They do so, however, only to justify their
original prediction. The concept had not been introduced in advance,
because they were uninterested in patients who were at low risk for
problems. Nor is there any detailed consideration of the cases misclassified as high risk, to see whether their successful coping was related
to the salutogenic notion of "engagement-involvement." This, then, is

an example of a study designed in pathogenic terms, constraining the authors to miss an opportunity offered by the data.

Tausig's study (1982) is not even a matter of missed opportunity. Completely methodological in concern, the study examines the relationship between a variety of uses of the Holmes-Rahe Life Events Questionnaire and the CES Depression Scale. Is it not, one must ask, a continued sole commitment to a pathogenic orientation that keeps us doing the stressor-illness studies? When Wolff and Hinkle introduced the concept in the late forties, it marked a major advance. Today, we learn little from such studies, however sophisticated the methodology may be.

The Healey et al. study (1981) is, for our purposes, parallel to Tausig's life events paper. They studied the stressful life events of 31 chronic insomniacs matched with 31 good sleepers. The former reported more events, more often reported a lifelong history of illnesses and somatic complaints, childhood problems, lower self-concept, and the like. We learn nothing about the good sleepers.

Very much in the same vein is Hansell's (1982) partly experimental studies of secondary-school students. Among whom, he asked, are blood pressures elevated in response to stressors? The hypotheses formulated—and largely supported—relate to school standing, social status, and parental involvement in school events. We learn that an accumulation of stressors elevate blood pressure, perhaps becoming chronic. But Hansell offers no suggestion—because he does not ask the question—about those who cope well with the stressors.

By contrast, Vachon et al. (1982) were concerned with testing the salutogenic hypothesis that breast cancer radiation patients would manifest less psychological distress when exposed to the supportive milieu of a specially designed residential setting. They contrasted 64 residential with 104 home patients. They learned that most women in both groups had low levels of distress to start with and did not change during treatment. Among those with low levels of distress who did change, fewer residential patients changed for the worse. Among those with high distress, again, fewer residential patients changed for the worse and more changed for the better. Unfortunately, there is no discussion about the patients who lived at home and improved without the structured support of the residence.

The final two symptom studies are consistent with a salutogenic orientation. In each case, the approach led to some theoretical advance. Hamburg and Inoff (1982) hypothesized direct relationships between knowledge about diabetes, internal locus of control, and successful diabetic control among 211 insulin-dependent children in a camp for diabetics. Two interesting findings emerged. Knowledge was inversely related to control, leading the authors to suggest that successful copers have less need for knowledge. Second, locus of control was differentially related to diabetic control among boys and girls. Boys with good diabetic control tended to be externals, while girls with good diabetic control were more likely to be internals. This finding leads to a reconsideration of sex role socialization and coping patterns.

Gardner's (1982) study of first-year medical students provides another example of a theoretical advance made possible by posing a salutogenic question. He compared two matched groups of students, assembling data on locus of control (focused on the past week) and perceived sources of stress on a weekly basis for 36 weeks. In addition to completing the weekly questionnaires, one group wrote brief essays, which were systematically commented on by a faculty member in a supportive manner. Gardner's key question, in this paper, was: Among whom does the feeling of being stressed *decline*? The data show, as hypothesized, that the essay group feels less and less stressed over time. But what is of interest and importance is that this group, i.e., the group presumably receiving social support from faculty, also manifested an *increase* in its score on external locus of control and decrease on internal. "When the external control is perceived as more stable than one's internal response," he writes, "it can be relieving to relinquish internal control" (p. 105). This finding is consistent with Antonovsky's (1979) proposal that a strong internal locus of control is not necessarily functional for a healthy outcome.

Behavior Studies

The final six studies to be considered refer to some behavior that can legitimately be ranked on a health successful-unsuccessful coping continuum. As noted, the majority of these are salutogenic studies. The one clear exception is the Sheehan et al. (1981) study of accidents and errors committed by nursing students. The independent variables include social supports and active coping responses as well as life events and depression. However, the former variables are considered in terms of how their absence leads to accidents and errors. Contrast this approach with one that assumes that the stressors of being a nursing student are likely to lead to errors and that seeks a positive explanation of the behavior of those low on errors.

Clarke, MacPherson, and Holmes' (1982) study of smoking behavior of Vermont seventh graders is also predominantly pathogenic. The theoretical rationale, linking external locus of control, learned helplessness, and smoking, is supported by the data. The low-risk group is highest on internal locus of control. But this is a residual finding, with no real attempt to understand why this should be the case. In the tradition of Seligman (1975), who wants to explain depression, the authors want to explain smoking. It doesn't occur to them that the explanation of nonsmoking poses at least as difficult a problem.

Defining the dependent variable in terms of successful coping is a necessary, though not sufficient, step in designing a salutogenic study. Benfari, Eaker, Ockene, and McIntyre (1982) seek to predict which subject will successfully stop smoking in a heart disease risk factor intervention program, but their independent variables—life events, security, type A, locus of control, anxiety, and depression—are largely in the tradition of pathogenic studies. Using factor analysis and stepwise multiple regression, they find that a combination of a low life events score and high self-reliance is highly predictive of success. As useful as the sophisticated statistical techniques are, they prevent us from analyzing the deviant cases, i.e., the men who stopped smoking "against the odds" (who were, perhaps, high on life events but high on self-reliance).

A salutogenic orientation does not, of course, guarantee positive results. Yanagida, Streltzer, and Siemsen (1981) tested the hypothesis that denial may be an important defense mechanism in helping dialysis patients cope well. Their first step was to distinguish between clear-cut compliers with fluid restriction instructions and clear-cut noncompliers. Subjects were then scored on denial by use of the Social Desirability Scale. It was found that both groups were equally high in denial as compared to the norms of healthy populations. Is denial, then, not functional for coping? Replication is needed. But once we start thinking in terms of what is functional, progress can be made.

Mills and Farrow (1981) suggest that transcendental meditation (TM) may be functional for successful coping. In a small experimental study of responses to a cold pressor test, they were able to show that those who practiced TM, though reporting no less pain, reported significantly less distress than nonmeditators.

Finally, we have included a study by Herman, Blumenthal, Black, and Chesney (1981), despite the fact that it does not attempt to explain a health, symptom, or behavior outcome. It is included because it attempts to elucidate the type B behavior pattern to answer the salutogenic question: Who doesn't get heart disease and why? In this paper, type B was described by use of the Gough Adjective Checklist. Type B people tend to be calm, quiet, cautious, silent, slow, and easygoing. This finding takes us one step toward a reasonable hypothesis about who will not get a heart attack. Of course, the type B person may be prone to cancer or depression, a "minor" detail that can be kept in mind only if one's focus is on the healthy.

DISCUSSION AND CONCLUSION

The first point that emerges from these studies refers to the dependent variable. Once a decision is made to study a given disease, a pathogenic approach seems to be inevitable, for concern is with that disease and only that disease. At this point, let us note unequivocally that we are not urging abandonment of the pathogenic approach. As a friend once remarked, "When I have cancer, I want to be treated for cancer, not for the sense of coherence." Our thesis is that she should *also* be treated for the sense of coherence—or whatever salutogenic variable turns out to be a powerful predictor of health. Nor is it enough to ask, "Who doesn't get disease X?" For, as we have noted, one may get disease Y, which may be as serious as disease X. The salutogenic alternative is intended to add the study of health to the studies of diseases.

Second, when one studies a given disease, one becomes familiar only with the literature on that disease. We do not read the work of, or talk to, others working on other diseases. Only by focusing on health can we make advances in developing a broad-range theory of successful coping that derives from familiarity with a wide range of studies on different diseases and health outcomes.

Third, we have seen that when one's focus is on an *undesirable dependent variable*, one's thinking tends to be oriented to studying *undesirable independent variables*. Given the predominance of the pathogenic model, we have found that even in salutogenic studies, researchers tend to define the dependent variable in terms of the absence of weaknesses rather than the presence of strengths.

The fourth point flows from the third. Stressors, by definition, are viewed as pathogenic. Only here and there do we find a hint that a stressor may be a challenge, giving rise to successful coping precisely because it makes unanticipated demands. This is disregarded particularly when one's hypothesis is supported. One then feels no need to look at the deviant case: The person who, subjected to a high stressor load, is nonetheless a successful coper.

Fifth, in a fair number of studies that use sophisticated methodological techniques to study associations, the very statistic prevents a close examination of the successful coper. We are exhausted, as it were, when we have established that we can account for so and so much of the variance. The conscious question that leads us to study the successful coper in detail may require simpler statistical techniques, on the one hand, and finer breakdowns, on the other. But it is dispensed with if we are content with what Louis Guttman has called "star worship" (personal communication)—results that obtain statistical significance.

Finally, we note that often, when salutogenic independent variables are included in a study, they are viewed as no more than buffers, mitigating the presumably negative effects of stressors. This implies that what we would really like is a utopian world free of stressors. Theories of coping, then, are only formulated with respect to this or that stressor. Hypotheses are neither derived from, nor tested across, a wide, disparate range of stressors.

In recent years, there are some indications that we are beginning to work at the problem of a broad-range theory of coping. The responses to the sense of coherence concept (Antonovsky, 1979); Bandura's self-efficacy (1977); Kobassa's work on hardiness (Kobassa, Maddi, & Kahn, 1982); Selye's use of the term "eustress" (1975); Moos' work on social climates (1979); and Silver and Wortman's work on coping with undesirable life events (1980)—all indicate that the pathogenic paradigm is losing its monopoly. Our goal in this paper has not been to prove the power of salutogenic thinking, but to plant sufficient questions in the minds of researchers, as well as practitioners, so that they will begin to critically examine the stress paradigm with which they work.

SECTION II

Risk Factors in Combat Stress Reactions and Post-Traumatic Stress Disorders (PTSD)

This section and the one that follows deal with combat-related stress conditions in soldiers and draw a distinction between an initial *combat stress reaction* and a subsequent *post-traumatic combat stress disorder*. They are similar in symptomatology, but the former is acute, fluid, potentially transient, and amenable to brief treatment, while the latter is potentially chronic, crystallized, and more refractory to treatment or to spontaneous remission. This distinction is not always made in the clinical and research literature. In the DSM-III (APA, 1980), for example two forms of the disorders appear, PTSD, acute and PTSD, chronic. The former refers to manifestations of the disorder with onset within six months of the trauma, and the latter to manifestations of the disorder with duration of six months or more. There is no reference in the former category to the two forms of the acute stress condition distinguished above.

The distinction is important because it has implications for prognosis and treatment. The chapters in this section make differential predictions with reference to this distinction. The working hypothesis is that situational factors (e.g., specific characteristics of combat and one's military unit) are more strongly associated with succumbing to combat stress reaction than personal factors (e.g., premorbid adjustment) and the reverse for failure to respond to initial treatment and entering a more refractory phase of the disorder. This issue is examined in the chapters comprising this section. Chapter 5, Chapter 6, and Chapter 7 deal with combat stress reaction, and Chapter 8 deals with post-traumatic stress disorder.

THE EFFECT OF BATTLE AND MILITARY UNIT CHARACTERISTICS ON THE INDIRECT/DIRECT COMBAT CASUALTY RATIO

Noy, Nardi, and Solomon in Chapter 5 propose that the number of men succumbing to combat stress reaction in a given group of combat soldiers is a direct function of two sets of variables:

The first is the number of direct casualties, i.e., the number of men dead or wounded in the operation. The intensity and traumatic character of stressors implied by a 20% direct casualty rate in a given military unit is greater than that of a 10% direct casualty rate. As a consequence of the higher direct casualty rate, there will be a correspondingly higher rate of indirect or psychiatric casualties.

The second is a series of situational factors whose presence provides stress inoculation or stress resistance against the deleterious effects of the combat situation. These include (a) the nature of the battle or combat (e.g., advance versus retreat) and its duration; (b) the clarity or comprehensibility of the mission or battle plan; (c) the extent of tactical support and the availability of proper equipment; and (d) confidence in the unit's leadership, and the unit's level of training and ability to work together.

The investigators provided independent judges with data on battle and military unit characteristics of four battalions that corresponded to the categories cited above. With no knowledge of casualties, direct or indirect, the judges correctly rank-ordered the four battalions whose actual psychiatric/direct casualty ratios ranged from nearly 1:1 to 0:12. This methodology recommends itself not only for demonstrating the efficacy of situational variables in accounting for the extent of psychiatric casualties *after the fact*, but also for predicting psychiatric casualties *before the fact*.

THE EFFECT OF INTRAPERSONAL AND INTERPERSONAL VARIABLES ON COMBAT STRESS REACTION

Whereas Chapter 5 deals with battle and unit characteristics affecting combat stress reactions, Chapter 6 focuses on variables within the soldiers themselves that made them high versus low risk for succumbing to a combat stress reaction. Solomon, Noy, and Bar-On selected *two entire populations* of combat soldiers who had participated in the earlier phase of the war in Lebanon: all known cases of combat stress reaction in the absence of physical injury and all known cases of physical injury without evidence of combat stress reaction. Their files were examined to provide data on five variables that constituted the high-risk profile.

The portrait of a high-risk soldier for combat stress reaction that emerged from these data was a man in the reserves, 26 years of age or older, with a low combat suitability score at time of induction, low educational level, and low military rank. Reservists were considered to be at a disadvantage for personal reasons such as (1) a lessened capacity with age for strenuous physical activity; (2) less resilience because of previous exposure to traumatic combat events in earlier wars; (3) greater conflict because of competing loyalties to their civilian family and to their military family; and (4) a more drastic and abrupt transition to combat duty when mobilized from civilian life.

They were also at a disadvantage because of adverse situational factors associated with military service in the reserves, as contrasted with the regular draft army (ages 18 to 21). Unit cohesiveness and confidence in leadership are lower in reserve units that serve one month per year as compared with regular units that are in continuous service over the three-year period of compulsory service for all young men. Reserve units are also reorganized from time to time; as a consequence, reservists may be relatively unfamiliar with one another and with their officers as they enter combat.

The other variables, combat suitability, educational level, and military rank, tend to be highly correlated and to constitute an index of one's military identification and commitment. At highest risk is a soldier with low educational level whose motivation for combat duty was low to begin with and who consequently served in a low military rank. Such an individual has less to lose by succumbing to a transient combat stress reaction than his opposite counterpart: an officer in the career army who was motivated to serve in the defense forces in general and in actual combat in particular, from the start.

THE LONG-TERM EFFECT OF A PRIOR
COMBAT STRESS REACTION ON
SUBSEQUENT EXPOSURE TO COMBAT:
EVAPORATION VERSUS SENSITIZATION

The frequency with which Israeli citizens are called upon to engage in war places a premium on conserving and utilizing the available manpower to the fullest. Hence, men who succumb to combat stress reaction and/or to a subsequent post-traumatic stress disorder in a given war are treated and are periodically reevaluated as to their capacity for future military service.

Men who have suffered combat stress reactions are assigned after treatment and follow-up to one of three categories:

1. They are reclassified as suitable once again for combat duty and are given appropriate assignments if they have recovered.
2. They are reassigned to noncombat duty (in support units serving close to the front lines, but not engaging in actual combat, e.g., driving fuel or ammunition trucks) if they appear to have suffered mildly incapacitating sequelae from their earlier stress reaction or disorder.
3. They are given an outright discharge from military service because of a crystallized psychiatric disorder.

These data are available on all Israeli soldiers, as are the follow-up data on service in a subsequent war.

In Chapter 7, Solomon, Oppenheimer, and Noy compare soldiers in the 1973 Yom Kippur War who had experienced combat stress reaction without physical injury to a randomly selected control group who had participated in the war without experiencing a stress reaction or a physical injury. They found that over twice as many (53%) of the former group had been reassigned to noncombat duty during the nine-year period (1973–1982) as compared with the latter (23%).* Similarly, the

---

*These figures indicate that given the nature of combat stress in the 1973 war and the character of treatment offered at the time, there was a significant fallout associated with the sequelae of the original stress disturbance. In the Introduction to Section Three, we indicate that treatment for combat stress reaction in the 1973 war was ineffective because it followed the civilian medical model rather than the military crisis intervention model utilized in the 1982 war. As a consequence, the chronicity of combat stress disturbance from 1973 on, in the form of reduced military capacity in 1982, is probably higher than it would have been if appropriate treatment had been offered in 1973. This is admittedly

percentage of men discharged outright for psychiatric reasons was 6% as compared with 2% for the control group.

What about the group that was still in combat-ready status in 1982? Follow-up of those who actually served in combat in 1982 indicated that only 10 of 1,000 in the former group succumbed once again to a combat stress reaction; 990 did not. The comparable data for the control group were only slightly better, 7 of 1,000. Given the conditions of the early phase of the war in Lebanon, these findings are encouraging and suggest that *for those who were considered combat ready*, the risk of a recurrence of symptomatology was not appreciably greater than for soldiers who had never experienced combat stress reactions before. These findings are all the more impressive, since they are based wholly on the resilience and renewed military capacity of soldiers who in 1982 were no longer young men by military standards and were reservists, 28 years of age and older.

PREMORBID ADJUSTMENT AND CURRENT FUNCTIONING OF COMBAT SOLDIERS WITH POST-TRAUMATIC STRESS DISORDER

The final chapter in this section examines the premorbid adjustment of men with combat stress reactions in the war in Lebanon who did not respond to forward-echelon treatment and were characterized by severe crippling symptomatology with a high probability of chronicity. In Chapter 8, Segal and Margalit first documented that their MMPI profiles at the time of admission to a special retraining unit for veterans with potentially chronic post-traumatic stress disorders (combat fitness retraining unit, CFRU) were highly disturbed and consistent with their diagnosed psychiatric status. The researchers examined the files of this group and ascertained that compared with normal controls, they were more maladjusted before entering military service. All received diagnoses on Axis II of the DSM-III indicative of a premorbid personality disorder. Finally, frequency of maladjustment in all earlier stages of life—childhood, adolescence, and young adulthood—and in their prior military service was tabulated and found to be far higher than the norm. Segal and Margalit conclude that soldiers whose combat stress reaction was refractory to treatment are at high risk for full-blown post-traumatic stress disorder because they were more vulnerable to begin with.

---

a conjecture, and follow-up over the next decade of soldiers with appropriately treated combat stress reactions in 1982–1984 will provide new figures of the post-traumatic stress disorder fallout after this form of treatment.

5

Battle and Military Unit Characteristics and the Prevalence of Psychiatric Casualties

SHABTAI NOY, CHEN NARDI,
and ZAHAVA SOLOMON

Investigators of combat stress reactions since World War II have concluded that the magnitude of combat stress is the major etiological factor responsible for psychiatric casualties and have identified group cohesiveness and group leadership as important buffering variables (Datel, 1977; Marlowe, 1979; Mullins & Glass, 1973; Noy, 1982, 1984). One way to investigate these relationships is to correlate the number of *direct casualties*, injuries or death caused by ballistics or explosives that occur in a given military operation, with the prevalence of the *indirect or psychiatric casualties* in that operation. Numerous studies have reported covariation between direct and indirect casualties and inferred that the latter is caused by combat soldiers experiencing stress commensurate to the direct casualties and becoming susceptible to combat stress reactions (Beebe & Apple, 1951; Levav, Greenfeld, & Baruch, 1979; Marlowe, 1979; Mullins & Glass, 1973; Noy, 1980).

The ratio of direct to indirect casualties is not constant, however, because of other battle characteristics that affect the prevalence of subsequent psychiatric casualties. First, there is the conduct and outcome of the battle. A battle is more likely to produce psychiatric casualties, all other things including number of direct casualties being equal, if it ends in failure and defeat than if it ends in success and victory.

Second, battles vary enormously in intensity and duration, as well as in number of direct casualties. Higher rates of direct casualties typically occur in crucial offensive or defensive protracted battles in which two sides are locked in an effort to break through versus to hold on. By contrast, lower direct-casualty rates are found in rapid forward movement or retreat operations (Noy, 1979; Stouffer et al., 1949). One may consider, however, these battle characteristics independent of the direct casualty rate in estimating the indirect psychiatric casualty rate.

Third, some military units may produce a far higher number of psychiatric casualties than would be anticipated on the basis of their direct casualties or battle conditions, because of the absence of such critical buffering factors as group cohesiveness and group leadership; and others a far lower number because of the presence of these factors.

If we take these relevant stressors and buffering variables into consideration, then we would expect cohesive groups with superior leadership and high morale engaged in successful, brief operations to have lower indirect/direct casualty rates. The present chapter examines this question in a retrospective study of the effect of battle and unit characteristics on the indirect/direct casualty ratio. The investigators examined whether independent judges were able to predict the rank order of psychiatric/direct casualty ratios in different military battalions on the basis of data on the battles in which they fought and their respective combat unit characteristics.

METHOD

Subjects

Four battalions of Israeli soldiers were selected. The data were drawn from the History Department of the Israel Defense Forces. Selection was based on analysis of the written accounts by battalion commanders of the battles in which their battalions had participated and was guided by the effort to ensure different kinds of battle experience. These data were then presented to seven judges working independently in the form of condensed categories that were censored because of military security. Six were mental health professional workers and the seventh, a nonprofessional. They were given data on relevant categories and instructed to rank-order the four battalions on each of these categories in terms of the expected ratio of indirect to direct casualties attributed to their rank order on these categories. These categories are presented in Table 1, in descending order.

Five sets of rank orders were obtained from each judge on the basis of the following categories of information:

1. Precombat preparation: Knowledge of the location of the enemy, knowledge of the mission, the occurrence of false alarms before the mission, and the commander's perception of the battalion's level of training.
2. Battle: Whether the battalion was under artillery fire, air attack, in a mine field, or was caught in an ambush situation, and whether civilian homes were being used by the enemy for shelter.
3. Support: The extent of tactical support, logistic support, and availability of proper equipment.

Each of the subcategories in the first three categories was ranked separately and a compositive ranking was given for each category.

4. Enemy: Estimate of the enemy's resistance.
5. Trust: Confidence in the battalion commander's judgment and battle orders and group cohesiveness.
6. Overall rank order: Each judge gave an overall rank order for each battalion after making the five above rank orders in an independent and serial fashion. The overall rank order was an intuitive judgment without effort to weigh systematically the relative importance of each of the five categories cited above.

The working assumption of the investigators was that the more the negative features characterizing a category, the higher the expected ratio of psychiatric casualties to physical for the battalion on that category. Similarly, the higher the rank across the five categories, the higher the overall rank assigned to a battalion. There was near unanimity of agreement of judges (95%) across all category ratings. By inspection, it appeared that each judge was more impressed by events taking place in the actual battle than by the other variables.

RESULTS AND DISCUSSION

The average rank orders for the five categories and for the overall category and the obtained psychiatric/direct casualties ratios are presented in Table 1. The battalion ranked first in psychiatric/direct casualty ratio was, indeed, characterized by the highest ratio, and so on for the other three battalions. We conclude that judges can predict the indirect/direct casualty ratio on the basis of information about battle and unit characteristics. The prediction was, of course, after the fact, and it is worthwhile to replicate these findings in prospective studies.

The unanimity of the judges in arriving at the rank orders of the battalions may be variously interpreted. It may be taken as confirmation of the objectivity, reliability, and validity of their independent evaluations. It may also be taken as evidence of their sharing a common orientation or bias toward these issues. Accordingly, an equal number of new judges who were wholly naive as to the purposes of the study and its rationale were instructed to rank the four battalions according to the same data base. Identical rank orders with equally high agreement were obtained from these judges.

Hence, we may conclude that it is entirely feasible (1) to predict the potential susceptibility of a given battalion to psychiatric casualties *before the fact* from a knowledge of their unit characteristics, cohesiveness, and leadership, and from an estimate of anticipated battle conditions and outcomes, and (2) to account *after the fact* for the actual indirect/direct ratio from these sources of information as they become complete.

Given the findings of this investigation and others cited above on the effects of situational and group variables, one may ask why the bulk of research on combat stress reaction until World War II and even thereafter was fixated on the individual personality predispositions of soldiers. The answer appears to lie in the psychodynamic bias of researchers and

TABLE 1
Judges Rankings of Battle and Unit Variables and Actual
Psychiatric/Direct Casuality Ratios

Battalion	A	B	C	D
Preparation	2	1	3.5	3.5
Battle variables	1	2	3	4
Support variables	1	2.5	2.5	4
Enemy variables	1.5	1.5	3	4
Trust variables	1.5	1.5	3.5	3.5
Overall ranking	1	2	3	4
Psychiatric/direct casualty ratio	1:1.2	1:2.5	1:10	0:12

practitioners. This contention is supported by the fact that the professional judges were more inclined than the naive judges to look for personality predisposition as an explanation of psychiatric breakdown. Both groups of judges were able, however, to rank the stressor variables successfully once they were asked to consider all the evidence, including the situational variables.

6

Who Is at High Risk for a Combat Stress Reaction Syndrome?

ZAHAVA SOLOMON, SHABTAI NOY,
and REUVEN BAR-ON

The rate of emotional distress is increased during and following combat (Mullins & Glass, 1973). On the basis of the experience of the American Army in World War II, it was concluded that no one is immune from the pathogenic effects of war (Beebe & Apple, 1951; Grinker & Spiegel, 1945), but that only a relatively small number of soldiers actually experience breakdown. Numerous research studies have been conducted to identify the factors that render some soldiers more susceptible to combat stress reaction than others. These studies have been largely unsuccessful in identifying a specific premorbid predisposition (Cooperman, 1973; Glass, 1957). What emerges from these studies is the conclusion that intensity and duration of combat are the major determinants of the onset of combat stress reaction, from which it follows that although soldiers differ in their reactions to combat situations, they will all theoretically succumb to combat stress if given a sufficiently long exposure to a sufficiently intense situation.

The reality of Israel's military situation provides, unfortunately, a unique opportunity to examine this question. As in previous wars, the 1982 Peace in Galilee conflict in Lebanon produced a number of psychiatric casualties. The diagnosis and treatment of these combat stress reactions were accompanied by careful documentation that lends itself to a thorough study of the demographic, military, and personality factors that may predict these combat-related casualties.

METHOD

Subjects

Two groups of combat-exposed soldiers were selected. The combat stress reaction group (CSR) consisted of *all* known psychiatric casualties identified in the earlier phase of the war in Lebanon. The term "combat stress reaction" includes all cases in which soldiers failed to function under fire, except when physically injured. It includes all manifestations of somatic, affective, and behavioral symptomatology attributed to war-related stressors by trained clinicians. The comparison group consisted of all soldiers who actively participated in battle and sustained physical injuries *without* psychiatric disturbance.

The size of the sample was so large as not to differ from infinity for statistical purposes. The actual sample size, percentage of the sample in each subcategory in the population, and any other details that provide information as to the size, structure, and tactics of the Israel Defense Force are classified information and its publication is strictly forbidden. Admittedly, this restriction prevents our answering certain questions. However, this disadvantage is offset by the advantage of having data on entire populations and subpopulations. These data permit us to make analyses within each subpopulation of the incidence of certain characteristics.

Materials

Data on combat experience and type of physical or psychiatric injury were obtained from the soldiers' medical files. Data on age, educational level, military rank, and type of military service were obtained from the soldiers' official army records. Four categories of military rank were used: privates and corporals; sergeants; senior sergeants; and commissioned officers. There are three types of military service: compulsory or regular service for three years required of all males aged 18 to 21, with the most capable, intellectually and physically, picked for combat duty; reserve duty required of all males after completion of regular service until age 55, usually for one month each year in the same units in which they served during their compulsory service; and career service for volunteers competitively selected for professional military careers following compulsory service.

A predictor of military performance was drawn from the official records. This was a composite score of combat suitability obtained at the time of induction. It is based on punctuality, sociability, independence, and motivation for service.

RESULTS

In order to assess differences between CSR and comparison groups, individual chi-square analyses were performed on the percentage breakdowns of the subcategories or levels of each variable within each group. Conclusions are based on the relative percentage of soldiers from each of the two groups on a given variable. The percentages of the various levels of each variable within CSR and comparison groups and the appropriate chi square are summarized in Table 1. All chi-square analyses yielded highly significant differences in proportions of cases. It may be noted that the 18-to-21-year-olds were twice as likely to become physically injured as psychiatrically disturbed. By the same token, soldiers 26 and older were far more likely to be psychiatrically disturbed than physically injured. We conclude that there is less risk of physical injury and more risk of psychiatric disturbance with increasing age.

Educational level operated in a similar manner. The lower the educational level, the greater the likelihood of psychiatric than of physical injury, and the reverse for the higher educational levels. The same trend was obtained for combat suitability with greater likelihood of psychiatric than of physical injury at the lower suitability levels, and the reverse for the higher suitability levels. With reference to military rank, reservists were more likely to be psychiatrically disturbed than physically injured, while the reverse was true for career and compulsory service. Finally, the same trend was found for rank: greater psychiatric than physical injury in the lowest rank, and the reverse for the highest.

DISCUSSION

The data indicate that all soldiers are not equally vulnerable to CSR. The composite profile of the soldier at highest risk for CSR is a reservist, 26 years or older, with a low level of education, low combat suitability, and low military rank. These findings are not consistent with those

TABLE 1
Distribution in Percentages of Psychiatric Casualties by Five Variables

Variable	CSR group	Comparison group	Chi square
Age (years)			df = 4, 109.49
18–21	20	42	
22–25	22	22	
26–30	34	19	
31–35	15	10	
36–55	9	7	
Total	100	100	
Education (years)			df = 2, 106.43
8	27	12	
9–12	67	80	
12 +	6	8	
Total	100	100	
Suitability			df = 4, 212.00
Very Low	9	2	
Low	20	9	
Medium	33	24	
Medium-high	29	40	
High	9	25	
Total	100	100	
Service			df = 2, 188.20
Reserve	80	46	
Compulsory	19	46	
Career	1	8	
Total	100	100	
Rank			df = 3, 86.67
Privates + corporals	63	45	
Sergeants	31	34	
Senior sergeants	3	4	
Officers	3	17	
Total	100	100	

reported in the American Army (Beebe & Apple, 1951), but are consistent with findings on Israeli casualties in the 1973 Yom Kippur War (Levav, Greenfeld, & Baruch, 1979).

The five variables may be regarded as two distinct clusters, each with highly interrelated variables. With respect to the first, age level and type of service, we may argue that reservists are more likely to experience psychiatric breakdown in combat for a number of reasons:

1. They are the oldest of the three service categories, and increasing age is associated with lessened capacity for strenuous physical activity.
2. They have probably fought in previous wars and repeated exposure to traumatic experiences may weaken their resilience.
3. They are required to undergo a more drastic transition from peacetime to wartime than soldiers in compulsory or career service.
4. The units in which they serve in combat are less cohesive than those of soldiers in compulsory service, and their interaction with army peers is more fragmented than that of the other two services. Since group cohesiveness is a buffer against combat stress reactions in stressful military service, the reservists are more at risk than the others.
5. They have a responsibility to their wives and children and probably emphasize their allegiance to their civilian family over their allegiance to their "military family." The younger soldiers in compulsory service are not married and may have a stronger allegiance to the military while in combat. Finally, the men in the career army have developed a dual allegiance in which their families concur more or less. The stronger the allegiance to the military family, the less the risk of CSR.

The three remaining variables—education level, combat suitability, and rank—are regarded by the Israeli army as interrelated predictors of military performance and provide a basis for selection and expectation. A soldier who at induction is found to have a low educational level and a low combat suitability score is likely to be placed in a service unit (e.g., truck driver, kitchen worker, ordinance clerk) rather than a combat unit (e.g., infantry, tank corps) and is likely to earn low military rank. This set of variables can lead to "a spoiled identity" (Goffman, 1963). Such a soldier has little to lose if at a conscious or unconscious level he decides to succumb to a stressful situation and to exit from the war zone. The fear of stigmatization is less aversive, the consequences to his military career are less costly, and the acute injury to his self-image as a noncombatant soldier is less severe.

Contrast his psychological situation with that of a soldier with a high educational level and suitability score at induction who is selected for an officers' course and after passing it successfully becomes a commissioned officer. Such a soldier has much more to lose because he has invested much more in his army career and in his self-image as a soldier, fighter, and officer, and the army has invested much more in him. He expects much more of himself and others expect much more of him. Failure to meet his responsibilities under fire and leaving the battlefield with psychiatric disability is much more threatening than the possible consequences of remaining, namely, physical injury or death.

In summary, the data suggest that breakdown in combat is associated both with personal characteristics of the soldiers and with environmental factors affecting them before and during stressful military service. The present design does not permit detailed analysis of etiology, course of CSR, and the relationship between the variables contributing to breakdown and to subsequent recovery. Longitudinal studies and multivariate analyses currently underway will shed greater light on these questions.

7

Subsequent Military Adjustment of Combat Stress Reaction Casualties: A Nine-Year Follow-Up Study

ZAHAVA SOLOMON, BRUCE OPPENHEIMER,
and SHABTAI NOY

The geopolitical situation is such that Israeli men participate in wars a number of times during their adult life. Hence, they are exposed to recurrent traumatic situations and are under great risk for developing combat stress reactions, if not during the first war encounter, then during the second or the third. Moreover, if they experienced a combat stress reaction in an earlier encounter, it is legitimate to ask whether this experience increased their susceptibility or inoculated them with regard to the next. The present study reports on the subsequent adjustment during the 1982 war in Lebanon of soldiers who experienced combat stress reaction in a previous war. It is the first report in an ongoing longitudinal project to assess facets of the long-term adjustment of soldiers who experienced combat stress reaction in the 1973 Yom Kippur War.

The research literature on the effects of recurrent stressful episodes indicates a sharp difference of opinion between two schools of thought:

stress evaporation versus cumulative residual stress (Eitinger, 1969, 1973; Quarantelli & Dynes, 1977). According to the former perspective, a soldier recovers from a transient psychiatric disability and returns to his premorbid level of functioning, none the worse for wear and no more likely to experience a new breakdown than a soldier who did not have an earlier breakdown.

One might even hypothesize an inoculation effect: if the disturbed soldier learned to cope with the consequences of the psychiatric breakdown and recovered, he is *better* able to cope with a recurrence of combat stressors than a soldier who has not developed the resources to recover. The latter argument is usually offered for a soldier who went through a stressful combat experience *without breaking down* and is subsequently presumed to be less vulnerable to a new combat situation than a soldier who did not have an earlier stressful combat experience, but it can be offered for one who did break down and subsequently recovered.

The opposing argument is that the consequences to mental health of severe stress reactions do not evaporate with the passage of time, but rather persist. The prior experience has weakened one's psychological resources so that the individual is both scarred and permanently more vulnerable, or at the very least more vulnerable for an extended period of time, than one who did not experience a prior severe stress reaction.

This question has not been examined in the research literature of military psychiatry, but there are some data bearing on the question. The psychiatric status of soldiers who experienced combat stress reactions in World War II was assessed in two follow-up studies, 15 and 20 years later, respectively (Archibald, Long, & Miller, 1962; Archibald & Tuddenham, 1965). These studies demonstrated that many soldiers who had experienced combat stress reactions did not recover, indicating that the stress did not evaporate.

Many more studies were done on the psychiatric status of former Vietnam combat veterans after discharge from military service as compared with that of noncombat Vietnam veterans or civilians. Some investigators found no evidence of lasting psychopathology in the combat veterans (Carr, 1973; Enzie, Sawyer, & Montgomery, 1973; Worthington, 1977). Other studies found striking differences between the former combat veterans and the control groups: more depression, greater inclination to violent behavior, greater difficulties in social and occupational adjustment, more trouble with the legal authorities, and greater sense of alienation (Pollock, White, & Gold, 1975; Stayer & Ellenhorn, 1975; Stuen & Solberg, 1972).

These conflicting findings cannot be easily reconciled. Inspection of the studies indicates, however, methodological differences in the selection of combat veteran and control groups and the strong possibility that the intense ideological and political debate that surrounded American engagement in the Vietnam War affected the selection, the overall research enterprise, and the interpretation of findings.

In any case, follow-up of veterans who were once exposed to a combat stress reaction and thereafter did not suffer a subsequent exposure does not answer the question of the effect of earlier traumatization on soldiers who are exposed to a combat experience some years later.

The present study poses three questions:

1. What proportion of those Israeli soldiers who experienced combat stress reactions in the 1973 Yom Kippur War recovered and were able to resume combat military duties in the reserve, what proportion were able to resume reserve duty in noncombat assignments, and what proportion were released from military service altogether?
2. What proportion of those soldiers who suffered a combat stress reaction in 1973 and engaged in combat in the war in Lebanon in 1982 suffered a recurrence of combat stress reaction?
3. Was the proportion of recurrent combat stress reaction in the latter soldiers greater than the incidence of combat stress reaction in the 1982 war for those combat soldiers who had not suffered combat stress reaction in the 1973 war?

METHOD

Subjects

The follow-up group consisted of several hundred soldiers (the exact number is classified) who were diagnosed by military psychiatric personnel as having suffered combat stress reactions during the 1973 war. This group does not include soldiers who sustained both physical injury and psychiatric disability or soldiers for whom the onset of combat stress reaction was after October 24, 1973, when overt hostilities on all fronts had ceased.

The control group consisted of soldiers who had participated in the 1973 war without experiencing combat stress reaction. Each control soldier was selected on the basis of his military identification number following that of a soldier of similar age and date of initial enlistment in the follow-up group. This method of selection was designed to randomize the effect of all variables that might affect adjustment in the 1982 war other than combat stress status in the prior war.

Test Scores

There were three dependent variables. The first was the soldier's profile or military health status on record immediately before the 1973 war and again before the 1982 war. This score is based on an assessment by the military medical authorities of the soldier's physical and mental fitness for military service. The range of profile scores was collapsed into three categories: fitness for combat, fitness for noncombat military service, and discharge from the army because of disability inconsistent with functioning in any service capacity. The second variable was whether the soldier actually participated in combat assignments in the 1982 war, and the third was the occurrence or nonoccurrence of combat stress reaction in the 1982 war.

RESULTS

The percentage of soldiers considered combat fit before the 1973 war was 94% and 83% for the follow-up and control groups, respectively. This difference follows from the fact that the follow-up group consisted of people who actually served in the 1973 war as a consequence of which they experienced combat stress reaction. Such a group would have a higher proportion of combat fit soldiers than a random group of soldiers some of whom were not called to serve at the front in that war.

Why soldiers with noncombat fitness ratings in the follow-up group (6%) were sent to the front and succumbed to combat stress reaction in the 1973 war may be explained by clarification of the noncombat fitness rating. It precludes participating in a fighting unit (infantry, tanks, artillery, etc.), but it does not preclude exposure to stressful war experiences, since soldiers with noncombat assignments drive ammunition trucks or provide other types of support close to the firing lines. On the basis of the fitness ratings prior to the 1973 war, the follow-up group consisted, if anything, of more soldiers with combat fitness than the control group.

The combat fitness ratings of the two groups on the eve of the 1982 war are summarized in Table 1. In the nine years that elapsed, over half of the follow-up group (53%) were now in noncombat duties and 6%

were discharged from military service as compared with 23% and 2%, respectively, for the control. This follows as a consequence of the combat stress reaction experienced by 100% of the soldiers in the former group and none of the soldiers in the latter. To confirm the basis of discharge from military service for the follow-up group, the medical files of the 6% discharged were examined, and in the majority of these cases (80%), these men were found to be suffering from severe psychiatric problems.

There was far less attrition from combat fitness status for the control group. Their attrition may be attributed to a variety of events occurring in civilian life (physical injuries, psychiatric problems) or in the army (reorganization of an aging military unit and reassignment of its members to noncombat support duties, etc.). We conclude that combat stress reaction led to a sharp attrition in combat fitness, but it is impressive to note that only 6% were actually discharged and that on the eve of the 1982 war, 41% were still considered fit for combat and the remainder available for support and possibly hazardous duties as well.

The percentage of soldiers in the follow-up and control groups who actually participated in combat in the 1982 war was 32% and 38%, respectively. Since only 41% of the follow-up group was considered fit for combat duty, this means that 32/41 or about 80% of the potential follow-up pool actually participated in combat. By contrast, only 38/75 or about 50% of the potential control group pool participated. We conclude that the participation in combat of follow-up soldiers was even higher than in the control group.

We now turn to the critical question, the rate of combat stress reaction in the 1982 war, 0.67% and 1.00% in control and follow-up group, respectively. This means that the baseline rate of combat stress reaction in the control group during the combat phase of the 1982 war was about 7 out of 1,000 men. For the follow-up group, all of whose members had suffered from combat stress reaction in the 1973 war and who now fulfilled combat assignments in 1982, only 10 out of 1,000 had a recur-

TABLE 1

Percentage of Soldiers in Fitness Categories in Follow-up and Control Groups before the 1982 War

	Combat	Noncombat	Discharged	
Follow-up	41	53	6	100
Control	75	23	2	100

rence of psychiatric difficulties, while 990 did not. This risk factor for recurrence is, indeed, higher than for the baseline rate, but it is clear that the overwhelming number of follow-up soldiers weathered combat experience in the war without recurrence of symptomatology. This conclusion should be regarded with some caution, since data on 1982 combat stress reactions were obtained for the early phase of the war in Lebanon only and delayed-onset cases were not included in either the follow-up or control group.

DISCUSSION AND CONCLUSIONS

The data appear to support the evaporation hypothesis, since many soldiers recovered from a severe crisis, returned to military service, participated once again in a highly stressful combat situation, and *did not succumb once again* to combat stress reaction. Since the risk rate for combat stress reaction was not appreciably higher in the follow-up group than the control, there is no support for the argument of heightened vulnerability in the former group.

These findings are consistent with those of Beebe and Apple (1951), who investigated the pattern of entries and exits of American soldiers in and out of their military units in World War II. They found that the chances of a subsequent psychiatric evaluation for soldiers who were evacuated from their units for psychiatric reasons and subsequently returned were no higher than for soldiers who were initially evacuated because of physical injury or illness.

Our findings provide tentative implications for the etiology of combat stress reaction. If we adopt the view that the key factors accounting for combat stress reaction are located within the individual, then we would expect the soldier who succumbed the first time to succumb repeatedly to combat stress situations. This was not the case for 99% of the follow-up group, who were exposed to two major combat experiences. Admittedly the first experience was far more stressful, on the average, than the second since the circumstances for the conduct of military operations in the two wars differed markedly. The Israel Defense Forces were caught by surprise with the outbreak of the 1973 war, but selected the time and place of initiating the 1982 war. This difference merely highlights the conclusion that the personal characteristics of the individual soldier are less important than external environmental circumstances in the occurrence of combat stress reaction. On the other hand, a small number of men who suffered psychiatric breakdown did not recover, and there is evidence that their condition may become chronic and generalized to many areas of civilian adjustment (Milgram, Arad, Toubiana, & Falach, 1984). It is highly probable that more effective treatment procedures applied at the onset of combat stress reaction and in subsequent treatment of recalcitrant cases will decrease still further the incidence of chronic sequelae of combat stress reaction.

8

Risk Factors, Premorbid Adjustment, and Personality Characteristics of Soldiers with Refractory Combat Stress Reactions

RUBEN SEGAL and CHAIM MARGALIT

Given the high recovery rate of soldiers with combat stress reactions who were in residence at the Combat Fitness Retraining Unit (CFRU), it is of interest to ascertain the premorbid adjustment and level of premorbid risk factors in these men prior to their breakdown in combat. If high levels of premorbid adjustment and low levels of premorbid risk factors are found, then we may conclude that the major contributing factors to their breakdown were situational in nature and that the recovery rate associated with their stay in the CFRU is impressive, but less than remarkable. If, on the other hand, we find low premorbid adjustment and high risk factors, we conclude that predisposing factors in these men contributed to their breakdown and recalcitrance to forward-echelon treatment. We would then regard the success of the CFRU in returning these men to military and civilian life as genuinely remarkable.

There is considerable controversy in the clinical research literature as to the importance of predisposing psychosocial stressors and premorbid personal social adjustment in reducing one's tolerance for handling combat stress without breakdown (Glass, 1949; Kardiner, 1959; Noy, 1978). There are two major clinical research approaches bearing on this question. In the first, we investigate, *after the fact*, soldiers who succumbed to combat stress reactions and ascertain their premorbid adjustment level and other premorbid risk factors. In the second, we identify, *before the fact*, soldiers at high risk for combat stress reaction and follow their adjustment during and after combat to ascertain what percentage of this group succumbed to the syndrome as compared with a group at low risk. On inspection, retrospective studies tend to be more successful in indicting premorbid risk factors than prospective studies, but the issue is by no means resolved, whatever the research methodology.

The present chapter deals with two aspects of this issue in a retrospective design. First, it asks what were the premorbid adjustment level and other premorbid risk factors in soldiers with exacerbated combat stress reactions who did not respond to forward treatment and eventually found their way to the CFRU? Second, it asks what are the intensity and kind of psychopathology manifested in the group on arrival at the CFRU? Third, it compares this presenting psychopathology with that of soldiers with severe combat stress reactions following the 1973 Yom Kippur War (Merbaum & Hefez, 1976).

METHOD

Subjects, Instruments, and Procedure

The soldiers who reached the CFRU are described in Chapter 12A (Section Three). They were compared with soldiers who served in combat units during the conflict in Lebanon, but did not succumb to combat stress reactions. The former group was given the MMPI in group during the first week of admission to the CFRU. The latter was given the MMPI in group at about the same time. The Hebrew edition of the MMPI (Butcher & Gur, 1974) was used, since previous research using this translation had demonstrated its reliability (Merbaum & Hefez, 1976). In addition, following their admission the CFRU group was intensively interviewed by an interdisciplinary team as to their premorbid history. The interviews were administered by clinical psychologists who were not working in the CFRU and were unaware of its purpose or rationale. They recorded those incidences in the history considered relevant to the current symptom picture and they utilized the DSM-III (APA, 1980) to record diagnoses for the first two axes of the DSM.

RESULTS AND DISCUSSION

Data of the Clinical Interviews

The following premorbid risk and premorbid adjustment factors were identified, and the number of soldiers falling into one or more of these categories was tabulated in percentages:

1. Early difficulties in interpersonal relations in the context of a pathological nuclear family (85%).
2. Difficulties in adjusting to school, poor habits of concentration, behavior disturbances, inconsistency in achievement (70%).
3. Difficulties in social adjustment and in intimate relationships as an adolescent and young adult (70%).
4. Problems in marriage and family life (70%).
5. Disciplinary problems during military service (60%).

These percentages are extremely high, far beyond the frequencies expected in a comparison group or encountered in the total population of soldiers in regular or reserve duty. Even allowing for overly zealous evaluations by the interviewers of premorbid psychopathology, these frequencies point to selective factors operating in those soldiers who both manifested combat stress reactions and did not recover during their stay in one or more forward-echelon treatment settings.

The diagnoses on the first axis of the DSM-III were consistent with an increasingly chronic condition in a post-traumatic combat stress disorder (PTSD). The vast majority of CFRU soldiers also received a diagnosis on the second axis, suggesting the presence of a premorbid personality disorder. The major disorders were anxiety, somatoform, dissociative, psychosexual, and adjustment.

MMPI Profiles

The MMPI standard scores for the three lie scales and for the 10 psychiatric scales are summarized in Table 1 for CFRU and control soldiers. Comparison of group means by t tests yielded differences favoring the control group over the CFRU group ($p < 0.01$) on the F lie scale and on 9 of 10 psychiatric scales, the only exception being the mania scale. The CFRU group was above the T-score cutoff of 70 on six of the psychiatric scales, while the control group was not above 70 on any. The elevation of these scales is consistent with a psychopathological picture characterized by anxiety, hostility, depression, negativism, passivity, demandingness, irritability, and alienation from others.

The score on the F scale is high, suggesting either pathology or an effort to respond in an unfavorable direction. Since the scores on the other two lie scales were within normal limits and inconsistent with a definitive set for "faking bad," the latter interpretation is unlikely. Moreover, Greene (1980) cites this specific lie scale pattern as consistent with chronic maladjustment in a patient population acknowledging personal problems and utilizing maladaptive defense mechanisms.

The MMPI scores of the CFRU group and of the Merbaum and Hefez group (1976), severe combat stress reactions from the Yom Kippur War, were compared. The scores of the latter group are also summarized in Table 1. There were no significant differences between the means of the two groups on any of the 13 scales. The Spearman rank-order correlation of the two sets of scores was extremely high (0.92, $p < .001$), indicating high agreement in the MMPI profiles of the two groups. It is concluded that the CFRU group presented a psychopathological picture on the MMPI consistent with PTSD and indicative of a poor prognosis. That the CFRU was able to discharge a group characterized by a high degree of psychopathology to military and civilian life after a residential stay of several weeks is properly seen as remarkable.

Merbaum and Hefez reported a relatively high frequency of premorbid personal problems (37%) and that 25% of their group had prior psycho-

TABLE 1

Mean MMPI Scores of CFRU, Control, and Merbaum and Hefez Groups

Scale	CFRU	Control	Merbaum and Hefez
L	53.0	50.5	54.2
F	75.0	59.0	77.6
K	52.1	56.1	49.6
Hs	84.0	61.4	75.4
D	87.6	55.8	84.4
Hy	76.5	66.5	72.3
Pd	69.6	55.1	72.4
Mf	68.9	54.2	67.3
Pa	74.1	60.9	73.9
Pt	77.8	57.7	82.7
Sc	93.2	62.4	90.0
Ma	67.5	63.7	60.8
Si	57.5	48.3	61.6

logical treatment. Since they do not describe the criteria used by their interviewers to obtain the frequency of premorbid problems, it is difficult to compare the data of the two psychiatric groups. Given the high frequency of premorbid factors in our group and the presence of a presumably premorbid personality disorder in nearly all cases, we concur with the conclusion of Merbaum and Hefez that premorbid factors reduce the ability of soldiers under stress to function adaptively and to recover quickly if their performance breaks down in the form of a combat stress reaction.

SECTION III

Treatment of Combat Stress Reactions and Post-Traumatic Stress Disorders in the War in Lebanon

The history of the treatment of combat stress reaction in Israel parallels that of the United States. In World War I Salmon (1919) found that if combat soldiers were given the opportunity to rest and unwind as soldiers, in uniform, close to the operations area, with the explicit understanding that they would be returning to combat duty, they did, in fact, do so. These lessons were forgotten in the 20 years between the World War I and World War II, with the result that hundreds of thousands of men were evacuated from the Mediterranean war theater in 1942 to hospitals far from the front, never to return to active duty. Only when manpower losses became intolerable were the principles of immediacy, proximity, and expectancy rediscovered and applied to soldiers with combat exhaustion, with impressive results.

Israel went through a similar experience. Large numbers of soldiers with combat stress reactions in the 1973 Yom Kippur War were evacuated from the front, given hospital pajamas and lodging in attractive seashore summer resorts, and were visited by well-meaning women of all ages, bringing home-baked cakes and gifts for the "patients." It is not surprising that few men returned to the battlefield after this kind of treatment and that many graduated from stress reaction to post-traumatic stress disorder.

In the aftermath of the 1973 war the appropriate conclusions were drawn. In the years that followed, the mental health branch of the Israel Defense Forces practiced the Salmon principles in extensive maneuver simulations. With the outbreak of the war in Lebanon in 1982, mental health teams were ready to apply these principles in forward-echelon treatment.

This section consists of four chapters dealing with the treatment of combat stress reactions and of post-traumatic stress disorders incurred in the war in Lebanon. The first provides empirical data on the clinical picture associated with these disorders and compares these data with the major symptoms noted in earlier Israeli and American wars. The second chapter documents the efficacy of brief forward-echelon "military" treatment over rear-echelon "civilian" treatment in returning men to their military units. The third describes a typical Israeli mental health team applying the classical "military" treatment. The fourth chapter describes in considerable detail the operation of a comprehensive residential treatment setting for soldiers with crystallizing post-traumatic stress disorder; these were soldiers who failed to respond to earlier forward-echelon treatment in 1982 and would have been evacuated to civilian hospitals and clinics for continued treatment, with poor prognosis as to their eventual recovery.

THE SYMPTOMATOLOGY OF COMBAT STRESS REACTION AND EXIT CRITERIA FROM AN INTOLERABLE SITUATION

In Chapter 9, Bar-On, Solomon, Noy, and Nardi tabulate the frequency of the symptoms that characterized a large random sample (30%) of all combat stress reactions in the first phase of the war in Lebanon. What emerged were disturbances in autonomic functioning, motor tension, emotion, cognition, and behavior that correspond to the formal criteria enumerated in the DSM-III. These investigators compared these symptoms with those noted in four other wars and attempted to demonstrate a correspondence between what was required by the military-psychiatric establishment for an honorable exit from combat on psychiatric grounds in a given war and the symptomatology exhibited by the veterans with combat stress reaction in that war. The exit ticket in World War I was labeled shell shock, and consistent with the hypothesis, symptoms associated with this term were prominent (e.g., tremor, noise sensitivity). In World War II combat exhaustion was the exit designation, and symptoms such as exhaustion, gastrointestinal upset, headache, and sleep disturbance came into prominence. In the Vietnam War symptoms consistent with the designation of transient adjustment reaction were discipline problems, aggressive behavior, and substance abuse.

There is no single explanation for the degree of correspondence. Given widespread knowledge of the requisite exit criteria in a given war, we may assume that selective attention was paid to these criteria by any and all of the following: the medical and psychiatric personnel diagnosing these conditions in the field and in the hospitals, office personnel summarizing case files of soldiers with incapacitating medical or psychiatric conditions, professional and research psychiatrists tabulating and interpreting the data, and last, but not least, the soldiers and officers in combat themselves. Labels influence behavior, and awareness of the "label effect" may enable psychiatric policy makers to select those labels and descriptors that best serve the interests of the armed forces and of the soldiers themselves.

EFFICACY OF FORWARD- VERSUS REAR-ECHELON TREATMENT

Notwithstanding the best of professional intentions, many Israeli soldoers who succumbed to combat stress reactions in the early phase of the war in Lebanon did not receive the planned brief forward-echelon treatment. Tactical and technical considerations in the height of combat dictated the airlift evacuation of some soldiers to the rear. Human error compounded the situation, and some soldiers were treated in Israel proper by medical and psychiatric personnel unaware of and untrained in the forward-echelon approach. Since the evacuation procedure was random with respect to the soldiers involved, a unique opportunity arose to compare the differential rate of return to one's unit as a function of forward versus rear treatment.

In Chapter 10, data on all psychiatric casualties during this period are analyzed. The percent of combat soldiers treated by the forward-echelon approach who returned in a few days to their unit was four times as great as the percent of those treated by mistake in a rear setting in Israel proper (59.0 versus 16.3). Noy, Solomon, and Benbenishti emphasize that the major factor responsible for this differential was expectancy. The factor was manifested in the prior training and current behavior of the personnel working directly with these soldiers and in a comprehensive treatment milieu conducted in a manner consistent with the expectation that the men would recover and return to their units.

THE THERAPEUTIC MILIEU IN A FORWARD FIELD STATION

In Chapter 11, Toubiana, Milgram, and Noy describe in detail the rationale and daily functioning of a typical forward field station. All features of the therapeutic milieu, from the decision of where to pitch the tents for lodging and who will pitch them to the implementation of the various treatment modalities, were guided by and subordinated to the expectancy principle. The mental health unit worked both with the combat soldiers who were in residence for three days at the most and with the medical personnel in the nearby field hospital. They also initiated contact with their soldiers' military units, and there were visits in both directions despite the short duration of the men's stay at the station.

Of the 15 men at this particular station, 14 returned to their units without further incident for the remainder of the year. A three-year follow-up indicated that two of the original 15 became disturbed a year or more later and were reassigned to noncombat duty, and that 11 actually served in reserve assignments (30 to 40 days) in 1984/1985. These findings are consistent with those reported in Chapters 8 and 10.

TREATMENT FOR POST-TRAUMATIC STRESS DISORDER: RATIONALE, FUNCTIONING, AND RESULTS

In Chapter 12, members of a treatment team (Margalit et al.) describe the rationale and functioning of a large rear-echelon treatment setting situated on a military base within Israel designed to handle men whose combat stress reactions were refractory to earlier treatment efforts near the front. The presenting symptomatology of these men was detailed in Chapter 8. The structure and daily functioning of the Combat Fitness Retraining Unit (CFRU) is described in Chapter 12A, with six subsequent subchapters detailing the various aspects of the program: behavioral milieu, behavioral group treatment, dynamic group psychotherapy, individual psychotherapy, physical activities, and a summary statement emphasizing the multidimensionality of the approach.

After a stay of 26 days, all men were discharged as improved and with no further need for hospitalization. Approximately one-third returned to their original combat units, and two-thirds to other noncombat assignments, with 7% of the reservists being given a psychiatric discharge. A follow-up two and a half years later indicated improvement for the regular soldiers in compulsory service (with two-thirds now in combat units) and a deterioration for the reservists, with only 22% now in combat units, and with 18% now discharged from the army for psychiatric reasons. Explanations for these differential changes in status over time in the two groups were not based on the obvious difference in age and physical fitness of the two groups, but rather on the difference in continuity of army service of the regular and reserve soldiers.

9

The Clinical Picture of Combat Stress Reactions in the 1982 War in Lebanon: Cross-War Comparisons

REUVEN BAR-ON, ZAHAVA SOLOMON,
SHABTAI NOY, and CHEN NARDI

Combat stress reactions refer to so wide a range of symptoms that it is difficult to ascertain whether the predominant features of combat stress reactions in one war differ from those of another and to propose explanations for obtained differences. The purpose of the present chapter is threefold:

1. To conduct a systematic survey of the observed symptomatology of Israeli soldiers who served in combat in the Lebanon War and were subsequently referred for emotional disturbance;
2. To compare this clinical picture with that described in the professional literature dealing with major wars occurring earlier in the century;
3. To offer an explanation for whatever differences might obtain in terms of the necessary *exit criteria* for leaving stress situations that become intolerable.

Qualitative and quantitative features of the combat-related symptomatology described in the research literature are related to the nature of the combat situation, its intensity and duration, the extent of loss of life and limb, the cohesiveness of the fighting unit, the character and conduct of military leadership, etc. (Grinker & Spiegel, 1945; Marlowe, 1979; Noy, 1978, 1980; Stouffer et al., 1949). If the stress-resistant and the stress-incapacitating factors in a given combat situation bring about an intolerable situation, the nosological label that refers to combat stress reaction and its descriptors then assumes a critical role. This label refers to those behaviors that are criterial for the diagnosis providing an exit from the situation and from the formal role of the combat soldier.

Our thesis is that in every evacuation from the battlefield, a collusion occurs both in the combat zone and thereafter in the military psychiatric unit between stressed soldier and the military and psychiatric authorities. When a soldier feels unable to go on with his mission, he initiates a dialogue with the organization and tries to communicate his inability in a way that will ensure an exit ticket from the battlefield without generating hostility against him. The organization understandably wishes to support the soldier in his combat role and to prevent his leaving the scene. For the soldier to leave the scene with the permission of the organization requires a particular form of collusion between the soldier and the gatekeepers. This collusion may operate on the conscious or the unconscious level, or both. In it commanding officers and military psychiatrists selectively perceive, and the stressed soldier selectively exhibits, the necessary exit criteria. This argument is developed more fully below and evidence is offered for its cogency.

METHOD

The first step was to review the literature on psychiatric casualties in World War I (Grinker & Spiegel, 1945; Menninger, 1948), World War II (Mullins & Glass, 1973), the Vietnam War (Figley, 1978a), and the Arab-Israeli War of 1973 (Adler, 1975; Arieli, 1974; Sohlberg, 1975). The most frequently reported symptoms are summarized in Table 1.

Subjects

The second step was to obtain precise frequencies of symptoms from Israeli soldiers in the Lebanon War. The clinical population consisted of all Israeli soldiers serving in Lebanon from June 6 to September 30, 1982 who were referred to psychiatric units for examination. Psychiatrists, psychologists, and social workers recorded the complete clinical picture

TABLE 1

Symptoms of Combat Stress Reactions in Different Wars

Symptom	Percentage	1982	1973	1968	1941	1919
1. Anxiety	55.9	X	X		X	X
2. Depressive affect	37.5	X	X			X
3. Sleep disturbance	33.9	X	X		X	X
4. Fear	33.7	X	X			
5. Social detachment	23.7	X		X		
6. Conversion reactions	21.8	X	X		X	X
7. Crying	21.1	X			X	
8. Decreased appetite	18.9	X			X	
9. Headache	18.8				X	
10. Exhaustion	17.2				X	
11. Psychomotor disorder	16.7		X		X	X
12. Dreams and memories	16.5		X			X
13. Tremor	13.3					X
14. Poor concentration	13.1					
15. Poor communication	11.9					
16. Dissociative states	11.4		X			X
17. Irritability	11.1					
18. Aggressive behavior	10.9			X		
19. Poor memory	10.7			X		
20. Noise sensitivity	10.4			X		X
21. Discipline problems						
22. Substance abuse					X	
23. Gastrointestinal				X		
24. Guilt feelings						
25. Constricted affect						

at the time, collected relevant collateral information, gave diagnoses, and made recommendations for therapeutic intervention. The exact number of soldiers and of mental health personnel is not cited here because of security regulations established by the Israel Defense Force, but suffice it to say that the numbers were large enough to permit statistical analyses and conclusions.

The men ranged in age from late teens to early forties. Since regular military service is confined largely to the 18-to-21-year age range, the majority of men were reservists. Most had served in combat roles and the remainder in supporting roles close to the front. They were being examined while the actual fighting was going on, shortly after the onset of their symptoms, and in mental health units in close proximity to the war zone, in accord with the well-established principles of immediacy, proximity, and expectancy of Salmon (Salmon & Fenton, 1929).

Procedure

Of this clinical population, 30% of the files were randomly selected for analysis in the present study and were scanned by two experienced mental health professional workers to yield a comprehensive checklist of the recorded symptoms. This exhaustive list was then trimmed by eliminating redundant descriptors. The final list was identical to that of Table 1 with minor variations. Six mental health professional workers collaborated in the final phase of the research in recording the frequency of occurrence of the descriptors from the checklist in the files selected for inclusion in the sample. Of these files, 11.0% were deleted because of unclear clinical descriptions, questionable evidence of an emotional disturbance, or symptomatology related to organic etiology (e.g., head injury).

RESULTS AND DISCUSSION

Of the soldiers in the sample, 69.0% were diagnosed as exhibiting a classical picture of post-traumatic stress reaction, and the remainder as exhibiting other situationally acute psychiatric disturbances. This distinction was discounted for two reasons: First, all symptoms were combat-related since none were in evidence in the military performance of these men prior to their participation in the Lebanon War. Second, no uniform set of criteria was adhered to by the many professional workers in arriving at their diagnoses of psychiatric disorders in general or of post-traumatic stress reactions in particular. Consequently, all were considered under the general rubric of combat stress reaction.

The percentages of these symptoms are summarized in Table 1 in descending order of frequency for this sample. The percentages add up to more than 100% because there were on the average four symptoms per soldier. Several of the symptoms require some elaboration. Fears appeared either as well-defined, war-related phobias (e.g., fear of touching weapons) or diffuse feelings of intense panic. Social detachment referred to both physical and affective withdrawal from others. Conversion reactions ran the gamut of limb paralysis, blindness, deafness, aphonia, and fainting. Psychomotor disturbances and disorders were about equally distributed between mild agitation and moderate psychomotor retardation, with the former frequently turning into the latter, but not the reverse. Disturbing dreams and memories were vivid, war-related, upsetting experiences and were a major cause of sleep disturbance.

Flashbacks were a frequently reported phenomenon in which one relived traumatic experiences, "seeing, hearing and even smelling the battle scene as if it were really happening all over again." Impairment in communication took the form of slow or of rapid speech, and of mumbling and stuttering. Stuttering, like enuresis, was usually a reactivation or exacerbation of earlier existing problems in childhood. Dissociative states ranged from verbalizations (e.g., "It didn't happen to me") to disoriented, even bizarre behavior (e.g., rolling on the floor and talking to a dead friend while going through the motions of trying to put together the pieces of the friend's dismembered body). The remaining behaviors on the list are self-explanatory. Those behaviors that occurred in less than 10% of the cases are presented at the bottom of Table 1 without percentages.

In order to compare the clinical picture of the five wars, the eight most frequently reported symptoms are identified by the letter X for each war (1982, 1973, 1968, 1941, and 1914, respectively). The only exception was the Vietnam War, where five symptoms were cited as frequent.

We propose that in stressful situations people engage in fight or flight or both alternatively. Just as fighting behaviors follow patterns established by military and societal training, the same is true of flight behaviors. The military establishment defines the various categories of flight behavior and establishes its response to each, according to its larger objectives. It understands that life-threatening situations lower the response threshold for flight reactions for all soldiers. Accordingly, it sets up a series of checks and balances, so as to permit evacuation, hopefully temporary (from the army's point of view), from the combat zone to a designated few men for prescribed reasons only.

We contend that the dominant clinical picture of each war is best understood in terms of the nosological label in use at the time and the "exit ticket" required for evacuation from the combat zone. An implicit understanding prevails in any given war between symptom presenters and symptom evaluators. In World War I, for example, the label was "shell shock." The requisite behaviors for this diagnosis reflected the consequence of this shock: tremor, noise sensitivity, and poor concentration, symptoms that were not cited for high frequency in any other war.

In World War II the term "combat exhaustion," or the colloquial term "battle fatigue," was used to refer to combat stress reactions. Incapacitated soldiers in World War II were sent to so-called "exhaustion units" for treatment. This label included such psychosomatic symptoms as physical exhaustion, gastrointestinal discomfort, and headaches, symptoms not noted in any other war. In addition, there were other symptoms associated with fatigue that were noted in other wars, e.g., sleep disturbance and decreased appetite.

This nosological label had gone out of use by the time of the Vietnam War. One of the few diagnoses in the psychiatric diagnostic manual in use at the time—the DSM-II (American Psychiatric Association, 1968)—that appeared acceptable to the military authorities to release men from duty was "transient adjustment reaction of adult life." This diagnosis appeared sufficiently benign and reversible so that the soldier was not stigmatized by the label. More important, from the military point of view, the term did not imply that fear, cowardice, or poor motivation was a sufficient cause for even a temporary release from one's military duties. Consequently, we should not be surprised that conduct and character disturbances, reflected in antisocial and/or aggressive behavior and in substance abuse, were the major symptoms cited. The exit ticket from the combat zone in the Vietnam War was more likely to be disciplinary rather than psychiatric and took the form of acting out, although acting up and acting in were also noted.

The two Israeli wars, the October 1973 Yom Kippur War and the 1982 Lebanon War, were similar with overlap on five of eight symptoms, and differed drastically from the other wars. Notwithstanding the widespread use of the term "helem krav" or battle shock, combat stress reactions were defined in mental health terms as transient psychiatric phenomena. In fact, exit criteria in the two Israeli wars were more "psychiatric" in character than those of the other wars discussed and gave prominence to fear, anxiety, and depression. If these were made freely available as exit criteria in the other three wars, the number of combat stress reactions would have soared. The Israel Defense Force has been able to acknowledge these widespread reactions as a basis for exit behavior because of strong societal and military pressures on soldiers to conduct themselves well in combat. Since the wars conducted by Israel are regarded as wars of national survival or national consensus, most Israeli soldiers regard those who are evacuated for nonphysical injuries as objects of sympathy or alternately scorn, but certainly not envy—hence, the relatively low percentage of psychiatric casualties in Israeli wars despite the wide latitude of the symptoms in the exit criteria, and the high percentage of soldiers with acute combat stress reactions returning to their units, as described elsewhere in this volume.

There are alternative explanations for the similarities and differences noted in the clinical pictures of these five wars, and the various explanations are not mutually exclusive. When we consider that verbal concepts affect our selective attention and our interpretation of what we see, it is not surprising that evaluators seeking to confirm or reject a hypothesis of combat stress reaction in a given case may overestimate the frequency of confirming symptoms and underestimate the frequency of symptoms that are not criterial. Similarly, soldiers unable or unwilling to persist in the combat soldier role select those features of the symptom panorama that constitute even a temporary respite from a situation they have come to regard as intolerable.

Awareness of the label effect may enable psychiatric policymakers to select those labels and descriptors that best serve the interests of the armed forces and of the soldiers themselves and may enable evaluators to achieve greater objectivity, comprehensiveness, and veridicality in their observations and diagnoses.

10

The Forward Treatment of Combat Stress Reactions: A Test Case in the 1982 Conflict in Lebanon

SHABTAI NOY, ZAHAVA SOLOMON,
and RAMI BENBENISHTI

The problem of combat psychiatric casualties was first described in the American Civil War, and treatment principles were first enunciated in World War I. Salmon (1919) implemented a treatment system in the American army based on lessons learned from the French and British, in which soldiers were treated at the front and promptly returned to their units. Glass (Mullins & Glass, 1973) described the approach as "enabling respite without severing the soldier from the natural support provided by his comrades." Artiss (1963) first coined the phrase "immediacy, proximity, expectancy" as a brief description of the major elements of forward treatment.

This treatment was implemented by the American army in World War I from the onset and in World War II from the Italian campaign on. In the Korean campaign, forward treatment was only introduced in the latter half of the conflict. The Israeli Yom Kippur War in 1973 was essentially without forward treatment, whereas in the 1982 conflict in Lebanon, forward treatment was introduced from the start. Thus, previous wars have provided ample opportunities to compare forward and rear treatments.

Clinical reports showed that when forward treatment was instituted, return to the units was high, while in its absence, discharge from military service and continued treatment in civilian facilities were high. In the latter half of the Italian campaign, after forward treatment was established, return rates to the units reached 70%. By contrast, in the early North African and Sicilian campaigns, the return rate was as low as 3% (Mullins & Glass, 1973; Spiegel, 1944). The same shift in return rate as a function of introducing forward treatment took place in the Korean War. In Israel only a small proportion of the psychiatric casualties in the Yom Kippur War returned to their units because of the lack of organized forward treatment.

Such reports clinically support the effectiveness of forward treatment, but they suffer from methodological handicaps. Usually all casualties in a given battle were given forward treatment or rear treatment. There was no situation in which both treatments were given to comparable groups from the same battle at the same time. One could claim, therefore, that the differential rates of return to the units were due to factors other than the location of the treatment and its associated components.

The 1982 conflict in Lebanon presented an excellent opportunity (albeit an unfortunate circumstance) for a controlled study of the effectiveness of forward treatment. The combat situation was such that some casualties within a unit were airlifted directly to the rear, while others were treated as planned in forward medical units. Furthermore, the reasons for the differential forms of evacuation were solely local, tactical, and technical conditions rather than medical considerations. Thus, this was a unique opportunity to compare the differential rates of return as a function of forward versus rear treatment.

METHOD

Subjects

Data on *all* individual psychiatric casualties in the early phase of the 1982 Lebanon conflict (June-September, 1982) were accumulated and computerized. *Post hoc* comparisons of the forward- and rear-treatment groups revealed no differences either in soldier attributes (IQ, motivation to serve, army duties, etc.) or in military unit characteristics. The forward-treatment population was subdivided into two subpopulations, treatment within Lebanon proper and treatment in Israel very near to the international border. The latter setting was also regarded as an instance of forward treatment since it was close to the staging center of the combat units at the onset of the campaign.

The rear-treatment population was also subdivided into two subpopulations: airlift and rear admissions. The first consisted of those soldiers airlifted by error to general hospitals at the rear, most of whom were then returned to an area near the international border as soon as the error was detected. The second consisted of men erroneously referred for rear treatment because they were on home leave at the time or because of faulty channels of evacuation. The latter were treated at the rear with no effort to return them to forward treatment.

RESULTS

The percentages of soldiers who actually returned to their military units after treatment were 59.0, 59.5, 39.5, and 16.3 for the four groups: in Lebanon, international border, airlift, and rear-admissions groups, respectively. It is clear that both forward treatments were better than both rear treatments, with better results for those airlifted to the rear and then brought back than for those treated in the rear (chi square yielded $p < .001$).

The rate of referrals to return to their units was actually higher (75 to 100%) in the forward-treatment settings than the rate of actual return. The difference was due to logistic difficulties in arranging for the soldiers to return to their units in a fluid and complex military operation. Some simply could not locate their units in the midst of battle; others had recovered sufficiently to leave the treatment centers, but not to search and locate their units on their own. These observations and the rate discrepancies do not detract from the above-mentioned differences in return rates, but merely indicate that under ideal return conditions, even more impressive treatment differences would have emerged.

DISCUSSION AND SUPPLEMENTARY ANALYSES

Given the present findings, three questions come to mind:

1. Of the three factors (immediacy, proximity, expectancy), which is the major factor within forward treatment that accounts for the higher return rate?

2. What are the mental health consequences of returning to one's unit during wartime?
3. What are the alternative explanations for these findings and how consistent are they with available data?

Expectancy Is Primary

Of the three factors, it is clear that immediacy is least important, since it was about equal in forward and rear treatment in the conflict in Lebanon. The airlift casualties sometimes began treatment even before those treated at the front. Of the two remaining factors, it appears equally clear that proximity is effective only to the extent that it reinforces the expectancy that the soldier will soon return to his unit. Admittedly, the greater the distance of the treatment center from the front, the greater the technical difficulty in implementing the referral that the soldier return to his unit, yet Israel is a small country and the difference in return time is a matter of a few hours, and not the crossing of an ocean.

There were, in fact, two treatment units in the rear that were only 200 meters apart. One was designed as a forward-treatment center for people who were erroneously airlifted to the rear and the other was designed as a second-echelon treatment center. Despite their proximity, the former unit that conveyed explicitly the expectancy of return to the unit in its treatment of the soldiers did, in fact, return a higher proportion of its soldiers to their combat units than the other.

We conclude that the important factor is the orientation of the psychiatric personnel, a factor that differs in forward- and rear-treatment settings in a number of respects:

1. Psychiatrists and psychologists in the forward settings are in uniform and readily identify with the needs of the combat unit to conserve manpower and not to be undermined by the phenomenon of men without physical injury leaving the unit and failing to return.
2. These professional workers are more likely to have received a forward-treatment orientation geared toward rapid treatment of transient incapacity. By contrast, personnel in civilian medical settings tend to attribute the psychopathology of combat stress reaction to personal characteristics of the soldiers themselves rather than to the stressful nature of the combat situation. Personal characteristics are typically regarded as traits of longstanding that are modified slowly and after considerable psychiatric treatment, whereas situational reactions are regarded as transient and temporary with rapid recovery. Hence, personnel in forward

and rear settings differ in their expectations about the course of the soldiers' symptom picture and its etiology and presumably communicate these expectations to their patients.

3. The psychiatric personnel working in the war zone experience anxiety and other combat stress reactions to some degree and tend to regard these symptoms as less pathological than do their professional counterparts in civilian settings far removed from the battlefield.

4. Many cues in the forward- and rear-treatment settings reinforce these differing expectations. Forward treatment takes place in a busy and bustling military setting, with weapons and men in uniform in view at all times. Rear treatment takes place in a quiet hospital setting with none of the cues associated with military life.

5. The health and illness labels that are used in the two settings also reinforce the corresponding expectancies. In a civilian hospital, patients are ill, whereas in the military setting men with combat stress reactions are not encouraged to regard themselves as ill.

The interplay of expectancy and proximity to the battlefield may be represented by an imaginary latitude line drawn across the northern part of Israel, the Upper Galilee region. All settings north of the line were forward-treatment settings in theory and practice and, indeed, had higher rates of return. All below the line were rear-treatment settings in these respects and had far lower rates of return.

Return to One's Combat Unit Sustains Mental Health

Several sources of information are consistent with the conclusion that return to the original combat units reduces the probability of a recurrence or exacerbation of the soldiers' former symptoms. First, only soldiers who did not return to their units were found to be in psychiatric treatment one year after the 1982 conflict. Second, in a follow-up study published elsewhere in this volume (Chapter 7, by Solomon, Oppenheimer, & Noy), we find that soldiers with combat stress reactions in the 1973 Yom Kippur War who returned to their combat units and actually participated in combat in the 1982 conflict in Lebanon were at no higher risk for combat stress reaction than a suitable control group: combat soldiers who had participated in the 1973 war without stress reaction and had now participated in combat in the 1982 conflict. These data are consistent with the conclusion that return to one's unit makes for mental health rather than for exacerbation of one's original symptomatology.

Age and Combat Status Affect the Return Rate

One may ask whether the success of forward treatment in returning the majority of soldiers with combat stress reaction to their units was at all related to variables within the soldiers themselves. What was the impact on return, even if minor, of premorbid personality characteristics and other variables within the soldiers themselves? A number of preinduction variables were examined and found to be unrelated to return rate. These included preinduction medical status, intelligence level, educational level, army performance prediction scores, motivation for service scores, and type of service (infantry, tanks, artillery, etc.). Even participation in battle was unrelated to return. The two variables that were highly related to return were the age of the soldiers and their combat status in the conflict. Younger men in combat status were far more likely to return than older men in noncombat status.

Relationship of Diagnosis and Treatment Variables to Return

Diagnosis affected return rate, since soldiers diagnosed as having combat stress reaction were more likely to return to their units than soldiers with psychiatric disturbance not attributed to combat. The probable explanation for this finding is that personnel oriented toward forward-treatment ideology felt obliged to return soldiers with combat stress reactions to their units. Psychiatric disabilities that were unrelated to combat did not fall within this category, since they were presumably related to personal weaknesses, and necessitated more conventional psychiatric treatment.

This relationship was found not only in front- and rear-echelon treatment settings, but even in civilian hospitals well in the rear, as soldiers who failed to return to their units from the first or forward-treatment setting were referred to the second and then on to the third. The only exception to this relationship were soldiers with combat stress reaction who were referred directly to the rear for treatment. Their symptomatology was so dramatic and severe that rear treatment was recommended from the start, and these serious cases proved to be recalcitrant to treatment during the war. As a consequence, fewer returned to their units than comparison soldiers who were referred to the same setting with noncombat psychiatric disability. Severity of symptomatology per se, however, was unrelated to return rate.

Soldiers with delayed combat stress reactions returned in smaller proportions to their units than soldiers with early combat stress reactions, presumably because the former were all treated in rear settings in which the rate of return is uniformly lower. Duration of treatment was also related to return to one's unit, with short-term treatment yielding a higher rate of return than long-term. This followed from the relationship between length of treatment and type of treatment, namely, shorter treatment in forward treatment and treatment of greater length in the rear. Thus, the number of treatment settings through which the soldier passed and the length of time he spent in each are inversely related to return rate, because of their relationship to the expectancy set within each treatment setting. In summary, these data suggest that expectancy exerts very powerful effects on the behavior of people coping with severe stress reactions, especially when these expectancies are strongly and unambiguously emphasized in the treatment milieu and when the people under stress are motivated to recover.

11

A Therapeutic Community in a Forward Army Field Hospital: Treatment, Education, and Expectancy

YOSEF TOUBIANA, NORMAN MILGRAM, and SHABTAI NOY

This chapter describes the functioning of a forward-echelon treatment unit for combat stress reactions during the conflict in Lebanon in the summer and early fall of 1982. As such it is typical of the many settings in which the principles of expectancy of return to one's unit, proximity to the front, and immediacy of treatment were realized. This particular unit was set up by nine mental health workers (four psychologists, three psychiatrists, and two social workers), sent into a battle zone in anticipation of a large number of physical casualties and, as a consequence, a large number of combat stress reactions. The combined unit established

The first author was a member of the mental health team whose functioning is described in this chapter. He wishes to express his appreciation to other members of the mental health staff for their collaboration in the treatment program (Y. Barg, R. Bar-On, N. Durst, D. Enoch, G. Haran, S. Hovel, A. Israel, M. Reiter, and M. Stern). He also expresses his gratitude to Janet Gool, mental health nurse from the Mental Health Community Center of Petach Tikva, for her help in the preparation of the manuscript. The second author was responsible for many of the ideas in the manuscript and prepared it in final form for publication. The third author, Head of the Research Unit in the Mental Health Department of the Israel Defense Force, provided follow-up data, reviewed the paper critically, and provided valuable suggestions.

itself about four miles behind the lines in a forward field hospital responsible for first aid, emergency surgery, and transportation of wounded soldiers to civilian hospitals in the north of Israel.

In describing the functioning of the unit, this chapter also deals with two major obstacles faced by the mental health teams of forward-echelon units in general: (1) evolving a unified approach despite differences in professional discipline and military rank (e.g., a social worker holding a higher rank than a psychiatrist) and in professional training and treatment orientation; and (2) establishing in soldiers with combat stress reaction the expectancy of rapid return to their combat unit, in the face of apprehensive and prejudicial attitudes of medical personnel in the setting (Enoch et al., 1983; Stern et al., 1983).

THE SETTING, THE PATIENTS, AND THE STAFF

Casualties arrived at the field hospital by helicopter or ambulance and were immediately evaluated in a central selection area for subsequent disposition. The medical authorities were confused, to say the least, when men without physical injuries appeared who were unable to respond appropriately to routine questions and whose behavior was unusual, if not bizarre. There were 15 such men among the medical patients. They displayed symptoms associated with post-traumatic stress reaction: anxiety, detachment, depression, shift in mood, autistic mannerisms, etc.

The mental health staff quickly separated these men from the physically injured patients and required them to work with the staff in putting up living quarters for staff and soldiers on the outskirts of the field hospital. These quarters consisted of makeshift tents to emphasize the temporary nature of the quarters in which the men were to live until they returned to their combat units only a few miles away. The men were housed close to the field hospital to emphasize that their condition did not mandate segregated quarters. They were not housed in the hospital itself so as to minimize the potential stigmatizing of these men by medical staff members who were as yet wholly uninformed about the nature of the combat stress reaction syndrome.

The tents of the soldiers were adjacent to those of their mental health officers to emphasize the close working and living relationships of both groups that were to prevail during their brief stay. The staff members elected to reside in these tents for still another reason: to develop intimate working relationships with one another as a cohesive professional group.

Most of them had known each other before in reserve duty or professional life, but they came from different professions, differed markedly in age, military rank, and command experience, differed in therapeutic approach in general, and had had different experiences in prior treatment of combat stress reactions in particular.

The major unifying force in the professional staff was their common acceptance of the expectancy principle: They were there to help the soldiers evacuated from the battlefield to return as quickly as possible to their units and to resume their military duties. All treatment modalities were subordinated to this goal, and all differences resolved with reference to it (as described in Glass, Artiss, Gibbs, & Sweeney, 1961; Mullins & Glass, 1973; Noy, 1984).

THE TREATMENT PROGRAM

The treatment program was similar in some respects to that of the Combat Fitness Rehabilitation Unit (CFRU) described elsewhere in this volume. It too consisted of psychodynamic and behavioral forms of individual and group therapy, sports, and other physical activities in an austere setting with military discipline. It differed, however, in a number of respects. It was forward rather than rear echelon. It was short term, a stay of a few days at most, rather than a standard stay of several weeks for all participants. Its proximity to the front was used to emphasize the expectancy principle more strongly than was possible in the CFRU. Given the close proximity to their military units, it was possible to establish contact with the unit by bringing the soldier out to his unit or by bringing his commanding officers or comrades-in-arms to him at the field station, even during the relatively short stay.

The treatment program for the men began with their initial contact with the mental health staff. The therapist:patient ratio was very high, frequently one to one, and each mental health officer functioned as therapist and military commander of a single soldier and as the liaison between the soldier and his direct unit commander and comrades. Each soldier was told forthrightly by his commander at the very beginning that after a short period of rest, he would become again an active soldier capable of returning to the front.

The milieu created by the mental health staff strongly reinforced this expectancy in a number of ways: The soldiers lived in field conditions and wore their uniforms. They had their meals in a communal military dining hall and were required to feed themselves properly regardless of any claimed infirmities or incapacities. They were required to maintain a proper military appearance and to conform to the grooming norms of the Israeli Defense Forces (that are relatively informal). They participated actively in the physical training. Each had a personal meeting with his therapist–commanding officer twice a day and attended group therapy sessions twice a day as well.

The group sessions held in the morning and in the afternoon were crucial for the recovery of these men and continued even as some of the members left to return to their units and an increasingly smaller number of men remained, three men some 60 hours after admission to the field station. While most of the men had not known each other before, they now found that they had similar stress reactions, intense feelings of anxiety and helplessness, and that they had shared similar battle experiences, including the sight of their friends wounded or killed. They reconstructed in the group sessions the main events that had transpired before, during, and immediately after the battle experience and were able to ventilate the feelings associated with these recollected experiences.

These mutual revelations brought about a marked decrease in feelings of guilt and shame that had overwhelmed them when they were evacuated from the front. Feelings of guilt and shame had arisen because these men had solved the basic conflict between fight and flight on the battlefield by leaving the scene. The mutual revelations and the professed goal of returning to their combat unit served to dispel these feelings and to reinforce goal-productive behaviors. Given differing recovery rates within the group, some soldiers announced their imminent intention to return and left the group a short time later, thereby strongly reinforcing the expectancy principle in the others. All participants in the group therapy session served as models for one another, and given the pressures toward goal-constructive behavior rather than the reverse, these behaviors were rewarded and emulated (Jacobson, 1975; Marshall, 1976).

The milieu within the forward-echelon unit and in the therapy sessions, individual and group, strongly emphasized such qualities as active coping, the friendship and solidarity of the military unit, and one's responsibility to others—qualities strongly emphasized by practitioners in the field (Marlowe, 1979; Spiegel, 1944; Steiner & Neumann, 1978). Visits to one's combat unit and visits by officers and friends to the field treatment unit served to remind the soldier that, despite his temporary incapacity, he still belonged to and was needed by them. The productivity of these contacts was enhanced by the briefing and guidance that the visiting officers received from mental health staff members before the visit. As a consequence, the recuperating soldiers rapidly regained the identity and the self-confidence consistent with returning to their unit.

The mental health staff was able to function in a comprehensive and effective manner because it ignored formal distinctions of military rank and professional status. Men with lower military rank than others assumed leadership roles by virtue of their recognized qualities and relevant expertise. There was autonomy in the formal therapeutic activities (individual and group psychotherapy) and collaboration and consensus in all other group activities. Intensive, constructive group meetings of all staff members provided mutual supervision and monitoring of all activities and opportunity for ventilation of anxieties and concerns.

Another difficulty that required constant group supervision was the tendency of therapists who were less experienced in treatment of stress reactions to adopt a developmental or historical treatment model (focusing on past events or on premorbid personality structure) instead of focusing on the ongoing emergency, on the recent traumatic stressful experience, or on anticipated functioning in the immediate future. If these historical models are not actively discouraged by supervisors, they may be applied in individual treatment, thereby strengthening the illness label that becomes attached to the individual.

COUNTERTRANSFERENCE IN STAFF AND VISITORS

Mental health staff members encountered another serious problem: powerful countertransference expressed in feelings of guilt about sending their patients back into combat, while they themselves were secure several miles behind the lines in noncombat assignments. In addition, staff members were older, married, and on reserve duty. Their patients were young, single (with few exceptions), and in compulsory service. The age and marital status differentials contributed to a big-brother or fatherly attitude toward the soldiers and to overprotective behavior, especially on the part of the less experienced officers. Overprotective behavior took the form of doing things for the patient that he should be doing for himself and was diametrically opposed to the treatment goal of restoring autonomous functioning. It was associated with the absence of the expectancy of ever regaining normal functioning and, in its place, creating an illness expectancy and an illness label.

Given the crisis orientation of the group, therapists met around the clock, identified the problem in one another, and dealt with it summarily by identifying those behaviors that were proscribed and by adhering to these prohibitions. They also were sensitive to overprotective behaviors toward their patients on the part of the "newly educated" medical staff and visitors and introduced precautions about these understandable reactions in their talks about combat stress reactions.

EDUCATION FOR ALL IN THE THERAPEUTIC COMMUNITY

Until recently medical personnel in Israel received little didactic or practical background and orientation in dealing with combat stress reactions. Hence, it was understandable, if not inevitable, that consternation, a feeling of professional helplessness, irrational fears, and other avoidant reactions characterized the members of the medical staff, physicians, medics, x-ray technicians, and other supporting paramedical workers when physically healthy men exhibiting bizarre behavior arrived at the field hospital.

The mental health staff recognized that treatment of the soldiers in a large and unsympathetic medical setting could not be successful, given the close proximity of the field hospital and the many opportunities for adverse contact between these men and the medical staff and medical patients at meals and other activities during the day. Accordingly, they developed a two-pronged approach: therapeutic interventions for their patients, as described in the preceding section, and an educational program for the medical staff to facilitate their treatment techniques and to prevent them from developing combat stress reactions in their own right.

The mental health staff launched into a series of formal and informal lectures on reactions to stressful situations in general and on combat stress in particular to all who would listen. At first they conducted lectures for the entire staff contingent. They met informally with medical staff and with all visitors arriving at the facility. They encouraged contact between their patients and the large medical staff in the field hospital. They contacted the officers and comrades of their patients in their original combat units, asking them to visit when possible, all the while emphasizing the temporary nature of their comrade's incapacity and his imminent return with their encouragement.

Medical staff and visitors observed the intensive treatment schedule and the movement of the 15 men in and out of the field hospital and

were favorably impressed. The medical staff came to acknowledge that
these soldiers had, indeed, reacted normally under the abnormal circumstances in which they found themselves and that their need for a
retreat of several days to restore their depleted physical and mental
resources was legitimate. The response of the staff and visitors indicated
that the educational program was successful in demystifying and de-
stigmatizing the problem. Two and a half years later the first author had
occasion to meet members of the medical staff in the course of reserve
duty and found that they persisted in the new attitudes and understanding that they had acquired earlier. He also received confirmation from
them that the lectures and informal talks had been helpful in *immunizing
them* (their words) from possible stress reactions. They were functioning,
after all, a very short distance from the front and might well have developed adverse emotional reactions, given the sounds of shelling
nearby and the kinds of medical experiences to which their work exposed
them.

THE CONTENT OF THE EDUCATIONAL APPROACH

In their formal and informal contacts, mental health staff members
attempted to convey the following information about the etiology, symptoms, treatment, and prognosis of combat stress reactions:

1. These reactions arise in any soldier in any or all of the following
   situations: when there is massive firing on the unit and considerable loss of life or injuries; when group cohesiveness and trust
   in the commander are lacking or have been disrupted; and when
   there is lack of knowledge about the goals of the operation or
   lack of prior preparation or experience (Marlowe, 1979; Steiner
   & Neumann, 1978).
2. Combat stress brings about a decrease in one's ability to endure
   and to perform properly under conditions of sustained stress.
3. Whatever the overt manifestation of the combat stress reaction,
   it is normal in the battle situation and will dissipate over time
   as the soldier resumes normal functioning in his military and
   civilian roles.
4. Men recover more rapidly if they are treated as responsible,
   healthy soldiers. They may develop serious difficulties when
   well-meaning people express sympathy or pity for their tem-

porary incapacities and thus assign them the role of patients, or when uncomprehending people call them cowardly or weak and recommend court martial.

5. The main features of the treatment program are the restoration of biological deficiencies (lack of sleep, food, rest, and calm), resumption of military life in a military setting, continued contact with one's former officers and comrades, opportunity for the sharing of battle experiences and ventilation of upsetting feelings, and an ongoing expectation that the incapacity is temporary, that the current treatment program is short-term, and that all members of the group will be returning shortly to their units to resume normal military activities.

RESULTS

The combined treatment and educational approach yielded remarkably good results. All 15 patients were referred back to their units after a stay of 36 to 72 hours. All but one remained there until the end of the hostilities. A follow-up several months later indicated that they had not been prematurely discharged from their military unit or referred for medical or psychiatric treatment. The fifteenth soldier did not function well in his unit and after a short stay was referred to the rear-echelon treatment unit (CFRU) that is described elsewhere in this volume. There he did well and was subsequently returned to his unit without further sequelae (see Case B below). These results parallel those reported by other front-echelon units and are confirmed by the overall report on front-echelon treatment of stress reaction in the conflict in Lebanon reported elsewhere in this volume.

A long-term follow-up of these men was conducted three years later. Their subsequent adjustment and functioning in the military were compared with that of a control group selected by computer. These were 25 soldiers serving in the same units and in the same military capacity during the conflict in Lebanon and with similar military proficiency scores on induction to the service. In nine instances there was one control per treatment soldier, and in the remaining six cases the number of controls varied from two to four per treatment soldier. In the case of soldiers in the treatment group who were serving in a different unit during the conflict, one control soldier was selected from their original unit and the other from the 1982 Lebanon unit.

Results were obtained for subsequent psychiatric treatment and combat profile. Of the 15 men in the treatment group, two men became disturbed a year or more after the conflict, one experiencing a brief psychotic episode associated with the death of a friend in combat and the other receiving short-term treatment for personal problems. These two men were subsequently assigned to noncombat duties. There were no cases of psychiatric disturbance in the control group. One man in the treatment group and two in the control group received lowered military profiles for medical reasons. As a consequence of these psychiatric and medical conditions and other circumstances (some units are not called up every year and some reservists are overlooked in a callup), the number of men who actually served in regular reserve duty (30 to 40 days) in 1984/1985 was 11 of 15 in the former group and 21 of 25 in the latter. We conclude from the long-term follow-up that the incidence of disability with consequent inability to serve in the armed forces was only slightly higher in the group that had experienced combat stress reactions than in the group that had not. The relative intactness of the former group may be attributed to the effectiveness of the forward-echelon treatment received.

ILLUSTRATIVE CASE STUDIES

Two case studies were culled from the 15 to convey the flavor of the contributing factors to the stress reaction and to the subsequent recovery.

A was a 19-year-old serving as an armored personnel carrier (APC) driver in compulsory service. In the late fall of 1982 after active and static combat, his unit was assigned a mission to capture a certain built-up area. Notwithstanding their anticipation that the mission would be accomplished without difficulty, they encountered heavy, accurate shelling. In a few minutes several APCs had exploded and their occupants were burnt to death or were killed by gunfire. Despite losing confidence in his commander's assessment of battle conditions and in the impregnability of the APC, *A* was able to assist in evacuating casualties. But when a close friend was killed during the evacuation, he reacted with a dissociative reaction, amnesia, mutism, and psychomotor retardation.

He was immediately evacuated to the installation, where he was able to discuss the traumatic events he had experienced. He noted the return to their units of other men who had suffered difficult combat experiences. He responded well to the visit of his commander and other members of his armored unit who came to the field hospital *in their APCs* at the suggestion of the therapist. With the encouragement of the professional staff and the patients at the field hospital, he was able to mount an APC and begin the resumption of military duties. Recovery proceeded at a rapid pace, and he remained psychiatrically well after returning to his unit. Two years later he still functions as a combat soldier in an armored unit without psychiatric restrictions and has participated in combat duties since his recovery.

Somewhat less successful was the course of recovery of *B*, a 30-year-old married man. During the conflict in Lebanon he was separated from his regular reserve unit and was assigned to a medical unit to serve as an ambulance driver. In this capacity he performed heroically, evacuating casualties and corpses. Two days later, he suffered a stress reaction characterized by anxiety, impulsive behavior, and resistance to returning to his assignment as ambulance driver.

During individual and group therapy sessions *B* recounted his war experiences emphasizing his feeling of helplessness, vulnerability, and fear of dying. The therapist acted as a participant, guiding model, inviting *B* to join him as he drove from the field hospital to the front on his way to give a lecture on combat stress reaction to *B*'s own commander and fellow soldiers in the ambulance unit. During this visit *B* responded well to encouragement from his comrades and soon returned to the unit as a driver. Unfortunately, his functioning deteriorated again, and he was evacuated to a rear-echelon treatment installation (CFRU) described elsewhere. Here he completed a three-week stay and was able to return successfully to reserve duty in Lebanon. A three-year follow-up finds him in the same military role as before after having completed several tours of reserve duty without further complications.

The differences in the course of recovery in the two men are instructive and may be attributed to any and all of the following differences between the two men.

1. *A* was young, in compulsory service, and he returned to his original unit where the desensitization process initiated during front-echelon treatment continued. The cohesive and continuous ties with his unit in compulsory service sustained him in his recovery. By contrast, *B* was in the reserves, served in an unfamiliar unit during the conflict, and was returning to a reserve-duty assignment that did not provide as much continuous exposure to sensitized stimuli as that of *A*.

2. There were clearly predispositional factors in *B* as compared with *A*. *B* had encountered problems with alcohol and drugs

and military discipline in his prior army service. *A*'s history prior to combat stress reaction was unremarkable.

3. *B* was married with commitments and loyalties to his wife and children, whereas *A* was single and more wholly committed to his military "family." Other chapters in this volume have noted the greater susceptibility of married men in the reserves to combat stress reaction as compared with single men in compulsory service.

CONCLUSIONS AND GENERALIZATIONS

The experiences described and the findings obtained in the present chapter are prototypical of other front-echelon treatment settings established in the summer and early fall of 1982 to deal with combat stress reactions in the war in Lebanon. These experiences and findings are generalizable to other societies in which a broadly based citizens' army engaged in war with an enemy generally regarded as threatening the survival of the society. That the conflict took place a short distance from the northern border of the country made the war legitimate in the eyes of most soldiers and the threat from the enemy a valid one. The social pressures that subtly reinforce the expectancy principle were strongly operating in this circumstance.

The techniques and findings of the front-echelon treatment are probably applicable in any situation, military or nonmilitary, characterized by some of the following traits: (a) in which the expectancy principle can be brought to bear in a convincing manner on individuals who have experienced severe stress of short duration; (b) who will participate in a treatment program with others who have been similarly stressed and with whom they may have had prior contacts or ties; (c) they will be returning to a community or social structure that is largely intact; and (d) the stressed individuals will continue to function in their customary roles once they recover.

Many civilian disasters are characterized, however, by several critical differing circumstances: First and foremost, civilian disasters often involve the destruction of homes and livelihoods, so that victims are not able to return to intact communities, but return to settings randomly ravaged and to citizens similarly traumatized. Second, the citizens suffering from stress reactions do not belong to an authoritarian or a voluntary organization that can command their allegiance and their obedience or can lay prior claims on their cooperation. Third, the expectancy principle works best when one can identify significant others in the setting whose expectancy for the recovery of the victims is regarded as a legitimate claim.

In summary, short-term treatment in a residential setting close to the site of victimization works best in people acknowledging the legitimacy of the treatment staff, the legitimacy of the group composition, and the legitimacy of expectations on them from one another, from the treatment staff, and from others in their community for their speedy recovery and return to normal routines. Keeping these criteria in mind, it may be possible to reproduce them to some extent in a large-scale disasters other than combat and to achieve beneficial results comparable to those described here.

12A

The Combat Fitness Retraining Unit

CHAIM MARGALIT, YOCHANAN WOZNER,
CHEN NARDI, RUBEN SEGAL, YAIR GOREN,
and YOSEF TRIEST

This is the first part in a series describing the Combat Fitness Retraining Unit (CFRU). This rear-echelon psychiatric unit was established early in the 1982 conflict in Lebanon to provide short-term treatment and rehabilitation of severe post-traumatic combat stress reaction in soldiers with poor prognosis following unsuccessful treatment in first-echelon settings. Described here are the physical setting of the CFRU, its therapeutic rationale, the soldiers who were treated there, and the principles governing the operation of the setting, the various interventions, and the follow-up. Other chapters in this series provide details on specific topics: the therapeutic milieu, individual and group psychotherapy, and dynamic and behavioral therapies.

BACKGROUND

The literature on the treatment of combat stress reactions refers to two major approaches: (1) treatment by military mental health workers in or near the combat zone, on the one hand, and (2) treatment by civilians in institutions and ambulatory settings far from the combat zone, on the other. The former approach developed out of the experiences of World War I, for the most part. Front-line intervention was established close to the war zone in accordance with Salmon's principles of immediacy, proximity, and expectancy (Salmon, 1919). Treatment included rest, gratification of physiological needs, individual and group psychotherapy that focused on present problems, abreaction of traumatic events, and the clear expectation that the soldiers would soon return to their units. Those soldiers who were treated without success in the first- and second-echelon settings and could not return to their combat units were treated in civilian settings.

The second approach was used in the early years of World War II and resulted in so high a rate of psychiatric casualties that it was abandoned. The Salmon approach was implemented after 1943 with great success (Baker, 1980; Glass, 1955, 1959; Kardiner, 1959; Mullins & Glass, 1973) and was used again in the Korean and Vietnam Conflicts (Allerton, 1969; Bourne, 1970; Strange & Arthur, 1967).

The State of Israel went through the same experience. During and after the 1973 Yom Kippur War, the Israel Defense Force provided treatment in civilian hospitals and recuperation centers within Israel that were far removed from front-echelon military settings. In these civilian settings treatment was dictated primarily by the professional orientation and clinical experience of the individual civilian therapists. This civilian treatment proved to be ineffective, and many soldiers did not recover or return to their units. Instead they suffered psychiatric sequelae after discharge from the army.

In the conflict in Lebanon in June 1982 an effort was made to return to the Salmon approach with immediate front-echelon military treatment of combat stress reactions. This program was largely successful and is described in earlier chapters in this section. The CFRU was established in a regular military training base to provide rear-echelon treatment for those who did not respond to front-line treatment because of the severity of their symptomatology and who were in need of continued treatment. The major aim of the approach was to prevent hospitalization in civilian psychiatric settings and the establishment of chronic symptomatology.

METHOD

Description of the Soldiers

Soldiers referred to the CFRU were functioning at minimal levels of adequacy and exhibiting many of the classical symptoms associated with post-traumatic stress disorder and/or severe adjustment disorders described in the DSM-III (APA, 1980). These included severe anxiety, psychomotor disturbance (agitation and/or retardation), sleep and appetite disturbances, dissociative and conversion reactions, apathy, and lack of volition. They ranged in age from 18 to 42, with 40% from the regular draft army (aged 18 to 22) and 60% from reserve units (aged 22+). All had been serving in combat or in service and logistic roles close to the front lines and had experienced traumatic battle experiences.

Subsequent psychiatric interviews indicated that 70 to 80% of these men, who were recalcitrant to front-echelon treatment, had prior histories of adjustment problems in civilian life and in their military service and had been diagnosed as personality disorders. Their premorbid civilian history is described in detail by Segal and Margalit in Section Two (Chapter 8).

Inspection of the overall *combat potential score* in the army files of these soldiers provided further evidence of premorbid factors contributing to a potentially chronic stress reaction. This score is based on a structured interview administered at the time of induction into military service and takes into consideration such motivational and attitudinal variables as motivation for combat duty, sense of personal responsibility, and identification with the Israel Defense Force. These scores are summed to yield an overall score on a scale from 1 to 5 (high) that is wholly independent of the physical fitness profile. All soldiers who reached the CFRU had received scores of 2.2 or better when they were inducted into the army, 2.2 being the lowest possible score consistent with assigning an able-bodied young man to combat or combat support duty. Only 15% of the group had attained, however, a score of 3.5 to 4.0. None had received scores above 4.0, and the remaining 85% were sandwiched in the relatively low range of 2.2 to 3.4. By contrast, in unselected soldiers with comparable duties, combat potential scores are normally distributed from 2.2 to 5.0. We conclude that these soldiers, who succumbed to combat stress reactions and failed to recover at front-echelon treatment stations, tended to come from the low end of the combat potential distribution.

Description of the CFRU

The structure and atmosphere of the CFRU was military in all respects, with well-defined rules and routines, and with military discipline. Most of the mental health personnel—psychiatrists, psychologists, and social workers—had had prior experience as combat soldiers in military units. The first two authors were in professional army service at the time and had been formulating a program for short-term residential treatment of soldiers with transient stress reactions under the auspices of the Army Mental Health Department at the Tel Hashomer Army Base. They were able to apply this program to the CFRU with the collaboration of the other mental health staff members.

The rationale and structure of such a unit is described extensively in the professional literature (e.g., Herz, 1979; Jaffe, 1975). Some of the treatment elements, drawn from the literature on short-term hospitalization, were introduced directly into the CFRU: formal military structure, therapeutic community structure, techniques of short-term crisis intervention, and multidimensional treatment. Two mental health officers and a physical education–combat trainer were assigned to each treatment unit or company consisting of 8 to 10 soldiers.

Treatment Principles

1. The milieu defined a spatial and temporal framework with well-defined boundaries, privileges, and responsibilities, and with a demand for the full-time and intensive participation of the soldiers.

2. The multidimensional treatment program utilized all of the following for the soldiers: military drills and skills that maintained discipline and soldiering proficiency; activities that maintained combat physical fitness (obstacles courses, field maneuvers and exercises, and target practice); individual and group sport activities; informal group activities and entertainment in the evenings; individual and group psychotherapy; behavioral therapy; couples counseling; and military and civilian community interventions.

3. The two-stage goal-directed treatment program consisted of two weeks devoted to intensive working through of traumatic experiences and two weeks devoted to rehabilitation and reintegration in the military and civilian communities. After this time soldiers were discharged from the CFRU.

4. The interdisciplinary structure of the staff and the variety of their treatment orientations contributed to an unusually rich therapeutic milieu with something for everybody by everybody: dynamic, behavioral, paradoxical, directive, pharmacological, etc.

5. Collaboration of the mental health staff and the combat and physical education staff was an essential feature of the program.

6. Each soldier was assigned a therapist who also served as his military commander during the treatment program. This deliberate overlap of two identities, which are kept separate in most treatment programs,

created an unusual kind of rapport between the two men and reinforced the military atmosphere of the therapeutic setting.

Timetable

The following timetable illustrates the daily schedule of activities in the CFRU:

06:30–06:45 : Reveille and morning exercises
06:45–07:45 : Breakfast and preparation for morning inspection
07:45–08:00 : Morning inspection
08:00–08:30 : Morning staff meeting with soldiers
08:30–10:00 : Combat and physical fitness activities
10:00–12:30 : Individual psychotherapy sessions
12:30–14:00 : Lunch and afternoon rest period
14:00–16:00 : Group psychotherapy
16:00–18:00 : Combat and physical fitness activities
18:00–19:30 : Dinner and family visits
19:30–23:00 : Evening group activities

Assessment Methods

Each soldier was systematically assessed during the treatment program and before discharge with respect to clinical status, interpersonal functioning, and level of motivation and participation in the combat and physical fitness activities. This took the form of individual and group interviewing, ongoing observations, and group testing (MMPI). A follow-up two and a half years later was based on current information in their files as to their military and psychiatric status.

RESULTS AND DISCUSSION

At Discharge from the CFRU

After an average stay of 26 days, all soldiers were discharged from the CFRU with an improved clinical picture and with no need for hospitalization. The treatment program was restricted to their period of residence at the training base, and there was no provision, unfortunately, for continuing treatment of any sort for these soldiers. In fact, few soldiers in regular duty received psychotherapy or counseling following their discharge. Only a few reserve soldiers sought psycho-therapy in civilian life, and in these rare cases for only a few sessions once a week. In the absence of continuing treatment for these soldiers, regular or reserve, we might well expect some deterioration in their condition over time.

According to official army records at time of discharge from the CFRU, 35% of the soldiers in regular service returned to combat status and 65% to noncombat status in support units. The percentages for the reservists were somewhat poorer, 32% and 61%, respectively, for combat and noncombat assignments, and 7% were given a psychiatric discharge. Considering that there was 100% incapacity in both groups at time of entry to the CFRU, these findings are very impressive. But did the effects of treatment last or did they dissipate over time?

After Two-and-a-Half Years

The picture two and a half years later provides evidence in both directions: improvement for the regulars and deterioration for the reservists. The percentages of CFRU regulars in the three categories—combat, noncombat, and psychiatric discharge—were now 66, 34, and 0, respectively, indicating that approximately half the soldiers in noncombat duty had shifted up to combat duty and none had shifted down from combat to noncombat or to psychiatric discharge. For the reservists, the reverse was true. The percentages of reservists in the three categories were now 22, 60, and 18, respectively. This means that there was a shift of 10% down from combat to noncombat or psychiatric discharge. The picture is somewhat mitigated by the fact that of the 18% with psychiatric discharge, there was a formal distinction with 6% regarded as permanent status and 12% as temporary status. Nevertheless, a substantial number of the reservists were experiencing severe work adjustment difficulties and were unable to hold a job or to maintain a reasonable standard of job performance. In summary, there was deterioration in the condition of the reservists over time and actual improvement in the condition of soldiers in the regular army.

An explanation for these contrasting findings may be found in the different military experiences of both groups following their discharge from the CFRU. The soldiers in the regular army returned to military service on a full-time basis until they completed their required service (three full years). During the two-and-a-half-year follow-up period most of them were in the service (at least part of that period) and were exposed daily to the drills, skills, weaponry, formal trappings, and informal camaraderie of military life. These experiences served to sustain their recovery from the earlier stress reaction and, if anything, to enable them to make further gains in military and in civilian adjustment.

The reservists had a different experience during the follow-up period. They served at best one month a year and the rest of the time were attempting to adjust to work, family, and social life away from the setting in which they had suffered an initially incapacitating post-traumatic reaction. In the absence of continuing formal treatment in civilian life and of informal desensitization and autonomous rehabilitation in army life, some of them suffered a decline.

From these data we infer that if the reservists had been kept in active service for an extended period following discharge from the CFRU, they might have been able to consolidate their earlier recovery or improve on it. Inspection of their files indicates, however, that as a group they were called to reserve duty during the follow-up period *even less* than reservists without a history of combat stress reaction. Of the reservist group, 39% were not called *even once during the two-and-a-half-year follow-up period* to serve in any capacity, despite the fact that the percent of reservists with psychiatric discharge ratings was only 18%.

Despite the shortcomings, the follow-up data provide impressive evidence for the lasting effect of participation in the CFRU: 100% of regulars and 82% of reservists functioning at a level sufficient to justify current or future military service.

12B

Behavioral Milieu of the Combat Fitness Retraining Unit

YOCHANAN WOZNER, CHEN NARDI, CHAIM MARGALIT, and RUBEN SEGAL

This paper describes the ecology or relationship between people and their environments in the CFRU and refers to the modifying milieu created and maintained by the staff to rehabilitate soldiers arriving from front-echelon settings with poor prognosis.

THE MILITARY MILIEU

Since the CFRU was set up in a regular military camp, all men were addressed as soldiers or cadets, but never as patients. They lived in companies of 8 to 10 in tents under the direction of their commander, a physical education trainer, and two mental health officers. These three were responsible for the around-the-clock activities conducted according to military routine. Soldiers were in uniform on the base, attended roll calls, and lived at all times under a military regime. Incoming soldiers were often unable to confirm with the regime because of their symptomatology, but they were made aware that their incapacity was temporary and that in a short time they would be functioning once again like soldiers. So strong was this modifying environment and its associated expectancies that after a short time on the base, soldiers who

136

continued to display symptomatic behavior were regarded by their comrades as deviant.

The following example illustrates this point. *J* was an army truck driver who periodically manifested severe regressive behavior, complained of headaches and pains in his hand (originally his entire hand was "paralyzed"), did not sleep with his comrades, and instead spent his nights outside the tent. Because he did not participate fully in the activities or conform to the norms, he came to be regarded by the others as deviant, his behavior was not accepted, and he received the appellation of "our nut case." *J*'s deviant behavior extinguished over time because there were few models in the CFRU for persistent, deviant behavior and many models for constructive behavior, and because the former was strongly discouraged by the staff, while the latter was consistently reinforced.

THE BEHAVIORAL MILIEU

The behavioral milieu was maintained through application of the following principles:

1. *The temporary duration of their stay.* Soldiers knew that they would be discharged after four weeks to return to normal military and life pursuits or to a chronic hospital setting.

2. *Internal locus of responsibility for outcome.* Soldiers were told that they were responsible for this decision, but that the staff was convinced that they would option for recovery and health and not for illness. Whenever a physiological complaint was voiced, for example, it was immediately examined, and when no physical cause was identified, the soldier was told that the problem was up to him to solve and that the staff was there to help. He was given to understand that he was an active partner in the rehabilitation process and not a passive participant or receiver of services.

3. *Repeated explanation and clarification.* All intervention methods were clearly explained to the soldiers, and if a soldier appeared not to understand, the explanation was repeated again and again in a matter-of-fact way. Staff members did not deemphasize their role as expert professionals, but they demystified their role and behavior so as to make the soldier an active and aware agent in his own rehabilitation. The particular symptoms of a soldier were interpreted to him as a *necessary stage for him* on the road to recovery.

4. *Informal fraternization within the military structure.* The staff members

were officers and were so treated, but there was a great deal of informal interaction with mutual help in numerous activities.

5. *The restriction of deviant behavior to individual or group treatment sessions.* Deviant behavior was strongly discouraged at all times day or night, except within the confines of the therapy hours.

6. *Continuous contact with former military units, family, and place of employment.* Soldiers were encouraged to visit their military units and to return home for brief family visits. By the same token, friends from their former units and their families were encouraged by staff to visit soldiers on the base. The older soldiers, reservists gainfully employed in civilian life, were encouraged to visit their places of employment. After careful planning with employers, soldiers were reintroduced to their former work activities for brief periods according to their estimated ability at the time. All visitors to the CFRU were encouraged to interact with the soldiers on a "normal" basis. Thus, spouses, children, friends, employers, and military commanders were incorporated into the rehabilitation process and constituted both a bridge and a magnet attracting the soldiers to the normal "outside." In addition, the attitude and behavior of the regular medical corps personnel toward the CFRU were positive and reinforced positive, goal-directed behavior both in the soldiers and in the staff.

APPLICATION OF BEHAVIORAL-MODIFYING MILIEU TO AN AVERSIVE TASK

Most of the soldiers declared on arrival at the base that they would never again hold a weapon, much less fire it. Staff members declared just as emphatically that each soldier would be shooting a weapon on the firing range before the end of their stay. This announcement was met by a chorus of mocking, resentment, cursing, and challenge. Staff members did not respond, but simply began walking about on the second or third day with different weapons. They would ask soldiers to instruct them in the loading and firing of a particular weapon. Inevitably at least one soldier would respond and would then be enlisted to "train" the others for the "weapons course." Soon there were many soldiers congregating around staff members assembling and loading weapons. Eventually the company marched to the rifle range where a regular instructor supervised the firing of weapons, with some men firing and others observing. Eventually nearly all soldiers handled and fired weapons before leaving the CFRU.

FOCUSED INTERVENTION IN SPECIAL SETTINGS

Apart from the tailoring of the environment for the special needs of the soldiers as a group and for individual soldiers, there were three special settings in which tasks were tailored and reinforcements provided on an individual basis. These were the physical education classes and the individual and group counseling sessions.

The physical activities were carefully graded and adjusted to the mastery level of the individual soldier, and every evidence of compliance and participation was consistently reinforced by the trainers, even vicarious observation by the nonparticipating soldier. In the daily individual session with his mental health officer, topics related to goal-directed, constructive behavior were discussed. Abreaction, desensitization, and support were variously provided as needed. In the daily group sessions goal-directed behavior was reinforced, and group cohesiveness and mutual responsibility were encouraged. Regressive behavior was permitted and presented to the group as a necessary stage in the recovery process.

THE SANCTION SYSTEM

All behaviors that were aspects of military life or were approximations in that direction were designated as goal-directed and were reinforced. Most reinforcements were social and symbolic and few were tangible, the exception being brief furloughs to leave the base for an evening or overnight. Since leaving the base to visit their former units, their families, or their places of employment were stages in their rehabilitation, some soldiers were encouraged to take these furloughs, while others were granted them as privileges.

Symptomatic behaviors were designated as counter-goal-directed and were punished. This usually took the form of verbal reprimand. Formal military punishment (restriction to the tent, forfeit of privileges, court martial) was rarely used, but the threat to use these punishments, if necessary, was present at all times, at least implicitly.

STAFF ACTIVITIES

Staff members were highly motivated in their activities and worked

12-to-16-hour days with rotating night duty for two staff members per company. They attended case conferences, group supervision, and business meetings daily. There was close cooperation between the physical-education trainers and the mental health officers, daily meetings, constant informal communication, and numerous *ad hoc* collaborative efforts.

For example, soldier N was confused, uncooperative, and wholly withdrawn from what was taking place around him. His trainer and mental health officer took him to the basketball court and began to throw the ball to one another, gradually involving N. After he played regularly for a time, he was able to establish verbal as well as nonverbal communication with them and with the others.

DISCUSSION AND CONCLUSIONS

Given the operating conditions of the CFRU, it was impossible to distinguish between the beneficial effects of the behavioral milieu per se and the effects of the many specific treatment modalities. Nevertheless, a number of conclusions are proposed.

First, the CFRU did not bring about any of the detrimental outcomes associated with residential treatment in an institution. It was very different from the "total institution" described by Goffman (1961) in its pluralistic, differentiated, and individualized approach. Since it existed for a short period and its patient staff ratio was high (3:1) and the size of the installation was relatively small, the stultifying effects of bureaucratization and anonymity were minimized.

Second, highly diversified interactions took place day and night, so that treatment proper was not confined to a single therapy hour without concern for the other 23 hours (Trieschman, Whittaker, & Brendfro, 1969).

Third, the CFRU was an integral part of an overall community (a military training base on which training was taking place daily) with clearly defined goals, rules, and positive and negative consequences of failure to achieve the goals or conform to the rules. This structure created a behavioral-modifying environment in which response contingencies appeared reasonable and predictable, with strong pressures toward constructive behavior and aversive consequences for deviant and regressive behavior (Wolins & Wozner, 1982).

Fourth, the success of the CFRU appears to confirm the validity of Vaihinger's "as if" philosophy (1924). He argued that goal-directed behavior requires our formulating a vision of what is not, but may be, and then believing that it will be and acting on the basis of this belief. The soldiers arriving in the CFRU were encouraged to believe that they were regular soldiers with transient symptomatology and that by performing the tasks of regular soldiers, they would, in fact, free themselves of their symptomatology and resume normal functioning. According to Stuart (1980), this fictional finalism, acting on the basis of beliefs that cannot be proven at present or are even contradictory to present experience, is necessary for all behavior and experience change in daily living.

12c

Behavioral Group Treatment

CHEN NARDI, YOCHANAN WOZNER, and CHAIM MARGALIT

Described here is a behavioral approach in group therapy of combat stress reaction that was utilized in the CFRU. Although behavioral methods have proven effective in individual treatment of combat stress reactions, there is little in the clinical literature on the application of behavioral methods in group psychotherapy. Moor (1945) treated soldiers suffering from nightmares in a group by asking each in turn to describe his nightmare, and after each description, he would talk about neutral topics. Saul, Howard, and Denser (1946) treated soldiers suffering from combat stress reactions by gradually exposing them in a group to war movies.

Kipper (1977) applied explicitly behavioral methods in his group treatment of veterans of the 1973 Yom Kippur War. He used two variations of systematic desensitization. In the first, he instructed soldiers in self-relaxation and gradual self-exposure to the anxiety-provoking stimulus. In the second, he instructed them to use this approach in dyads, two soldiers with different phobias helping one another in simultaneous exposure to the stimulus. He argued that the presence and encouragement of the other increased one's motivation to achieve behavior change and reinforced one's effort to change one's behavior. Marafiote (1980) recognized the potential of the group to maximize behavioral principles in treatment of combat stress reactions and tailored group therapy for veterans with delayed combat stress reactions displaying such symptoms as social withdrawal, limited verbal expression, rapid heart beat, and breathing difficulties.

142

THE TARGET BEHAVIORS FOR CHANGE

In the CFRU there were two separate clusters of behavioral problems, phobic behaviors and depressive behaviors. The former cluster included flight and avoidant behavior associated with irritability, sleep disturbance and nightmares, and somatic complaints. The latter consisted of social withdrawal and reduced physical activity, lack of interest in recreation and group activities, and a dramatic decline in activity level in all areas (military, family, sex). The fear-provoking stimuli were noises (e.g., gunfire, airplanes, explosions, engine noise) and intrusive scenes (e.g., the sight of injured soldiers, the sight of weapons, blood, open and closed spaces).

THE RATIONALE OF GROUP BEHAVIORAL TREATMENT

Group belongingness and group cohesiveness have been shown to be major support systems for people in crisis situations, whether in civilian life in coping with unemployment or in military life in coping with basic training or with combat operations (Goodacre, 1953; Jones, Hornick, & Sells, 1972; Noy, 1978; Stouffer et al., 1949). If these group characteristics buffer its members against adverse stress reactions, then one might argue that they may be beneficial in the treatment medium offered those who succumbed to these kinds of reactions.

There are at least four major paradigms of behavior change: classical conditioning, operant conditioning, cognitive behavioral modification, and modeling. A number of features of the group treatment setting facilitate all four behavioral paradigms. These include the following:

1. The group generates more potential solutions for the problems of group members than any one member can generate on his own. Since all of the group members are coping with somewhat similar problems, they may have firsthand knowledge and in concert suggest solutions that any one member might not have considered.

2. Although all group members have some symptoms in common, all have some unique symptoms that are not shared by the others, and different intensities and variations of the common symptoms. This means that each member is likely to find another who is less disturbed by some of the anxiety-provoking or depression-reinforcing stimuli that are so distressful to him.

3. Behavior modification of group members by group members can take place outside the treatment hour. In the case of the CFRU, soldiers accepted problem-solving assignments from one session to the next with a commitment to report on the success of their efforts the following day. In any given assignment for a soldier, other group members were often involved in reinforcing and modeling roles.

4. Reinforcement in a group by different group members in a self-help group is more effective than reinforcement by a single individual, especially when the reinforcement is forthcoming from other soldiers who have shared similar traumatizing experiences and similar symptomatology. Group members can challenge one another, criticize one another's defensive maneuvers and self-serving rationalizations, and offer direct advice without engendering the hostility aroused against the professional interloper. Moreover, any one group member can be regarded as an outsider who cannot understand what the soldier is going through because no two situations are alike. This kind of rationalization breaks down, however, when 8 to 10 men are in the room and no one can claim wholly unique traumatic experiences, unsurpassed suffering, and irreversible incapacity.

5. Since group members are progressing, each at his own pace in the process of rehabilitation, everyone finds someone more advanced than he in some respects and someone less advanced in others. In effect, each member can offer every other member his own tale of successes and failures in self-rehabilitation and can invite the other to learn from his experience.

6. The group provides social interaction both in the treatment hour and in other formal and informal group activities during the day. The reinforcement of social interaction and of verbal and physical activity is strongly indicated in mitigating the intensity of depressive reactions where social withdrawal and inactivity are major symptoms.

One could argue that these group features could militate against rehabilitation with each soldier reinforcing psychopathology in the other, as commonly occurs in closed psychiatric wards. In the CFRU, however, there was unrelenting pressure by the therapists toward constructive, healthy behavior with reinforcing consequences and equally strong criticism of deviant symptomatology. In the group treatment sessions, psychopathology was tolerated, but only as a step toward recovery. The therapeutic atmosphere of the CFRU encouraged the soldier to blame external circumstances for his stress reaction and to assume personal and group responsibility for recovery and return to military and civilian duties. This kind of atmosphere permeated the group sessions as well guaranteeing positive reinforcement of constructive behavior rather than of symptomatology.

CASE ILLUSTRATIONS OF BEHAVIORAL GROUP TREATMENT

Each of the illustrations below, drawn from the notes of the group therapists, can be interpreted in terms of one or more of the four behavioral paradigms or in terms of other behavioral or psychodynamic paradigms of behavior change. The authors do not assert that only behavioral explanations account for the therapeutic import of the behaviors described in these anecdotes, but rather wish to illustrate the particular advantage of the group setting in the explicit application of behavioral principles.

1. A soldier refused to make a trial visit to his place of employment. He was afraid he would lose control and physically attack one of the other workers. Another group member said:

"Look, I also had a problem like that and worked it out. So in the beginning I would come in for a short visit and eventually stayed longer and longer."

2. A soldier had developed a phobia about weapons and was unwilling to assemble a rifle prior to shooting it on the range. One member recommended and subsequently demonstrated the gradual approximation approach to the task. Another suggested that he think of the rifle as a collection of pieces of steel and wood and described in detail a personal monologue of his own mastery of the phobia.

What are you scared of? After all, this is just a few pieces of wood and steel. I know very well how to operate it. I've done this hundreds of times in the past and am able to do it now. I took the rifle in my hand, aimed at the target, and said to myself that I am not shooting at a person now, but just at a paper target. I'm shooting now at my fear and destroying it, I won't let my fear control me. I pulled the trigger and shot. I was happy that I could do it.

3. One soldier attained a position of leadership in the group, was very supportive of the efforts of others, and offered them assistance in coping

with their problems. During one session, he was challenged by one of the others, "If you are such a big hero (and helper), why don't you deal with your fear of weapons?" After a brief silence, the group leader asked him the same question. He hesitated and then stated that he would take the first step that very night (sleep with his rifle under his bed).

4. A soldier afraid to go into town was accompanied the first time by another group member. A soldier who refused to read newspapers for fear of receiving information about the war was helped by a friend who initially read him newspaper articles that did not deal with the war and gradually exposed him to articles with more and more war content.

5. A soldier whose weapon jammed at a critical moment in combat blamed himself for the death of his friend. Other group members helped him to think more rationally about the event:

> Your depression will not return your dead friend to life. Therefore, it fills no need. There is no connection between the jamming of your gun and the death of your friend.

6. A 35-year-old reservist came under heavy artillery fire, and a number of his friends were wounded or killed. At first, he helped the wounded, but later collapsed and was evacuated in a dissociated state. After unsuccessful treatment in two prior settings, he was admitted to the CFRU depressed, withdrawn, and at times wholly unresponsive to the environment. This loss of contact would occur whenever there was reference in his immediate environment to war-related stress or to weapons. He was brought back to social contact only when someone touched him and simultaneously called his name. During the group sessions that dealt with these issues, it was agreed that he would be touched and called by name whenever he stared at the floor. This reinforcement pattern increased his participation in the group discussions and in dealing with traumatic cues outside the session.

In summary, these illustrations convey the flavor of a behavioral group therapy treatment in a residential military setting in which group members functioned as cotrainers or surrogate therapists for one another and achieved substantial behavior change that persisted on follow-up months later.

12D

Dynamic Group Psychotherapy

YAIR GOREN, YOSEF TRIEST,
and CHAIM MARGALIT

Psychotherapeutic interventions are more effective when the functional characteristics of the therapeutic setting are related to, and correct for deficiencies in, the corresponding characteristics of the setting that gave rise to the presenting problem. This principle applies both to a long-term situation giving rise to neurotic traits in the client and to a single traumatic situation giving rise to a traumatic stress reaction.

An example of the long-term problem is the indecisive and bitter client whose father was a critical and rejecting figure. This client gains insight and acquires a new repertoire of behaviors in a therapeutic setting in which a male therapist provides a less critical and more accepting male model. An example of the situational problem is the client who was devastated by a humiliating public experience and is now very anxious and ineffectual in many similar situations. He recovers confidence in social situations by reliving or rehearsing elements of this experience in the course of group psychotherapy and by enacting new social situations and achieving more satisfactory outcomes.

This principle underlies many types of psychotherapy, but is especially explicit in some therapies, e.g., family therapy, client-centered counseling. The preferred treatment is in a situation similar to the one that gave rise to the problem, except that positive features in the second compensate for negative in the first. In this section this principle is illustrated with respect to dynamic group psychotherapy as the treatment of choice for combat stress reaction.

The goals of *individual* therapy for post-traumatic combat stress reaction are typically formulated without an explicit effort to duplicate in
the treatment setting those conditions that prevailed in the premorbid
setting in which the symptomatology emerged. Grinker and Spiegel
(1945) cite as goals: restoration of the soldier's self-esteem as a soldier
and thwarting the development of dependency and the adopting of the
role of sick person. They cite the conventional techniques of establishing
transference, abreaction, and insight without regard for matching the
treatment setting with the setting in which the breakdown occurred.

The core problem in post-traumatic combat stress reaction is (a) the
breakdown of the military group relationship of which the soldier was
a part and (b) the consequences of this breakdown. The major goal of
treatment is to repair, restore, or recreate this relationship. This relationship—a system of rules, roles, privileges, and responsibilities—is
the mainstay of a man's identity and a major support system in the
course of his military service both in highly stressful situations and in
boring and monotonous ones.

The *manifest* relationship of men in their military unit is damaged or
destroyed by war and attendant injury and death. The *latent* interpersonal representation of this relationship within the individual is undermined when the soldier succumbs to combat stress reaction, thereby
breaking the bond between him and his comrades and commanding
officers. The goal of treatment is to restore the manifest relationship
when it is humanly possible (when the number of physical casualties
has not decimated the unit), but especially to restore the latent relationship of the soldier to his past, present, or future military unit. In our
view, this goal is better achieved by helping the soldier to overcome a
feeling of alienation and loneliness from the military unit and to reestablish warm interpersonal relationships in the course of *group psychotherapy* with a group of men also recovering from combat stress reaction.

Rosenheim and Elizur (1977) and Walker and Nash (1981) recognize
this problem and propose the compensatory solution when they specifically emphasize group psychotherapy as the vehicle for overcoming
alienation and isolation and for promoting the expansion, as contrasted
with the contraction, of interpersonal relationships. They emphasize the
importance of the supportive group setting in legitimizing the public
expression of anxiety, rage, aggression, hate, and frustration, thus reducing feelings of shame and guilt. They do not, however, sufficiently
explicate or capitalize on the special nature of the *military group setting*
in which the breakdown occurred and in which the optimal healing
experience should take place.

COMBAT STRESS REACTION AS FLIGHT FROM
THE MILITARY FAMILY

In basic training and in subsequent service young men become members of a "military family" (see Dasberg, 1982) in which the members assist and protect one another against failure and the consequences of failure, whether in peacetime military duties or in wartime. This family relationship is a support system *par excellence* enabling each man to perform effectively in his own niche and enabling the group to function effectively in its own right. This contract is upheld by the individual members so long as it appears to serve both their individual and collective interests.

In many combat situations, however, a conflict arises in which the better interests of the group appear to run counter to the better interests of the members in general or of a particular member. To follow orders, to fight on, to remain with the group is to risk injury, captivity, or death. To flee is to avoid these consequences, but to suffer others—guilt, moral opprobrium, and court martial for dereliction of duty. One resolution of this avoidance-avoidance conflict is to leave the scene by succumbing to a combat stress reaction or breakdown. In so doing, one breaks the group contract, abdicates his responsibilities to his military family, abandons his group identity, and suffers initially acute and possibly chronic crippling psychiatric symptoms. In return he avoids the total loss of all controls and he preserves his own life.

WHY DYNAMIC GROUP PSYCHOLOGY IS
THE TREATMENT OF CHOICE FOR COMBAT
STRESS REACTION

Soldiers enter group therapy as emotionally disturbed individuals with fragmented and spoiled (in Goffman's sense) military identities and leave far less disturbed with reconstituted and rehabilitated military group identities. When they are capable of rejoining the larger military family once again, both physically by returning to their unit or to a new and appropriate unit for them, and psychologically by reidentifying once again as members of the military family, they are largely symptom free or on the way to becoming symptom free and are at peace with themselves and with their civilian and military families. This is the belief that motivates mental health officers working in forward- and in rear-echelon treatment units.

This rehabilitative process can best take place within group therapy: men who are initially group members in name only become, in fact, *group members* and reconstitute their military identity by creating a genuinely cohesive group from the isolated, alienated, and bitter individuals who confront one another on entry into the group setting.

Consider some of the following elements of all therapeutic situations that are better handled in soldiers with combat stress reaction by the medium of group therapy.

Projective identification is a well-known defense mechanism in which an individual projects onto others those aspects of himself that are ego alien. This mechanism is frequently encountered in combat stress reaction because of the basic conflict between preservation of honor, self-confidence, and group cohesiveness and the preservation of life at all of these costs. The group context of other men with similar problems enables one to gain emotional distance from his own projective identifications by observing in action those of others in self-disclosure and in role playing.

Protective containment refers to the limits that are imposed on impulsive or other forms of unacceptable behavior by the structure of the group setting. The group with its leader, its rules and regulations, its permissiveness, but clear setting of limits, provides an opportunity for the expression of intense, socially unacceptable emotions without fear of group-endorsed hostile criticism, and without fear of loss of control. Fear and aggression, guilt and depression can be expressed and catharsis can be achieved without any threat to one's fragile sense of control.

Group cohesiveness is valuable in any therapeutic context because it reduces the sense of loneliness and alienation from others, emotions that are counterproductive if not destructive to all human relationships. It is especially important to achieve in the case of men for whom military group cohesiveness was often the *raison d'être* of their efforts to cope in threatening situations. It is understandably easier to achieve in a group setting.

Social comparison or perceived similarity between people is an important therapeutic feature. It is a universal antidote to alienation, and it reassures one that unacceptable aspects of oneself are human. Social comparison and mutual observation and self-disclosure permit us to rephrase the well-known statement *Nothing human is alien to me* by saying, *Everything in me that appears alien is human.*

Traumatic separation from others is a common experience in many life crises. The feeling that one has been deserted by others can be paralyzing and prevent positive behavior change. A group setting is more efficacious than an individual treatment setting for reuniting the individual with lost entities.

GROUP PSYCHOTHERAPY IN THE COMBAT FITNESS REHABILITATION UNIT

Group therapy was an integral part of the four-week CFRU program. Each group of 8 to 10 soldiers met daily for two hours and was led by two therapists identified as military personnel. The pace and level of discussion in the group was intensive and immediate. Soldiers had arrived because things were wrong with them, but things would be made right and now was the time for making them right. Therapists regarded their role as reversing the group disintegration process that produced overt psychopathology in the soldiers and that accounted for their coming to the CFRU.

There were four phases of group therapy. Each is discussed below and examples are provided from the CFRU experience.

Resistance

In the initial phase the soldiers did not want to deal with the precipitating traumatic experience and by the same token did not want to establish meaningful contact with one another. They were narcissistic, depressed, hostile, and passive as if to say, "Nobody can understand what we went through or can help us."

The group leaders explained the therapeutic contract and were greeted by silence and mutual avoidance. Silence was interpreted by the leaders,

It seems to be difficult to share war experiences with one another. Perhaps there is the feeling that these experiences are too traumatic to reexperience and that it is difficult to share them with others, particularly with strangers.

or

It appears that the silence means: Don't touch me, don't come near me, I am dangerous.

In a second group meeting a young soldier named Yehuda joined the group. He became extremely anxious and vomited while sitting in his military truck because of rumors of infiltrators. He was less disturbed than the other members of the group and was a young, suggestible, innocent person. When he joined the group, he said, "What happened to you? You all seem to be in mourning." When no one responded, he turned to the group leader and asked, "What [by implication, *terrible thing*] happened to them?"

Leader: You can' talk to each other.
Yehuda: You must have had very difficult experiences. [He turned to the leader.] They all seem to be fighters [combat soldiers], they must have had it very rough, not like me. I only came close to the war and could not take it. What's with you guys?

Avi [dramatically]: I am ready to talk about the size of my shoes, not what's happening to me.
Leader: There is a conflict here between the need to share and know what happened to everybody and the fear of baring feelings and sharing traumatic experiences. . . . Yehuda seems to be saying that you are guarding a treasure that you are unwilling to share with such as me.

Reactivation and Abreaction

The ambivalence about withholding or expressing emotionally charged experiences broke down during this phase as soldiers became more active, more angry, and critical especially about army leadership. By the end of this phase, most members had shared their traumatic experiences with one another.

In the fourth session Danny announced that he was willing to talk about what happened to him. His tank was lost behind enemy lines because of a radio communication failure. He and his friends abandoned the tank and hid in the home of a Lebanese family. At night while PLO fighters were searching for them, they deliberated whether to fight, surrender, or commit suicide. Danny convinced the others to surrender, and they were subsequently captured. Because Danny was wounded, he was separated from the others and eventually was released; the others were killed. As he told his story he appeared alienated and distant.

The response of the group was rage. Avi spoke furiously and insisted that he should have fought with hand grenades, "Why didn't you commit suicide?" To this remark, Danny said, "You are nuts," and slammed the door as he left the room.

The group returned to this topic that night, and Danny began to talk emotionally about what had happened. The leaders offered several interpretations:

1. Danny's conflict was between suicide and surrender. A combat stress reaction is itself a kind of surrender so that, in fact, all members of the group had surrendered.
2. Danny had chosen surrender, but his emotional isolation was a kind of a living death because he seemed to feel as if something had died inside.
3. Participating in group therapy was a form of captivity because the soldiers were forced to struggle with painful alternatives and could not legitimately leave the scene.

Group Cohesiveness

As soldiers began to share their experiences, they began to acquire the characteristics of a cohesive group. Their mood became less dysphoric, at times even euphoric. They began to depend on the group, to develop group pride and greater self-esteem.

The group attempted to understand why Avi thought Danny should have committed suicide. Avi explained that he was upset that the PLO would spare anyone, because he himself had stood guard over PLO prisoners and had fantasized inflicting cruel punishment on them. Cognitive consistency required that they be cruel and not spare an occasional Israeli prisoner of war. Since there were such exceptions, he felt ashamed about his thoughts.

Another group member, Benny, a signal corpsman, expressed concern that he was responsible for the communication failures that caused Danny's tank to go astray and that he had indirectly contributed to the death of Danny's three friends. Benny further explained that he had broken down upon entering a house from which shots had been fired on them. He found there only the bodies of two men in civilian clothes and was upset that he might have killed civilian hostages, while the terrorists had escaped the back way.

There was increasing camaraderie in the group, laughter, and casual conversations at all hours. They began to help one another. They even invented a humorous name for themselves, "The Cuckoo's Nest."

Separation

As members came to the end of their prescribed stay, they began to emphasize self-reliance rather than exclusively group reliance. They began to deal with pretraumatic problems, their future plans, difficulties in their marriages, conflicts with their parents. As the awareness that they would soon be leaving set in, the euphoria decreased and some of the old symptoms surfaced. The soldiers had to work through their fear of returning to army life. They also had to learn to live with an altered self-concept, a more realistic one perhaps, but a self-concept that included real guilt over unworthy behaviors.

Uri was still suffering from nightmares in the third week of stay at the CFRU and having difficulty in relating to others. Group members took responsibility for waking him each morning even though they suspected that he was taking medication on the sly. One confirmed this suspicion and said that he had "stolen" Uri's medication. The leader suggested that all wanted to help Uri, whom they regarded as a therapeutic failure and a medication-dependent patient, but were anxious because he represented the illness within each one of us that we fear would not be successfully cured. Group members accepted this interpretation in a tense manner.

The same group arrived late for the following session. The leader interpreted their lateness as resistance and upset over the preceding meeting. Group members became very angry, some insisting that the leaders wanted to make them sick again, others despairing at the failure of therapy. The leaders interpreted these feelings as related to difficulties in separation. After a silence, group members became less sad and angry and discussed realistically their individual therapeutic gains.

Summary

The destructive process initiated by the combat stress situation is arrested and reversed by a complementary constructive process represented in the daily group psychotherapy sessions. The group situation is the preferred setting for treatment here because it duplicates the group setting in which the soldier was traumatized. In both settings there is a group of soldiers engaged in a group enterprise. In the first, things go well until exposure to combat and the ensuing stress reaction and its consequences. In the second, things start off badly, but end well with the achievement of group cohesiveness and the restoration of a supportive military identity in the group members. Once this goal is achieved, group members are able to return to the victimization setting, to join authentic military groups with military assignments, and to function well once again.

12E

Individual Psychotherapy

CHAIM MARGALIT, RUBEN SEGAL, and
YAIR GOREN

There are two major groups of clinical papers relating to individual psychotherapy with combat stress reaction cases. One refers to work carried out in outpatient civilian clinics after the war and the other to work during the war and often in front-echelon units. The clinical literature in the former group emphasizes specific psychodynamic conflicts, characteristic ego defense mechanisms, and specific stages of psychotherapy such as abreaction and catharsis (Arieli, 1974; Dasberg, 1982; Egendorf, 1978; Ferenczi, Abraham, Simmel, & Jones, 1921; Figley, 1978b; Freud, 1955; Howard, 1976; Lidz, 1948; Lifton, 1973; Plesset, 1946; Shapira, 1967; Shatan, 1973).

The literature in the latter group emphasizes models that attempt to integrate the above-mentioned aspects of psychotherapy by cross-referencing the symptoms characterizing clients, the therapeutic focus and content, therapist and client roles, and the therapeutic strategies at each stage of psychotherapy (Benyakar & Noy, 1975; Grinker & Spiegel, 1945; Neumann, 1974; Weisman, 1982; Williams, 1980). Described here are the symptoms, foci, roles, and strategies that characterized the stages of individual psychotherapy with soldiers admitted to the CFRU with severe and potentially chronic reactions to a recent combat stress experience. Their symptoms were regarded as a reactivation of earlier personal problems in view of a premorbid history of difficulties in adjustment in civilian and military life.

PRINCIPLES OF INDIVIDUAL
PSYCHOTHERAPY IN A UNIQUE SITUATION

The form of individual psychotherapy conducted at the CFRU may be described as intensive, short-term, goal-directed crisis intervention for soldiers with post-traumatic disturbances. The therapeutic relationship established between the soldier as client and his commanding officer as therapist is unique in many respects. First, it is in direct conflict to the conventional therapeutic wisdom that the therapist is a professional stranger who sees the client in a highly circumscribed setting (time and place) and has no other direct contact with him. In the CFRU the *therapeutic contract* was one hour daily for four weeks, but there was additional *therapeutic contact* between the two men day and night for the entire period. They dined, exercised, and socialized in close quarters from initial admission to ultimate discharge.

Second, the therapist was the client's commanding officer and in a position to administer rewards and punishments for the client's actions. In some societies and armies, the therapist's rank might have contributed to a superior-inferior relationship in which the therapist commanded the soldier to recover along lines defined by the officer. Given the informality characterizing Israeli society in general and the Israel Defense Force in particular, this was not a likely eventuality.

Moreover, Israeli officers are drawn by merit from all walks of life and all ethnic groups and are expected to provide a personal example to their cadets. The command that is traditionally given by the officer in the face of the enemy is "Follow me" and not "Advance, men." In keeping with this tradition, the mental health officers, with few exceptions, and all physical education–combat trainers had served as combat soldiers in previous wars. These men were able to appreciate the soldier's reaction to combat stress and other aspects of military life. They attempted to establish a relationship of intimacy and mutual responsibility for the success of the CFRU and provided ongoing immediate feedback to their soldiers throughout the course of the program.

Individual therapy served an additional function in the program in that it complemented the daily group therapy session. The latter was an intense group experience in which the soldier may have been understandably reluctant to air certain topics and express certain feelings before his fellow soldiers. These topics and feelings could, however, be brought into the individual session.

METHOD OF DATA COLLECTION AND
CONTENT ANALYSIS

All therapists kept notes on the course and content of all their therapy sessions. A team of mental health professionals analyzed these notes for common features in content and sequence over time. Given the large number of soldiers and therapists, the similarities that emerged from this analysis were impressive and are reported below according to the symptomatology, defense mechanisms, therapeutic foci, and therapist role that characterize each phase. These features are summarized briefly in Table 1 for schematic purposes.

PHASE ONE: ABREACTION

In post-traumatic combat stress reactions the traumatic experience arises from intensive exposure to the horrors of war with heightened emotional arousal associated with the reality and surreality of injury, death, and survival. The symptom picture includes many of the following: anxiety, confusion, disorientation; agitation and startle reaction versus psychomotor retardation and stupor; intense and labile emotion. In attempting to cope with this traumatic experience soldiers typically use denial and repression, detachment and isolation, and dissociative and conversion reactions. The therapist role at this time is empathic, supportive, and even directive in order to elicit abreaction, cognitive reorganization of the trauma, reduction of emotional intensity, and working through feelings of loneliness, helplessness, fear of death, and fear of loss of control. In the course of the cognitive and emotional playback that characterizes abreaction, the soldier comes to rely less and less on the above-mentioned defense mechanisms.

PHASE TWO: WORKING THROUGH TRAUMA-
RELATED CONFLICTS

The soldier and therapist attempt to work through the underlying conflicts related to the war trauma: flight versus fight, and guilt feelings over being evacuated from the battlefield without visible physical injury and thereby abandoning his fellow soldiers and jeopardizing their lives

TABLE 1

Phases, Symptoms, Defense Mechanisms, and Therapeutic Foci in Individual Treatment

Phase	Symptomatology	Mechanisms	Foci
Phase One: Abreaction	Symptomatology: Anxiety, agitation and startle reaction versus psychomotor retardation and stupor, confusion, disorientation	Mechanisms: Repression, denial, dissociation, isolation	Foci: Working through fear of death, loss of control and loneliness experienced, reduction of emotional intensity of combat experience, cognitive reorganization of the events; supportive, directive, shifting from active to passive role
Phase Two: Working through current conflicts	Symptomatology: As above, but also disturbances in sleep and appetite, grief work, depression, guilt feelings	Mechanisms: Decline in those mentioned above, but also projection, displacement, rationalization	Foci: Analysis of the traumatic experience and its implications for feelings of failure, helplessness, injury to self-concept; therapist restructures conflicts and reflects "objective" reality, moderates and reflects aggressive accusations and other transference phenomena and monitors own countertransference

TABLE 1 (continued)

Phase	Symptomatology	Mechanisms	Foci
Phase Three: Working through premorbid conflicts	Symptomatology: As above, but also somatic complaints, interpersonal isolation, occasional rage and acting out	Mechanisms: Shift to introjection of aggression and guilt and projective identification as forms of resistance to working through	Foci: Relating premorbid intrapsychic conflicts to present, broadening the client's awareness of unknown, threatening aspects of his personality, and integrating them in the present, reflection of transference and present and past coping styles; encouraging the client to achieve new integration and more mature coping now and in future
Phase Four: Preparing for separation and the future	Symptomatology: Reactivation of anxiety, anger, and depression in anticipation of termination and separation	Mechanisms: Phobic reactions, somatization, regression, acting out	Foci: Focus on present and future, shift from intrapsychic to interpersonal, working through anxieties about future challenges and separation from therapist and CFRU

and limbs. The symptoms that characterized phase one persist, usually with less intensity, but other symptoms may now appear: sleep disturbances and nightmares; loss of appetite; depression, sadness, guilt, and a mourning reaction. In this phase the soldier focuses on existential aspects of life and death: the sense of personal helplessness, the feeling of being abandoned by those who died or were injured, and the inability to deal with one's aggressive impulses during and after the crisis situation. In order to cope with their guilt feelings, aggressive impulses, and frustration, soldiers make extensive and intensive use of both projection and introjection as well as the defense mechanisms cited earlier. The therapist attempts to define more clearly these conflicts and associated feelings and to clarify what actually happened in battle in order to put events in their proper perspective, to reduce guilt feelings, and to mitigate the injury to masculine self-concept. In replaying the actual events of the battle, the prior combat background of the therapist is crucial for credibility and mutual trust. He reflects back the transference of the soldier toward him and monitors carefully his own countertransference (that of a reservist in a noncombat role toward a combat soldier who upon recovery will return to combat). He serves as a target for the anger and accusations of the soldier, but remains encouraging and supportive.

PHASE THREE: WORKING THROUGH
PRECOMBAT CONFLICTS

The symptom picture of the previous phase persists, namely, depression, sadness, guilt feelings, interpersonal isolation and withdrawal, and occasionally attacks of rage and acting out. The therapist focuses on those premorbid conflicts that were reactivated by exposure to the present traumatic situation. The goal is to learn the psychodynamic explanations for the severity of this particular stress reaction to the traumatic situation. An effort is made to examine important factors affecting personality development during one's formative years: problems in early object relations and identification; experiences of rejection, abandonment, and alienation; gender identification and psychosexual development; and the character of one's interpersonal relationships. The therapist encourages the soldier to assess the discrepancy between real self and ideal self and to bridge the gap through reinterpretation of the past and the present.

The ideal self is typically characterized as the epitome of strength, courage, independence, masculinity, and effective coping with little or no need of help or advice from others, and with little need to experience or to discuss personal problems. The real self suffers by comparison since it is characterized by doubts about one's masculinity, by personal inadequacy in coping with personal problems, and by dependency, passivity, and hypersensitivity. These self-denigrating attitudes and behaviors arise because of the perceived failure to play a heroic role in combat. Because they are intolerable, they are projected onto the therapist, the military establishment, the family, and one's peers.

Anger and frustration are increased by the soldier's resistance to the shift in focus from the current trauma to premorbid conflicts and to the increased insight that accompanies this focus. A major task of the therapist at this time is to continue to absorb the anger and frustration of the soldier as well as to function as a mirror reflecting the soldier's efforts and success in gaining insight and in resuming control over himself and over events in his environment. The therapist accepts the soldier's weaknesses, emphasizing their human and universal character, and expresses confidence in the soldier's ability to achieve new and more mature ways of coping with life stressors. The eventual goal proposed to the soldier is reintegration in military and/or civilian life at a higher level of awareness and adequacy than before.

PHASE FOUR: APPLICATIONS TO PRESENT AND FUTURE CHALLENGES

The therapist focuses on rehabilitation and termination of therapy. This focus activates some earlier symptoms—anxiety, anger, somatic problems, and depression. These symptoms are now associated with the anticipation of termination of therapy and of the stay at the CFRU. Some soldiers, especially older reservists, engage in phobic ractions, regression, and acting out because of their anxieties over reintegration into the complexities of their civilian and military life circumstances. The therapist permits expression of these symptoms even as he encourages and directly moves the soldier toward entry into the world outside the CFRU. Extensive contact is made with family, employers, and military unit commanders, and trial visits are arranged. Therapy deals both with the anxiety over separation and with the apprehension over returning. The therapist is suggestive, directive, even demanding. In termination the two men deal with all aspects of separation anxiety—from the CFRU, the staff, the therapist, and the other soldiers in his company. Countertransference may be especially strong in the therapist as the soldier returns at his recommendation to combat duty in the very military units in which the original traumatic experience occurred.

CASE PRESENTATION

In order to illustrate empirically the therapeutic approach used in the CFRU, we selected a representative clinical case, that of Erez, a young paratrooper in regular service. Quotations from the admissions interview are included to convey the nature of the trauma that he was experiencing and the coping mechanisms that he was using.

Battle Anamnesis During Initial Interview

At the outbreak of the war in Lebanon, Erez was completing a junior-officer course in a combat paratroop unit. He was an exceptional trainee and possessed enormous physical and emotional stamina. Erez and his comrades landed from the sea in rubber dinghies to capture a bridge-head.

The landing went pretty quickly and I felt well. I wasn't afraid at all. I was a squad leader, an example to everyone. I encouraged the others, I functioned well.

In the last stage of the operation the force split, the company commander was injured, three of Erez' best friends were killed, and he and the others found themselves near the medical treatment unit.

It started to get difficult. Terror began to get the better of me. I was surrounded by the injured and the dead. I had to continue to fight, I was the best soldier in the course, I couldn't be a disappointment. I began to think about death. I felt lonely, defenseless, the commander was hurt, my friends were either killed or injured.

Erez overcame these feelings and was traveling in an armored personnel carrier waiting to enter combat in a built-up area when he suffered another panic attack, more intense than the first.

I thought that this was the end, we would all die here. What irresponsibility to send us on a mission like this. I was tense, paralyzed, indifferent. I didn't want to eat. The doctor and the platoon commander asked me what had happened. I couldn't disappoint them and destroy my image, so I told them I had a problem of conscience, of ideology. [Later] I felt choked, paralyzed, but I had to prove to the officers that I was able, I felt all kinds of sensations, trembling, sweating, I couldn't control body functions. I felt a deathly terror.

Eventually the company completed its combat assignment and Erez was given a short leave to his home on a kibbutz. He withdrew into his house and into himself.

I couldn't show them [kibbutz friends and family] that I was weak. I thought that this was a temporary crisis and that I would get over it alone. I tried to force myself to forget the thoughts, the images, and the events.

There followed an increase in the frequency of nightmares, fears, and thoughts about death, including thoughts about suicide. When his leave was up, he returned to his unit and was referred to a company physician who noted the severity of his reaction and referred him to the CFRU. Parenthetically, we may observe that if he had received front-line treatment immediately following the military operation, he would have developed far fewer and far less intense symptoms. Because of the delay and the leave far from the front lines, his condition deteriorated and mandated the referral to the CFRU. The tests administered at admission (MMPI, 16PF, and DAP) yielded a picture identical to the clinical picture described above: anxiety, apathy, dysphoria, inability to concentrate or to function as a soldier, preoccupation with war experiences, inability to sleep, and suicidal ideation.

Clinical Anamnesis

Erez began his recollection of the past by referring to thoughts of death and suicide (on both a philosophical and a personal level) when he was in the fifth grade. He was in psychotherapy for one year at a regional mental health center for kibbutz members. He interjected that during the war, he suddenly recalled Erez, the little boy of that period, and the memory paralyzed him completely. After the year in therapy, he functioned poorly and was tense, pressured, and withdrawn. He deliberately kept distance between himself and his age peers and almost never entered class.

Another difficult period was in adolescence when he cut himself off from his friends, engaged in philosophical and ideological problems, and spent time with the overseas volunteers on the kibbutz. He came to despise them because of their materialistic way of life. He began to read about, feel, and behave according to the image of the "new Jew" as contrasted with the "diaspora Jew" (a Jew living outside of Israel). In his search for personal and national identity, he engaged in extremely different behaviors at one and the same time. On the inside, he felt himself lacking in confidence, worried, isolated, withdrawn, and fearful of people. On the outside, he was a group leader of youth and a talented athlete. Erez entered the army with the expectation that here he could realize his fantasies of masculinity and fitness and his ideological beliefs about the "new Jew." During his military service he became close to his commanding officers, was a prominent and exceptional soldier, took risks, accepted difficult assignments, demonstrated bravery and strength, but "Suddenly, the whole building collapsed. I can't accept that I am capable of being afraid."

His parents had immigrated to Israel from Arab countries when they were children. His father is a teacher and educator. His mother suffers from a "mysterious" nervous illness, the precise nature of which is unclear to Erez, and she barely works. The home atmosphere in the kibbutz is tense, "walking-on-tiptoe" with an "overly cautious" interaction between parents or with Erez. There is warmth, and he feels close to his father but maintains distance from his mother. He does not share his current problems with family members and goes home only when he feels better. He was reluctant to broaden the discussion about his family, noting that he is the eldest with a younger brother 10 years old.

Treatment by Phases

In the beginning, Erez sat crying and trembling, but insisted that he did not want to discuss his experiences and that he would overcome them alone (repression, denial, isolation). Slowly, with the active direction of the therapist, he reconstructed the traumatic battle experiences in minute detail and with great emotional intensity. Over seven sessions he reviewed these experiences and the associated feelings of being an abandoned, helpless little boy and achieved fairly complete affective catharsis.

In the second phase of treatment, he attempted to assign responsibility for his predicament to his officers and to the government, and then to occupy himself with ideological issues (projection, rationalization, intellectualization). The therapist pointed out to Erez that these behaviors reflected underlying defense mechanisms, whereupon he shifted with great emotional intensity to his disappointment with himself as a man and as a soldier. He became passive, withdrawn, and sad, focusing on the experience of personal failure. He expressed strong guilt feelings about the friends he had abandoned because of cowardice and inability to fight. He recalled that he fired his weapon once during the entire operation. He described the death of a close friend and of searching for him under fierce enemy fire at great personal and inappropriate risk since it was known that the friend had actually been evacuated from the battlefield and had subsequently died. He described wandering around as the shells fell as if playing Russian roulette and was forcibly pulled under cover by his friends. The therapist was supportive and empathic, reflecting back to Erez his harsh self-perceptions.

The third phase began about the tenth session. Erez was very depressed as if in grief and mourning and expressed suicidal ideation. He tended to introject guilt and aggression and at the same time to overidentify with the grief of the other soldiers in the CFRU, while denying his own problems (projective identification as a defense against committing himself to greater self-awareness and personal integration). Erez rejected the therapist's interpretations of his defense mechanisms and became very angry.

At this juncture, the therapist decided that it was necessary to overcome his own countertransference reaction (to be supportive and overprotective) and to circumvent resistance and regression in Erez by adopting a very assertive and directive role. He drew Erez into a discussion and effort to understand his early intrapsychic conflicts within the family circle and their implications for his reactions during battle. The major goal of treatment was to reduce the enormous discrepancy between real and ideal self-image by making superego internalizations more flexible and less punitive. These internalizations represented his identification with an idealized image of his father and with the ego ideal promulgated by the kibbutz society of the soldier hero. He became more accepting of the child within and of the fears and weaknesses associated with the child, and he integrated this aspect of himself into a more realistic self-image. With these insights he became more cooperative with friends and therapists, involving them in his experiences and even expressing aggression in a more comfortable and free fashion than before. He also invited his parents to visit and spoke to them about himself, something he had never done before. With a dramatic improvement in his behavior and a marked reduction in overt symptomatology, he began to speak with optimism about the future.

The fourth, and last, phase of therapy dealt with the decision about future military service. Erez had to resolve a serious personal dilemma, whether to return to the paratroopers and to the facade of combat ready masculinity or to accept reassignment to a noncombat, rear-echelon unit and the acknowledgment of personal weakness. He chose an assignment between these two poles, an operational military unit that operates close to the front, but does not actually engage in combat. He agreed to continue treatment and request reevaluation of his military service in half a year. Separation from the therapist was difficult for both, despite the fact that the therapist was spared the personal crisis that therapists face when a treated soldier returns to combat status during an ongoing war.

DISCUSSION AND CONCLUSIONS

Several conclusions follow from our work with soldiers in individual psychotherapy. First, the symptom picture, psychodynamic changes during the course of treatment, and changes in the treatment strategies by therapists are remarkably similar across the literature cited earlier on World War I and II, Vietnam, and the Yom Kippur War. The descriptive model presented above in schematic form and in the case history resembles other models cited in the clinical literature.

Second, post-traumatic combat stress reaction may be regarded as a special case of the more general phenomenon of post-traumatic reactions of whatever origin. There are many common elements (clinical picture, psychodynamic conflicts, treatment strategies) between the general case and this specific class of stress situations (Brull, 1974; Horowitz, 1976; Menninger, 1977).

Third, there are some unique features to combat stress reactions in particular:

1. The necessity to select and adapt interventions for the individual client from a wide range of treatment possibilities.
2. The emphasis on the two aspects of treatment of combat stress reactions—short-term crisis intervention and long-term rehabilitation. The first emphasizes situational factors affecting coping behavior during the crisis, an intrapsychic focus, and a some-

what restricted interpersonal focus. The latter emphasizes a broad focus on the community, the family, and one's place of employment.

3. The intensity of client resistance and therapist countertransference in a military treatment setting. The therapist, currently performing a noncombatant role, is treating a soldier who upon recovery returns to life-threatening combat duty in wartime. Considerable sensitivity and self-awareness are required of the therapist in these circumstances, far more than are required in civilian mental health settings after the war.

12F

Physical Activities in Rehabilitation

CHAIM MARGALIT, YOCHANAN WOZNER, and RUBEN SEGAL

Physical activities in the form of team sports and combat training were emphasized from the start in the CFRU program for several reasons:

1. The research literature provides some support for the positive effect of physical activity on emotionally disturbed people, particularly psychiatric patients in a residential setting (Curreton, 1963; Dadson & Mullens, 1969; Davis, 1947; Morgan, 1969). The soldiers in the CFRU were in residence for several weeks, so that we could anticipate beneficial effects from physical activity in groups becoming cohesive over time. Findings of the studies cited above suggest that physical activities alleviate inner tension, provide a basis for relaxing without the necessity of consuming tranquilizers, increase self-confidence, and improve one's motivation to interact with others and to cooperate with other treatment programs. One of the few reports on the effect of physical activity on recovery from combat stress reaction (Inbar, Weingarten, & Bar-On, 1974) suggests that participation in sports and other physical activities is helpful both in diagnosis and in prognosis, and that the greater the physical activity elicited from the soldier, the greater the speed and extent of recuperation.

2. Members of the mental health staff were convinced of the value of physical activities in rehabilitation and intended from the start to institute them both for the soldiers and for themselves.

DESCRIPTION OF THE PROGRAM

The extent of time devoted to individual and group activities was considerable. Sport activities included soccer (the Israeli national sport), volleyball, basketball, free gymnastics, exercises with equipment, running and jogging, swimming (sea and pool), and walking trips. Combat training activities consisted of drills, practice with weapons and live ammunition, and topographical tracking. Relaxation skills were taught and practiced.

These activities took place twice daily, in the morning from 8:30 to 10 A.M. followed by a brief rest period and a session of individual psychotherapy, and in the afternoon from 4 to 6 P.M. after the group therapy session. In addition, there were morning exercises associated with reveille and light sport activities after the evening meal.

OBSERVATIONS ON THE EFFECTS OF
PHYSICAL ACTIVITIES

Intrapersonal Effects

One of the consequences of combat stress reaction is a loss of self-esteem and doubts about one's masculine identity and about one's ability to cope with challenging and/or threatening situations. Physical activity was a means utilized by some soldiers to reestablish coping skills and to regain self-esteem in one area, a given sport or combat-related activity, and to generalize from success in the one area to other areas. Physical prowess is a major dimension of the masculine identity of men, especially young men. Evidence of adequacy in physical activities was found to be reassuring and restorative.

An example in point was *E*, a swimming champion before enlistment. He found in the pool and the sea innumerable opportunities to demonstrate his premorbid prowess in swimming and to receive thereby the admiration and encouragement of peers and staff members. He then began to join in the less familiar sport activities, and also to participate more freely in the individual and group therapy sessions as well.

M was an excellent marksman, in the infantry with special commando training. During the battle he was cut off from his unit and was alone without food and water under heavy shelling for two days. When found, he was extremely anxious, withdrawn, and reluctant to handle weapons again. He was slowly "nudged" by the physical instructor to participate in the activities and was repeatedly asked to "help out" in weapon training. His progress was reflected in his gradually being able to show others how to shoot and in regaining his marksman skills. He achieved excellent scores and became "the Sharpshooter" of the CFRU unit.

H was a 38-year-old soldier who witnessed the death of his commanders by a direct hit of their jeep by a rocket. He was admitted to the CFRU in a serious depression and wholly isolated from his surroundings. On the third day he participated in a basketball game and failed to make a basket despite numerous attempts. With group support, he redoubled his efforts, ran faster, and tried harder, eventually making a basket. This achievement brought on demonstrations of support and happiness on the part of team members. It also suddenly produced in him an extreme emotional release in the form of a loud shout, a show of happiness, and physical exhaustion, following by an emotional breakdown and abreaction: He began to cry and to retell his traumatic war experience.

The Interpersonal Effect

Combat stress reaction is usually accompanied by a sense of alienation or estrangement from one's peers and military unit. One frequently experiences a deep sense of guilt because he has chosen "flight" over "fight" in a situation in which group solidarity is called for. Physical activities provide corrective experiences because they encourage the development of interpersonal relationships and require split-second decisions about cooperation and self-reliance in competitive team situations. Given the importance of sensitive and flexible timing in making the experience a gradual one, we tried to select experienced physical instructors who would have not only the skills of support and reinforcement, but also the flexibility to permit graceful decline of the invitation to participate and withdraw.

Physical Activity Reduces Drug Intake and Symptom Frequency

Many soldiers were well on their way to psychiatric drug dependency by the time they were admitted to the CFRU. During the time between the traumatic event and their arrival at CFRU, they were given tranquilizers in the benzodiazepine group. These drugs were deliberately withheld at the CFRU and the soldiers were told that physical activities were a better means of achieving a relaxed state of mind and body. The continued consumption of medication was regarded by the group as a negative phenomenon, and group pressures toward participation in physical activities were strong, so that after several instances of participation in physical activities, soldiers experienced a healthy tiredness and a relaxed state, consequences that were inherently reinforcing. In special cases of severe depression (8% of the cases), 100-to-150-mg doses of the tricyclic group were given daily.

Diagnostic and Prognostic Consequences

The behavior of soldiers in the physical activities was an important source of information about their progress and was frequently at variance with their apparent progress or lack of progress in other activities, e.g., psychotherapy. These disparate sources of information were shared at case conferences.

An example is Y, a parachutist, who arrived at the CFRU in a severe depressive state. He was openly negativistic and refused to cooperate in any form of activity. During his stay he became more open in his individual psychotherapy sessions, but persisted in passive and uncooperative behavior at all other times. Several days before his anticipated discharge, we were seriously weighing sending him to another setting for continued treatment, when a dramatic change occurred in his behavior during physical activities. He began to perform at an excellent level that surprised his peers and the physical instructor. When this change was reported during a case conference, his therapist discussed with him returning to his former unit. He did so, even participated in combat activity with his old unit, and remains to this day (two years later) a regular reserve member of this unit.

In conclusion, we found physical activities to be highly useful in the treatment of combat stress reactions. We strongly urge that they be incorporated as an integral part of any treatment plan for people suffering from acute stress reactions from sources other than combat when these people are assigned to a residential setting for significant periods of time.

12G

A Multidimensional Model for Treatment of Post-Traumatic Stress Disorders: Summary Statement

YOCHANAN WOZNER and CHAIM MARGALIT

Presented here is a conceptual model for the demonstrated treatment efficacy of the CFRU. It suggests that the CFRU is a promising treatment modality for people suffering from severe disturbance in functioning after a traumatic experience, whether in military or civilian life.

The symptoms that characterized our clients were wide ranging and included behavioral excesses/deficits in intrapersonal and interpersonal spheres and in cognitive, affective, and behavioral life areas. These symptoms may be regarded as evidence of impaired mastery in one or more subsets of the individual's life system. This system is represented by three intersecting circles representing the intrapersonal (micro), interpersonal (mezzo), and social (macro) levels of functioning, current and future, and is described in Figure 1. If we examine the seven subsets that emerge from the intersection of the three, we find in clockwise order:

1. Intrapersonal with cognitive, affective, and behavioral content
2. Interpersonal with behavioral content
3. Social-political behavioral content
4. One's beliefs, attitudes, and perceptions about society at large

5. One's beliefs, attitudes, and perceptions about family, friends, and other primary relationships
6. Behavior related to social roles and functions
7. Moral and transcendental content

This list describes all possible loci of symptomatology and of the corresponding avenues for stress-related interventions. It is clear that symptoms cut across a number of subsets and that interventions affect more than one subset. The various interventions (dynamically oriented and behaviorally oriented psychotherapy, individual and groups sessions, physical drills and exercises, etc.) used in the CFRU were not assigned to different life subsets. It is reasonable to hypothesize, however, that the dynamic therapies are more germane to the intrapersonal subset (1), behavioral therapies to the cognitive and behavioral (1, 2), group sessions to the interpersonal (2), physical drills to the behavioral (6), and lectures and meetings to social attitudes (3). Any given intervention is

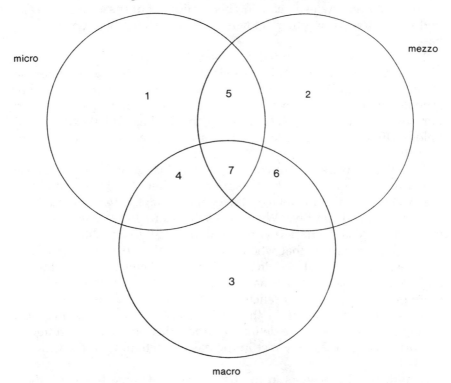

Figure 1. Ecosystem subsets.

far richer in its implications than its *a priori* assignment to a given life subset.

THE DYNAMICS OF THE CFRU

No single intervention or activity within the CFRU was unique. The claim for uniqueness can only be applied to the overall atmosphere in which all these activities took place with intense effort and involvement in a relatively short time span. Ordinarily a residential treatment setting brings about adverse iatrogenic effects in the residents, but there were several reasons why these adverse side effects did not occur in the CFRU:

1. There was no opportunity for stigmatization either before entering or after leaving the CFRU. The setting did not exist beforehand and ceased to exist when the last client left. Individual clients may have introduced their own stigmatizing perceptions, but these were not elicited or reinforced by other soldiers or by staff members on the army base.

2. The setting was regarded positively by the professional staff, who were far more optimistic about the efficacy of the CFRU than professional staffs of residential settings (psychiatric hospitals, prisons, boarding schools, or other "total institutions") tend to be. Staff members were perceived as "universal reclaimers" in the Wolins and Wozner terminology (1982) who, nevertheless, had a tolerance for compromise and for setbacks.

3. Activities were structured so as to enhance growth in all life areas rather than in one area at the expense of another. The former approach is a system in which the total of the feedback loops between the various life subsystems is positive: When one subsystem grows, the subsystem with which it is connected is also enhanced. By contrast, a negative feedback loop implies that when one grows, the other diminishes. To achieve the former goal, certain conditions must be met: (a) goal-directed and counter-goal-directed behaviors must be clearly distinguished; (b) there must be a graduated sanction system for both kinds of behaviors; and (c) significant others in the larger world outside the immediate setting must support these definitions and sanctions. These conditions, set forth in Figure 2, were met in the daily functioning of the CFRU.

Goal-directed behaviors in the CFRU were of three types: (1) those required by the setting, e.g., adhering to the daily program; (2) those

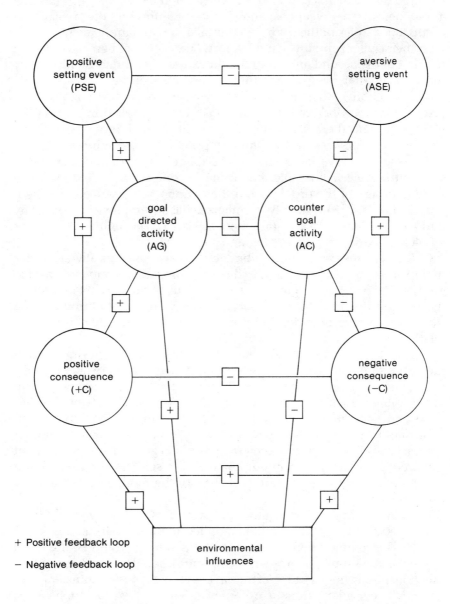

Figure 2. Normatively appropriate reward-and-punishment internat.

required by the distinctly military character of the setting, e.g., standing at parade, carrying weapons; and (3) those required by the civilian and occupational roles of the soldiers, e.g., talking with family members and with their civilian employer and fellow workers. As soldiers moved from the first to the second and on to the third, they expanded their mastery from initially narrow to increasingly broad areas of life.

The sanction system in the CFRU was more implicit than explicit (except for prescribed military sanctions). It was applied in a variety of ways, e.g., the therapist reinforcing certain behaviors in the therapy sessions, conversation in the dining room reinforcing self-reliance and reprimanding regressive behavior. Discipline was firm and unambiguous, but flexible. All people who came in contact with CFRU soldiers were informed of the program and their support was actively solicited. This included visiting family members, civilian employers, and army buddies. The military and professional staff of the military base was wholeheartedly behind the program.

CFRU staff members tried to bridge the gap that typically separates therapists from clients and creates distinct, competitive, and even hostile groups. Despite the different value orientations and expectations that the two groups brought to the setting, they were able to bring about a collective experience and warm camaraderie with mutually supportive relationships.

Despite the interdisciplinary character of the CFRU staff, drawn from the various mental health professions, staff members were able to enlist one another's help in carrying out their treatment programs. Group supervision at least twice weekly helped to resolve professional differences and disciplinary animosities. Most important was the commitment of all staff members to the success of the enterprise rather than to their professional allegiances or to their own personal goals. This commitment was infectious and was communicated to the soldiers themselves and was an important element in the efficacy of the modifying therapeutic milieu.

It is our considered opinion that the principles and the practical techniques used in the CFRU could be applied to nonmilitary settings and clients. The common denominator of such a setting would be the effort to rehabilitate human beings who temporarily sought the haven of dysfunctional behavior because of the aversive nature of a transient, but potentially chronic, traumatic experience. Several possible applications come to mind: newly released prisoners of war or political hostages, victims of near-miss industrial accidents or airplane accidents, citizens victimized by events such as Three Mile Island or Love Canal.

SECTION IV

Performance in Highly Stressful Situations

The five chapters that comprise this section all deal with intrapersonal and interpersonal variables affecting performance in strenuous and demanding physical activities. Chapters 13, 16, and 17 deal explicitly with military life (performance under fire in basic training, serving as a POW in a Syrian prison, and parachute jumping, respectively). Chapter 14 (motivation in anaerobic maximal physical exertion) and Chapter 15 (performing simple and complex learning tasks in extreme heat in the presence of and competing with other participants) deal with issues whose implications for military training are readily evident.

EXPECTANCY OF INJURY AND PERFORMANCE IN DANGEROUS SITUATIONS

In Chapter 13, Keinan assesses the subjective probability of a soldier that he would incur physical injury in a variety of risky situations. He found (a) that this expectancy differentiated volunteers for a high-risk combat unit from men serving in a conventional combat unit and (b) that it adversely affected performance in a highly stressful combat simulation experience. He concluded that men with high confidence expectancy, i.e., a low expectancy for personal injury in dangerous tasks, become less anxious in stressful situations involving physical danger and attend better to the details of the tasks at hand and as a consequence perform far better. This measure is recommended for inclusion in selection batteries to be administered to volunteers for dangerous training courses and missions. Several questions could then be answered: (1) whether success in the course is associated with initial expectancy level and (2) whether taking the course lowers the original expectancy level.

In a broader sense, confidence expectancy as defined here is an example of the kind of personality trait recommended by Rotter (1975) as possessing optimal validity: not so narrow that it is valid only for a specific life situation identical to that investigated in the original study, and not so broad that it has no validity at all, whether for specific situations or for a general class of situations.

THE EFFECT OF MOTIVATING CONDITIONS ON MAXIMAL PHYSICAL EFFORT

In Chapter 14, Geron and Inbar describe how manipulating certain motivational conditions enhanced maximal physical performance in a brief anaerobic task by young soldiers. Performance on trial two of riding a bicycle ergometer at maximum speed for 30 seconds was examined in eight groups. In the control condition, performance on trial two fell below that of trial one in a number of respects, but it remained unchanged or was enhanced when there was feedback about one's achievement in trial one, when intrinsic motivation to succeed was elicited, and when people were competing with one another. Conversely, the absence of feedback, the threat of punishment, the presence of nonparticipating onlookers, and other variations did not arrest the decline or actually contributed to a further decline.

The study illustrates the facilitating effect of two variables on one's subsequent achievement effort: (1) information about one's prior achievement level, and (2) the presence of others performing the same difficult tasks. Where competition between individuals serves to enhance performance, its effect is due in part to the contribution of these other variables.

THE EFFECT OF COMPETITION AND THE PRESENCE OF OTHER PERFORMERS ON PERFORMANCE UNDER HEAT STRESS

In Chapter 15, Zakay, Epstein, and Shapiro reach similar conclusions using a different stress paradigm and different kinds of performance measures. They found that performing complex perceptual, motor, and memory tasks under heat stress was enhanced by the presence of others performing these tasks simultaneously. As a consequence, they did as well under the heat condition as subjects in the cool, comfort condition.

The explanation for performance facilitation as a function of the presence of other performers was couched in terms of anxiety reduction and more effective attentional responses. Why people are less anxious when performing a difficult task in a highly stressful situation in the presence of coactors performing the same task is unclear. Mere spectators may be perceived as anxiety-provoking because they may appear as critics of the subject's efforts, but coactors may evoke positive emotional reactions since they are making comparable strenuous efforts and presumably know how difficult these tasks are.

The further introduction of competition to the coaction paradigm did not contribute to better performance per se, but unlike coaction alone, it lowered physiological stress induced by the heat condition as measured by heart rate, rectal temperature, and sweat rate, possibly by reducing situational anxiety. These findings hold implications for military training and for performance in other strenuous and demanding occupations.

COGNITIVE AND BEHAVIORAL SURVIVAL STRATEGIES IN SOLITARY CONFINEMENT AS A POW

Numerous studies have documented the long-term consequences of privation, torture, solitary confinement, and other stressful experiences associated with serving as a prisoner of war in a hostile enemy environment. A review of this research literature may be found in Hunter (1978), who documents the severe, chronic maladjustment that may result from cruel and inhuman captivity for a significant period of time. Veterans returning from prison camps in Korea or Vietnam became extraordinarily vulnerable both to physical and to psychological health problems in the course of their incarceration. Some were significantly disturbed when they were freed. Others became disturbed months and even years later, displaying delayed reactions associated with their heightened vulnerability (Segal, 1974).

In Chapter 16, Shachak analyzes his own captivity and efforts to cope with imprisonment in a Syrian prison during and after the 1973 war. That he is today an effective professional person and derives satisfaction from family, social relationships, and work may follow from the kind of person he is and the kinds of coping mechanisms that he used during his eight-month captivity. As may be easily ascertained from reading his description of captivity, the circumstances of his imprisonment were reminiscent of the cruel treatment received by American POWs in Korea and Vietnam.

Shachak was able to reduce the stressful aspects of his incarceration by engaging in what he termed "componentiality" or breaking up reality into different life spaces and activities and as a consequence was able to live an enriching and unusual rich life despite the harsh, deprived, and regimented existence of an Israeli POW in an Arab prison.

He attempted both to find meaning in his suffering (Frankl, 1962) and to minimize this suffering by a number of strategies: (1) introducing structure in his cell (transforming simple materials into more elaborate objects that enhanced the quality of life even in the abysmal conditions of the POW camp); (2) organizing his daily activities (diary, calendar, daily schedule, makeshift chess game); (3) selecting those guards with whom he would establish a relationship in order to receive certain necessary privileges (toilet, water, medical care); (4) avoiding other guards to whom he gave private and colorful names to express his distaste of them and his confidence that he could handle the situation, despite their hostile presence; (5) making plans for the future after release; (6) communicating whenever possible with other Israeli prisoners, despite the risk of severe punishment individually and collectively; and (7) conducting imaginary conversations with loved ones and with God, and imagining holiday gatherings at the appropriate seasons.

Shachak's experiences should be of interest to people interested in the long-term consequences of being a POW or a hostage of terrorists. They can serve as examples of creative, effective behaviors. These behaviors transcend the constraints of the setting and reflect courage, steadfastness, and creative problem solving in men making the best of a difficult situation and minimizing for themselves the known adverse consequences of being a POW. His is a humanist-existential approach with some intellectual and philosophical underpinnings, and his concrete examples illustrate without excessive elaboration survival strategies for hapless POWs.

This writer compared Shachak's account with that of the Presbyterian missionary Benjamin Weir, who was held in solitary confinement in Beirut for 16 months by Shiite revolutionaries (*The Washington Post Magazine*, October 13, 1985). The differences between the two men and the circumstances of their incarceration were many: Weir spoke Arabic fluently, had spent many years in Lebanon, and was sympathetic with the struggle of the revolutionaries. He was never beaten or tortured and his confinement was relatively benign. On the negative side, he was a much older man, was incarcerated twice as long, and had no contact with fellow hostages for most of his lengthy captivity. Despite these differences, both men described remarkably similar strategies to maintain their emotional and cognitive equilibrium.

THE RELATIONSHIP BETWEEN COHERENT APPRAISAL OF PERFORMANCE IN A HIGHLY STRESSFUL TASK AND TASK PERFORMANCE

In Chapter 17, Shalit and his military psychology colleagues in Sweden investigate the predictive validity of a self-report cognitive appraisal scale about parachute jumping with reference to the quality of the jumping performance by the appraiser. Their scale is based on a sequential adjustment model that is more elaborate than the primary/secondary appraisal model of Lazarus (Lazarus & Folkman, 1984) and involves three phases and three modalities. The phases are appraisal of threat, mobilization of resources, and deliberate and planned execution. The three modalities are cognitive, affective, and instrumental. Shalit attributes the modest predictive validity obtained for the model to methodological difficulties and to the obvious contribution to criterion performance of variables not accounted for by the model. Shalit has used this model to advantage in other military research, and its larger implications for coping with nonmilitary stress situations invite further research.

13

Confidence Expectancy as a Predictor of Military Performance Under Stress

GIORA KEINAN

Recent theoretical approaches to the study of stress have shifted emphasis from definitions of stress in terms of situational or stimulus variables (e.g., Miller, 1953) to the viewing of stress as an inner state that evolves from interactions between the organism and its environment (e.g., Endler & Edwards, 1982; Lazarus & Launier, 1978; Lehman, 1972). The growing prominence of this interaction approach to stress research has generated numerous investigations concerned with individual differences in sensitivity and response to stressors. Salient among these are studies of cognitive variables that mediate between stressors and individual's responses, and particularly, of the individual's *expectations* concerning his relationship with the environment and his ability to cope with stressful situations. Thus, McGrath (1972) viewed stress as stemming from a perceived imbalance between demands and capabilities and emphasized the significant role played by the individual's expectations in determining such imbalance. Lazarus (1966) maintained that an environmental demand will induce stress only if the individual expects that he will be incapable of adequately coping with it.

The critical role played by persons' expectations in determining their perception of and reactions to threats motivated the present study, which sought to identify an expectation that mediates behavior and performance under stress. The study was designed to serve a twofold purpose: first, to further understanding of the determinants of performance in stressful, dangerous situations; second, to develop an instrument for the selection and classification of individuals for dangerous tasks and occupations.

In attempting to set expectation-based predictions of behavior, one should take into consideration the potential effects of the generality of expectations. Overgeneralized expectations are relevant to a wide range of situations and events but, because of their generality, have a low predictive power. On the other hand, expectations that are overly specific, though potentially highly predictive, are reduced by their specificity to limited applicability (Rotter, 1954, 1975). Consistent with Rotter's analysis, the present study evaluated performance under stress in situations that involve threats to physical integrity as a function of the expectation that physical damage may occur. This particular expectation falls in the midrange between the overgeneralized and the excessively specific: On the one hand, the expectation is quite general as individuals might encounter a wide range of risky situations. On the other hand, the expectation concerns a clear and sufficiently focused outcome (physical integrity) and thereby promises accurate behavior predictions.

A theoretical model, dealing with the expectation of incurring physical damage and its effects on individuals whose physical integrity is threatened, was developed by Kern (1966). This model posits the existence of two opposite attitudes that affect the individual's coping with threats to physical integrity: (1) The *confidence attitude* stems from one's expectation that he has the ability to cope with the environment and thereby remove or neutralize the threat. A strong confidence attitude orients the individual toward situational cues related to the control of the environment. The *despair attitude*, on the other hand, consists of the expectation of having to bear the impact of the physical threat. When prominent, this expectation orients the individual toward external danger stimuli or to internal cues of anticipated injury.

The intensity of each of the two attitudes is a function of two components: a general or background component and a specific or situational one. The former refers to the totality of the individual's past experience with situations involving threats of physical injury. Repeated experiences of success or failure in neutralizing threats evolve, in adulthood, into a relatively stable background component of confidence or despair. The specific component, on the other hand, derives from the characteristics of a particular event, which convey information about the intensity of the threat and the feasibility of attentuating or removing it.

Although Kern's model provides a useful framework for analysis of the individual's expectations and their effect on his behavior in the face of threats, two of its key assumptions are questionable. First, Kern stresses the role of actual, direct experience in the shaping of attitudes and completely overlooks the impact of indirect, vicarious experience, i.e., expectations drawn from watching, reading, or hearing about physical threats. Second, and most important, Kern assumes that the confidence and despair attitudes comprise separate, independent dimensions. This assumption implies the inconceivable, namely, that the two attitudes can grow strong or weaken simultaneously—for instance, that an individual might expect to be physically injured and yet expect the threat to be neutralized or be entirely removed. It would appear more reasonable to assume that the two attitudes comprise opposite poles of a single continuum.

The above reservations have led to a redefinition of the expectation of physical injury, to be henceforth referred to as "confidence expectancy." The confidence expectancy is the individual's subjectively assigned probability of his incurring serious physical injury (grave wounds, first-degree burns, suffocation, loss of consciousness, or death) in a situation where his physical integrity is threatened. This expectancy is more precisely defined by the following characteristics, some of which derive from Kern's model while others were formulated by this author.

1. The confidence expectancy develops on the basis of the individual's direct experience with situations involving an actual threat to his physical integrity as well as on indirect experiences with such threats.

2. The confidence expectancy consists of a general component, based on the total direct and indirect experiences of an individual with situations where his physical integrity was threatened, and a specific component, based on his direct and indirect experiences with a particular kind of stressful situation.

3. The extent of experience that an individual has gained with a particular stressful situation determines the relative weights of the general and specific components that compose his confidence expectancy. The more shallow the experience the individual has had with a particular situation, the greater the weight of the general component in shaping the confidence expectancy regarding this particular type of situation.

4. The confidence expectancy derives from a cognitive evaluation, which can be carried out even when the individual is not emotionally or physically aroused. Consequently, this concept fundamentally differs from those of fear and anxiety. It is possible, for example, for an individual to judge the risk of his being injured as high without being frightened or anxious.

5. Realistically, there are few instances in which no relationship exists between an individual's performance level and the intensity of stressors to which he is exposed. It is, therefore, assumed that confidence expectancy is related to the evaluation of one's performance level, quality of skills, and ability to cope with threats.

The central premise of this study was that the behavior of individuals who are exposed to threats to their physical integrity would be influenced by the level of their confidence expectancy. It was more specifically assumed that in dangerous situations, individuals who have a high confidence expectancy would focus on the task at hand, while those low in such expectancy would direct their attention to the danger stimuli and attempt to avoid them. On the basis of this assumption, it was predicted that an inverse relationship would be found between the level of an individual's confidence expectancy and the stress he experiences and a direct relationship between the former and the quality of his performance in the face of physical threats.

METHOD

Subjects

Members of the Israel Defense Force ($n = 806$) participated in the study. The sample was drawn from five subpopulations: (1) *Navy Crew Sample*. This sample contained 157 members of the Navy who had served on seagoing vessels for at least two years. The majority had taken part in the 1973 Yom Kippur War. (2) *Naval Cadets Sample*. This sample consisted of 104 trainees in the navy cadets course. (3) *Commando Sample*. There were 125 candidates for a voluntary commando unit, a line of service known to be particularly difficult, as it demands great physical and mental exertion. The candidates were for the most part new recruits, who had been in the army for about a week, and were undergoing screening for the unit. (4) *Two Infantry Samples*. These samples included 420 soldiers serving in regular infantry units during their basic training. Sample A included 125 recruits, and B included 295 recruits.

Instruments

Confidence Expectancy Questionnaire (CEQ). This questionnaire was designed to measure individuals' confidence expectancy in situations where their physical integrity is threatened. Each item specifies an activity characteristic of military service, which was selected to meet the following criteria:

   a. The activity exposes whoever engages in it to a relatively high risk of physical injury.
   b. It is habitually performed by soldiers in all branches of military service, both in war and in times of peace.
   c. The extent of risk created by each activity is negatively related to the proficiency with which it is performed.

In order to ascertain that the activities chosen would be subjectively perceived as risky, each of 30 activities was judged on a nine-point scale, ranging from 1 ("no risk of injury") to 9 ("very high risk of injury"). The judgments were carried out by the Navy Crew Sample subjects whose experience, including first-hand combat experience, was assumed to assure valid judgments. On the basis of these judgments, 29 activities that received mean scores higher than 3 ("small chance of injury") were selected.

The respondent to the CEQ was instructed to imagine that he was about to participate in each military activity listed, having received the relevant, essential training, and rate the risk of his being seriously injured while performing each activity. In order to facilitate the respondent's admission of injury expectations, he was told that it is only natural to anticipate physical injury in dangerous situations. The respondent was further assured that his responses would have no effect whatsoever on his military career.

Frequency of Activity Performance Questionnaire (FAPQ). This questionnaire was designed to assess the frequency of respondents' past participation in assignments involving physical danger. The activities presented in the questionnaire are voluntary. It was therefore assumed that an individual who had freely chosen in the past to repeatedly undertake dangerous tasks succeeded in neutralizing or removing the danger they entail and, consequently, that such an individual would score higher in confidence expectancy than a person who performed a few such tasks or none.

The questionnaire was built on the basis of Kern's Background Activity Inventory (1966). This inventory includes, however, numerous activities that are alien to the Israeli culture. It therefore had to be redesigned to better fit local customs. To this end, subjects of Infantry Sample A were asked to rate the frequency with which they have engaged in each of 44 activities, and the type and extent of injury likely to be sustained in each activity. Activities in which at least 70% of the subjects have never engaged and/or were judged to be only minimally dangerous were screened out.

The final questionnaire consisted of 28 activities such as roller skating, diving, and eating unwashed fruits. Respondents were asked to rate the frequency of their past participation in each activity on a nine-point scale, ranging from 1 ("never participated") to 9 ("participated very frequently"). The responses obtained in Infantry Sample A yielded an alpha reliability coefficient of 0.88.

Social Desirability Scale. Crowne and Marlowe's (1960) Social Desirability Scale measures the tendency to reply in the direction of socially approved responses, whether or not the answers are descriptive of one's personality.

Rotter's I-E Scale. Rotter's (1966) locus of control questionnaire assesses the degree to which individuals perceive a direct relationship between their behavior and ensuing reinforcements.

Peer Evaluation Questionnaire. Each soldier was asked to give the names of three fellow soldiers from his platoon who, in his opinion, would perform best in situations involving physical threat (e.g., combat), as well as three others who would perform worst in such situations. The questionnaire stated that this information would be used for research purposes only, and that neither the respondent nor his peers would be adversely affected by the answers given.

Platoon Commander Evaluation. Platoon commanders were asked to evaluate their soldiers with respect to performance in stressful situations, where their physical integrity was threatened. Nine-point scales, ranging from 1 ("very poor performance") to 9 ("very good performance"), were employed for these evaluations.

The Trench Test. This test constituted a partial simulation of combat conditions. The subject, equipped with an automatic rifle and two ammunition magazines with six rounds each, was asked to move in a standard IDF fortified trench (see Figure 1). Inside the 1-meter-deep trench, two 6-meter-long "shooting zones" were designated with white marking tape. At a distance of 10 meters for each shooting zone, a cardboard target shaped like the upper half of the human form was set

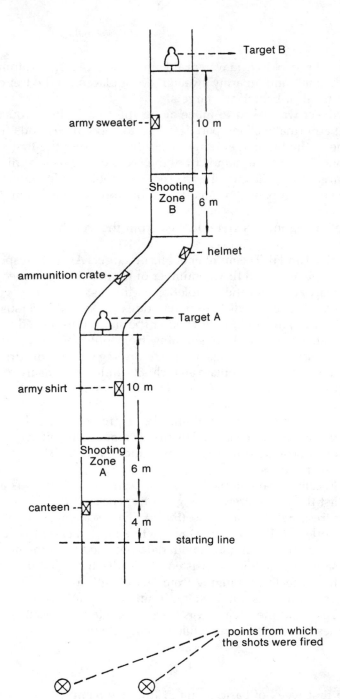

Figure 1. The fortified trench.

up. Five military objects (a water canteen, an army shirt, an ammunition crate, a helmet, and an army sweater) were placed on the trench floor, either in front or behind the targets.

The subject was asked to move along the trench, in a crouched position, at a normal walking pace. He had to shoot the rounds from one magazine at the first target (target A), while crossing the first shooting zone (zone A), and the rounds from the second magazine at the second target (target B), while crossing the second shooting zone (zone B). The subject was accompanied by an officer who moved behind him throughout the test.

The following indices were derived from the trench test.

1. Hits I and II: The number of hits on targets A and B, respectively.
2. Magazine I and II: The number of rounds that remained in each magazine after the completion of the test.
3. Obedience: A dichotomous index ("obeyed" versus "disobeyed") that indicated whether the subject disobeyed any of the instructions, such as shooting from outside a shooting zone, failing to change magazines, or stopping while in the firing zone. It was decided to obtain an inclusive index to measure obedience to all instructions, as only a very few subjects disobeyed each particular instruction.
4. Commander's Observation: The degree of stress displayed by the subject, as evaluated by the accompanying officer, was rated on a seven-point scale (1 = "under no stress"; 7 = "under severe stress").
5. Recall: Upon completion of the test, the subject was asked to list the items strewn along the trench.
6. Stress Self-Report Scale (SSRS): This scale was derived from Kerle and Bialek's (1958) Subjective Stress Scale. The latter was adapted to local norms with data obtained from the naval cadet sample. The SSRS consisted of 13 adjectives that indicated different feelings, ranging from "excellent" to "very frightened." The scale was administered immediately following the Trench Test, and the subject was asked to circle the adjective that best described his feeling while moving along the trench.

Procedure

In the first week of basic training, Infantry Sample B was given the CEQ and the FAPQ. The former was readministered 20 days later to 80 members of the same sample. The repeated testing was carried out in order to evaluate the test-retest reliability of the CEQ. Eighty additional members of the sample were asked to complete the SD and I-E scales.

In order to test for the "known-groups analysis" of the CEQ, it was administered to the Commando Sample. As already noted, service in this voluntary commando unit is extremely taxing, both physically and psychologically. Hence, to the extent that the CEQ is a valid instrument, it should distinguish between volunteers to this unit and members of the Infantry Sample.

Approximately three and half months after administration of the CEQ, the Trench Test was carried out. Soldiers from Infantry Sample B who participated in the test were randomly divided into an experimental group consisting of 166 soldiers and a control group of 83 soldiers (a ratio of 2 to 1).

The experimental group performed the test under conditions that were designed to elicit considerable psychological stress. To create the impression that the test is extremely dangerous, a stretcher on which several bandages and a medic's kit had been placed was set up in a conspicuous position close to the entrance to the trench. Next to it, an intravenous fluid feeding bag was hung on a rod, and a medic was seated alongside. At a distance of 10 meters from the starting line, on slightly higher ground, lay two squad commanders, armed with automatic rifles aimed at the trench.

The test was carried out as follows: Each soldier approached the trench alone and stood next to the starting line. The task was then explained to him by an officer from his unit. The soldier was told, in addition, that while he was moving along the trench, live rounds would be fired overhead. It was emphasized that his posture must remain crouched while he moved so that his head would not rise above the edge of the trench, otherwise he was likely to be hit by the overhead fire. The commanding officer went on to emphasize that the training at hand was one of the most dangerous and warned the soldier to exercise extreme caution.

Following the commanding officer's instructions, the soldier was approached by the medic, who asked for his blood type. This question was designed to draw the subject's attention to the medical equipment in the area and to reemphasize the risk of physical injury. Subsequently a dry-run drill was held. The subject moved along the trench in a crouched posture, and the commanding officer followed him, pointing out the shooting zones and targets and telling him when and in what direction to shoot.

When all explanations and instructions had been given, the subject returned to the starting line and began the test proper. Throughout the test, the squad commanders fired continuously in the direction of the trench. However, they shifted their angle of fire to assure a margin of safety; that is, the bullets did not go directly over the subject's head but close nearby. In the debriefing session, the subjects reported that the change in the angle of fire went unnoticed and that, on the contrary, they were certain that the bullets were flying directly overhead.

The subjects in the control group performed the test in the absence of both overhead gunfire and medical equipment. Nothing was said to them by the commanding officer to arouse apprehension. The control group was introduced into the study, (1) to determine the extent to which the experimental condition was indeed stressful, and (2) to assess whether the CEQ does in fact test the variables it purports to. To the extent that the inventory is valid, it should yield higher correlations with performance of the Trench Test indices in the stressful experimental condition than in the control condition.

Upon the completion of the test, each soldier, whether in the experimental or control condition, approached the experimenter, who was hidden from the view of those shooting in the trench. The experimenter explained to the subject that he had participated in a psychological experiment. He then asked the subjects to complete the recall and SSRS scales. After answering the scales, the subject was asked to move to an isolated location from which it was impossible to communicate with those who were still awaiting the trench test.

Two weeks after administration of the Trench Test, the Peer Evaluation Questionnaire was answered by 94 subjects from Infantry Sample B. At the same time, platoon commanders were asked to evaluate soldiers of the same sample.

RESULTS AND DISCUSSION

CEQ Reliability

Various indices show the CEQ to be highly reliable. A .95 alpha reliability coefficient was found in data obtained from Infantry Sample B subjects. Item-total correlations ranged from .54 to .72. Test-retest reliability, over a lag of 20 days, was .80.

CEQ Validity

The validity of the CEQ was assessed in a variety of ways: concurrent validity, construct and discriminant validity, and predictive validity.

Concurrent validity was evaluated by comparing the CEQ scores obtained in the Commando Sample with those found in Infantry Sample B. It was assumed that members of the first sample, who are typically exposed to greater risks and more severe threats, would show a higher confidence expectancy. This assumption was supported: The CEQ scores were significantly higher ($t = 6.49$, $df = 498$, $p < .001$) in the Commando Sample than in the Infantry Sample.

Construct and discriminant validity were assessed by correlating CEQ scores with SD, I-E and FAPQ scores. A correlation of $-.08$ ($n = 80$, NS) was found in the first case. The absence of a correlation between the two indices indicates that the CEQ does not yield a measure of social desirability but rather of genuine expectations.

Previous research (Heaton & Duerfeldt, 1973; Lefcourt, 1966) gave support to the expectation that CEQ scores would be related to the individual's locus of control (I-E scores). It was specifically assumed that a person with an internal locus of control, who is characteristically self-confident, would show a strong confidence expectancy. However, contrary to this assumption, the CEQ–I-E correlation turned out to be nonsignificant ($r = .12$, $n = 80$). This raises two possibilities: one, that confidence expectancies are indeed independent of locus of control; two, that Rotter's scale is invalid for the measurement of locus of control in nonstudent populations. Evidence supporting the latter possibility was offered by Nowicki (1972).

The CEQ was found to be negatively correlated with FAPQ scores ($r = -.26$, $n = 291$, $p < .01$). The latter index was the frequency with which individuals had voluntarily engaged in risky activities. It appears, then, that individuals who had repeatedly undertaken such activities succeeded in neutralizing and removing the threat involved in their performance and have developed, in turn, a higher confidence expectancy than individuals who had seldom performed activities of this kind. This finding is entirely consistent with the rationale that guided the development of the CEQ. It should be noted, however, that the correlation between the CEQ and FAPQ scores is quite low, suggesting that the confidence expectancy does not derive exclusively from direct experience with risky activities. Vicarious experience might play a significant role in the development of such expectations as well.

The primary criterion for the evaluation of the CEQ validity, i.e., its predictive validity, was the Trench Test. In order to employ the latter test as a criterion, it was necessary to ascertain that it constituted, in effect, a stressful situation. The various indices yielded by the Trench Test, in the experimental and control conditions, are shown in Table 1.

As expected, the "hits" indices, which primarily assessed hand-eye co-ordination and reaction time, were significantly lower in the experimental than in the control group. Subjects in the latter condition were apparently more efficient, as evidenced by the finding that they used more ammunition, at least in shooting zone A. In addition, subjects in the control condition followed instructions more closely, reported less stress, and were rated by the commanding officer as less stressed than their counterparts in the experimental condition. Taken together these indices suggest that the stress manipulation applied in the experimental condition was, indeed, effective.

Interestingly, the recall index failed to reveal a significant difference between the two conditions. This finding is inconsistent with results obtained in previous studies that showed that an increment in stress

TABLE 1

Differences between the Mean Scores of the Control and Experimental Groups on the Indices Produced in the Trench Test

Index	Group	Mean	SD	t, χ^2
Hits I	Control	1.65	1.25	4.17**
	Experimental	1.01	1.06	
Hits II	Control	1.53	1.17	3.46**
	Experimental	1.02	1.03	
Magazine I	Control	0.02	0.22	2.32*
	Experimental	0.19	0.85	
Magazine II	Control	0.17	0.82	1.00
	Experimental	0.29	1.06	
Recall	Control	2.25	1.55	1.57
	Experimental	1.95	1.41	
Obedience	Control	1.93	0.26	$\chi^2 = 3.18*$
	Experimental	1.83	0.37	
Self-report	Control	3.66	2.10	3.61**
	Experimental	4.73	2.25	
Commanders' evaluation	Control	2.35	1.60	3.75**
	Experimental	3.26	1.88	

*$p < .05$,** $p < .001$

The number of soldiers in the control group ranged from 81 to 83 and in the experimental group, from 157 to 166.

disrupts the performance of peripheral tasks (Bursill, 1958; Hockey, 1970; Weltman & Egstrom, 1967). One may hazard the speculation that the military artifacts scattered about in the trench were not sufficiently out of context to attract the attention of either the experimental or control subjects.

Table 2 presents the correlation between the CEQ and Trench Test indices. It can be seen that significant correlations, ranging from .34 to .48, were obtained in the experimental group between the CEQ and the hits indices, SSRS scores, and the commanding officer's evaluations. By contrast, in the control group, the CEQ correlated with the hits indices only. In addition, the latter correlations were significantly lower than those obtained in the experimental condition. It appears, then, that the CEQ effectively predicts both the level of performance and the stress experienced by individuals in situations that pose threats to their physical integrity. The different correlation patterns obtained in the experimental and control conditions indicate that, as intended, the CEQ predicts quality of performance under stress rather than quality of performance in general.

Further evidence regarding the CEQ's predictive validity derives from its correlation with Platoon Commander Evaluations and the Peer Evaluations Questionnaire. It will be recalled that these two instruments were administered to assess individuals' overall quality of performance in stressful situations that involve physical threats. The correlation between the CEQ and the Platoon Commander Evaluations was $-.34$ ($n = 174$, $p < .001$). The CEQ's correlation with the number of times

TABLE 2
The Correlations between CEQ Scores and the Indices Obtained
in the Trench Test

Index	Experimental Group	Control Group
Hits I	-0.44***	-0.22*
Hits II	-0.40***	-0.20*
Magazine I	0.05	0.08
Magazine II	0.11	0.08
Recall	-0.02	0.08
Obedience	-0.12	0.08
Self-Report	0.34***	0.14
Commanders' observation	0.43***	0.10

*$p < .05$, ***$p < .001$

individuals were voted by their peers as "best performers" in stressful situations was $-.21$ ($n = 93$, $p < .001$), and with the number of "worst-performer" votes, $-.50$, $p < .001$). These significant correlations indicate that the CEQ is quite valid even when the criterion consists of long-term acquaintances rather than of an isolated event that involves acute stress.

In conclusion, the present results affirm the theoretical propositions concerning the centrality of the confidence expectancy as a mediator of individuals' ability to overcome psychological stress and perform effectively in the face of danger. Aside from its theoretical significance, this affirmation is important from a practical point of view. Confidence expectancy can be employed as a predictor of performance in risky situations. The CEQ might thus prove to be a valuable device for the screening and selection of individuals for tasks and occupations that threaten their physical integrity.

14

Stress and Motivation During Maximal Physical Performance

EMA GERON and OMRI INBAR

This study investigated the conditions under which heightened motivation facilitates or interferes with coping in physically stressful situations. According to the inverted-U-curve hypothesis, heightened motivation increases arousal level beyond the optimal range and brings about decrements in performance. Since the introduction of additional motivating stimuli has been found to facilitate performance in some stress situations (Lundberg, 1982; Lundberg & Frankenhauser, 1978), it appeared worthwhile to examine a variety of motivating conditions to differentiate facilitatory versus detrimental effects on the repetition of a maximal physical effort.

METHOD

Subjects and Procedure

Two hundred soldiers (aged 18 to 22) were divided randomly into 10 groups and instructed to perform the Wingate Anaerobic Test (Bar-On, Dotan, & Inbar, 1977). This task consisted of riding a bicycle ergometer at maximal speed for 30 seconds. Subjects were told that the purpose of the test was to determine their physical fitness and that they should do their best in riding at maximal speed. Trial one on the ergometer was identical for all subjects, each performing individually without further instructions. Trial two was different for the eight experimental groups with regard to the motivating conditions.

1. Each subject in the first group (M1) was given the results of trial one (number of revolutions during the 30 seconds), asked to set his goals for the second, and then performed by himself. This constituted the *intrinsic motivation condition*.

2. Each subject (M2) was given personal feedback on trial one and performed on trial two after being given an assigned goal (5% higher than his previous effort). This constituted the *extrinsic motivation condition*.

3. Each subject (M3) in the *audience effect condition* did trial two in the presence of the others as passive spectators and without any information as to his performance on trial one.

4. Each subject (M4) in the *competition condition* was yoked in trial two with another whose performance on trial one was equal to his own. The two men were informed of this fact and instructed to compete for the higher achievement, with no one else present during the competition.

5. Each subject (M5) in the *punishment condition* performed by himself and was told that his performance on trial two was being monitored and compared to that of trial one, with electric shock introduced if he fell below trial one for each five-second interval.

6. Each subject (M6) in the *reward condition* competed with two or three others who were similar on trial one performance for a piece of cake. Only subgroup members were present during the competition.

7. Each subject (M7) competed with a member of the other of two teams in a *group competition condition* (Zander, 1975) with prizes (cinema tickets) given to the team whose total number of revolutions was highest. All were present as subject pairs competed, and they cheered on their team members. Subjects were not informed of their trial one achievement, but the trial two results were written on a board in the view of the competitors.

8. Subjects (M8) in the *social responsibility condition* were asked by an authority figure present during trial two to do their best for the good name of the institution in what was otherwise a noncompetitive situation.

The remaining two groups were controls and merely repeated trial one a second time.

Measures

The effect of the various motivation conditions was examined on four kinds of variables:

> *Performance variables*: Mean power output in watts (MP), peak power output (PP), and fatigue index (FI) recorded by the downslope of performance in percent terms.
>
> *Galvanic skin resistance* (GSR): Measured by the basic resistance level (in units of 250 ohms) before and after each of the trials.
>
> *Flicker fusion frequency (FFF)*: Number of critical light flickerings for one second before trial one and after both trials. FFF and GSR were regarded as arousal level indicators.
>
> *Performance attitudes*: After each trial a questionnaire was administered. The first three questions (task difficulty, personal effort level, and task readiness) were rated on a five-point scale, and the last two questions (personal goals and feelings) were rated qualitatively according to three response categories.

RESULTS AND DISCUSSION

The Effect of Trial One on Trial Two

The "pure" effect of simply repeating trial one a second time following a 90-minute rest period was first examined. Several changes were noted:

1. A significant decrement was noted in peak power output, 673 watts versus 690 ($p < .05$).
2. There was also a decrease in the magnitude of the relationship between peak output and fatigue index, $r = .41$ in trial one and a nonsignificant level in trial two.
3. Changes in a negative direction were noted on the GSR and FFF measures suggesting a reduction in arousal level, but these differences did not reach formal significance.
4. There were similar differences on the attitude scales, with task difficulty rated higher on trial two and with fewer definitive goals (conveying self-confidence, concentration, and controlled behavior) expressed on trial two ($p < .01$).

There were no other differences either in levels of mean power output or the fatigue index or in the relationships of the various performance variables. We conclude that the stress of repeating a maximal effort after a relatively lengthy recovery period was adverse rather than facilitating.

The Effect of the Motivating Conditions

Analysis of the eight experimental conditions indicated that there were two categories of influence. Audience effect, punishment, and social responsibility (M3, M5, M8) all reflected the kind of detrimental stress effect reported for the controls, decline in the correlation of PP and FI and in GSR. By contrast, competition, reward and group belonging (M4, M6, M7) exercised a positive, facilitating effect. These conclusions were based on data summarized in Figures 1, 2, and 3 on the PP variable, the relation between PP and FI, and on the GSR. In these figures changes are presented as percents from the baseline performance on the task in trial one.

If we examine these figures in detail, we find that PP was unchanged in two of the three conditions in the detrimental category and higher in all three conditions of the facilitating category. Similarly, the magnitude

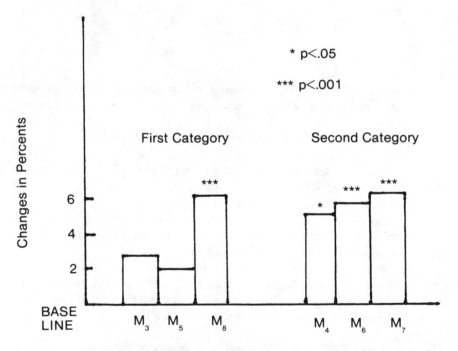

Figure 1. Motivational influences on peak power output.

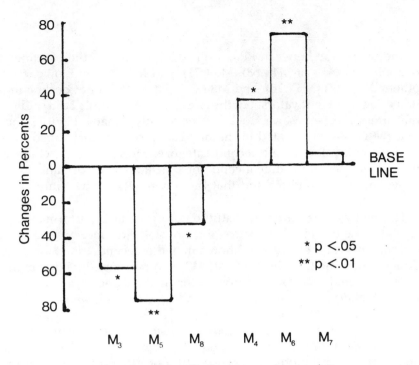

Figure 2. Motivational influences on the correlation between peak power output and fatigue index.

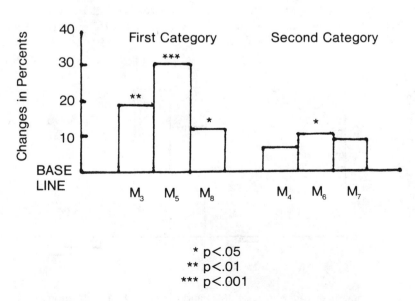

Figure 3. Motivational influences on galvanic skin resistance.

of the correlation between PP and FI was higher than the baseline cor-relation ($r = .41$) for M4 (.58), M6 (.71), and M7 (.44) and lower for the others: M3 (.17), M5 (.10), and M8 (.32). That PP did not decline in the first category of motivators, but the correlation of PP and FI did, indicates that stress affects these variables independently. Finally, Figure 3 shows that the GSR was elevated in the first category and unchanged in two of three motivators in the second category. Overall, we conclude that the competitive motivational conditions facilitated performance on the above-mentioned indices and that the others were either unhelpful or detrimental.

The motivational effects on attitudes toward task performance par-alleled those of the performance and physiological measures. M4 sub-jects in the competitive condition rated the second trial as no more difficult than the first. By contrast, M3 who performed before an audi-ence evaluated trial two as more difficult than one, rated their own efforts higher, and evaluated their readiness to perform as lower ($p < .05$ in all comparisons cited).

The effect of the intrinsic versus extrinsic motivation condition was complex. On the one hand, PP and GSR remained constant from trial one to two. On the other, the correlation of PP and FI rose and there were changes in attitudes toward performance reflecting facilitation in coping, as shown in Figures 4 and 5. Subjects in the intrinsic motivation condition did not report trial two to be more difficult than one (in the detrimental stress conditions trial two was reported to be more difficult);

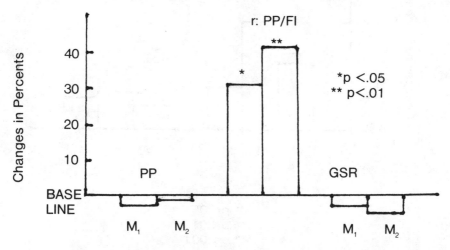

Figure 4. Influences of the intrinsic (M1) and extrinsic (M2) motivation condition.

the effort level remained unchanged, but the readiness to perform was actually higher ($p < .01$). For both groups, intrinsic and extrinsic, there was a positive change in emotional attitude in trial two ($p < .01$), indicating that these conditions affected one's subjective experience primarily and not their actual performance. It is possible that the absence of performance facilitation in these two conditions derived from the brief duration of the maximal effort. Some investigators (Bosel & Otto, 1981; McGrath, 1972) have emphasized the importance of specificity in the relationships of certain classes of stressors and performance-mediating variables. In the present instance, we may hypothesize that intrinsic and extrinsic motivation will exercise positive effects on physical performance during stress situations of long-term duration.

CONCLUSIONS

The major finding of the present investigation is that competition in and of itself is not detrimentally stressful and may even facilitate performance. Specific attention must be paid, however, to the other motivational variables associated with a particular competitive situation.

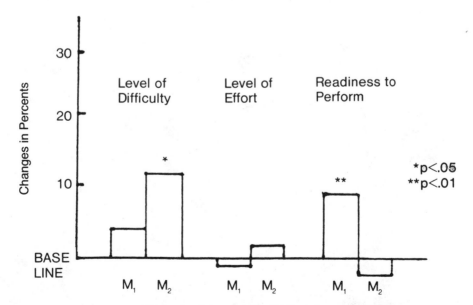

Figure 5. Influences of the intrinsic (M1) and extrinsic (M2) motivation condition on the attitude toward the performance.

The presence of an audience, the punitive consequences of failure, the fear of failure, and the weight of social responsibility may exercise positive effects on maximal physical performance in competitive situations characterized by relatively low stress, but cannot be recommended as mediators in situations of high stress. The same was found for intrinsic and extrinsic motivation, which contributed primarily to an improved subjective experience (a consequence of importance in some contexts), but not to an improvement in performance.

Overall, the conclusions reached in this study are specific to short-term maximal effort and not to long-term efforts. As such, they are more applicable to some forms of athletic competition and not to others. They are also less applicable to the kinds of physical tasks that soldiers are routinely called upon to perform in military training and in combat situations. There are, however, special situations both in civilian and in military life where maximal physical effort may be mandatory, and here we find that the various motivating conditions either maintained or increased peak performance above that of baseline, whereas mere repetition of the effort after a lengthy rest period trial in the absence of any such motivators decreased it.

15

The Effects of a Coacting Setting and Competitive Motivation on Performance Under Heat Stress

DAN ZAKAY, YORAM EPSTEIN,
and YAIR SHAPIRO

The concept of stress refers to a complex psychobiological process which is generally initiated by a situation (stressor) that is potentially harmful, dangerous, or frustrating (Spielberger, 1982). Environmental conditions such as noise and elevated temperatures might act as stressors and cause stress on both physiological and psychological levels. Schlegel (1980) defined heat stress as the total load on an individual from both environmental and metabolic sources, and heat strain as the resulting biochemical, physiological, and psychological adjustments made by the individual. The assessment of human performance under heat stress has and continues to be of practical importance in the fields of commerce, aviation space technology, and military training.

Early experimental research on the effects of elevated temperatures on human performance can be traced back to the works of Viteles and Smith (1946) and Mackworth (1946). The former attempted to determine the effects of heat and noise on the efficiency of workers in a bridge chart room aboard a seagoing destroyer, and the latter tested the performance of telegraph operators at five levels of heat stress. Both studies showed gross decrements in performance as a result of heat.

Subsequent research has shown that the original conclusions were somewhat optimistically parsimonious, and in some recent studies findings have been complex and heat has been found to facilitate performance (for extensive review see Bell, 1981). Bell (1978) noted that research concerning the effects of heat on performance has shown mixed results of decrements, increments, or no differences, depending on the type of task. Dixon, Copeland, and Halcomb (1980) conducted an extensive survey of relevant literature and concluded that high environmental temperatures cause performance decrements on tasks involving such factors as vigilance, tracking, visual discrimination, spatial relations, manual dexterity, and fine-control sensitivity. They concluded as well that reaction time was not affected and that those psychomotor factors which show a temperature effect generally do so at approximately 87°F. Epstein et al. (1980) examined complex psychomotor task performance after two hours of staying in conditions of 88°F and 95°F. When compared to a comfortable 70°F condition, even highly motivated subjects were unable to maintain performance efficiency in the heat.

Heat was found to affect not only psychomotor and cognitive performance but social behavior as well. Russell and Ward (1982) report that unpleasant temperatures decrease attraction toward and willingness to help strangers and increase willingness to harm them. Cunningham (1979) found that when temperatures were moderate, and the more sunshine there was, the more generous people were. Similarly, Carlsmith and Anderson (1979) found that civil riots were more likely when temperatures were unpleasantly high. Calvert-Boyanowsky, Boyanowsky, Atkinson, Gaduto & Reeves (1976) report that aggression occurs more indiscriminately in a hot room than in a cold room. Russell and Ward (1982) suggest that the effect of heat on social behavior can mainly be accounted for by changes in affect. However, the exact mechanism by which heat stress influences performance is not clear. Bell (1981) concluded that the effect of heat on task performance involves at least three separate mediators: body temperatures, arousal, and attention. Some researchers (e.g., Poulton, 1970; Provins, 1966) attribute performance decrements on reaction-time tasks to changes in arousal. A debate exists among researchers in regard to the relationship between physiological and psychological effects of heat stress. Wing (1965) supports the view that heat stress degrades mental performance sometime before physiological tolerance limits are reached. This view is attacked by Hancock (1981), who claims that decrement in mental task proficiency is a function of imminent thermophysiological collapse. Hancock suggests that the absolute level of tolerance may be susceptible to alteration from various factors such as acclimatization, subject motivation, and specific task motor skills.

A phenomenon that has somewhat similar effects on performance to those of heat stress is that of social facilitation, defined as the facilitation or inhibition of performance due to the presence of an audience (Cottrell, 1968). It was found (for extensive reviews see Bond & Titus, 1983; Cottrell, 1968, 1972; Geen & Gange, 1977) that audience and coaction setting has been associated with performance decrements about as often as with increments. Allport (1924) noted that social facilitation seems to occur mainly when task demands are simple. This complex state of affairs was explained by the drive theory introduced by Zajonc (1965). According to that theory, the presence of conspecific organisms as either coactors or a passive audience produces drive that leads to facilitation of performance on tasks involving well-learned responses and inhibition of performance on tasks involving poorly learned responses. This is because an increment in general arousal is produced. As a result the emission of dominant responses is facilitated at the expense of subordinate ones. "Accordingly, in tasks in which the emission of dominant responses improves performance, the presence of others is facilitating but in those in which emission of dominant responses would be 'incorrect,' the reverse of social facilitation should occur" (Geen & Gange, 1977, p. 1268). Empirical support for Zajonc's drive theory was obtained in many studies (e.g., Blank, Staff, & Shaver, 1976; Cottrell, Rittle, & Wack, 1967; Matlin & Zajonc, 1968). Bergum and Lehr (1962) and Morrisette, Hornseth, and Shellar (1975) concluded that performance of individuals in teams is superior to that of isolated individuals in vigilance tasks. Evidence from studies involving physiological measures of arousal such as palmar sweating and muscle action potential (e.g., Chapman, 1973, 1974) has also been generally in support of an arousal theory.

One conclusion based on Zajonc's drive theory is that social facilitation should influence differentially the performance of new and poorly learned tasks and that of well-learned ones. This conclusion was empirically supported by Hunt and Hillery (1973). However, the nature of influence of drive produced by social facilitation on behavior is not clear. One possible explanation, which was supported empirically by Geen (1976a), was that increased drive leads to a narrowing of the range of cues utilized in performing a task and hence helps the performer in avoiding irrelevant cues. Nevertheless, it should be emphasized that Zajonc (1965) thought that the drive was produced by the "mere presence" of others. A different approach, which contradicts the "mere presence" hypothesis, was introduced by Cottrell (1968, 1972). His point of view is that arousal is elicited by passive observers only to the extent that the performing individual feels apprehensive over implicit or explicit judgment of his performance by those observers. In contrast to Zajonc's drive theory, the implication of Cottrell's hypothesis is that the presence of others is a learned source of arousal based on the expectation of potential positive or negative social contingencies for performance. Numerous studies have been conducted to decide between the "mere presence" and the evaluation apprehension hypotheses. Geen and Gange (1977) concluded that "from research with humans, there is strong evidence that evaluation apprehension is an immediate antecedent of socially induced drive. Nevertheless, a fair amount of evidence indicates that audience settings may increase drive without producing such learned fear" (p. 1268).

Some explanations of the social facilitation phenomenon that are not rooted in drive theory can be found in the literature. Sanders and Baron (1975) have suggested that the presence of conspecifics may increase arousal level by distracting the subject from the task. However, Geen and Gange (1977) note that this point of view cannot explain how social facilitation can lead to improvement in performance. Another nondrive approach is suggested by Duval and Wicklund (1972). Their point of view is based on their theory of objective self-awareness. An objectively self-aware person is in a state in which attention is focused entirely inward and as a result his/her level of performance on a task is increased. Duval and Wicklund thought that social facilitation is produced because the presence of coactors on an audience might enhance objective self-awareness. However, Geen and Gange (1977) note that this theory accounts only for performance increments in social settings, but not for performance decrements. They conclude that "drive theory remains the most parsimonious for explaining both increments and decrements in performance in terms of a single set of constructs" (p. 1268).

The purpose of the present study was to test the influence of a coacting setting and of competitive motivation on performance of simple and well-learned psychomotoric tasks under heat stress conditions. It was hypothesized that under such conditions subjects would be able to perform such tasks on the same level as under comfort conditions. The rationale for this hypothesis was that according to Bell (1981), arousal and attention are two major mediators which are deteriorating because of heat stress on the one hand, but improved because of social facilitation effects on the other.

A coacting setting was defined by Bell, Loomins, and Cervone (1982) as a situation of "two or more persons performing a task simultaneously but independently" (p. 20). It was found that a coacting setting can foster increased drive by enhancing perception of competition (Laughlin & Jaccard, 1975; Martens & Landers, 1969). Hence, it is plausible to assume that competitive motivation is a factor that increases social facilitation effects. This assumption is supported by the finding of Geron and Inbar (1983) that competitive motivation helped subjects in overcoming stress while performing physical exercises. Hence, it was further hypothesized in the present study that by emphasizing competitive motivation in a coacting setting, social facilitation will be increased as compared to a coacting setting without an emphasized competitive motivation. The significance of this study lies in its potential applied implication in war (e.g., tank crews) and peace (e.g., teams working under extreme heat conditions).

METHOD

Subjects

Fourteen males with average age of 19 years volunteered to participate in the experiment. All underwent a medical examination, and five were rejected because of problems such as high blood pressure.

Apparatus

A climate chamber was used in which it was possible to control temperature levels.

Experimental Conditions

Four experimental conditions were included in the experiment.

1. Comfort conditions in a coacting setting (CM).
2. Heat stress conditions with the aid of personal cooling systems in a coacting setting (CL).
3. Heat stress conditions in a coacting setting (HS).
4. Heat stress conditions in a coacting setting and emphasized competitive motivation (HC).

The Coacting Setting

The experiment was designed so that social facilitation would be ensured on the basis of the mere presence and the evaluation apprehension hypotheses. All nine subjects were seated together in the climatic chamber, and each one performed each task individually but simultaneously. The effect of an audience and of evaluation was maintained because a medical assistant was present in the chamber at all times. Performance was recorded for each subject.

The CM condition. In this condition comfort climate with a temperature of 75°F, relative humidity level of 50%, and speed of airflow of 0.3 meter/record was maintained in the chamber.

The HS condition. In this condition severe heat stress was maintained in the chamber, with a temperature of 122°F, relative humidity level of 30%, and speed of airflow of 0.3 meter/second.

The CL condition. In this condition the climatic parameters in the chamber were the same as in the HS condition, but the subjects wore personal cooling systems, which decreased the effect of the heat stress.

The HC condition. In this condition, eight subjects were tested under CL condition and only one subject tested under HS condition. In other words, eight subjects wore personal cooling systems and one subject stayed in the room under the heat stress conditions without any aid.

It was assumed that the competitive motivation of this single subject would be increased because he would like to prove his ability to cope with the heat despite his being under inferior conditions. This assumption was indeed validated by interviewing the subjects after the experiment.

Physiological Measures

Heart rate (HR) and rectal temperature (T_{re}) were recorded every 10 minutes by an ECK apparatus and a thermistor (YSI-401), respectively. Sweat rates (SR) were calculated from pre- and postexperimental differences in weights, corrected to water intake and urine output. The physiological status was calculated by the physiological strain index suggested by Hall and Potte (1960):

$$SI = \Delta HR/100 + T_{re} + SR \text{ (units)}$$

Where SI is the physiological strain index; HR is the elevation in heart rate (beats per minute); T_{re} is the elevation in rectal temperature (°C); and SR is the sweat rate (kg).

Psychological Tests

Forms recognition and identification. A slide of 1 of 10 previously learned forms was exposed on a screen for a period of four seconds, on a camouflaged background. The subject was requested to identify the form and to press, on a keyboard consisting of five keys, the correct key according to rules learned earlier. The keyboard was connected to a Rockwell A 65 microprocessor, which controlled the stimuli presented and recorded the responses automatically. The time taken for a correct response (accurate to 0.001 second) and the number of errors made were recorded.

Hand dexterity and eye-hand control. These were measured by a ring task (Meir & Vardi, 1972) in which the subject had to thread small rings onto a spike, first with the right hand and then with the left. Speed was measured manually by the tester.

Digit/symbol test (Meir & Vardi, 1972). This was intended to measure level of concentration and learning ability. At the top of a page were presented nine digits, under each of which was a different symbol. The subject had to match a random series of digits with the corresponding symbol. The number of correct matches in 90 seconds was recorded.

Digit span test. This was intended to test memory. Single and double digits were read by the experimenter. On a given cue, the subjects had to write down the digits in the order presented or in reverse order. The number of correct digits was recorded.

Subjective comfort. Every 30 minutes each subject recorded his level of comfort on a five-point scale.

PROCEDURE

The subjects went through a process of acclimatization for three days, four hours/day, after which they were tested during 13 days under the various conditions. Each subject was tested twice under comfort conditions (*CM*), twice under heat stress (*HS*), once under heat stress in the high-competition condition (*HC*), and eight times under heat stress conditions with the aid of a personal cooling system (*CL*). By this procedure it was possible to evaluate the performance under the four experimental conditions and to compare it within each subject. During each experimental trial, which lasted for four hours, subjects were seated on straight-back wooden chairs. A medical assistant was present in the chamber at all times, and two qualified testers, a male and a female, administered the tests in the chamber after the second and the third hours. A water bottle was available *ad libitum*. Before the experiment itself a learning phase was conducted, in which subjects learned to perform all tasks at a maximal level under regular conditions. This was done in order to eliminate learning and carryover effects and because, as reported earlier, social facilitation is effective mainly on well-learned and familiar tasks.

RESULTS

The following physiological measures were calculated for each subject: the average rectal temperature (T_{re}), the average heart rate (HR), and the physiological status (SI).

The following psychological measures were recorded: the average recognition time (RT) and average number of errors (E) in the recognition test, time needed for the completion of the ring test (RN), number of correct matches in the digit/symbol test (DS), number of correct digits in the digit span test in normal order (CD) and in reverse order (RD), and the average subjective comfort (SC). The means and standard deviations of all physiological and psychological variables are presented in Table 1.

Each variable was analyzed by a one-way analysis of variance with repeated measurements $(df = 3, 24)$. Significant effects were found only in regard to HR $(F = 4.73\ p < .01)$, SI $(F = 4.82\ p < .01)$, SC $(F = 4.78$ $p < .01)$, and RT $(F = 3.02\ p < .05)$. Specific comparisons performed by means of Schéffé tests revealed significant differences, which are presented in Table 1.

DISCUSSION

The results obtained are in support of the hypothesis that a coacting setting and competitive motivation help an individual in coping with a heat stress situation. However, it was found that the increment in coping capability due to competitive motivation is manifested mainly by a decrement in level of physiological strain and not necessarily by an increment in task performance. It was found that performance on all tasks was not decreased significantly under heat stress conditions with social facilitation (*HS*) as compared to comfort conditions (*CM*) or to the two other experimental conditions (*CL* and *HC*). Only recognition time was significantly longer under heat stress conditions (*HS*) in comparison to comfort conditions (*CM*). These results are consistent with those reported in the literature (e.g., Bell, Loomins, & Cervone, 1982).

The fact that subjects succeeded in maintaining the same level of performance under all experimental conditions reflects the social-facili-

TABLE 1

Means, Standard Deviation, and Schéffé Tests
According to Experimental Conditions

		Experimental condition			
		HS	HC	CL	CM
Tre[0]	$\overline{X}$	38.21	37.37	37.05	36.57
	SD	.50	.49	.47	.18
HR	$\overline{X}$	111.44$_a$	85.33$_b$	73.11$_b$	66.00$_b$
	SD	10.52	6.54	8.07	4.91
SI	$\overline{X}$	3.09$_a$	1.93$_b$	.80$_{b,c}$	.26$_c$
	SD	.48	.34	.23	.08
RT	$\overline{X}$	2979.22$_a$	2179.44$_b$	2610.33$_a$	2709.55$_a$
(milliseconds)	SD	635.58	549.06	970.23	419.82
E	$\overline{X}$	.13	.08	.07	.12
	SD	.04	.09	.06	.03
RN	$\overline{X}$	8.85	8.56	8.47	8.61
(seconds)	SD	5.70	10.03	6.07	4.87
DS	$\overline{X}$	67.36	75.00	71.66	65.66
	SD	10.01	25.96	16.30	9.57
CD	$\overline{X}$	5.71	5.11	5.55	5.37
	SD	1.31	2.14	1.33	1.34
RD	$\overline{X}$	4.61	4.88	4.44	4.96
	SD	.96	1.90	1.81	.89
SC	$\overline{X}$	1.35$_a$	1.33$_a$	3.05$_b$	3.77$_b$
	SD	.52	.50	1.01	.87

df in all comparisons are 3, 24.
Significant differences ($p < .05$) were found between conditions denoted by "a" and conditions denoted by "b" and "c."

tating effect caused by a coacting setting. This effect helped subjects in overcoming the destructive effects of the heat stress. On the other hand, the competitive motivation does not seem to help subjects in achieving better performance. However, this might reflect a ceiling effect since all tasks were well learned before the experiment itself. The destructive effect of heat stress was clearly manifested on the physiological level, a finding that is consistent with those of Evans (1979). The physiological strain of subjects was found to be significantly higher under heat stress conditions (*HS*) than under all other three experimental conditions. However, in the condition of increased competitive motivation (*HC*), the physiological strain was much more closer to that of the control conditions (*CM* and *CL*) than to that of heat stress (*HS*) despite the fact that a coacting setting was maintained in it and that subjects were exposed to the same heat stress conditions in the two experimental situations (*HS* and *HC*). In other words, because of social facilitation caused by the coacting situation, subjects in the *HS* conditions invested much effort and thus succeeded in maintaining high level of performance, but the effort invested caused a high level of physiological strain. On the other hand, when competitive motivation was added on top of mere coacting (the *HC* condition), high level of performance was maintained, but the "price" paid on the physiological level was significantly reduced, although the physiological strain was still significantly higher as compared to that found in the control situations.

It is of interest to note that the subjects were aware of their internal condition: The reported subjective comfort was the same under heat stress with mere coaction (*HS*) and under heat stress with coaction and competitive motivation (*HC*) and in both cases significantly lower than under the two control conditions. It might be concluded that both coacting and competitive motivation help subjects to maintain high performance level, but competitive motivation influenced, in addition, the level of physiological strain.

It is suggested here that this specific influence of competitive motivation might be explained by reduction in state anxiety. The relationship between state anxiety and performance level was demonstrated in regard to ocean diving environment, which is considered to be an environmental stressor similar to heat. Situational anxiety has been found (Baddeley, 1967; Biersner, Dembert, & Browning, 1980; Mears & Clearly, 1980) as the major factor that interacts with depth to cause decrement in the performance efficiency of simple manual dexterity tasks in the open ocean underwater environment. Ursin, Baade, & Levine (1978) note that the influence of situational anxiety on diving performance is well understood because the individual response to a stress situation depends on how one is able to cope with the situation, how the danger is being met by adequate responses, and how one evaluates the situation. Geen (1976b) found that the presence of an audience produced performance decrements on a difficult task to a greater degree among subjects with high test anxiety than among those with low test anxiety. Schachter (1959) as well as Wrightsman (1960) found that under certain conditions the presence of conspecifics leads to reduced anxiety.

Spielberger (1966, 1972) emphasized the role of the context in which a potential danger is encountered in determining the extent to which it is perceived as threatening and, as a consequence, on the level of state anxiety produced. Accordingly, it is suggested here that a state of competition creates a context under which an environmental stressor is perceived as less threatening. One possible mechanism by which this influence might be explained is that of attention, since in the context of a competition attention might be directed inward and as a result only a small amount of attention is paid to environmental cues. This suggestion is in line with the view of Duval and Wicklund (1972). Similarly, Epley (1974) suggested that anxiety reduction in social settings may be the result of distraction by the audience, which interferes with attention to the fear-provoking stimulus. Another possible explanation was introduced by Geen and Gange (1977), who wrote that "decreased arousal may occur during stressful situations as a result of the presence of others because the persons present are conditioned stimuli for emotions that are incompatible with fear, anxiety, anticipatory frustration, etc." (p. 1274). It is plausible to assume that competition is a state in which anxiety is perceived by subjects as an incompatible response. However, it should be remembered that the effect of competitive motivation is dependent on personality traits, as found by Geron and Inbar (1983).

The present study indicates that coacting settings and competitive motivation might be used in order to improve coping with environmental stressor. However, the exact mechanism responsible for this effect as well as the methods for optimal utilization of competitive motivation should be the subjects of future investigation.

16

Componentiality as a Survival Strategy in a Total Institution: Case Study of a POW in Solitary Confinement in a Syrian Prison

ORI SHACHAK

In the concentration camp every circumstance conspires to make the prisoner lose his hold. All the familiar goals in life are snatched away. What alone remains is "the last human freedom," the ability to choose one's attitude in a given set of circumstances." (Allport, in Frankl, 1962, p. xi)

TOTALITY IN TOTAL INSTITUTIONS

The situation of a prisoner of war (POW), who is cut off from the outside world and held in solitary confinement for a prolonged period

I am grateful to Haim Hazan who developed the theoretical framework on which this study is based and who encouraged me in writing and analyzing my experiences in this way. I also wish to thank Margo Tepper-Schotz who helped me to translate this paper from Hebrew.

of time, represents an extreme case of an inmate in a "total institution." This term was coined by Goffman (1961) to describe a general model for institutions such as army barracks, mental hospitals, monasteries, prisons, POW camps, and concentration camps.

The total institution is distinguished by a number of characteristics not found together in other kinds of institutions: (1) All aspects of life are conducted in the same place and under the same single authority. (2) Each phase of the inmate's daily activities is carried out in the immediate company of a large number of like-situated persons. (3) All phases of the day's activities are tightly scheduled, and the entire sequence of activities is imposed from above by a system of explicit formal rules and a body of officials. (4) The variously enforced activities are brought together into a single rational plan designed to fulfill the official aims of the institution. In effect, the central feature of total institutions is the breakdown of barriers ordinarily separating different spheres of the individual's life. This breakdown of barriers is defined as "totality."

Wallace (1971) uses the term "totality" to refer to the degree of control that the staff of the institution exercises over the inmates. In his view, the total institution represents an extreme case of power relations and social control in which the inmates are wholly dependent on the staff. Most of the literature on the total institution refers to this definition (McEwen, 1980).

Another aspect of totality refers to the construction of social reality and the creation of the individual's identity within social boundaries. Totality is described as an adaptive strategy in a situation of powerlessness in which one compensates for a lack of major resources by concentrating all available resources in one mainstream of social action. In employing this strategy, however, individuals must pay the high price of denying personal idiosyncrasies and their former social identities (Hazan, 1981).

The coercive nature of the total institution tends to cause totality and the breakdown of the individual's personal identity through processes of "mortification of self" and "contamination" (Goffman, 1961). Through these processes, inmates are stripped of the "props" they have chosen to define their identity in the past. They are forced to engage in activities incompatible with their self-concept; things they consider personal and intimate (i.e., their bodies, their thoughts) are brought into contact with alien and contaminating things; their world becomes unidimensional; and they themselves assume the identity of powerless persons.

COMPONENTIALITY VERSUS TOTALITY:
DIFFERENT WAYS TO CONSTRUCT SOCIAL
REALITY

By contrast, the world outside the total institution is highly differ-entiated. Individuals interact with different people in many places and in different ways and come under the jurisdiction of various authorities. They define and experience their own identity in terms of autonomous units that are not necessarily dependent on each other. Berger, Berger, and Kellner (1973) define this world as one of "multiple realities" or a "componential" world. Componentiality constructs social reality by en-abling individuals to use and/or to adapt for their own purposes re-sources from various spheres of social reality.

Structural features in the environment contribute to the bringing about of a total as contrasted with a componential world. The physical barriers of a prison, the lack of major resources required by the prisoners, the routine of daily living, and the imbalanced relationships between pris-oners and guards contribute to a total life-world (Goffman, 1961). By contrast, an urban life-style and highly differentiated technological pro-duction increase the division of labor in society, the heterogeneity of roles, responsibilities and privileges, and permit the emergence of a componential life-world (Berger, Berger, & Kellner, 1973).

What role do individuals play in creating their world? Do they simply surrender to social forces beyond their control and accept the terms of the total or componential society in which they find themselves? Berger, Berger, and Kellner (1973) show that people in componential complex societies choose among different identities. However, complexity can cause alienation and the loss of identity. Goffman (1961) documents that inmates in a total institution preserve a part of their original identity by establishing informal relationships ("underlife" or "secondary adjust-ment," in his terminology) among themselves that substitute for the formal system of relationships prescribed by the total institution.

Hazan (1981) regards totality and componentiality as opposite poles on a continuum of strategies used by people according to their definition of a situation and their perception of reality. A componential life-world can be constructed in a total institution, and totality may exist in a highly compartmentalized and complex social environment.

An example of totality as a survival strategy may be seen in elderly people in an old-age home who participate throughout the day in reli-gious activities to prove adequate social functioning (Hazan, 1981). An example of componentiality in a total institution is the power exercised by the inmates of a maximum security prison, such that the staff cannot direct daily activities without the prisoners' active cooperation (Sykes, 1970). The ties of inmates with influential people, relatives, and friends outside the institution affect their interaction with the institutional staff (Greenberg, 1982; Hazan, 1980). Another example is the ability of prisoners to preserve self-identity by finding meaning in their suffering even under the harsh conditions of a concentration camp (Frankl, 1962); the search for meaning becomes a major resource for living and a survival strategy for those lacking other resources.

A CASE STUDY

Introduction

The purpose of this case study was to analyze the life-world of a POW held in solitary confinement as a dialectic process of negotiation between the prisoner and his environment. The study indicates how componentiality as a survival strategy enabled the prisoner to preserve his identity and to establish a componential world within a total institution. The study is based on my own experiences as a POW in Syria in 1973–1974.

I served as a fighter pilot during the 1973 Yom Kippur War. My plane was shot down over the Golan Heights on October 7, 1973, and I was captured by the Syrians. Four of the eight months of imprisonment were spent in solitary confinement, and the intensity of this experience left its impression on me for a long time afterward. Rereading the few notes that I made during this period helped me to recall many details that I had forgotten in the interim. Because of the passage of time, I am now able to view these events in a more balanced, less emotional perspective. This personal experience enabled me to penetrate the life of the inmate in a total institution and to closely observe this world, including the part that is usually hidden from the researcher, the prisoner's consciousness.

Physical Conditions in the Prison

I was held in four different cells and frequently moved from one to another. These cells are described below in some detail to show how these structural features affected, but did not determine, my life experience.

"The Drawers." A few days after my capture I was brought to a small cell (length, width, and height in meters, 1.7 × .6 × 1.8). It had no windows and there was no opening of any kind in the door. The darkness was almost total except for a faint ray of light that filtered into the cell. I was forced to lie down on the concrete floor handcuffed and was informed by the guards using hand signals that I was not to stand up. I felt as if I had been put into a drawer, so I named this cell "The Drawers." Lying on the floor in handcuffs was painful, but I soon discovered that the handcuffs were not locked, so I released one of my hands and changed the position in which I was lying. I heard sounds and groans from the cells next to mine and realized that there were other Israeli POWs with whom I could communicate. I was given *pitot* (Arab bread) filled with *hummus* (chick pea spread), white cheese, or jam three times a day. Whenever I was taken from this and subsequent cells, my eyes were covered so that I could not see what was happening around me.

"The Grey Cells." I named this type of cell after the color of the walls, a light grey. It was relatively large (3 × 2 × 3 meters) with a boarded-up window. The door was metal and had a small peephole. A light was on 24 hours a day. I received three thin woolen blankets, spread one on the tiled floor for my "bed," and used the other two to cover myself. I was given a personal mask to wear whenever I was taken from the cell and also used it when I wanted to sleep. Food was delivered three times a day. Breakfast usually consisted of two thick *pitot* with olives, cheese, sardines, or jam, and tea. I would divide up the *pitot* and eat them during the day. Lunch consisted of rice or *burghul* (a kind of wheat), some meat, and fruit. Potatoes or soup was given out at dinner. This appeared to be standard army food and was distributed to inmates in all the prisons in which I was held, except "The Drawers." The food was served in a bowl; sometimes I was given a spoon, but usually I had to eat with my hands.

"The Upper Cells." These cells were located on an upper floor of the El Maza military prison. This I understood because they were called *a'aliyyin* (upper) by the warders and I was led up many stairs to my cell. The six or seven cells in this section were connected by a narrow corridor at the end of which were the toilets. Each cell was about 2.5 meters square and 2 meters high. The door, which had a peephole, was made of thick wood. Light from the outside corridor entered the cell through a window above the door. I was in this cell during the month of De-

cember, and despite the cold weather and occasional snow, I was clothed in a uniform made from thin material and did not have shoes or socks. I had only one woolen blanket with which to wrap myself when I slept on the concrete floor.

"The Lower Cells." This was the most comfortable cell of all. I was there for two of the four months of solitary confinement. There were nine similar cells located on the ground floor of the prison. It was relatively large (4.5 × 2.5 × 3 meters). There was a concrete slab in one corner on which I could lie and above this on the wall a concrete shelf on which I kept the "possessions" I had accumulated: bowl, spoon, bars of soap, pair of underclothing, towel, and pajamas. In the other corner was a "Turkish" toilet (a hole in the floor) and a water faucet, facilities that did not exist in the other cells in which I stayed. I used the water to wash my eating utensils, my clothes, and even the cell floor. In the course of time, conditions improved further and I was given three blankets and a pair of shoes, still later a mattress and warm woolen clothing.

Interactions Between the POW and the Warders

The enforced physical confinement and the need for necessary resources that were in the hands of the warders influenced the nature of my interaction with them. A few examples follow.

A water faucet and a toilet are necessary resources for a POW. Since these facilities were lacking in most cells, I tried to find a "good" warder who would answer my requests. I came to recognize the different warders and discover how each would respond. Sometimes, I had to pay a price for their assistance. When I was held in "The Drawers," the guards would take me out whenever I asked. I would call out "W.C." and the guard, whom I called "The Englishman," because he knew a few English words, would answer, "What do you rid?" (the word *urid* in Arabic means "want," so the sentence was really a mixture of English and Arabic and meant "What do you want?"). Then he would open the door and I would repeat "W.C."; he would blindfold me, lead me to the toilet, take off the blindfold, and wait outside.

The guards were less cooperative in providing me with drinking water. When I would call the guard and ask for water, he would enter the cell and ask what I wanted, then go out and come back with a glass of water. My frequent requests for water apparently disturbed his conversation with the other guards or some other activity, and he often became angry with me and hit me for being bothersome. On one occasion after I had finished in the toilet, the guard did not blindfold me, but let me to an adjacent room in which there was a sink and water faucet. He permitted me to drink as much as I wanted. This was probably the best solution for me because now I was able to drink water frequently (whenever I was taken to the toilet) and no longer had to depend on the guards, so it became a routine.

I came to a similar arrangement with the guards in "The Grey Cells." However, not all the guards treated me the same way. One, whom I called "The Black One" because of his black hair and large moustache, did not let me remove the blindfold when I was in the toilet. He left the door open, stood nearby, and it seemed to me that he was watching. I felt humiliated in this situation and asked him to take off the blindfold. He became angry and refused, saying, "Be'ayunak tikhra?" ("Do you shit with your eyes?"). After this episode, I refrained from calling to the guards when he was on duty. He may also have discerned my reluctance to have any contact with him, and he also refrained from any contact with me. One day, however, "The Black One" was on duty all day and his partner was "The Bad One," who would hit me and make fun of me whenever he entered my cell. Therefore, I did not ask to be taken to the toilet the entire day and in the evening urinated into my food bowl when I could restrain myself no longer. I also tried to drink my urine because I was very thirsty.

Being taken to the toilet was also a problem in "The Upper Cells." My relations with the guards were shaped by their readiness to take me to the toilet. The shifts were fixed, and I quickly learned who was the guard on duty and responsible for the cells in a given shift and who would come on next. This enabled me to choose whom I would ask to take me out. When the guard on duty was "Stand Abu-Rah," my chances of going to the toilet were nil. He would treat me very badly (*Rah* in Hebrew means bad). Whenever he entered my cell, he yelled at me to stand up, so I gave him a name combined of English, Hebrew, and Arabic meaning "The father of evil yelling at me to stand up." When I would ask to be taken out, he would open the door and sign to me "Wait" or "Later" and then leave and not come back. I came to interpret this sign as meaning "Wait for the guard on the next shift" and stopped calling him.

Another guard, whom I named "The Good One," took me out whenever I asked, did not hurry me, and permitted me to drink as much water as I wished. He would frequently come into my cell, leaving the door open a crack (possibly for fear of being caught with me), and we would converse. Other guards would also talk with me, but their conversations would be short. The guard would say, *"Shu?"* ("What?") and sign to his shoulder asking my military rank. I would reply, *"Nakeeb"* ("Captain"). The guard: *"Shu. Phantom o Skyhawk?"* ("What fighter plane did you fly?"). I: *"Phantom."* The guard would ask, *"When Darabt?"* ("Where did you bomb?"). I would pretend that I did not understand this question, but would answer at last. The guard would then hit me because I had, in his words, bombed innocent civilians, and leave. This type of conversation was repeated a number of times with these guards, but only a few times did it progress beyond what I have recounted.

"The Good One," on the other hand, would hold long conversations with me. I told him that I was a member of a kibbutz (collective settlement) and explained at length what a kibbutz was. He listened intently and could not believe that in Israel a pilot could be a *fellah* (farmer). I spoke of my family and friends and he of his life and home, saying that he longed to return at the end of his military service. At times, we even discussed political subjects. I invited him to visit me in Israel, and he offered to reciprocate if peace were ever achieved. A few times *even he* hit me at the end of our conversation, but I persisted in initiating conversations with him.

Despite the closed cell, I could sometimes see what was happening outside and studied these phenomena carefully: which guards were on duty, some idea of the construction of the prison, and the different staff and Arab prisoners who provided the various services. I came to understand the formal and informal hierarchy within the prison, including a few Arab prisoners who received specially favorable treatment.

Most guards did not follow prison rules strictly. They did not explicitly break rules as did the few who entered my cell for conversation while on duty, but they engaged in roughhousing, e.g., throwing snowballs at each other on cold winter days or wrestling among themselves for amusement. One guard, whom I called "The Good Uncle," adhered to most of the rules. He was about 40, tall, and had a large, black moustache. During his watch, he would stand in one place and answer prisoner calls quickly, but would refrain from any contact with POWs beyond what was required. He never struck me and on the following occasion was very helpful.

I needed a doctor because my wounded foot had swelled and was painful. This happened during the time I was undergoing intensive interrogation, and my efforts to obtain medical attention came to naught. I would pound on my cell door, display my wounded foot to the guard, and ask for a doctor. The guards, at best, paid no attention to my request and, at worst, hit me for my "insolence," with one guard spitting on my foot and signing "to cut it off." After three days of fruitless efforts, "The Good Uncle" came on duty. I decided that he would be the one to bring the doctor. I waited until he lit a cigarette and seemed comfortable and relaxed, and then began to pound on my cell door as hard as I could, yelling, "Doctor! Doctor!" When the guard opened the door, I pleaded that he bring me a doctor. He looked at my foot, signed that I should wait, and returned with a medic. The next day a doctor came to treat me.

Interactions with the Other POWs

I succeeded in communicating with my fellow prisoners and shared experiences with them, in spite of the physical isolation. In the next cell to mine in "The Drawers" was Itzik, a navigator from my squadron who was captured the same day. We had known each other superficially, but we now held long, intimate discussions. He spoke of his wife's pregnancy and his concern for her. He complained that it was "boring" in prison, but we both agreed that it was better to be bored than in pain, since we were not interrogated or tortured while we were in "The Drawers." Interrogation was usually accompanied by severe torture, such as electric shocks and whipping.*

In another cell was a pilot captured several days after us. From him we received more up-to-date news of the war. I learned that two of my friends had been killed in the fighting. Another soldier from an armored division recounted the tank battle in which he was captured. His hand was wounded, and the stench from his wound was evident to all. He was afraid that his hand would have to be amputated because he had not received any medical attention, and he asked my advice. I gave what advice I could, although I was not convinced of its value, because I felt it was my duty to help another person whose situation, if anything, was worse than mine.

Helping a fellow prisoner and relating to him as one in need improved my own situation, psychologically speaking. By these actions I left the category of "an unfortunate" and became "a helper." A similar shift in orientation took place in the El Maza prison when I saw guards bringing in a POW with his head covered whose leg had been amputated. I sat

---

*I have refrained from commenting on interrogation, although it was an integral part of my entire prison experience, because it pertains to military security. I have also refrained here from giving any information that could harm other POWs who are currently in Syrian prisons or who may be there in the future.

on my ledge and cried. I was angry at the Syrians for the way they were treating this man, I pitied him, but I was also glad that I was in good health and better off.

Communication with the other POWs in the El Maza prison was not easy. Sometimes I would tap on the walls and hear answering taps. These were usually not more than signals of mutual identification and encouragement, which I would make when my neighbor was brought back from interrogation. Once I heard someone whistle Israeli songs. I joined in and we whistled together for a while. Suddenly, my cell door was opened and I heard another cell door being opened. We had been caught. Guards entered my cell, tied me up, covered my eyes, and one guard slapped my cheeks a number of times. Afterward, the blindfold was removed and I was warned against whistling again. I must emphasize that I knew that the guards might hear us and that we would have to pay for it when caught, but I still chose to whistle. There were occasions when I was successful in holding long conversations in a loud voice with other prisoners. We would begin by whistling an Israeli song, call to each other by spelling out our surnames so that we would not be easily identified by the guards, and we would then talk. Each would tell how he was captured and report on his health and how he kept himself occupied. Even so, we were sometimes caught and beaten.

There were a few occasions when I deliberately limited the boundaries of my world. Once I became ill with the flu during the winter. I decided to conserve my energy by lying on the ledge that served as my bed and refraining from any conversation. Since I did not reply when my friends called to me, they assumed that I had been transferred to another cell. One saw a medic enter my cell and told the others that I had been taken away and that a wounded prisoner had been brought in my place. After several days I felt better and called out that I had been there the whole time. They found it difficult to understand why I had ignored their calls. My insistence in adhering to the decision to remain silent appeared ridiculous to them, but was essential to me as evidence that I was in control of my life circumstances.

The POW Alone

I was alone most of the time since interaction with guards and with fellow prisoners was limited. Although space and other material resources were in short supply, time was virtually unlimited. Thus, the organization of space and time and my few material possessions became major factors in constructing a componential world in prison.

In the absence of the usual means of measuring time that are available outside, I had to observe the passing of day and night by using the cues of prison life: distribution of food, changing of the guard, and the carrying out of routine activities (e.g., taking showers and the washing of floors by, and family visits for, the Arab inmates). I scratched a line on the wall each day in order to keep track of the days of the week. I could not remember the date of my capture, but I knew that it was a Sunday and I counted time by weekly units from that day.

The one occasion on which I lost the orderly passage of time illustrates the importance of timekeeping to me as a POW. When I was in "The Upper Cells," I had an intestinal problem that became so severe I could not sleep a whole day. I must have become very weak, because I fell asleep the next afternoon. When I awoke, I waited for supper and was surprised to find two *pitot* that were always given for breakfast. The other food items were also not those of the evening meal. My conviction that it was night began to waver, but I found it difficult to believe that it was morning or that the guards would have let me sleep through supper. I thought about this for many hours, not knowing whether it was day or night. Only when lunch was distributed was I finally convinced that I had slept through the afternoon and night. In retrospect, I considered this a "gain" in time because every passing day brings one closer to eventual release. Not being aware of the passage of time through sleeping becomes a "gain" and not a loss of time.

In dealing with time, I made various calculations to estimate the length of my stay in solitary confinement. The day that I would be released from prison seemed far away, and I was sure that before then, I would be put in with the other POWs. I decided that one month was about the right interval and counted the days until the anticipated event. I would lengthen or shorten my hypothetical waiting period according to the "signs" that I felt validated my calculations. For example, an improvement in conditions, such as blankets or warm clothing, was interpreted as a sign of impending reunion, while the renewal of interrogations was a sign of the opposite.

One day my cell door was opened too early for supper, but I brought my bowl to the door anyway. The guard pointed to a stack of 10 bars of soap on the floor. I took one, but he pointed to the stack and said, "*Hud lakh kullu*" ("Take them all"). This surprised me, and I said, "*Hada l'sanah?*" ("For a whole year?"). I sat on my ledge and pondered why the authorities had given me so much soap and interpreted it as a sign that my stay in isolation would be lengthy.

Each day as the sun set, I would gaze at the rays of light that came in through the window and wait for them to disappear. Another day of captivity had come to an end and I would scratch another line on the wall and make a mental summary of the day's events. I would interpret the events in the light of the guards' behavior to me and try to predict what could be expected in the coming days. These "summaries" were carried out as "conversations" with God, or with close personal friends and family. I would also write imaginary letters to them, tell them about myself, give them advice, and tell them to do certain things at home: taking care of bank accounts, obtaining permits, and buying things for the house. When deep in thought, it was as if I were with them outside the prison.

I would also celebrate holidays and special events. On Hanukkah, for example, I imagined myself lighting candles; I sang songs and saw myself playing with a *dreydl* (spinning top) and eating *latkes* (the traditional potato pancakes of the holiday). In similar fashion, I celebrated family birthdays, my wedding anniversary, and so forth. I also reconstructed my past, remembering events of my childhood which, today, I can no longer recall. I also made plans for the future, studying at the university and building my dream house. I even "planned" a national road network, water reservoirs, and other projects for the State. In this manner, I was able to ignore the immediate surroundings and escape beyond the barriers of the prison.

I also made use of my limited possessions to organize time and space. I would exercise daily for a long time. I would jog about two kilometers in my cell. I frequently cleaned the cell and, when it contained a water faucet, would wash my clothes daily. Eating was not the mere satisfaction of physical hunger, but an event extending above and beyond the time spent eating in the outside world. It was a lengthy ritualized activity from the anticipation, the receiving of food, the washing of hands, to dining. With my spoon I whittled figurines from the bars of soap I was given. I tore off the pocket of my checkered pajamas and played chess on it, using pieces of orange peel to play the "white" against the "orange." I was able to write a brief diary with improvised materials and spent a great deal of time transferring the elastic band on one pair of underpants to the other pair that lacked the band.

DISCUSSION

Research has shown that total institutions are more open than they first seem (Greenberg, 1982; Hazan, 1980). Extension of the social network of inmates beyond the confines of the institution makes it possible for them to construct a world of multiple realities. POWs find themselves in a very different situation when placed in solitary confinement under constant supervision and without toilet facilities, water, or the other material resources found in abundance outside the prison. Despite these restricting circumstances, POWs succeed in creating a componential world through redefinition of the situation and negotiation and interaction with their social environment, i.e., the guards and fellow prisoners.

POWs can exploit their limited material resources to compartmentalize their world. Worthless things, which the institution does not control, can acquire meaning and become important. Even the denial of free access to toilet facilities, water, and medical care can be transformed from means of intensifying totality into incentives promoting componentiality.

Time, at the POWs' disposal in unlimited quantities, is at first sight unvaried and boring. However, prisoners can imbue various events with meaning and can organize a daily routine that decreases uncertainty and introduces variety and multidimensionality into their world.

The prison itself is not a monolithic authority, and prison guards are not anonymous creatures carrying out instructions from above. POWs can break down the barriers between themselves and the guards by relating differentially to them and characterizing the guards as human beings, thus making it possible to negotiate to obtain necessary resources. This humanization also reflects back on the prisoners themselves, both because they can then characterize themselves as human beings and because the guards tend to return the humanizing behavior, thereby aborting the dehumanization process described by Goffman (1961). There is a price for this humanizing interaction with the guards: physical blows or going without toilet facilities or water for a day. The willingness of the POWs to pay it demonstrates their ability to make choices freely among various alternatives.

Regardless of the price, POWs further compartmentalize their world and preserve their original identities by communicating with fellow prisoners. Wall tapping, whistling patriotic songs in unison, and having conversations enable the POWs to identify with others. Maintaining contacts with the various worlds outside of prison (country, friends, and family) can also be achieved through imagination. The prisoners preserve their past and plan for their future. In the present they envision themselves in the preprison world to which they hope to return.

Hazan (1981) has indicated that in situations of powerlessness, people with limited resources may choose totality as a survival strategy (e.g., an elderly person in an old-age home). How were the POWs able to choose componentiality as a survival strategy in an institution structurally more total than an old-age home? The explanation appears to be that elderly people cut themselves off from the outside world because they do not expect to ever return to it. The POWs, by contrast, regard their present situation as temporary. They preserve their past and plan for their future. As their world expands beyond the confines of the prison, the POWs' daily experiences are compartmentalized in reality as well in their own consciousness. Under these circumstances, POWs do not assume the identity of powerless anonymous inmates, but keep their own identities.

17

Coherence of Cognitive Appraisal and Coping in a Stressful Military Task: Parachute Jumping

BENJAMIN SHALIT, LEIF CARLSTEDT, BERIT
STAHLBERG CARLSTEDT, and INGA-LILL
TALJEDAL SHALIT

This study tested a model formulating the relationship between coherent preappraisal of performance and adequacy of performance in a stressful military training exercise: the first parachute jump made by Swedish officer cadets. Previous studies on this topic (Fenz & Epstein, 1967; Ursin, Baade, & Levine, 1978; Vaernes, 1982) related performance effectiveness on this task to unconscious appraisal as assessed by projective tests (e.g., Thematic Apperception Test, Defense Mechanism Test). The rationale underlying this approach is that in a given situation, the most important determinant of coping behavior is the coper's personal, subjective evaluation of the situation (Baade et al., 1978). The objective nature of the situation is not without importance since it may determine the best *possible* outcome and since the less the congruence between the objective situation and the subjective perception of the situation, the lower the potential for effective coping. Research (Baade et al., 1978) has shown that poor performance in parachute jumping is associated with the use of repression and isolation, defense mechanisms assessed by the Defense Mechanism Test (Kragh, 1960).

The distortion of preappraisal of stressful situations because of unconscious defense mechanisms may be termed *perceptual defense* and appears to fall within an early phase of the perceptual process and to set limits on what will be appraised by the coper. Later conscious phases of the perceptual process have been investigated by Lazarus (1966) and the present investigators. Lazarus described a three-stage appraisal model: Primary appraisal determines whether the situation is perceived as benign or threatening, secondary appraisal determines whether the individual feels that he or she can cope with the threat, and tertiary reappraisal focuses on the results of the coping behavior.

The present investigators propose a more detailed model for the perceptual process that takes place after the initial unconscious perceptual defense. This sequential adjustment model (SAM) describes three phases: *appraisal*, in which the situational stimuli are evaluated and their implications for the coper understood; *mobilization*, in which personal resources for dealing with the situation are assessed and readied; and *realization*, in which the utilization of perceived resources is clarified and the plan for coping behavior determined. Each of these phases is processed with reference to three modalities: *cognitive*, or the structure and clarity of the situation; *affective*, or the emotional implications to the coper; and *instrumental*, or the coper's response style or way of dealing with the situation.

The three phases times the three modalities generates a nine-stage matrix described in Table 1. Each of the nine squares in the matrix is represented by a question about the perceptual process that must be answered by the coper before effective coping can occur. The answer

TABLE 1
Sequential Adjustment Model

	Process Phase		
Modality	Appraisal	Mobilization	Realization
Cognitive	Is this SOMETHING?	Do I UNDERSTAND?	HOW shall I do?
Affective	Does it CONCERN me?	Do I WANT it?	Shall I COMMIT myself?
Instrumental	Can I EFFECT it?	Am I READY?	DO it.

may be given quickly and with minimal deliberation or very slowly after fully conscious deliberation. The spatial configuration of the model is a spiral in which each phase is a separate loop and the modalities are located on a vertical axis.

The term sequential in the name of the model refers to the assumption that the appraisal of each stage sets a limit for the effectiveness of the appraisal of the stage that follows. If a perceptual process does not clear a given phase, the sequential process is derailed and no further coping behavior will occur. If the answer to the question in cell 2 (Does the situation concern the coper?) or the answer to the question in cell 5 (Do I want to do the behavior in question?) is negative, then further processing does not occur. By a feedback loop one can then return to the beginning to reevaluate the stimuli at that stage. If the consecutive answers to all stages are affirmative, then processing is effective and the resulting task performance will be correspondingly effective, assuming that other variables necessary for effective performance are present.

Comparisons may be drawn between the Lazarus model and that described here. His primary appraisal is equivalent to SAM stage 2, secondary appraisal to stage 3, and reappraisal after stage 9. Lazarus regards stage 1 or cognitive appraisal of the initial situation and its coherence versus its ambiguity as a part of primary appraisal (Folkman, Schaefer, & Lazarus, 1979). Shalit (1982) has shown that ambiguity adversely affects subsequent coping stages, so that it might well be regarded as an earlier independent stage.

Two formulations of the SAM model were evaluated here. The *conjunctive* formulation hypothesizes that poor processing in any stage sets limits for the adequacy of the subsequent stages. An unbroken process of affirmative answers to all nine stages is a necessary, but not a sufficient, condition for good performance, whereas a broken process is a sufficient condition for a poor performance. The *compensatory* formulation hypothesizes that each stage contributes to the final outcome or performance and that a later stage may compensate for inadequacies at an earlier one.

METHOD

Subjects

Subjects were 106 Swedish officer cadets in a training course in parachute jumping in which they made several compulsory jumps from the training tower and after two weeks made an elective jump from the air.

Instruments and Procedure

Two instruments were used. The Wheel Questionnaire was constructed by Shalit (1978) to map coherent appraisal of a given situation. It consists of an open-ended questionnaire, shaped like a wheel, in which respondents listed those factors that characterized a stressful criterion situation (in this instance, the forthcoming parachute jump from the air). Their responses were scored for structure rather than content and yielded three indices of perceptual coherence (structure, involvement, and control) corresponding to the first three stages of SAM. These indices were found to predict effective performance in different military tasks (Shalit, 1982).

The second instrument was the Disposition Questionnaire consisting of 10 questions, two questions each for stages 4 to 8 in SAM. These questions are presented in Table 2. A pilot study had shown that the actual presentation of the questions in the stage-consistent order was *not* perceived by naive respondents as corresponding to a preconceived logical system and was, therefore, retained in the present study. Each question was scored on a four-point scale with 4 the best choice.

The structural relationship between the five pairs of questions and the requirements of the model was examined by smallest-space analysis with a Kendall tau correlation matrix (Guttman, 1968). It was found that the two questions representing each stage were closer to each other than to questions representing the other stages. Each pair of questions may be viewed as representing a differently perceived domain or stage. Other features of the analysis were consistent with the hypothesized structure

TABLE 2
Disposition Questionnaire

Question	Response pole	SAM stage
1. Do you feel there is something more you would like to *know* about the jump?	Nothing/great deal	4
2. Have you *understood* what you should do?	Nothing/all	4
3. How much do you *want* to jump?	Very much/little	5
4. How much does jumping *attract* you?	Very much/little	5
5. Are you mentally *prepared* for the jump?	Very much/not at all	6
6. Are you mentally *ready* for the jump?	Very much/not at all	6
7. Do you feel you can *cope* with the situation?	Completely/not at all	7
8. Do you know how to *handle* the situation?	Completely/not at all	7
9. Would you like to *continue* with parachute jumping?	Definitely/not at all	8
10. How important is it for you *to jump well?*	Very much/not at all	8

of the model and are discussed in detail elsewhere (Shalit, Carlstedt, Stahlberg Carlstedt, & Taljedal Shalit, 1983).

Criterion response was an assessment of the jump by an experienced instructor on a 10-point checklist referring to the jumper's positioning, angle of limbs, head, etc. This assessment was made immediately after the jump and yielded a five-point rating scale with 5 as best. The instructor was unaware of the cadet's responses on the two questionnaires. The Wheel Questionnaire was administered one day before the jump and the Disposition Questionnaire in the airplane immediately prior to the jump.

RESULTS AND DISCUSSION

In the first conjunctive analysis, each stage was designated as cleared or not cleared, i.e., that the respondent had or had not attained sufficient perceptual coherence at that stage. For stages 1 to 3, not cleared scores were based on previous research (Shalit, Carlstedt, Stahlberg Carlstedt, & Taljedal Shalit, 1982). These were $> .3$, $< .4$, and < 2.0 for structure, involvement, and control indices, respectively. For stages 4 to 8 in the Disposition Questionnaire, a pair of questions yielded a range of scores from 2 to 8, with 4 or lower categorized as not cleared. On this basis, all respondents were dichotomized as belonging to one of two groups, those who demonstrated an uninterrupted sequence of cleared stages and those who had not cleared one or more stages.

Jumping effectiveness was also dichotomized into a good (scores 4 and 5) and poor category (scores 1 to 3), with 26 subjects, or 24.5%, falling into the former category. A 2×2 table of sequentials/nonsequentials and good/poor jump yielded a chi square of 8.46 ($p < .01$). Only four of the 42 nonsequentials were good jumpers, while 22 of the 64 sequentials were good jumpers.

In a compensatory analysis, the respondents were ranked in accordance with the weighted sum of their answer pairs for the eight stages. The weighing was based on multiple regression with jump performance as criterion. The ranked scores were dichotomized into groups comparable in number to the sequentials and nonsequentials of the conjunctive analysis. The resulting 2×2 table yielded a chi square of 4.27 ($p < .05$). In this analysis, eight of the low coherence group were rated as good jumpers, twice as many misses as in the conjunctive analysis. Accordingly, there is modest confirmation for the hypothesis that sequentiality of stages in coherent task appraisal contributes to an effective performance above and beyond the contribution of the various stages cleared.

There is a methodological explanation for the relatively small advantage of the conjunctive approach over the compensatory one and for the failure of so many cadets with a sequential stage response pattern to jump well (over two-thirds). This explanation refers to the use of gross dichotomizing of appraisal and jumping behavior. Our analysis treated all stages as of equal weight. A stage that was not cleared earlier in the sequence was treated the same as an uncleared stage later in the sequence. Moreover, clearing a stage was treated as all-or-none rather than as a continuous distribution. To obtain an indication of the relative importance of each stage, a partial profile analysis was conducted for each respondent (Levy, 1980; Shye, 1978). In this analysis of the relationship between the stages cleared and not cleared for each individual relative to jumping effectiveness, the data indicated that the greater the sequentiality, the more effective the jumping even within the sequential and nonsequential groups. Sequentiality accounted for 14% and 10% of the explained variance in criterion for the two groups, respectively.

Use of more sensitive rating scales and more refined statistical techniques might raise the predictive power of sequentiality of stages in the appraisal model, but there is an upper limit for the effect of psychological variables on the criterion task. It is reasonable to assume that intrapersonal variables are more cogent in the first jump than in subsequent ones, but even in the former many extrapersonal and interpersonal variables affect jumping performance, e.g., force and angle of wind, sheer physical ability, level of training, and social parameters of the training and test situation. Notwithstanding these strictures, the use of the proposed model to diagnose the phase and/or the modality of the perceptual process in which the respondent's behavior was inadequate is recommended both to enhance predictive validity of screening devices in training programs and to identify and treat remedially those aspects of the overall process in which given individuals are insufficient.

One might argue that predictor and criterion measures from early phases of training might increase the predictive validity of the model. This was not found to be true. All cadets made five tower jumps and gave their responses to the SAM instruments in advance. No relationship was found between coherent appraisal and tower jumping because of the uniformly high appraisal scores. No relationship was found between effectiveness of tower jumping and jumping from the plane. Accordingly, we conclude that future research should concentrate on constructing more sensitive instruments and on delineating additional psychological variables mediating between coherent task appraisal and task performance.

SECTION V

The Effect of War on Civilian Populations

A theme that runs through the first three chapters comprising this section is blaming the victims: Either the victims are blamed by others or blame themselves for the predicament in which they find themselves. This theme is implicit in the first of two chapters dealing with terrorism and explicit in the second. The first deals with terrorism as a general phenomenon affecting Israeli society (Chapter 18), and the second with the specific experiences of adolescents who were held as hostages in a bloody episode that occurred six years earlier (Chapter 19). This theme runs through the third chapter, in which the original settlers of the Yamit region attempted to cope with the victimization experience imposed on them by their own government in evicting them from their homes as a condition of the Egypt-Israel Peace Treaty (Chapter 20).

The next chapter (Chapter 21) discusses many aspects of the stressors affecting civilians in Israeli society during war and relates them to an ecologically based model of stress resistance. It subjects so-called social support systems to more critical scrutiny, both theoretically and empirically, than has been true in the voluminous literature on this concept until now. It highlights the importance of high personal self-esteem and a conviction of personal mastery in stressful situations in buffering the individual against potentially overwhelming stressors.

TERRORISM: WHOM DO YOU BLAME AND
WHAT DO YOU DO ABOUT IT?

Friedland and Merari (Chapter 18) analyze the rationale of terrorism
as an act of psychological warfare. Its perceived threat is greater than
the actual physical threat that it poses either to the individual or to the
society as a whole for several reasons: first, because it undermines the
individual's sense of control over his fate from threats to his physical
safety; and second, because it undermines the citizen's belief that his
government can and will protect him against attack. From the point of
view of the perpetrators of terror, the intended victim is the government
itself whose policies they wish to influence and shape to their advantage.
They elect to achieve this goal by victimizing small numbers of citizens
in highly public, dramatic acts. Ultimately the government and its policies are under attack and are the true victims, especially if the concessions demanded jeopardize the national self-interest or threaten the very
existence of the state in the long run.

Terrorist goals are often achieved when the victimized citizens and
the potential victims in society at large conclude that the concessions
that they are asked to make are not as great as the anxiety they currently
experience. In the case of the Arab-Israeli conflict, Friedland and Merari
conclude that most Israelis believe that the concessions demanded are
so extreme that they cannot be met. Consequently Israelis tend to harden
their political attitudes about moderate concessions that might otherwise
be made, if these were, in fact, being demanded by the terrorists.

There are many conflicts in the world, however, in which terrorism
is highly successful in cowing a local population and assuming control
of the government or in coercing the government to accept terrorist
demands. If we assume that the terrorist demands are illegitimate, then
we must conduct our own war of minds with the members of the society
under attack to reduce their pressure on the government to make these
dangerous concessions or outright capitulation. We must explain the
Stockholm syndrome (Ochberg & Soskis, 1982) to the largest possible
audience so that its effects are kept to a minimum.

The syndrome describes the positive identification of the hostage with
the captor to reduce the apprehension that follows from rejecting the
captor and the cause he or she champions. If the hostage identifies, then
he or she assumes that others will also see the justice of the captor's
cause and will make the necessary concessions to bring about one's
release. If, on the other hand, the hostage rejects the captor and what
he stands for, then one assumes that others will do the same, with the

result that the hostage will be killed. Given these alternatives in a prolonged situation of life-threatening stress, it is understandable that many people succumb to the former, anxiety-reducing alternative. This phenomenon written large may also apply to the behavior of an entire society, especially one for whom the issues and the concessions demanded do not loom large in importance. To counteract this phenomenon, one must educate the public as to the implications of concession, the limitations of sovereign power to protect citizens against all forms of international terror, and the necessity for adopting a realistic resignation that some problems are not wholly solvable, while some solutions are worse than the problems they were designed to solve.

TERRORIST VICTIMIZATION: LONG-TERM CONSEQUENCES

Three developments have contributed to a greater awareness of the consequences of brief, highly stressful situations. First, the raising the consciousness in the West as to the sequelae even of brief terrorist episodes without injury or loss of life. This has occurred because of the proliferation of these episodes, their presentation on television because of their high human interest, and their fictional dramatization in novels, plays, and movies. Although these presentations do not emphasize the sequelae of the terrorist attacks, they excel in dramatizing the uncertainty, suspense, and horror of the spectator-participants in these episodes. The viewer then draws his or her own conclusions as to how one would respond in the short and long haul to such an experience.

Second, there have been a number of other acts or threats of acts of violence on people that have captured the public imagination: Victims of violent crime against persons, rape, evacuation of peoples from ecologically contaminated areas (e.g., Love Canal, Three Mile Island) are a few of the examples that come to mind.

Third, the society as a whole has become well aware of the delayed and long-term consequences of combat stress by witnessing the post-discharge adjustment and behavior of Vietnam War combat veterans. The term "post-traumatic stress disorder" has been widely applied to this phenomenon and, to an increasing extent, to the other forms of victimization, albeit episodes of brief duration, cited above.

In Chapter 19, Ayalon and Soskis conducted a long-term follow-up of the adjustment of five survivors of one of the major terrorist attacks to take place in Israel, the murder of 22 adolescents and the wounding of 56 others on May 16, 1974. These young adults were asked to assess those intrapersonal and interpersonal behaviors that helped or hindered their coping with the active crisis and with the aftermath of the terrorist attack in the six years that followed. All behaviors were classified on three continua: (1) behaviors performed by oneself or others; (2) during the crisis or since; and (3) the positive or negative impact of these behaviors on effective coping.

If one examines the content of the verbatim responses given by one of the interviewees, it is apparent that she is suffering from a mild-to-moderate case of post-traumatic stress disorder as evidenced by her fears, phobic reactions, hypersensitivity to sudden noise, and strong, but vague, apprehensiveness about the recurrence of such an attack. The reasons for these chronic sequelae may be found in other responses given by this young woman and by the other interviewees:

1. The terrorist attack was highly traumatic, not only because of the number of dead and injured, but also because they felt they were abandoned by the adults. Some adults escaped at the onset and the remaining adults failed to function as leaders. There was no leadership during the 16-hour tense period before the Israel Defense Force attacked.

2. The survivors were forgotten in the immediate aftermath of the attack. After all, they were alive, possibly uninjured, whereas countless others were seriously injured or dead. In the annual memorials to the victims of this particular episode, these survivors felt left out, as if their continuing suffering and heroic efforts to reconstitute their lives were not worthy of note.

3. There was a half-hearted effort to bring the survivors together as a self-help group, but it was unsuccessful. In retrospect, treatment from the beginning should have been group oriented both for the initial stress reactions and for the subsequent chronic symptoms that were consistent with post-traumatic stress disorder. Survivors saw themselves as insiders, and age peers and adults as outsiders. This was an astute and psychologically understandable perception, but they never developed the group cohesiveness to gain enough from being insiders to compensate them for what they lost by exposure to the traumatic event.

4. The survivors also suffered from internal schism because of disagreement and lack of clarity as to the distribution of funds given by a well-meaning public to facilitate the recovery and rehabilitation of the survivors. Some were resentful and others were guilty about a possibly inequitable distribution of these funds. Financial compensation should have been handled in a public and responsible manner so as to contribute to group cohesiveness and to individual rehabilitation.

5. The responsible adults in the community, e.g., the teachers and members of the mental health professions, were untrained in these matters and implied that the survivors either were malingering or were neurotically preoccupied with themselves. These unfortunate interactions alienated the survivors and encouraged them to blame themselves for their chronic symptomatology.

VICTIMS OF WAR AND VICTIMS OF PEACE

If the victims of terrorist attack or other acts of war do not always receive the sympathetic and enlightened treatment that they merit, then the victims of peace are even more neglected or maligned. The major theme of Chapter 20 (Toubiana, Milgram, and Falach) was that the settlers of the Yamit region evicted from their homes to restore all of Sinai to Egypt were hapless victims of the peace process.

There was no professional or public recognition of the anguish over leaving homes and farms built with their own hands. A pioneer way of life they had enjoyed for nearly a decade with the blessings and praise of the society ended with the razing to the ground of all buildings. The former settlers were themselves calumniated in the national media for placing greed above country in pressing for steep financial compensations and in trying to thwart the road to peace. Understandably, they reported significant symptomatology during the uncertain waiting period, from the government commitment in 1978 to withdraw from Sinai to final implementation in 1982, and a reduction of symptomatology after the uncertainty was resolved and they had begun to rebuild their lives and communities. Because of the group character of these communities, settlers were able to withstand the pressure toward self-blame or alienation from society rather well. Nevertheless, their status as victims of the peace process was not recognized until very recently. The implication for the mental health field is clear. A person being evicted from his home is a victim even if one's politics and behavior under stress are not attractive to the society at large or to members of the media or the mental health professions in particular.

WHAT SUPPORTS THE HOME FRONT
DURING WAR?

Most comprehensive theories of stress and coping emphasize social resources along with personal resources as buffers to the direct effect of stressful life situations on the physical and mental health of individuals and on their functioning during crises and thereafter. In Chapter 21, Hobfoll attempts to refine the concept of social support systems by integrating the concept within an ecologically based model of person-environment fit. In this model memories of past traumatic experiences as well as apprehensive expectations of future traumatic experiences and losses exercise a disruptive effect, no less than the current appraisal of the ongoing crisis. The model is dynamic in that appraisals, value orientations, and coping behaviors evolve and are modified by changing events and their consequences. There are also changes over time in the kind and amount of support systems needed and the support systems that are available.

In addition, Hobfoll examined some of the implications of his theory in studies of the effect of personal and social resources on emotional upset in adult civilians at the height of the war in Lebanon and found that certain kinds of social support increase rather than decrease an adverse emotional reaction. In a second study a year later, as the war was winding down, he found that male students were more affected by personal war-related events than women students and related this finding to the different military roles and identifications of men and women. These and other findings served to accentuate the heuristic value of his comprehensive stress model and to recommend its application to stressful events and crises other than war.

18

The Psychological Impact of Terrorism on Society: A Two-Edged Sword

NEHEMIA FRIEDLAND and ARIEL MERARI

The last 15 years have been marked by the proliferation of political terrorism, which has reached an unforeseen incidence. Terrorism has proved to be a more serious problem than anticipated (Jenkins, 1982a), and it challenges both policymakers, burdened with the design of countermeasures, and social scientists, who are called upon to explain it.

Terrorism's unique nature is revealed by two phenomena. First, public perception of the threat and danger of terrorism seems to be disproportionate to terrorists' actual capabilities.

> No band of terrorists is a match for the smallest standing army or indeed any metropolitan police force. None can command the resources of the tiniest nation. *Yet terrorism has been characterized as a worldwide menace.* (Kupperman, 1982, p. 27, italics ours)

Second, terrorism, more than any other form of warfare, has an impact on a target group immensely larger than that of the immediate victims and often on populations beyond that against which the terrorist act is directly aimed (Mickolus, 1977). Taken together, these phenomena suggest that terrorism bears primarily on individuals' perceptions, on the "public mind"; in other words, it is a form of psychological warfare.

The psychological impacts of political terrorism are potentially manifest in individuals' emotional and attitudinal responses. In the realm

243

of emotions, the fear and concern for personal safety that terror tactics might give rise to is a revealing indicator of their effectiveness. One could argue, of course, that terrorists' ability to sow widespread fear hardly needs proof as it is obvious that violence and particularly the terrorists' hallmark, randomly targeted violence, are anxiety inducing. It should be noted, however, that terrorism has claimed relatively few casualties to date, and that in most countries the actual probability of incurring harm from terroristic activity is only a fraction of, say, the risk of death or injury in vehicle accidents or common crimes. Hence, the power of terrorism to intimidate should not be taken for granted.

Intimidation and the induction of fear are not the ends of terrorist activity but rather means to effect political change. Their violence is predicated on two assumptions: (1) Violent action can force the causes pursued by terrorists into the forefront of an indifferent public's awareness. (2) Faced with the choice between continuing violence and acceptance of the terrorists' demands, the public might opt for the latter. Thus, the attitudes that the targets of political terrorism develop toward its perpetrators, their objectives, and the actions that ought to be undertaken vis-à-vis them constitute telling measures of the effectiveness of terrorism.

The study reported herein examined the reactions of the Israeli public to terrorism. During 1979, the calendar year in which the study was conducted, 271 terrorist incidents took place in Israel and the administered territories, resulting in 23 dead and 344 injured (Merari, 1983). The study assessed the degree of fear and concern for personal safety caused by terrorist activity in Israel, attitudes toward political solutions to the Palestinian problem, and attitudes toward various counterterrorist measures.

METHOD

The attitudes of Israeli citizens toward terrorism were surveyed during April and May 1979. The results of the survey were classified until recently. The survey was conducted under the auspices of the Jaffee Center for Strategic Studies, Tel-Aviv University. The survey items were designed to assess fear and concern for personal safety, attitudes toward the PLO and possible solutions to the Palestinian problem, and attitudes toward various counterterrorist measures. These items were incorporated in a public opinion poll that is routinely administered, every two weeks, by the Israel Institute for Applied Social Research.

Sample and Procedure

The survey was administered twice, on May 6–8 and May 27–29, 1979, each time to 500 respondents. These were sampled from the adult Jewish population in the four largest cities in Israel (Jerusalem, Tel-Aviv, Haifa, and Beersheba). On April 22, while preparations for the study were underway, a hostage incident occurred. Terrorists broke into a housing complex in Naharia, a town in the northern part of the country. A young girl was killed in the process. The terrorists then tried to escape, taking hostage the girl's sister and father. The two were killed by the terrorists after the latter realized that they had been intercepted and were surrounded by security forces. Four survey items, designed to assess the degree of fear and concern elicited by terrorist acts, were administered within four days of this incident, on April 24–27, to a sample of 500 respondents. One of the four items was administered again during the two survey periods in May. In sum, three items were administered to 500 respondents, one item to 1,500 respondents, and 13 items to 1,000 respondents.

RESULTS

Fear and Concern for Personal Safety

Table 1 contains data that describe the levels of fear and concern expressed by the respondents. The data in this table were collected immediately after the Naharia incident, and they depict an extremely high level of worry and concern. Ninety-three percent worried about terrorist incidents in the country at large, and 88% about terrorist actions against Israelis abroad. A smaller, though still large, proportion of the sample (73%) was extremely worried or worried about the possibility that terrorist acts might be perpetrated in their vicinity.

The high degrees of worry and concern may be attributed to the temporal proximity to an actual incident. A comparison of the responses given to item 1 within 96 hours after the Naharia incident and several weeks later suggests, however, that the high level of worry was only partially due to such temporal proximity: Seventy-nine percent expressed, immediately after the Naharia incident, extreme worry or worry that they or members of their family might get hurt from terrorist actions. This proportion declined only slightly, to 73%, several weeks later.

The levels of fear and concern were only marginally affected by dem-

TABLE 1
Degrees of Worry Expressed Immediately after the Naharia Incident[a]

Item	Extremely worried	Worried	Somewhat worried	Not worried	Not at all worried
1. Are you worried about the possibility that you or members of your family might be hurt by terrorist actions?	48	31	11	7	3
1a. Several weeks after the incident.	36.5	36.5	14.5	8.5	4
2. Are you worried about terrorist action in the country at large?	68	25	5	2	0
3. Are you worried about terrorist action in your vicinity?	48	25	13	10	4
4. Are you worried about terrorist action against Israelis abroad?	49	39	7	3	2

[a]All values in this and subsequent tables are percentages.

ographic variables. The proportion of females who expressed extreme worry (item 1) was higher than the proportion of males (79.11% versus 66.02%, respectively). Worry was also related to educational level: 87.69% of those with an elementary education, 74.81% of those with a secondary education, and 60.87% of those with university education expressed extreme worry or worry.

Attitudes Toward the PLO and Possible Solutions to the Palestinian Problem

The data presented in Table 2 show that an overwhelming majority held negative attitudes toward recognizing the PLO as the legitimate representative of the Palestinian people and toward the establishment of an independent Palestinian state. On the other hand, more than half favored granting autonomy to the inhabitants of the West Bank and Gaza Strip. These regions, which are heavily populated by Palestinians, have been occupied by Israel since the 1967 Six-Day War. None of our respondents was an inhabitant of these regions.

Items 8 to 10 were designed to relate the above political attitudes to the effects of terrorism. The relevant data are depicted in Table 3. More than 90% of the respondents regarded terrorism as a reason to deny the PLO a representative status and to avoid political change in the areas occupied by Israel, be it the granting of autonomy or the establishment of an independent Palestinian state.

Attitudes Toward Counterterrorist and Retaliatory Measures

The data presented in Table 4 indicate that the majority of respondents supported the adoption and use of extreme counterterrorist action. Countermeasures that do not endanger civilians or innocent bystanders received stronger support (see items 13, 15, and 17). Yet action that might result in the killing of innocents was also substantially supported (e.g., item 16).

Demographic variables had some effect on the degree to which the various countermeasures were supported. The violent suppression of riots was more frequently favored by males (86.87%) than by females (78.57%). The demolition of houses was more strongly supported by religious (84.75%) than by nonreligious respondents (77.5%). In addition, a higher proportion (91.1%) of the religious respondents than the nonreligious ones (83.96%) favored the imposition of curfews.

The most persistent effect of demographic variables can be attributed to the respondents' levels of education. The relevant data are presented

TABLE 4

Degrees of Support for Various Counterterrorist Measures

Item	Strongly support	Support	Oppose	Strongly oppose
To what extent do you support the				
11. Demolition of houses that harbored terrorists?	56.5	23.5	14.5	5.5
12. Forceful suppression of riots in areas occupied by Israel?	50	32	14	4
13. Deportation of individuals who held contacts with terrorist organizations?	62	28	8	2
14. Imposition of curfews?	48.5	38.5	9.5	3.5
15. Retaliation against terrorist bases, provided it does not endanger civilians?	70.5	24.5	3.5	1.5
16. Bombing of terrorist bases, even if it jeopardizes civilians?	44	31.5	19	5.5
17. Assassination of terrorist leaders?	73	19.5	6	1.5

TABLE 2
Degrees of Support for Political Solutions

Item	It definitely should	I think it should	I think it should not	It definitely should not
5. In your opinion, should Israel recognize the PLO as the Palestinians' representative?	3	8	14	75
6. In your opinion, should Israel grant autonomy to the inhabitants of the West Bank and Gaza Strip?	18.5	39	18.5	24
7. In your opinion, should Israel consent to the establishment of an independent Palestinian state in the West Bank and Gaza Strip?	4.5	8	19.5	68

TABLE 3
The Effect of Terrorism on Willingness to Accept Political Solutions

Item	It is certainly a reason to	I think it is a reason to	I think it is a reason not to	It is certainly a reason not to
In your opinion, is terrorism a reason to or a reason not to				
8. Recognize the PLO as the Palestinians' representative?	1	3	18	78
9. Grant autonomy to the inhabitants of the West Bank and Gaza Strip?	1.5	6.5	20.5	71.5
10. Agree to the institution of an independent Palestinian state?	1	2.5	18	78.5

in Table 5. Although the differences among the categories are quite small, the overall pattern of results suggests an inverse relationship between individuals' educational level and the degree of support for extreme counterterrorist measures.

DISCUSSION

The present investigation sought to assess the psychological reactions of a public that has been exposed for a considerable length of time to the threats and actions of terrorists. The survey was designed with a view to the essence of terrorism, that is, the attempt to alter through intimidation a target population's attitudes and behavior. Accordingly, particular attention was given to the emotional and attitudinal impacts of terrorism, as well as to the relationship between the two.

Regarding emotional impacts, the data suggest that terrorism's ability to intimidate and to induce worry and concern exceeds disproportionally the actual damage it causes. As already noted, in the year of the survey, 271 incidents occurred, resulting in 344 injured and 23 dead. The actual probability of being victimized by terrorist activity, especially in the cities sampled, was extremely low, estimated at less than one-twentieth of the likelihood of being hurt in a road accident. Yet a large majority of the respondents expressed worry about the risk of personally incurring the consequences of terrorism. It might be that in the case of terrorism, the randomness of the threat and particularly its perceived *uncontrollability* dramatically enhance its impact. Thus, although the risk of vehicle driving may be far greater than the danger of terrorism, the car driver is usually reassured by a subjective feeling of control, which the potential victim of terrorism lacks.

TABLE 5

Degrees of Support ("strongly support" + "support") for the Various Countermeasures, According to Different Educational Levels

	Elementary	Secondary	University
Demolition of houses (item 11)	86.36	81.57	71.82
Deportation (item 13)	93.40	91.19	85.19
Curfews (item 14)	90.82	88.44	83.96
Bombings (item 16)	83.16	75.84	63.16

The survey results indicate that terrorism has failed to produce the change in attitudes sought by its perpetrators. A majority of the respondents was opposed to recognizing the PLO, to political solutions to the Palestinian problem, and regarded terrorism as a sufficient reason to reject such solutions. Most respondents favored, instead, the reliance on extreme counterterrorist measures.

The hardening of Israelis' attitudes toward terrorists and their objectives was also revealed by the respondents' unanimity of opinion. Response distributions were only marginally related to demographic variables. The effects of such variables were only manifest in the context of attitudes toward counterterrorist measures, and within this context, only the respondents' educational level yielded a consistent effect.

Taken together, the data concerning the emotional impact of terrorism and its effects on attitudes did not bear out the rationale that governs terroristic action: Despite the widespread concern and worry revealed by these data, there was no evidence of any willingness to politically concede to terrorists. On the contrary, and as already noted, the majority advocated the adoption of harsh measures against terrorists. Thus, at least insofar as Palestinian terrorism and the Israeli public are concerned, terrorism proves to be counterproductive.

This finding raises more general questions regarding the effectiveness of terrorism as a tool designed to achieve political change, and about the validity of the intuitively compelling assumption that popular willingness to accept such change is a simple, direct function of the depth of fear induced by terrorist acts. Some doubt about the validity of this assumption derives from research on the attitudinal or behavioral impacts of fear-arousing acts (e.g., Janis & Feshbach, 1953; Leventhal, 1970; Mewborn & Rogers, 1979; Rogers, 1975; Rogers & Mewborn, 1976). More specific doubts stem from the low incidence of political changes that can be unequivocally attributed to terrorism. Recent history shows that cases in which terrorists have succeeded in obtaining their principal political goals are rare. In most of them, terrorism was used in the course of campaigns for national liberation, conducted against colonial powers. Such were the cases of the Jewish struggle against the British in Palestine, the Ethniki Organosis Kypriakou Agoniston (EOKA) against the British in Cyprus, the Mau Mau against the British in Kenya, the Front de la Libération Nationale (FLN) against the French in Algeria, and the Frente de Libertacao de Mocambique (FRELIMO) against the Portuguese in Mozambique. In all these cases, terrorism played a decisive role in wearing out its target populations to the degree of accession to the terrorists' demands. Characteristically for these examples of terrorist success, however, the importance of the issue at stake was far greater for the terrorists than for the targeted populations. For the latter, conceding to the terrorists' demands was relatively inconsequential.*

The preceding examples along with our survey data suggest that the determination of a target population to adhere to its political positions in the face of terrorism is governed not only by the perceived intensity of the actual and potential terrorist assault, but also by the perceived importance of the positions under threat. The joint effect of these two factors is schematically presented in Figure 1.

The curve presented in Figure 1 comprises by no means a "best fit" to empirical data. Data of a kind and range that are needed for empirical curve fitting are currently unavailable. The curve should, therefore, be regarded as a convenient, graphic representation of a theoretical proposition.

Two characteristics of the proposed curve are noteworthy. First, it represents a departure from the commonly held assumption that the public's willingness to concede is *linearly* related to the intensity of terrorism. This assumed linearity might have been valid if the cost of adherence to its positions were the sole determinant of the public's resolve to resist terroristic pressure. There are grounds to propose, however, that the relationship between individuals' willingness to alter their attitudes and behaviors and the intensity of attempts to forcefully induce such change is shaped by two conflicting factors (e.g., Brehm, 1966; Friedland, 1976). On one hand, utilitarian considerations and the cost of resisting change tend to produce a positive relationship between individuals' readiness to change and the intensity of raw power that is brought to bear on them. On the other hand, threats are usually perceived as illegitimate modes of influence, and they, therefore, promote resentment and resistance. This effect might be particularly potent when terrorism is employed to compel political change. Moreover, the more insistent the influence attempt (e.g., the more violent and persistent the terroristic campaign), the stronger the target's reluctance to abandon its attitudinal or behavioral positions.

Combining the conflicting effects just described, we propose that public resistance to terrorism is a curvilinear function of the intensity of the

---

*The successful terrorist and guerrilla campaign of the Zimbabwe African National Union (ZANU) and the Zimbabwe African People's Union (ZAPU) against the white Rhodesian regime is a clear exception. This case was unique, however, in at least two important respects. The whites were desperately outnumbered and were incapable of eliciting foreign or international support for their position. Thus, although they were struggling for vital issues, they could not realistically hope to prevail.

latter: Within the range of low to some moderate level of terrorist-action intensity, the public's willingness to yield to terrorist demands is negatively related to the intensity of terrorism. Within this range, in other words, the intensity of terrorism is insufficient to make the public reconsider the costs and benefits of adhering to its political positions vis-à-vis the issue in question, but is sufficient to challenge the public and to create popular animosity toward both terrorists and their causes. Thus, under conditions of low-to-moderate terror intensities, terrorism might result in a radicalization of public attitudes in a direction contrary to the terrorists' interests. Yet, beyond a certain threshold of suffering, popular steadfastness is likely to erode. Past this threshold, the more intense the terrorists' assault, the less resistant to concessions the public is likely to be.

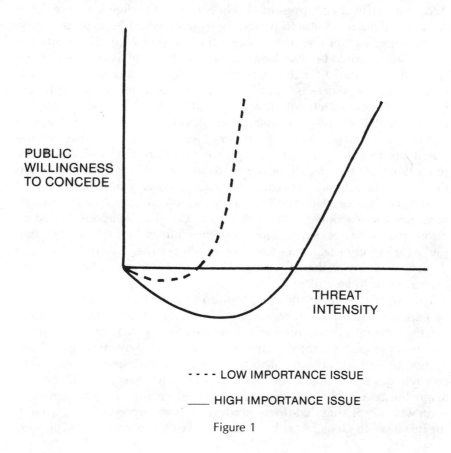

Figure 1

The second characteristic highlighted by Figure 1 is the *interactive* effect of the intensity of terrorism and the publicly perceived importance of the concessions demanded by terrorists on the public's willingness to concede. Two parameters of the proposed interaction ought to be noted. One, the greater the perceived importance of the issue at stake, the higher the location of the critical threshold referred to above, i.e., the function's inflection point on the intensity-of-terrorism dimension. Two, the greater the perceived importance of the issue at stake, the steeper the negative part of the function and the more moderate its positive part.

One may argue that the results of the present study are inconsistent with the functions shown in Figure 1, in that a process of radicalization in the public's relevant political positions appears to have taken place, despite a high degree of expressed concern about the effects of terrorism. According to the theory presented above, in a case of high fear of terrorist activity, public readiness to politically concede could be expected to be in the rising part of the curve, above the value of zero. This apparent inconsistency could be due, however, to the possible inadequacy of the survey methodology for the measurement of emotional states. The validity of such measures is typically threatened by semantic ambiguities. For instance, the statement "I worry about terrorism" could connote an emotional state ("I fear terrorism"), but it could also be the expression of a negative *attitude* toward terrorism. Hence, one cannot rule out the possibility that the widespread concern about terrorism reflected more the salience and centrality of the issue in the public's awareness than the degree of intimidation caused by it. Thus, it is not clear to what extent the measured public concern was indeed accompanied by behavioral fear reactions such as taking to carrying weapons, avoiding public places, or even emigrating from the country. It might well be that the actual level of fear was considerably lower than suggested by our data, that is, lower than the critical threshold that must be surpassed for terrorism to be effective.

The Israelis' support for the adoption of antiterrorist measures may be explained as a natural consequence of their almost total opposition to any form of political reconciliation with the PLO. However, from a different perspective, the extreme measures favored by our respondents appear to be disproportional to and quite unwarranted by the minor concrete damage brought about by Palestinian terrorism to date. Noting again the relatively small number of Israeli victims of terrorism, it is somewhat surprising that three-quarters of those surveyed were willing, for instance, to go as far as bombing terrorist bases *even if civilians were jeopardized*. Thus, to account for such widespread support of radical counterterrorist action, it is necessary to take into consideration three additional factors.

The first factor consists of public attitudes toward the terrorists' goals. That is, the Israeli public's support for extreme action might be a function not only of the actual damage caused by terrorists, but also of the ultimate political ends they strive for: in the case at hand, the annihilation of Israel. We suggest, in other words, that terrorists' stated objectives might be a more important determinant of public reaction than their proven ability to accomplish them.

This points to a second, general factor: It seems reasonable to assume that foreign terrorists challenging a state would draw a more unanimous and extremely negative public reaction than internal ("domestic") terrorists. This assumption rests not only on the known tendency to direct aggression toward the outgroup more readily than to the ingroup (see Tajfel [1982] for a review) but also on the truism that the very definition of internal terrorism as "internal" implies the existence of a political or ideological schism within society. Internal terrorists, in other words, are usually allied, ideologically or politically, with some segment of their society and therefore enjoy some measure of popular support.

Third, the greater leniency of response to internal as compared to foreign terrorist acts could also be due to different meanings that might conceiveably be attached to the two types of terrorism. Foreign terrorists, being part of an outgroup, are likely to be regarded as an "enemy" and their tactics construed as acts of "war." Such perceptions legitimize the adoption of ruthless and even brutal countertactics, as it is normatively accepted that states of war permit the relaxation of common moral and ethical constraints. By contrast, domestic, internal terrorists, who are members of the ingroup, are often regarded as social deviants or political criminals rather than as adversaries. Therefore, in responding to their acts, the standards adhered to must differ from those which apply to the former case, that of a warlike confrontation with foreign terrorists.

Terrorism appears, in conclusion, to be a two-edged sword. Our interpretation of the data suggests that terror tactics can be effective tools of political influence only when the actual or perceived threat exceeds a certain critical threshold. Below this threshold, terrorism is not merely ineffective but appears to cause a hardening of attitudes and a crystallization of opposition to the causes pursued by terrorists. Needless to say, the present analysis is by no means exhaustive. Our propositions, for one, primarily derive from the Israeli experience, which is probably unique in some important respects. Their applicability to other cases must, therefore, be verified. Second, a target public's resolve to withstand terrorist pressure is clearly affected by more than the two factors our model employs. For instance, the availability of effective counterterrorist measures, public hope and confidence that authorities are capable to release it from its predicament, or the degree to which concessions to terrorists bear on each individual's fate might importantly affect public steadfastness in the face of terrorism. We submit, however, that such factors are particular instances or corollaries of the more general, intensity-of-threat and issue-importance dimensions.

19

Survivors of Terrorist Victimization: A Follow-Up Study

OFRA AYALON and DAVID SOSKIS

As a form of victimization, political terrorism is at the same time personal and public. In a world concerned with nuclear mass destruction, contemporary terrorism has most often focused its violence on individuals or small groups of people. Yet political terrorism, in contrast with conventional assault or murder, is also inherently public. Terrorists *use* their victims to extort something from a third party, such as a target state, or to bring their cause to the center of public awareness through publicity in the mass media (Hacker, 1976; Jenkins, 1982b). They can do this best in societies that place a high value on individual human lives, and they often choose particularly valued groups, such as children, as their victims.

Coping with terrorist victimization by individuals and groups can be carried out on many levels, adapting Caplan's model of primary, secondary, and tertiary prevention (Caplan, 1964).

On the state level, *primary interventions* involve policy making to resolve the conflicts that lead to terrorist incidents and security measures to protect high-risk populations. *Secondary interventions*, which occur after hostages have been taken, include: (1) hostage negotiation and various assault options (Bolz, 1983), and (2) attempts to control the media and thus limit the terrorists' access to publicity. *Tertiary state interventions* include the interrogation, trial, and sentencing of terrorists both as a potential deterrent and as a booster of public morale.

On the clinical/social services level, *primary interventions* involve the development of relevant coping skills in the general population and in high-risk groups (e.g., self-defense directories, hostage behavior guides and training). *Secondary interventions* include therapeutic debriefing of hostages and crisis intervention with victim families and in the affected community. *Tertiary interventions* include extended treatment of post-traumatic stress disorders and rehabilitative services (Ochberg & Soskis, 1982)

Of these various types of intervention, tertiary clinical and social service programs have been the least developed to date. This may be due to the paucity of adequate long-term follow-up studies of victims of political terrorism and to emotional difficulties experienced by therapists engaged in these interventions (Ayalon, 1979, 1982a). Yet these studies are warranted since data from other groups, such as crime victims (Bard & Sangrey, 1986; Symonds, 1975) and American prisoners of war (Segal, 1974; Ursano, Boydstun, & Wheatley, 1981), have indicated that long-term psychological effects are common following these forms of victimization.

The collection and publication of long-term follow-up data on victims of terrorism have also been hampered by other factors: (1) As the dramatic events fade from the front pages, victims report a diminution of interest and sometimes, unfortunately, of help. (2) Involved clinicians are justifiably reluctant to publish data on readily identifiable patients. When this is done in an exploitative way, it exposes victims to a second victimization of callousness and labeling (Symonds, 1980), to which they are particularly sensitized in light of the major role played by the publicity of their plight in the terrorists' instrumental manipulation of the original hostage incident.

Longitudinal data on coping by former hostages have come from autobiographical accounts (Fly, 1973; Jackson, 1973) and from several published clinical studies (Hillman, 1981; Jacobson, 1973; Sank & Shaffer, 1979; Stöfsel, 1982; Strentz, 1982). A notable study is the detailed report by Ochberg (1982) on the experiences of the Dutch newspaper editor Gerard Vaders during and after the capture of a train on which he was a passenger by South Moluccan terrorists in 1975. This report is unique in its in-depth perspective on Vaders' individual efforts to cope with the event and its aftermath and on their interaction with family and social factors. As a journalist, Vaders was willing and able to share his experiences with others. Like other "successful" victims, he was also able to join in efforts directed at helping future victims and has participated actively in programs of the Dutch government directed toward this end.

Our data consist of structured follow-up interviews six years after the event with survivors of one of the major terrorist attacks ever to take place in Israel. The study focuses on the survivors' own subjective assessments of the personal and social factors that helped or hindered their efforts to survive during the attack and to cope in the aftermath.

HISTORICAL BACKGROUND

On May 15, 1974, around midnight, three armed Palestinian terrorists infiltrated the Israeli town of *M* from across the Lebanese border. After shooting at a passing van on the main road, they invaded an apartment building, killing in their beds a father, pregnant mother, and four-year-old boy, and severely wounding a five-year-old girl. Leaving the apartment, they shot at an old man on the street and proceeded to the local school, intending to hide there and wait to capture the children arriving in the morning. The school was not empty, however. One hundred and five teenagers and 10 adults from a religious high school in a nearby town, *T*, were on a school outing and were camping in the school building that night.

Upon reaching the school grounds, the terrorists forced one of the teachers to take them inside the building. The terrorists then occupied the school, holding over 100 captives at gunpoint. At the onset of the attack 17 pupils and six adults (three teachers, two guides, and the bus driver) escaped from second-floor windows. Several others were released later with messages to the negotiators outside. The escape route was soon barred by the terrorists, leaving as hostages over 80 children and three adults, two teachers and a nurse.

The next day pressures mounted on political decision makers to succumb to the terrorists' demands. Negotiations were conducted without results until the deadline given by the terrorists expired. The incident was concluded after 16 hours when the Israeli Defense Forces stormed the building. During the rescue raid the terrorists executed 22 children and wounded 56, shooting them at close range. The three terrorists were killed during the operation.

The hostages' families, residing in the neighboring town *T*, endured 12 hours of anguished suspense, having learned from the radio about their children's plight. Some of them rushed to the site of the attack and were witnesses to the traumatic results.

In the first hours after the assault, shock and chaos reigned. The population of *M* reacted with open expressions of grief and rage. Funerals in *M* and *T* were accompanied by violent outbursts directed not only at the terrorists but also at government representatives who were felt to be responsible for the security failure.

The bitterness of the victims' families was aggravated by a sense of accumulated deprivations. The residents of the two communities had several features in common: Most were refugees from Arab countries, immigrating to Israel in the late fifties and early sixties. They had large families to support and on the whole were considered socially disadvantaged. The families of the hostages were traditionally religious.

A previous study by Ayalon (1983) on the effects of terrorist attacks on Israeli communities has explored factors that contributed to their resilience or vulnerability. During the years 1974–1980 14 terrorist raids involving the capture and killing of hostages were launched against Israeli civilian communities: towns, villages, and kibbutzim. These varied in pretraumatic levels of communal organization, cohesiveness, self-reliance, and sense of purpose. Adaptive responses occurred in communities that were small, homogeneous, well established, autonomous, and self-reliant (e.g., kibbutzim). Adaptive community responses did not occur in communities overburdened with stresses of acculturation, alienation, economic difficulties, and political inferiority. The *M* and *T* communities fell in the latter category. In addition to these negative predisposing factors, the communities of *M* and *T* were exposed to a level of trauma and loss quantitatively much greater than that which occurred in other terrorist incidents of the same period (Ayalon, 1982b). Consequently, the immediate effects of the terrorist attack were much more severe and the resolution of the crisis more difficult.

METHOD

Data for the study were collected by means of structured interviews conducted in Hebrew by the senior author in the subjects' home community in Israel. Five subjects (two men and three women) were chosen randomly from an alphabetic name list of survivors. One choice had to be repeated, as the person could not be located. All consented to be interviewed. Two subjects were interviewed individually; the remaining three were interviewed together at their request. All interviews were tape-recorded with informed consent from the subjects for their publication as a contribution to research. The transcribed interviews were translated into English for analysis.

The interviews were structured by means of a series of open-ended questions to provide responses describing each of the eight possible combinations of the three dimensions of victim coping:

1. *Self versus others* refers to the different contributions to survival and coping of cognitive and emotional intrapsychic processes and behaviors initiated by the victim versus the expected or actual behavior of others (according to Soskis, 1983).
2. *Short versus long-term* refers to whether the coping responses occurred during the active crisis (the attack, the period of captivity, and the rescue raid) or thereafter until the present. The latter time period is the setting for some secondary and for all tertiary interventions.
3. *Positive versus negative* refers to the subjective evaluation by the survivors themselves as to whether the reported behavior was helpful to them in survival and coping or not. These subjective assessments do not always correspond with preconceived evaluative or diagnostic criteria. Moreover, the same behavior (e.g., talking to the terrorists) was evaluated as positive in the short-term, but negative and disturbing in the long-term perspective.

It is thus necessary to explore the various combinations of these dimensions to provide a realistic picture of victim coping.

The question format was: *What did you/others feel, think, or do during the attack/later that was helpful/disturbing to you?*

The complete interview protocols were first reviewed by each author independently, and appropriate categories were constructed for presenting the data. The two sets of categories were then combined and reconciled until a consensus was reached between authors.

RESULTS

Before the pooled data are presented in the form of general-response categories, the edited verbatim transcript of one subject's responses to the study questions is presented to provide some sense of the richness of the primary data. Rivka (a pseudonym) was 17 at the time of the attack, 22 at follow-up. She is currently married with one small child. She was injured during the assault and required several operations before recovering. After leaving the hospital she returned to school, and eventually graduated from a teachers' seminary and took a teaching job in special education. She sought and received psychotherapy for a one-year period following the attack. Rivka kept a diary regularly before the attack and made entries in it while recovering in the hospital. She was interviewed in her apartment. Her husband was present during part of the interview and cared for their baby at other times. Rivka was eager to talk and did so eloquently.

Self/Short-Term/Positive

1. I tried to pass the time by thinking about my childhood. I visualized pictures of myself from the age of three or four and pictures of my home, my family, the school, my boyfriend.
2. I remember my father always saying to me: "When there is any trouble, don't stay in the middle; always stay in a corner." I kept my place in the corner of the room, with my back to the wall.
3. I vowed that I'll read the Psalms every day and light a candle for Rabbi David Ben Moshe [a Moroccan Rabbi admired by Rivka's uncle] if I get out of this place alive. During the day I read the Psalms and secretly prayed to God to take us out and free us from these bloodthirsty murderers. He did hear my prayers.
4. One girl kept whining and I tried to calm her down. I told her things would change for the better, and with God's help, we would get out of there.

Self/Short-Term/Negative

1. After we had been kept hostage for hours, one of the terrorists looked for a student to take a written message to the police station. The terrorist was looking into my eyes, as if waiting for me to volunteer to go out. I wanted very much to go, but my whole body felt paralyzed and my tongue would not move. I was thinking that I did not know where the police station was located and that I would be shot on my way out. So I stayed, and in the end suffered so much and got wounded as well.

Others/Short-Term/Positive

1. There was someone who got killed later. He took care of us, comforted us, calmed us. He gave us water and divided our food equally. It really was very encouraging.

Others/Short-Term/Negative

1. There was someone who tried to organize us against the terrorists. He had many ideas on how to attack them; I didn't think they were reasonable. Each time he came up with a new idea, everyone became panicky. The girls in the room cried and begged him not to do it. It made us nervous.

Self/Long-Term/Positive

1. In the hospital, a week later, I started again to write in my diary using my uninjured arm. . . . [Rivka read a diary passage from her hospitalization describing negative premonitions before and during the trip: I had had the feeling that something bad was going to happen, but I tried to wave it off as a crazy idea. . . . On our way to M we climbed a rock. I had to fight a drive to tumble and to break a leg so I'd be sent back home. I wish I'd done that. Arriving at the school I felt a heavy load on my chest, could not participate in the games, could hardly sleep. I was waiting for something to happen. When the terrorists came, I was awake and somehow I was not surprised. I only wish I had shared all those feelings with someone before the attack. . . .] I felt lousy for not having acted on these warnings; everything could have been different now. But writing it all down was a relief.
2. Whenever someone asks for volunteers to run an errand, I immediately do so. For instance, once the principal asked one of the teachers to bring something from the other room; I jumped up to leave the room. I have a feeling that if I go out on an errand, I will somehow benefit from it.
3. I am always full of fears, but some thoughts of what happened helped me to pull myself together. Recently while I was teaching in the classroom there was a sudden loud noise. I thought: shells, bombing, or sonic boom? Instinctively, I ran to the door

in the middle of the lesson. But when I reached the door, I suddenly remembered that I had children in the class and was responsible for them. I then immediately returned to my place in the classroom. It reminded me of how our teachers left us; I had been terribly angry with them at the time. I will *not* do the same thing.

Self/Long-Term/Negative

1. I found it very difficult to go a few yards away from home. My mother would go out to throw out the garbage and I would call, "Mommy, Mommy," just like a baby. I wouldn't even let her go shopping. About six months later I stepped out of the house. . . . Even now I never travel to dangerous places.
2. My life today is affected by what happened in *M*. I wake up on hearing even the slightest noise. I immediately run to the window to see what is going on. A few times when I woke up in the middle of the night I ran right to the door, to escape. Then I suddenly remembered that I was at home and the door was locked. I took my baby out of bed and held him. I also woke my husband and he had to calm me. These things happen quite frequently, whenever a strange noise reminds me—not to mention real "katyushot" [Russian-made rockets fired by Palestinian terrorists into Israel].
3. When I was looking for an apartment, the only thing I thought about and also told my husband was: "I should not live on the first floor—too dangerous, too close; the second floor—maybe I won't have enough time to hide; the third floor is the best, because the terrorists won't make it up there." That's why I chose the third floor.
4. When I'm alone in the house in the evening, I start to worry: If they enter, where would I hide? What would happen if the child cries? They would hear him.
5. We have a gun in the house. Although I am afraid to touch it, I run to it when there is even the slightest noise, as though it could take care of me. This happens almost daily.
6. I have a very insecure feeling about the future, tremendous fear. If I buy a new dress or something for the house, I will use it immediately, because I might not be able to use it later.
7. Six years have passed, but to me it seems as though it happened yesterday. Time isn't on my side. Six years—that's for an outsider, a stranger, but not for someone who went through it.

Others/Long-Term/Positive

No responses.

Others/Long-Term/Negative

1. The social security doesn't help at all. I am not the sort of person who raises hell, so I didn't get any help. I deserve it, though, because I can't fully use my injured arm and it's difficult for me to take care of my child.
2. A lot of money was collected from contributors, but none of it reached us. These contributions caused tension in our relationships with each other in the group. Some do not even say hello on the street because they are afraid the other person will find out how much money they received and from whom.
3. The teachers in our school did not understand us. When we cried in class or could not concentrate, they would blame us for taking advantage of what had happened, and for being lazy.

For the first six months after the incident Rivka described herself as regressed and essentially homebound. Despite the persistence of event-related fears, startle responses, and catastrophic expectations, she has adapted well in the important developmental areas of work, interpersonal relationships, and family. She was able to derive benefit from keeping a diary, a coping mechanism also utilized effectively by the Dutch journalist Gerard Vaders during the Moluccan train incident in 1975. Rivka was also able to use "some thoughts of what happened" to arrive at effective compensatory coping with later stressful events that reminded her of the incident and triggered fearful behavior. She was distressed by the lack of direct benefits to her from organized helping programs and by the perceived insensitivity of school personnel to psychological problems of the surviving students immediately after the incident.

It is of interest that one of our subjects was the volunteer student who left with the message referred to above. Although spared from injury during the assault, this other person suffered frustration and guilt over isolation from peers, including long-term emotional and behavioral effects ("until this day I feel lousy"). The contrast of these two accounts illustrates the profound dilemma in coping during crisis and later adaptation posed by hostage incidents for even the healthiest victims.

The pooled data from all subjects are summarized in Table 1. The number of subjects making each response is given in parentheses.

TABLE 1
Coping Responses

Self/Short-Term
  Positive
    Helping/taking care of other hostages (3); seeking physical safety (2); nervous eating (2); trying to influence terrorists (2); sustaining effort despite wounds (2); suggesting attacking terrorists (1); believing he/she would be rescued (2); thinking only of self (2); palliating imagery (1); religious thinking and behavior (4); jokes/humor (1)
  Negative
    Feeling trapped/incapacitated by danger (3); defensive sleeping and unawareness (2); misidentifying terrorists as Israeli soldiers (2); feeling worried or guilty about parents (2); anger at teachers fleeing and abandoning the hostages (1); frustration/guilt at separation from peers (left with message) (1)

Others/Short-Term
  Positive
    Heroic friend who got killed took care of us (3); direct physical rescue (2)
  Negative
    Hostile or inconsistent behavior by terrorists (3); abandonment by teachers (3); unrealistic plans to attack terrorists (2); insincere efforts to calm hostages (2); nobody helped at all (2)

Self/Long-Term
  Positive
    Helping other former hostages (2); sharing with other former hostages (2); safety-seeking rituals (2); compensatory behaviors (2); denial/avoidance of incident (2); self-reliance (1); religious faith/observance (1); keeping a diary (1); anger/revenge (1); physical injury externalized problems (1)
  Negative
    Discomfort/insecurity with survival (3); phobias/catastrophic expectations (2); startles easily/is hyperalert (2); sleep/dreaming disturbed (2); remembering incident "like yesterday" (2); anger at teachers who fled (2); upset by reminders of incident (2); incident-related guilt (1); lack of trust (1); identity confusion (1)

Others/Long-Term
  Positive
    Family support/care (1); care by physicians (1); vocational help from officer in military (1)
  Negative
    Harassment/blame (4); insensitivity/lack of understanding (3); ineffective psychological services (3); ineffective social/financial services (3); labeling/stigmatization as victim/survivor (3); selfishness/lack of caring (2); lack of survivor group cohesiveness (2)

Religious thinking and behavior was the most frequently mentioned self-initiated, short-term, positive coping response. Significantly, although only one subject mentioned religious faith or observance as a long-term positive factor later in the interview, two other subjects mentioned positive short-term religious perspectives in their descriptions of coping while a hostage. Other helpful cognitive factors (such as palliating imagery and belief in rescue) are clearly analogous to traditional religious behavior, but may be true of many secular people in life-threatening crisis situations.

Helping or taking care of other hostages was reported by three of five subjects as a behavior helpful to *them*. This response was also valued in long-term coping. The adaptive role of religious, ethical, and altruistic behavior in high-stress captivity experience has been commented on in other situations (Ochberg & Soskis, 1982; Soskis & Ochberg, 1982) and by other authors (Frankl, 1955; Sledge, Boydstun, & Rabe, 1980; Stockdale, 1978). Negative "self" factors mentioned by the group were predominantly maladaptive defensive adaptations (e.g., sleeping, unawareness, misidentification of terrorists) to the overt threat of the hostage situation, reactions observed in other hostage incidents (Ochberg, 1982; Strentz, 1982).

The contribution of others to one's short-term coping was seen as less significant and more negative by our subjects than their own coping response. This is reflected in the number of responses (17 "other" versus 33 "self") and the preponderance of negative responses (12 negative versus five positive) in "other/short-term." Two subjects felt that nobody had helped them at all during the incident. Three of our subjects, however, mentioned the sustaining role of one heroic friend described by Rivka who "stood by the window and talked all the time. He transferred what the terrorists told him to the soldiers downstairs. He took it on himself to organize the gang. He brought us water and food. He could have escaped when the terrorist wasn't looking. When he saw the terrorist start to shoot, he jumped on him. The terrorist shot five bullets into him." Another subject described him aptly as becoming "like a father to us. . . . I'll never forget him for as long as I live because he helped me a lot and also helped my brother."

The preponderance of negative behavior by others is largely accounted for by the hostile and inconsistent behavior of the terrorists and by the perceived abandonment of the students by their adult teachers and guides. The vacuum in group leadership was reflected in the predominantly negative evaluation of plans to attack or thwart the terrorists.

On long-term coping, too, "self responses" are more frequent than "others" (33 versus 23) and are balanced for positive and negative (15 versus 18). "Other" responses are overwhelmingly negative (20 versus three positive).

Although the study interviews did not include focused clinical inquiry, scrutiny of the five protocols revealed that three clearly meet the current diagnostic criteria for post-traumatic stress disorder (APA, 1980), the remaining two subjects reporting several of the characteristic symptoms (e.g., catastrophic expectations, startle response, sleep disturbance, lack of trust).

The number of positive responses of others to long-term coping was disappointingly small. Three, including Rivka, were unable to name *any* positive response of others. Family support and physician care were mentioned by one subject and vocational help from an officer in the military by another. This distressing situation may be atypical but is nevertheless unacceptable to anyone assessing the adequacy of victim services.

Our subjects had no trouble, on the other hand, identifying many negative behaviors of others relating to the formal clinical/social services interventions.

For our subjects the lack of help from clinical and social services forms part of a broader negative picture of others' responses ranging from insensitivity and selfishness to active harassment and blame, and leading to their perception of the victim/survivor role as stigmatized. Although this tendency to harass and blame victims may seem incomprehensible on a superficial level, it has been observed in other settings (e.g., Bard & Sangrey, 1986). Perhaps the clearest analogy of this phenomenon is Lerner's "just world theory" (1977), in which observers of victimization who were powerless to help tended to attribute fault or undesirable traits to the victim. The observers' "just world" view is maintained, but the victim suffers "a second injury" (Symonds, 1980). In addition to the insensitivities and critical behavior of agencies, professional workers, and lay people, the suffering of our interviewees was clearly increased by their lack of cohesiveness.

DISCUSSION

The victim of terrorism could literally be anybody. Both the method and the message of terrorist attacks violate the rules of war and select innocent civilians and even children as their targets. Although these attacks are not a major source of mortality in our contemporary world, their effect reverberates far beyond those directly killed or harmed, and it is incumbent upon us to learn all we can from each one.

The incident that led to the victimization of our subjects was a particularly harsh and dramatic one. Moreover, our subjects were exposed to an additional dimension of victimization through the escape of most of the teachers and guides early in the incident. These factors magnify the negative effects of the incident, but the basic situation and its stressors are shared by hostage incidents everywhere. Several conclusions emerge from our study that can be fit into the scheme of primary, secondary, and tertiary interventions outlined earlier.

Although the present study bears most directly on clinical/social service interventions, it has several implications for governmental interventions as well. On the secondary level, the work of hostage negotiators is facilitated by a knowledge of what is going on "inside" the incident, including the reactions and coping efforts of hostages and their interactions with the hostage takers. Moreover, one or more hostages are often released during the course of an incident with messages or for medical reasons. The interrogation of the subject in the present study who was released with a message was hampered by his frustration and guilt at being separated from his peers. Attention to this psychological issue in the interviewing of released hostages will enhance their ability to help the authorities.

On the tertiary-state level, former hostages are a crucially involved group in reacting to legal and ceremonial efforts by government to deal with the aftermath of a terrorist incident, in terms of both deterrence and maintenance of public morale. One of our subjects highlighted this issue:

> All the important government officials came to the last memorial ceremony, five years after the disaster. They spoke and paid special attention to the parents of the dead. But they did not even mention, did not even say one word about those who were injured and about the other pupils. This really hurt me.

Survivors need to be included in ceremonial recognition, an inclusion that helps them and improves morale in all who live in the victimized communities. The importance of sensitive planning in such situations was highlighted by events surrounding the return of the American hostages from Iran, when some Vietnam veterans expressed anger and resentment at the contrast in their welcomes. Thus, official statements, ceremonies, and welcoming programs should be planned to include references to and recognition of other groups of victim–survivors whose traumatic memories may be revived by the current incident.

On the clinical/social services level, the present study provides a number of recommendations for primary interventions on behalf of high-risk groups. Coping while a hostage is clearly aided by religious thinking and behavior or other strategies aimed at maintaining meaning and hope, and by sharing with and caring for other hostages. Other helpful strategies include (1) humor, which has been mentioned repeatedly as a sustaining perspective by other former hostages and captives, and (2) efforts to record and "witness" the event through diaries or journals (Ochberg & Soskis, 1982). On the negative side, the study supports the advice given in most training courses that efforts by the hostages themselves to overpower their captors are likely to be dangerous and unsuccessful. Ayalon (1978) has undertaken the development of a manual of teaching materials for children at risk of war-related emergencies that emphasize a primary prevention approach. It may also be useful to familiarize possible victims with the range of common symptomatic sequelae experienced by former hostages. Although this carries the risk of "suggesting" symptoms, it may alleviate the secondary anxiety and feelings of isolation caused by their onset. In view of the high incidence of symptomatic sequelae in our study group, the potential benefit of such interventions may outweigh the risk.

The results of the present study support the need for active secondary interventions immediately following hostage incidents, such as those employed with the American hostages released from Iran. In that situation, the decision was made to detain the hostages in Germany for therapeutic debriefing before allowing them to be reunited with their families. Such an intervention may provide a crucial therapeutic opportunity for group work, since, as in our own sample, the group itself may not show much internal cohesiveness or, as in the case of the American returnees from Iran, may scatter widely geographically after release.

The same risk/benefit considerations of suggesting symptoms versus mitigating their impact (mentioned earlier in reference to primary interventions) apply to the process of therapeutic debriefing. It may be particularly important to focus on cognitions or behaviors that were positive in terms of short-term coping, but may entail negative consequences in the long term. One of our subjects felt helped by her efforts to communicate with her terrorist captors:

> I walked over to one of the terrorists who understood Hebrew and asked him why he was doing this. When he said that he

wanted to liberate his friends from prison, I asked if he did not think that there were other means of achieving this. I wanted to influence them to change their minds.

Later, however, the subject saw this behavior as negative:

Today, when I look back and think that I actually spoke with the terrorists, with those murderers, I feel awful. How could I even speak with them?

Some early therapeutic working through of feelings about behaviors that might have been helpful in their surviving or coping may help alleviate later inappropriate guilt. This same shift in the evaluation of hostage behavior is likely when the Stockholm syndrome (positive feelings or identification with terrorists and negative feelings toward the authorities) has been prominent (Strentz, 1982). The Stockholm syndrome was not a significant feature with our subjects, however, because the terrorists were cruel and inconsistent with these hostages.

The tertiary interventions provided were evaluated by the ex-hostages as negative:

Although they tried to form a group right after the incident to help us, it failed. It didn't continue. I don't think it helped me.

Although these efforts were not successful, we believe that this remains a worthwhile pursuit for former hostages. The unique and severe nature of terrorist victimization may make it difficult to share with family or friends. A group setting provides opportunities to share feelings about the incident and its aftermath and to explore and reformulate dependency attitudes and expectations from interpersonal relationships. Rivka herself distinguished between "insiders" and "outsiders," and the former group may well be a crucial stress-resistant resource of support. Major efforts should be made to bring former hostages together even for a brief period. An example would be the "reunion" arranged by the American government for the former Iran hostages in April 1981.

The difficulties in arranging therapeutic groups and the problems of geographical dispersal, as well as the variety of individual long-term adaptations, highlight the importance of locally available individual counseling and psychotherapy as a tertiary intervention. Clinicians working with former hostages will require some preparation for the special needs of these clients and will benefit from familiarization with the range of symptoms of post-traumatic stress disorder and of the short- and long-term coping responses that hostages typically manifest. Some traditional psychotherapeutic approaches may not be useful with this group. One subject was given a standard response when she spoke to her psychology instructors about therapy: "If you want to get treatment, go ahead; if you don't want to, it's OK too." She interpreted this to mean that she was the only one who could help herself and that others were not interested or available. For people whose sense of basic trust may have been severely challenged, an active, warm, and committed approach is important. Promises or reassurances need to be backed up for people susceptible to feelings of bitterness and of abandonment. The same person commented:

> I was told that when I graduated, they would assist me in finding a job. But meanwhile no one does anything; no one helps me to find a job. They shouldn't have promised to.

Former hostages are likely to require and benefit from active help with vocational readjustment and rehabilitation, especially when accustomed settings or activities are associated with traumatic memories and when self-esteem has been shaken.

The traditional approach to the psychotherapy of post-traumatic stress disorders includes the effort to help the patient work through the event and the reactions it aroused. Often the trauma is retold and/or relived many times within the therapeutic relationship. This repetition requires a *continuing* therapeutic relationship for its beneficial effect.

> After the attack, psychologists and counselors came. We had to tell and retell everything that had happened. I don't think it helped at all. . . . I don't even recall their names except for one. The social workers kept changing every month or two.

Administrative considerations are often invoked to explain this discontinuity, but it probably also involves the strains on therapists confronting victims of major catastrophes.

The long-term maintenance of therapeutic continuity is needed if specific cognitions and behaviors are to be evaluated accurately in the broad perspective of the patient's psychic structure, developmental needs, and realistic life situation. Before attempting to "treat" a nondisabling symptomatic or compensatory behavior, the clinician must determine what, if any, resources are available to replace its current function and whether it is in fact harmful. One of our subjects provided an example of such a "symptomatic" behavior, which she evaluated as positive, that might well be left alone.

> During the rescue operation one of my friends caught me and threw me out of the window. Since then I have felt that the window is the safest of all places. Whenever I am at a party, or anywhere else, I always place myself near the window. When I returned home from the hospital, I moved my bed next to the window. The window provides me with a sense of security.

Rivka's need to volunteer for errands falls in a similar category.

Four of our five subjects mentioned family as important in their coping. The families of former hostages will require support and guidance in helping their victim–members handle post-traumatic stress disorders and in reestablishing the family equilibrium. Often, the families themselves are exposed to extremely high levels of stress during and immediately after the incident. They too are victims and may require treatment. Family members provide the "frontline" social support system for former hostages and may be the only social support for some survivors.

Whether social support is seen as directly protective against the pathogenic effects of high-stress situations (Caplan, 1981) or as effective in ameliorating depressive or other symptoms (Aneshensel & Stone, 1982), it is a resource that must be fostered. Three of our subjects mentioned a relatively inexpensive but powerful and long-remembered intervention: the importance of being visited regularly when confined to the hospital.

The opposite of social support is the harassment and blame reported by four of five subjects. Clinicians must be on guard against victim-blaming aspects of their own countertransference, which, according to Lerner (1977), may be a relatively universal human tendency. He found that blaming the victim could be significantly lessened by any procedure that caused observers to identify with the victim: even simple instructions to "imagine yourself in the victim's place" (Lerner, 1977). Clinicians can utilize this technique themselves and seek to foster it in significant others who tend to blame former hostages. On the broader social level, publicity for victims and their portrayal as the stars and heroes of media accounts and dramatizations may have far-reaching effects. Although terrorists may be more glamorous than victims, it is the victims who have the more important lessons to teach us, and they should be given the opportunity to do so. Our subjects, and other victims of terrorism, have suffered and been scarred by their experiences. Yet they have managed to cope and to go on with their lives, making the best of the worst.

20

The Stress and Coping of Uprooted Settlers: The Yamit Experience

YOSEF TOUBIANA, NORMAN MILGRAM,
and HERZL FALACH

The phenomenon of being forcibly uprooted from one's home and having to resettle elsewhere is widespread. Urban renewal and the razing of old neighborhoods, political persecution and the forced emigration of people from their homeland to a new country constitute a major source of stress for many groups and countless individuals in all continents (Coelho, Yuan, & Ahmed, 1980). The deleterious effects of having to cut ties with one's familiar surroundings and to establish new ties in unfamiliar and possibly threatening settings are well documented (Tiryakian, 1980). As a consequence, a literature has accumulated on crisis intervention at the primary, secondary, and tertiary levels to facilitate the coping of displaced persons in an uprooting-resettling crisis (George, 1974; Kutash, 1980).

The present chapter is divided into two parts. In Part One, we investigated the adjustment of a group of evacuees shortly after they were evicted from their homes, and we related their adjustment to intra- and interpersonal stress-resistant factors (Toubiana, Milgram, & Falach, 1983). In Part Two, we concluded from these data and clinical observations that government officials, members of the mass media, and especially members of the community mental health field did not appreciate and consequently did not meet the mental health problems of these evacuees. In documenting this conclusion, it was necessary to provide considerable detail about the political controversy in which the former settlers were enmeshed. Recommendations were made to prevent professional insensitivity from occurring in future crises involving uprooting and resettling.

THE RAZING OF YAMIT

The present chapter deals with a unique group of evacuees—the former settlers of the Yamit region in the Northern Sinai who were evacuated as part of the peace settlement between Israel and Egypt in 1982. They differed from the kinds of evacuees typically reported in the literature. On the positive side of the ledger, they were not the disadvantaged, the poor, the elderly, or the ethnic minorities. On the contrary, they were largely cohesive young families, middle class, and prosperous by the country's standards. Moreover, they were being afforded the opportunity to settle in a nearby region as an intact community or to settle elsewhere on a family basis with full financial compensation.

On the negative side, their forced eviction was enacted by the government and supported by the majority of citizens in the very society that had encouraged their settling there to begin with. Moreover, the legitimacy of the ideological motivations for their settling in Yamit was now challenged, and their status in society plummeted sharply from that of pioneers to opponents of the public good and exploiters of the public treasury. In following their uprooting, we capitalized on a natural phenomenon to investigate their adverse stress reactions in relation to the changing uncertainties of their situation, their social cohesiveness, motivations, and support systems.

A HISTORICAL INTRODUCTION

The Yamit region is located on the northeastern tip of Sinai and the Mediterranean Sea bordering on Israel and the Gaza Strip. Several years after Israel occupied Sinai in the Arab-Israeli War of 1967, Israeli citizens were encouraged to settle in the region and to establish the city of Yamit and numerous agricultural settlements in the Yamit region, some collectivist (kibbutz) and others based on individual enterprise. Settlers had diverse motivations for coming to the region, ideological and materialistic, and all were endorsed by the society. Whatever their motivations, these communities were successful on all counts: People were prosperous and happy and were highly regarded by their fellow citizens living elsewhere in Israel.

This peaceful, idyllic world was shattered, ironically enough, by the national search for peace. When Anwar Sadat of Egypt made his historical visit to Jerusalem in November 1977, negotiations commenced for a peace treaty between the two countries. In September 1978 the Israeli parliament committed the nation to a gradual withdrawal from all of Sinai, the final stage of which was to be the evacuation of the Yamit region and the relocating of the settlers elsewhere in Israel. For the next three and a half years the settlers were in a quandary with potential for enormous pathological repercussions for several reasons:

1. It was not altogether certain that they would actually be uprooted. There had never before been a single instance of an Israeli settlement being uprooted because of political considerations. Moreover, significant, vocal groups within the government and the society opposed the treaty with Egypt or insisted that the treaty could be achieved without sacrificing Yamit itself.

2. During the delicate and protracted negotiations and step-by-step evacuation of Sinai, the government urged the settlers to remain in Yamit and to continue business as usual so as to maintain pressure on Egypt to live up to its commitments to the peace treaty. Yamit was to be retained as a trump card and surrendered to Egypt only when it became clear that the Egyptians were honoring their commitments.

3. During the tortuous negotiations and successive evacuations, some young people actually established new settlements in the Yamit region in order to thwart the return of the area to Egypt. These people, called *resisters* in this paper, lived, worked, and raised their children in the Yamit region for nearly three years. Their presence and the support that they received from some elements within the government and the society encouraged the original settlers to believe that in the end they would be able to remain in the region.

This tense and uncertain waiting period ended abruptly in April 1982 when Israeli soldiers forcibly evicted resisters and the remaining settlers from their homes in actions that were widely publicized on national television. After the eviction the settlements were razed to the ground.

PART ONE: AN EMPIRICAL STUDY

This study was conducted one month after evacuation of the Yamit region. The following questions were examined:

1. *The extent of symptomatology reported by settlers and resisters for the long waiting period and the immediate aftermath.* Given the traumatic character of the uprooting experience, we predicted substantial distress in settlers and resisters in both time periods and a reduction in symptomatology in the aftermath of the evacuation as compared with the tense, uncertain waiting period. We also predicted that the resisters would exhibit less distress than the settlers because their particular religious and nationalist motivations and support systems buffered them against the incursion of anxiety, depression, hostility, and other disruptive emotional reactions.

2. *The relationship of symptomatology to planning in advance for new eventualities.* Research has shown that planning and preparing in advance facilitate coping with long-term crisis situations (Coelho et al., 1980). Accordingly, we predicted that settlers who planned in advance for the eventual evacuation and were actually in their new homes by April 1982 would be less disturbed than settlers who delayed their resettlement programs and were in temporary quarters in the aftermath period.

3. *The relationship of symptomatology to social cohesiveness of group members.* We assumed that settlers sharing long-standing communal ties with their current group would cope better with the stress of uprooting and resettling than settlers lacking such ties. Accordingly, we predicted that settlers moving en masse to their new homes and communities would report less symptomatology than isolated settlers who had splintered off from their original groups and were now joining largely intact groups in establishing their new homes.

4. *The relationship of symptomatology to the kind and intensity of one's original motivations for settling in the region and to the extent of the fulfillment of these motivations.* We predicted that the stronger the motivations and the more these motivations were thwarted by uprooting, the greater the symptomatology. More specifically, we predicted that ideological motivations would be more strongly associated with symptomatology than materialistic ones. This prediction followed from the assumption that ideological motivations were more threatened by the uprooting experience, since materialistic motivations could be satisfied after suitable financial compensation in some other location.

5. *The relationship of symptomatology to the kind and intensity of support*

systems utilized by settlers and resisters during the establishment of their homes and to the erosion of these support systems during the uprooting process. Research has suggested that support systems facilitate coping with stressful situations by providing help in solving the urgent problems at hand and by buffering individuals against disruptive emotional stress reactions (Lieberman, 1982). Accordingly, we predicted that continued availability and utilization of support systems would be associated with a lower level of symptomatology.

Method

Subjects. Respondents were 100 former inhabitants of agricultural communities in the Yamit region. Subjects were about half male and half female. Most were married with both husband and wife responding. The majority (*n* = 80) constituted the settler group and had been living in the region from the very beginning. Mean years of residence was 7.51 (SD = 1.78). Respondents were between 28 and 48 years of age (mean age = 35.96), and their formal education was high school graduate or above. They were divided into four approximately equal subgroups. There were the *early resettlers*, already living in their new homes when evacuation finally occurred, and the *late resettlers*, residing in temporary housing south of Ashkelon while their new homes were being built. Each of these subgroups was further subdivided into *old-timers*, from the original group of founding settlers, and *newcomers*, who joined from founding groups that had broken up.

The resisters (*n* = 20) were younger (mean age 27.25), their educational background was religious-nationalist, and they had settled in Yamit three years earlier. They were uprooted from their homes in the final stages of the evacuation, and soon after they relocated to a new settlement in close proximity to their former homes in Yamit.

The cooperation of the respondents in filling out the prepared questionnaires was obtained through their leaders. The first author contacted leaders of five collective settlements, arranged for group sessions to explain the purpose of the study, and distributed the questionnaires directly to many respondents and indirectly to the others via their leaders. The percent return of completed questionnaires was 83%.

Measures. Criterion measures of coping included the following instruments: the Johns Hopkins Symptom Check List (SCL-90), developed by Derogatis (Derogatis, Lipman, Rickles, Uhlenhuth, & Covi, 1974); the Life Satisfaction Scale developed by Cantril (1965); and several indices of current attitudes, feelings of alienation from society, and reported ability to resume normal vocational pursuits.

The SCL-90 consists of 90 items yielding scores on nine symptomatic scales including anxiety, depression, etc. One scale (psychotic ideation) was deleted because its blatantly bizarre content was unsuitable for the respondents of the present study. Several items were dropped from the other scales because of content unsuitability, and the remaining 70 items were translated into Hebrew and provided scores on eight scales (listed in Tables 1 and 2) and one overall score of emotional upset. Respondents rated each item on a five-point scale from not at all bothered (1) to very much bothered by the symptom (5). They were asked to refer to the preceding week. Their overall score was regarded as an index of symptomatology in the aftermath period. Alpha correlation coefficients of the eight scales for settlers were found to be satisfactory: They ranged from .64 to .88, and the coefficient of the overall score was .92.

Four of the eight scales were considered especially sensitive to changing life circumstances and to reflect *state* rather than *trait* characteristics (Spielberger, 1966). These were scales of anxiety, depression, hostility, and somatization. The four remaining scales were regarded as referring to more stable characteristics that are less sensitive to change in crisis situations. These scales were obsessive-compulsive behavior, paranoid ideation, phobic anxiety, and interpersonal hypersensitivity. Accordingly, four items were selected from each of the first four scales and were combined to constitute a state scale rated with reference to the waiting period preceding the evacuation from Yamit. Respondents were first instructed to rate their symptomatic behavior on the 16-item scale for the waiting period and then to rate their behavior on the entire 70-item scale for the aftermath period.

Cantril (1965) instructed subjects on his life satisfaction scale to rate current, past, and future life satisfaction on a 10-rung ladder with 10 representing the optimal life and 1, the poorest. In our adaptation, respondents were instructed to rate their satisfaction before the government announcement to evacuate the region, their current satisfaction, and their contemplated satisfaction three years hence. Troubling concerns during the waiting period, measures of alienation from society during the uprooting process, and assessment of ability to resume normal work pursuits were also obtained.

The motivational scale consisted of five statements, each describing a different motivation for settling in the Yamit region. These were: (1) ideological—nationalist, socialist, and/or religious; (2) strategic—creating a permanent buffer zone between Egypt and Israel; (3) political— preventing the return of the settled area to Egypt; (4) personal—the challenge of settling in a new and barren area and making it fertile; and (5) materialistic—the search for a higher standard of living. Each statement was rated on a four-point scale from very important (1) to not at all important (4). Respondents also rated each statement on a four-point scale with reference to the extent to which each motivation was actually being fulfilled before the evacuation, with complete fulfillment rated 1 and none, 4.

The support system scale consisted of six sources of support designated in the research literature (Lieberman, 1982) as relevant to our situation: (1) the nuclear family; (2) the extended family elsewhere in Israel; (3) community leaders; (4) group cohesiveness; (5) personal ideology and belief system; and (6) national consensus, i.e., the ideological and moral support of the government and the society as a whole. Respondents rated each source of support on a four-point scale from very efficacious (1) to not at all efficacious (4). They were instructed to rate each source of support first for the period when they first settled in the region and second with reference to the waiting period of the uprooting process.

Results and Discussion of Data

Symptomatology during the waiting period. Per item means and standard deviations (in parentheses after the means) of the four crisis-sensitive scales for settlers and resisters are summarized in Table 1. Norms on American psychiatric outpatients and nonpsychiatric controls (Derogatis et al., 1974) are presented in Table 1 for comparison purposes. On inspection, we note that the scores of the settlers are comparable to those of the psychiatric reference group, and those of the resisters are comparable to those of the nonpsychiatric reference group. One-way analyses of variance of the four scales for settlers and resisters yielded highly significant F values ($p < .001$). Why the resisters reported that they were symptom-free during the tense waiting period, while the settlers reported a moderate amount of emotional upset, may be attributed to the differing motivations of the two groups. This issue is discussed in a subsequent section.

The highest means were reported for anxiety and depression followed by hostility and bodily complaints. One implication of the high internal consistency of the overall scale (alpha = .90) consisting of items from four different scales (anxiety, depression, etc.) is that people who reported that they were frequently anxious also reported that they were

TABLE 1
Means and Standard Deviations of State Scales in Waiting Period

Scale	Settlers	Psychiatric	Resisters	Normal
Anxiety	2.90 (1.08)	2.47 (.88)	1.45 (.55)	1.30 (.37)
Depression	2.88 (.94)	2.79 (.94)	1.55 (.58)	1.36 (.44)
Hostility	2.41 (.96)	2.10 (.93)	1.34 (.33)	1.30 (.40)
Somatization	2.05 (.94)	1.87 (.75)	1.08 (.15)	1.36 (.42)

frequently depressed, hostile, and physically uncomfortable (e.g., headaches, stomach upset). The nonspecificity of the emotional stress reactions of the settlers suggests (1) that these symptoms were state characteristics elicited by the stress situation rather than trait characteristics occurring across many different situations and (2) that they would decline in the aftermath period when uncertainty ceased and the stark reality of evacuation and its consequences confronted the settlers.

The settlers identified up to three problems troubling them during the waiting period. Their answers fell into three categories: uncertainty about the future (52%), concern about physical destruction of their homes (26%), and feeling rejected by the society because of allegations that they were holding out for unconscionable financial reparations (22%).

Symptomatology in the aftermath period. Means and standard deviations were computed for the 16 items in the overall SCL scale of 70 items that had been rated for the waiting period. Means and standard deviations for the four state scales for the settlers were 1.92 (.69), 2.24 (.79), 1.66 (.67), and 1.65 (.62), respectively. When t tests of correlated means were computed between waiting and aftermath period, highly significant reductions in the frequency of these symptoms were found on all four scales ($p < .001$). These frequencies were still well above those of the resisters or the nonpsychiatric reference group. The resisters remained at the same low frequency of symptoms as before.

Per item mean scores and standard deviations of the four trait scales of the SCL for settlers and resisters are summarized in Table 2, together with the norms of the reference groups. By inspection we note that the scores of the settlers are comparable to those of the nonpsychiatric and well below that of the psychiatric reference group. From these findings we may conclude that the settlers as a group were not pathologically disturbed individuals to begin with, and that their emotional upset during the waiting period and afterward represents their reactions to an ongoing collective and personal crisis. The mean scores of the resisters were so low as to suggest the possible use of denial in their emotional experience, in their self-report, or both.

Early versus late resettlers and newcomers versus old-timers. Two-way analyses of variance, early × late resettling and newcomer × old-timer, were computed on all symptom scales in the waiting and aftermath period for the settlers. Being an old-timer remaining with one's pre-evacuation group did not affect the symptomatology directly. There was

TABLE 2
Means and Standard Deviations of Trait Scales in Aftermath Period

Scale	Settlers	Psychiatric	Resisters	Normal
Obsessive-compulsive	2.12 (.91)	2.47 (.91)	1.24 (.61)	1.94 (.78)
Paranoid ideation	1.85 (.78)	2.16 (.92)	1.00 (.00)	2.09 (.85)
Phobic anxiety	1.22 (.44)	1.74 (.80)	1.20 (.40)	1.23 (.31)
Interpersonal sensitivity	1.70 (.72)	2.41 (.89)	1.08 (.57)	2.03 (.85)

a significant interaction ($p < .001$), however, reflected in a higher frequency of emotional distress in one group as compared with the other three: the newcomers who joined an early resettling group. Apparently for these people, the stress of resettling with its struggles and its invidious comparisons with the halcyon days of Yamit was greater than the compensation of having begun their resettling ahead of the late resettlers. That there was no disadvantage for the newcomers as compared with the old-timers in the late resettlers may be attributed to the timing of the self-report: They were apparently enjoying a moratorium of two months during which time they were becoming acquainted with old-timers in temporary quarters and did not yet have to cope with actual resettlement in their new community.

Settlers and resisters on other measures of coping. The other coping measures also confirmed the better adjustment of the resisters over the settlers. Their life satisfaction in the aftermath period was higher, 7.14 (1.84) versus 5.41 (1.59) on the 10-rung ladder ($p < .05$). They reported a lower social alienation score, 1.25 (.40) versus 1.65 (.54) on a three-point scale ($p < .01$). They resumed their normal work and living habits better, 3.56 (.73) versus 2.17 (1.00) on a four-point scale ($p < .001$). Clinical observations by the first author of settlers and resisters were consistent with these self-reports. One month after the evacuation the settlers were less confident, less content, and less able to resume normal functioning than resisters. Moreover, 70% described themselves as feeling alienated from the society as a whole because of the criticism expressed against them in the media. One optimistic note was their high life satisfaction in the past, 7.00 (1.72), and their still higher projected life satisfaction for the future, 8.24 (1.72).

Motivations for settling in Yamit. Means and standard deviations of motivations for settling in Yamit, their importance, and the degree of their fulfillment before the evacuation crisis are presented in Table 3. One-way analyses of variance were computed by motivation for the two groups. With the exception of national security, which was relatively important for both groups, all other F values were highly significant ($p < .001$), indicating marked differences between groups. It may be noted from Table 3 that for settlers, the most important motivations were standard of living and personal challenge, and these were the least important for the resisters. By contrast, the most important motivations for resisters were ideological and political (preventing the return of Sinai to Egypt).

TABLE 3
Means and Standard Deviations of Motivation Scores

Motivation	Importance		Fulfillment	
	Settlers	Resisters	Settlers	Resisters
Ideological	2.03 (.92)	1.00 (.00)	1.79 (1.04)	1.13 (.40)
Strategic	1.78 (.85)	1.93 (.96)	1.55 (.95)	1.85 (1.09)
Political	2.96 (1.27)	1.13 (.35)	3.05 (1.28)	1.87 (.81)
Personal	1.54 (.79)	3.36 (.74)	1.33 (.70)	2.15 (1.14)
Materialist	1.25 (.60)	3.47 (.92)	1.20 (.60)	2.85 (1.29)

The relative importance of motivations was largely recapitulated in their fulfillment, with the same order of means for both variables. Correlations were computed between importance and fulfillment scores by motivation, and highly significant correlations were found for nearly all motivations ($p < .001$). In general, the more important the motivation, the more likely it was rated as fulfilled, except for standard of living. This means that some settlers who placed great importance on standard of living were disappointed in this regard and that others who placed little importance on it reported fulfillment beyond expectation.

Relationship of motivations for settling to symptomatology. The relationship of the motivation scores to symptomatology and to other coping indices was examined. Given the restricted range of scores on these variables for resisters, analyses in this section were restricted to settlers. Correlations of importance scores to symptomatology in both waiting and aftermath periods were in the predicted direction: the more important the motivation, the greater the emotional upset, the greater the sense of alienation from the society, and the greater the difficulty in resuming work and household routines ($ps < .05$). All correlations were of modest magnitude, in the .20-to-.33 range. The only exception was standard of living, whose importance was unrelated to symptomatology or any of the coping indices. This may be explained in terms of the financial compensation given to all evacuees. This compensation minimized the threat to standard of living and thereby neutralized adverse effects arising from such threats. Correlations with fulfillment scores were in the predicted direction, but did not reach formal significance.

The resisters as a group were an exception to the relationship between the importance of motivations and the extent of symptomatology. Since they emphasized ideological and political motivations that were ultimately fruitless—with the return of Sinai in general and Yamit in particular to Egyptian sovereignty—one might expect them to experience far greater emotional disturbance than the settlers themselves. After all, the resisters had come to Yamit for the express purpose of preventing that which took place in April 1982. Yet one month later, their symptomatology was similar to that of a control reference group that had not been exposed to a long-term crisis situation. It became clear in discussions with them that their expectations, attributions, and interpretations of events insulated them against disappointment, self-blame, depression, or even anger. When one examines this group's leadership, social support systems, and ideology in terms of Festinger's criteria (Festinger, Riecken, & Shachter, 1956), one can understand why prophecy did not fail.

The resisters had, indeed, hoped to thwart the return of Sinai to Egypt, and they acknowledged that their efforts were not successful in this regard. They believed, however, that the success of the venture was not wholly in their hands and that a higher power would determine the immediate and the ultimate outcome of the struggle. In fact, all believed that someday they would be able to return and to settle once again in a Yamit under Israeli sovereignty. Eviction was only a temporary setback.

Even the temporary setback was in their eyes a victory of sorts. One of the motivations behind their acts of civil disobedience in Yamit was to demonstrate the extent of opposition to returning other territories occupied in the 1967 war to Arab sovereignty. For them as for most Israeli citizens, Jerusalem and Judea and Samaria (the West Bank) are far less negotiable than Sinai. One could imagine the escalation in civil disobedience if these more important regions were candidates for evacuation. The resisters felt that they had made a point that would not be quickly forgotten by the government, the society as a whole, and interested foreign observers. As a consequence, they were able to settle within Israeli borders in the nearest possible place to their former homes in Yamit, without emotional distress.

Support systems and their implications. Means and standard deviations of the efficacy of the various support systems for both groups during initial settlement and during the uprooting experience are summarized in Table 4. In the settlement period they reported that the nuclear family, the personal belief system, and group cohesiveness were important sources of support that bolstered them in their coping efforts. National consensus and the extended family were seen as providing less support. The major difference between groups was the greater support forthcoming from group leadership for the resisters. This is understandable since resister settling was a far more audacious act against the national consensus than settlement by the settlers many years earlier in accord with national consensus at that time.

When we compare efficacy of support systems for settlers in the settling and uprooting periods, we find that during the crisis the extended family became more sustaining than before ($p < .05$), and the national consensus less than before ($p < .01$). The efficacy of the national consensus also declined for the resisters ($p < .05$). Correlations between efficacy of support systems in the two periods were high for all support systems ($p < .001$), except the nuclear family and the national consensus whose correlations over time were not significantly different from zero.

TABLE 4
Means and Standard Deviations of Support Systems in Two Periods

Support systems	Settlers		Resisters	
	Settling	Uprooting	Settling	Uprooting
Nuclear family	1.12 (.43)	1.11 (.35)	1.23 (.75)	1.43 (.94)
Extended family	2.33 (1.04)	1.95 (1.06)	2.94 (1.01)	3.13 (1.13)
Community leadership	2.33 (.96)	2.08 (1.04)	1.56 (.89)	1.67 (.98)
Group cohesiveness	1.59 (.84)	1.76 (1.02)	1.50 (.89)	1.47 (.92)
Personal ideology	1.56 (.82)	2.00 (1.12)	1.00 (.00)	1.07 (.26)
National consensus	2.42 (1.08)	3.41 (1.12)	2.67 (1.10)	3.69 (.85)

This means that the sustaining support of the nuclear family during the settling period for some respondents was not necessarily available for them during the crisis, and the reverse: The nuclear family became more sustaining during the crisis than in the earlier, less stressful period. The same inconsistency was noted for national consensus, which was less available for many during the crisis than before.

Conclusions

An assessment of symptomatology one month after the evacuation does not permit us to draw definitive conclusions about the long-term consequences of a stressful experience. A follow-up study one year or more later will provide more definitive conclusions. This follow-up study has been undertaken and will be reported in a future publication. On the basis of the present data, however, we may conclude that the settlers showed considerable emotional upset during the uncertain waiting period, displayed a reduction in symptoms in the aftermath, but were still emotionally upset. They were especially bitter about the criticism expressed in the mass media about their efforts to thwart the evacuation or to receive adequate (in their eyes) financial compensation for their loss of homes and livelihoods.

In general, settlers with strong motivations for settling in Yamit and without efficacious support systems were more disturbed than those with weak motivations and strong support systems. The major exception was the entire resister group, whose strong ideological and political motivations and flexible belief system insulated them from the trauma of evacuation in the immediate aftermath of the evacuation.

There is an apparent contradiction between the generalizations about the importance of motivations and about the efficacy of support systems: The importance of one's belief system is a *negative* factor in the generalization about motivations, while the sustaining power of the belief system is a *positive* factor in the generalization about support systems. The contradiction is more apparent than real. If the original belief system strongly motivated the original settling behavior, but is now shattered by the new reality, there is, understandably, an adverse effect on one's adjustment. If the belief system survives the crisis and retains its sustaining influence in a new or flexible manner, there is a positive effect on adjustment, as seen in the case of the resisters. In assessing the availability of stress-resistant factors in people under crisis, it is important to distinguish between motivation and support systems and between belief systems at two points in time, before and during the crisis, and to evaluate assets and deficits appropriately.

PART TWO: RECOMMENDATIONS FOR
THERAPEUTIC INTERVENTION

Several implications for therapeutic intervention follow from these
conclusions and from supporting clinical observations.

The Role of Government: Honesty About Uncertainty

First, uncertainty imposes an enormous burden on the coping abilities
of people in a long-term crisis. The uncertainty experienced by settlers
was in part dictated by the political considerations of the government
in its negotiations with Egypt. If government officials were more aware
of its potentially deleterious effect, however, they might have been able
to formulate a more helpful policy as a guide for the settlers. Such a
policy might have dealt directly and openly with the deliberate ambiguity
of the government's policy. It was possible to be honest with settlers
and to encourage the option of staying as long as possible with the
strong likelihood of eventual evacuation, but to acknowledge and support the right of settlers to select the option of early resettlement. Settlers
who elected to remain until the bitter end would regard themselves as
patriots and would be so regarded by their fellow citizens. Settlers pre-
ferring a less ambiguous option would leave earlier in the uprooting
process and be spared the stressful uncertainty. Settlers would have
paid a lower psychic price whatever option they selected, and they
would have been less of a target for public calumny.

*The Role of the Mass Media: Trial Without Jury and Without Expert
Testimony*

It was quite evident from a casual examination of the news coverage
and editorial commentary in the major Israeli newspapers and on television that there was no sympathy or understanding of the anomalous
situation in which the settlers found themselves. They were frequently
confused with the resisters to their psychological disadvantage. Their
original motivations for settling in Yamit were delegitimized, even
though these motivations were not exclusively materialistic and included
national security and ideological considerations as well. If the public
media were more aware, they might have permitted the settlers to express their distress at the unfortunate predicament in which they found
themselves: the first victims to pay the price of the peace. If there had
been judicious consultation and more balanced reporting and interpretation of the behavior of the settlers in the media, their public image

would have been more positive. The settlers would have experienced less of a sense of alienation from the larger society and would have paid a lower psychological price.

The Role of Community Mental Health in Crisis Intervention

Community mental health professionals have a consultant role both in advising government officials as to the effects of their policies on affected groups at high risk, and in informing the mass media of the effects of their reporting and interpreting of these events on these groups. The mental health community at large did not identify Yamit settlers as victims and did not offer support. There were a few isolated efforts to contact other Sinai evacuees (Horshovsky & Scheffer, 1983), in Sharm Al Sheik and Nueva, for example, whose evacuation aroused little attention or controversy because of their small numbers and remote location. These exceptions proved the rule: There was no professional concern during the lengthy waiting period or in the aftermath for the larger body of Yamit settlers.

As a consequence, the settlers were not encouraged to organize as self-help groups for mutual support in coping with the enormous stress of uncertainty and relocation. There was little effort to identify settlers who were more at risk than others and to offer them preventive treatment or instruction in stress management. Although the life of an entire community was being threatened and that community in its original form actually disappeared, there was no thought about assistance in anticipatory grief work or in grief work after the fact.

The plight of these evacuees during the waiting period is only now, belatedly, being recognized as similar to that of families of soldiers missing in action. Considerable research (Teichman, 1975) has shown that these families are seriously disrupted by having to cope with the uncertainty of the final status of the missing soldier. MIA families are regarded as at risk and are often the target of preventive mental health interventions. The Yamit settlers were not so fortunate.

Blaming the Victim in Community Crisis

Their situation is remarkably like that of veterans of the Vietnam War (Haley, 1978; Lifton, 1978). These veterans returned home after a chronic stress situation to an ungrateful society. They bore internal (psychic) injuries for which no one was willing to assume any responsibility or to show sympathy and understanding. Years after their return the mental health field has awakened to their predicament and to its responsibilities. The same trend is beginning to evolve in Israel with reference to the Yamit settlers. We are becoming aware that ideological controversy and one's personal position with respect to it may cloud professional judgment about people who are experiencing societal victimization and associated traumas. The victimization and the trauma are authentic problems worthy of our attention regardless of the merits of the case and the behavior of the affected groups in attempting to prevent the evacuation or in negotiating for financial compensation.

This is the most important generalization forthcoming from the Yamit experience, i.e., the importance of raising the professional consciousness of mental health professional workers about unrecognized victims in crisis situations associated with political or ideological issues. Mental health professionals were as remiss as government officials, the mass media, and the society as a whole in failing to recognize the untenable and difficult crisis in which the Yamit settlers found themselves during the lengthy waiting period and thereafter. The fact that the settlers by and large received adequate, and in some instances unreasonably large, financial settlements did not insulate them against the stress of uprooting and relocation.

The resisters present even more of a challenge to community mental health professionals precisely because they appear to have been symptom-free during and immediately after the evacuation, and they elicited even less sympathy and professional concern. If anything, their actions earned them the animosity and opprobrium of many mental health professionals, who tend to adopt a liberal, secular as opposed to a conservative, religious orientation.

We conclude that all groups subjected to the stress of uprooting and relocation are proper targets of professional concern regardless of the political and ideological stance they espouse, the behavior they exhibit during the crisis, and the extent of the financial compensations they receive.

21

Civilian Adjustment to War-Related Stress

STEVAN HOBFOLL

One can recall being a child and looking at soldiers with an admiration reserved especially for them. They seemed strong, even invulnerable. They were very much adults, only perhaps more powerful members of that species. Like John Wayne, they also seemed to be loners. One didn't see the family behind the man. Looking at them now that we are adults, however, we are struck by their youthfulness. For the most part, they are young men just out of school. Being older and having families ourselves, we are painfully aware of them as sons, brothers, husbands, and fathers of young children.

This view of the soldier as separate from family is also evidenced in the lack of research on those closest to the soldier. Despite the fact that millions of Americans were touched by the loss or serious injury of a loved one in Vietnam, for instance, there is little empirical testimony to this fact (Figley, 1978b). These victims of the war suffered their losses in the privacy of their own homes, not on the battlefield.

This chapter focuses on the effect of war-related stressors on civilians in Israel. The goal, as is common in stress research, is to understand the stress process and to predict which individuals can most effectively withstand the deleterious effects of war-related stress, and which individuals cannot. The chapter has two parts. First, a number of theories

Writing of this chapter was made possible, in part, by grants provided by the Center for Absorption of Scientists, Ministry of Absorption, Israel, and the Israel Foundation Trustees–Ford Foundation.

that try to explain how people react to stress in general and that relate to the theme of person-environment fit in particular will be considered. This perspective emphasizes that stressful situations affect people differently depending on their capability to meet specific demands produced by stressors. In the second section, preliminary studies of the effects of war on civilians, which derive from this theme, will be presented.

THEORETICAL ISSUES

The Stress of War for Those at Home

Before presenting the relevant theories and empirical studies, the context of the civilian in Israel needs to be described. Almost all males in Israel serve in the regular army from the ages of 18 until 21 and continue in active reserve duty until age 55. Main-line units are filled with both regular army and career army troops, and these units usually are the first in action and the last to depart. Reserve units, however, are also actively involved in combat roles.

Women, except the very religious, serve for two years from age 18 until 20. They may have to do reserve duty until they are married. They are not assigned combat roles, but may find themselves near combat areas. They learn how to use personal weapons and are often used as instructors for jobs as diverse as combat paramedicine or tank gunnery.

These circumstances have visible effects on Israeli civilians. For one thing, they are aware of the reality of war. Having learned to handle weapons, they know their destructive power. Having seen Israel from a military view, they know something of its strengths and weaknesses. Living and traveling in the country, they are well aware of its small size and of the fact that it faces hostile nations.

Non-Israelis may see the Israel-Arab conflict as small compared to involvements in which America or Europe may potentially be involved. Israelis do not. Israel was attacked in 1973 by "the equivalent of the total forces of NATO in Europe . . ." (Herzog, 1984, p. 230). By the afternoon of the first day, the Egyptians had crossed what was thought to be an impregnable barrier in the south, and the Syrians were approaching major population centers in the north. Although Israel quickly regained these territories and pressed into Egyptian and Syrian territories, the initial Arab successes clearly made their point.

Perhaps the most important Israeli characteristic stemming from these special circumstances is that everyone in Israel feels personally involved with war. During Israel's brief modern history, there has been little peace. Wars are the norm, and wars of attrition bridge the gaps between full-scale wars. It is almost impossible not to have an extended family member in the military at all times. Thus, the personal distance that Americans may have felt from Vietnam, or the English from the Falkland Islands, is not part of the Israeli experience.

Theories of Resource and Demand Fit and War-Related Stress

One of the first theories of person-environment fit was proffered by McGrath (1972) in his classic conceptual definition of stress. McGrath defined stress as a state of imbalance between environmental demand and the response capability of the organism. He defined demands as requirements that stem from situations. They may be internal, as when we must "grin and bear it," or external, as when we must complete a report or fight a battle. Response capability, in turn, is seen as a product of the resources individuals possess and their ability to call on these resources to meet situational demands. Resources may be any source of aid or support, be it funds, a strong physical constitution, a good friend, or a strong will.

McGrath further emphasized that psychological stress is a function of the importance the individual assigns to failure to meet the demand. The higher the perceived personal cost of failure, the more stress will be felt. In situations where the cost of failure is less significant, a severe demand-versus-resource imbalance would be less stressful.

Stress exists not so much in the objective imbalance between demand and response capability, but in the subjective evaluation of this imbalance. Lazarus (1966) emphasizes that cognitive appraisal (see also Lazarus & Folkman, 1984) of a demand-versus-resource imbalance is the necessary condition for psychological stress. In other words, the objective reality is not nearly as important as individuals' perceptions of their circumstances.

The theories of McGrath and Lazarus offer a formal scheme for evaluating the tremendous demands that war makes on civilians. The foremost fear is that a loved one may be killed or seriously injured in the fighting. Such a fear imposes a tremendous threat to civilians. Moreover, there is little that civilians can do to directly counteract this threat. Since the individual cannot directly affect the threat, he or she must rely mainly on emotion-focused coping strategies to aid stress resistance.

Emotion-focused strategies include limiting psychological distress by redefining the situation, altering one's appraisal of the possible consequences, or denying the nature of the threat.

Although traditional psychoanalytic literature has considered denial to be necessarily indicative of psychopathology, partial denial may have some positive effects. This is especially the case in the early phase of confrontation with massive stressors (Lazarus, 1983). The following case example illustrates the temporary efficacy of partial denial:

> One woman, a social science faculty member, was convinced that her husband's unit did not cross the border into Lebanon despite considerable information to the contrary. She argued that had he been sent to Lebanon he would have telephoned first. She further argued that his being in a reserve unit meant that he would be held back until the war progressed to a later stage. Since he was in an antiaircraft unit, finally, she convinced herself that he would be guarding Israeli's frontier on this side of the border. She spent the first two weeks of the war reasonably serene, despite the fallacies and weaknesses of her arguments. When she learned that her spouse's unit had been engaged in intensive combat near the outskirts of Beirut, she became quite anxious. Interestingly, she said that she had been expecting this would happen sometime and that she could cope with it.

Perceptions of Stress: Their Link to Trait Beliefs

The Lazarus and McGrath theories imply that perceptions come first and conclusions as to the degree of stress follow. My own observations from the war lead me to the supposition, however, that a process of negotiation occurs at the same time as appraisal, but in the opposite direction. That is, people attempt to arrive at an appraisal of the situation that is consistent with their beliefs about themselves. What allows individuals to arrive at such an evaluation may be an internal discussion designed to convince themselves that their trait beliefs apply to their current situation. In other words, they carry out an argument in order to arrive at their original premise, a premise they held before beginning any cognitive search.

A typical television news show during the war illustrates how these negotiations take place. Following a broadcast of the scanty hard facts of the day's events, a panel of experts is presented. There is an expert for everyone's tastes: a professor for those who value the ivory tower, a battle-proven retired general for the military-minded, and a journalist who is held in popular esteem because he is known to seek the story behind the story. Panel members analyze the situation. When opinions seem weak, allusions are made to informed sources. Following the appraisal of each participant, there are questions and criticisms.

After an often heated argument, one of two things occurs. Either there is a natural rapprochement of viewpoints, which leads to a shared reappraisal of the degree of stress (the threat versus our nation's ability to meet this stress), or a glib commentator ties together the various conflicting viewpoints to make a convincing unified stance. In both cases the final conclusion is at the very least guardedly optimistic. This negotiation process occurs in our living rooms, in workers' cafes, and in office coffee klatches. It also occurs in our minds.

Research by Kobassa and her colleagues (Kobassa, Maddi, & Courington, 1981; Kobassa & Puccetti, 1983) and theoretical notions of Antonovsky (1979) also may be interpreted as suggesting that this backward appraisal occurs on the individual level. Hardy individuals (Kobassa et. al., 1981), for instance, tend to appraise situations as challenging rather than threatening, and as meaningful rather than meaningless. They see themselves as capable of meeting these challenges. Antonovsky's (1979) sense of coherence implies a similar process, namely that those with a sense of coherence have a positive appraisal of outcome from the outset. For them, it will work out as well as may be expected and to their own best interests.

A study by Coyne, Aldwin, and Lazarus (1981) illustrates this point on the clinical level with reference to underestimating or underevaluating one's social support. Despite the substantial social support they received, depressed women appraised their support systems as inadequate. Others have also noted that depressed persons have stable expectations of their poor ability to withstand stressors (Arieti, 1970; Janoff-Bulman, 1979). This reminds one of the adage "Don't confuse me with the facts, my mind is already made up."

It is not implied that this reverse appraisal process results in an altogether foregone conclusion. Rather, it would seem that this process of negotiations toward a belief-guided situational assessment occurs together with a more straightforward appraisal process. For depressed people, on one hand, or hardy people, on the other hand, the situational appraisal may be highly related to their trait beliefs. Others who have less stable beliefs about their ability to meet situational demands in general may be more influenceable and their personal traits may play less of a part.

Person-Environment Fit: Past, Present, and Future

In Caplan's (1983) reformulation of his person-environment (P-E) fit theory (we will call it P-E fit theory to distinguish it from the general case of person-environment fit), he emphasizes that past experiences with P-E fit are related to present and future evaluations. While his theory has inspired a great deal of research in past years, his reformulation was motivated by the small amount of absolute predictive power of the model. He attributes the relatively low predictive success of the original P-E model to a lack of emphasis on past and future P-E fit. Caplan argues that a concentration on the here and now alone ignores the extent to which people may continue to be stressed by their past and may already be stressed by what has yet to occur.

His reformulation has special implications for war. North America today is confronted for the first time since the Civil War to threats to civilians as a result of the borderless war of international terrorism. Although the actual chances of being involved in a terrorist attack are statistically negligible, Americans' sense of vulnerability has been awakened. The June 1985 hijacking of a TWA carrier from Athens caused Americans to relive the anguish and humiliation of a similar ordeal, when American embassy officials were held hostage for over a year in Iran. This past P-E fit also affected anticipated fit of America's ability to confront terrorism. The same yellow ribbons were tied to mailboxes indicating families' longings for the return of their loved ones, and news broadcasts aired familiar scenes of press conferences held by terrorists and officials. These similarities serve as reminders that link the past, present, and future.

Individual traits may also affect the stability of P-E fit over time. Israelis, for example, may hold a general and stable consensus of the ability of the country to withstand the vicissitudes of war and terrorism (Guttman & Levy, 1974). Past, current, and anticipated fit may be said to be consistent and decidedly positive. Still, significant events may change such traits and therefore change stability of perceptions of fit from one time to another. The 1967 Six-Day War's rapid and one-sided success in Israel's favor had lulled Israelis into a view of their inviolability. However, this relative stability was for a period shaken by the initial accomplishments of the combined Arab forces in the 1973 Yom Kippur War. The professionalism and sophistication of Arab troops and the lack of preparedness of Israeli forces resulted in an anxious national reaction.

This may be compared with the reactions of anxious individuals. Specifically, high trait-anxious persons tend to view the future as uncertain and ambiguous, a state that they perceive as noxious (Archer, 1979). Caplan (1983) asserts that this leads to their making unstable and inconsistent estimates of past, present, and future P-E fit. So, it might be expected that trait-anxious Israeli wives would be expected to make unstable current and anticipated assessments of P-E fit regarding their ability to withstand the stress of war. Like Israelis after the initial setbacks of the Yom Kippur War, their current and past assessments of P-E fit would not necessarily result in anticipated future perceptions consistent with the actual outcome (i.e., success) of the past.

It can be seen from Caplan's formulation that perceptions of P-E fit may vary in their stressfulness and consistency over time. The brief examples cited here illustrate how his dual axes of stressfulness (i.e., degree of P-E fit) and consistency of past, present, and future evaluations may be applied to war-related stress research. Such thinking may be particularly compatible with cross-cultural research on war, as the model provides a common structure by which different cultures can be compared.

The Importance of Process

The cognitive appraisal involved in stress reactions is no single-frame photograph, but a moving sequence of events. Following initial appraisal of threat, on one hand, and of perceived resources, on the other, a number of things may alter the balance. Individuals may act to change the situation; the stressor may change in intensity; and circumstances may alter the value of success or failure. Reappraisal continues during the entire process (Lazarus, 1966; Lazarus & Folkman, 1984). Since the degree of stress is the perceived imbalance between threat and resources, appraisal of stress level vacillates.

Process is emphasized in Lazarus and Folkman's (1984) reformulation of Lazarus' (1966) original coping model. This is highlighted in their definition of coping, which they write is the "constantly changing cognitive and behavioral efforts to manage specific external and internal demands that are appraised as taxing or exceeding the resources of the person" (p. 141).

The process of coping is illustrated in their recent study on students' efforts to secure social support in conjunction with changing environmental demands (Folkman & Lazarus, 1985). Following the course of an examination, they found that the type of support students received was related before the examination to information support. Information support seeking dropped dramatically after the examination was over. In contrast, emotional support seeking was low during the anticipatory stage, rose after the examination, and stayed elevated after grades were announced. They argue that this indicates that coping is an active process that evolves in response to environmental demands.

A similar thesis was proffered in a study of adjustment to outcome of pregnancy (Hobfoll & Leiberman, in press). In this investigation it was found that the relative facility of social support versus personal resources (i.e., self-esteem) was related to the type of demands different circumstances placed on women. Originally, women whose circumstances were consistent with receipt of social support (e.g., following premature delivery) were aided by intimacy with their spouse. However, women whose circumstances limited the accessibility of social support (this was seen to be the case for spontaneous abortion) were aided solely by their own possession of high self-esteem. After the lapse of three months, only self-esteem was effective for either group. It was reasoned that this is related to expectations that after a given time people are expected to stand on their own two feet. This study illustrates how the environment affects adjustment because of both the differing and evolving nature of the person-environment interaction.

War and terrorism, too, are stage events that quickly evolve. Each new report brings involved family members to optimistic peaks or crushed hopes. As the war or terror-related sequences unfold, different coping strategies are devised and applied. The environment changes, and individuals change their environments. The process model serves as a warning not to oversimplify the nature of the stress at hand. Instead, one must consider its dynamic attributes and the interaction of the environment, cognitions, and coping behaviors. The emphasis on process provides an essential dimension to the study of war-related stress. Such efforts are necessarily complex, but there are a number of studies to date of other stressors that provide a point of reference (Hobfoll, 1985b).

An Ecologically Based Model of Stress Resistance

Hobfoll and his colleagues (Hobfoll, 1985a, 1985b; Hobfoll, in press; Hobfoll & Leiberman, in press; Hobfoll & London, in press) have developed a process model of stress resistance, termed the model of ecological congruence. Their thinking is based, in part, on seminal work on the ecology of human psychological systems by Kelly and his colleagues (Kelly, Snowden, & Munoz, 1977) and on the stress models of Lazarus (1966), McGrath (1972), and Pearlin and Schooler (1978). The ecological congruence model is distinctive from other stress models in that it is more comprehensive. It places less emphasis than these others on cognitive appraisal, but a wider role is allegated to individual traits and personal and cultural values. Like these other theoretical frameworks though, it highlights both the importance of process and the interaction between the individual and the environment.

The model suggests six essential dimensions of the stress-resistance process. The overall ecological fit of these dimensions determines the valence of effect of the resources. The term "valence of effect" is used to emphasize that ecologies are sensitively balanced and that changes at any dimension will affect the overall outcome. The dimensions are: resources, needs, time, strain, perception, and values (see Figure 1).

According to the model, combinations of resources may be combined to affect strain. Resources include those attributes or properties of the individual and the environment that may be employed to reduce threat. However, the actual outcome may be positive or negative. The nature of this relationship is dictated by the extent resources meet the task and emotional demands confronting the individual. The fit between resources and demands can be illustrated by a lock-and-key analogy whereby resources are defined only in respect to their congruence with specific environmental demands. Situations may require application of combinations of resources in order to unlock the sequence of evolving demands. The wrong key may not only fail to unlock the door, but prevent the trial of other keys, and so it is with resources.

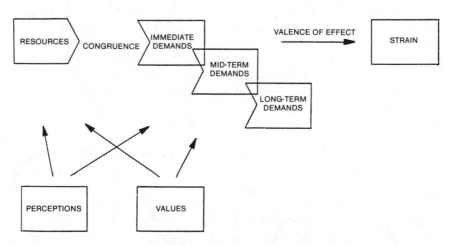

Figure 1. The model of ecological congruence.

Time is another major dimension of the model. This includes both time since the event's occurrence and time in terms of the developmental stage of the individual. Time since the event's occurrence implies that following the event there is a sequence of varying stressors that are moderated by the individuals involved, their coping efforts, and secondary events. Thus, a victim of a heart attack may be further stressed by resultant financial problems and sexual dysfunction. His behavior and that of his support system may exert their influence on the course of events from the moment the possibility of threat occurs.

Time must also be evaluated developmentally in terms of the individual's place in the life-span and the individual's personal emotional development. A very sage kibbutz friend, on approaching his eightieth birthday, put it this way, "I used to be excited going to the fields with a gun on my back not knowing if I will plow or fight, but now I am only scared when I see my grandsons go to war."

Stress resistance is also moderated by individual and group perceptions and values. It is reasoned that these perceptions are more constant than the theories of Lazarus or McGrath imply. Specifically, it is argued that to a great extent they are products of individuals' world view. To use a metaphor, they are only tempered, not forged, by situational factors. A balance between cognitive and personological approaches is consistent with a significant body of recent literature on stress resistance (Hobfoll & Leiberman, in press; Kobassa & Puccetti, 1983; Lefcourt, Martin & Selah, 1984). This literature clearly indicates that personal traits play a large role in predicting evaluations of attributes of stressful situations.

Values are not emphasized whatsoever in other stress-resistance theories. The model of ecological congruence ascribes an important role, however, to individual, group, and societal values. It is argued that values affect all aspects of the stress process. They shape our choice and utilization of resources, define what is stressful to us, and confine the breadth of acceptable coping strategies. Cheating on an examination, for instance, may be perceived as potentially helpful, but morally impermissible.

Values that are expressed by a society may also impinge on individuals when such values take the form of sanctions. Some examples of this include difficult divorce laws, religious tenets involving abortion, and laws involving drinking. More subtle sanctions, such as ostracization by family for working instead of being a housewife, may be no less potent than proscribed ones. Whether subtle or blatant, values provide a framework that influences the nature of our perceptions and the diversity of what we might consider to be justifiable behavior. Moreover, by limiting potential coping efforts, the sanctions themselves may become stressors. In this way people may feel stressed and confined, leading to an increased feeling of helplessness.

EMPIRICAL STUDY OF THE MODEL OF ECOLOGICAL CONGRUENCE

Two empirical studies were carried out in order to test facets of the model as they pertain to war-related stress. They are separate cross-sectional investigations, but are based on a common theme and common instruments. The first study was performed immediately at the onset of the Israel-Lebanon war, and the second study one year later. Although different samples were employed, a cautious attempt will be made to link the respective findings.

Study One

Rationale and methodology. In the first study, emotional responses of 56 women were examined during the first week of the war (Hobfoll & London, in press). These women each had a loved one involved somewhere in the conflict. In most cases, their husbands, sons, and brothers had been mobilized on less than 48 hours' notice. Accurate information about where the loved one was located was unavailable to them.

We had originally thought that personal resources—namely, self-esteem and a sense of mastery—and social support would both aid stress resistance. These resources have been found in numerous studies to be related to more healthy emotional responding in the face of significant stressors (Brown, Bhrolchrain, & Harris, 1975; Hobfoll & Walfisch, 1984; Pearlin & Schooler, 1978). Self-esteem was defined as the stable belief that one possesses positive qualities and is worthy of love and positive regard. Mastery was defined as the stable belief that one can usually affect one's environment toward a positive outcome. Social support was defined as information provided by the acts of others that leads us to feel that we are esteemed and loved, and that we are a part of a network of caring individuals (Caplan, 1974; Cobb, 1976).

It was also consistent with the model to distinguish between two dimensions of social support, intimacy and support actually received. Intimacy implies having close relationships in which individuals feel secure, loved, appreciated, and able to disclose personal matters. We examined women's reported intimacy with their closest friend and closest family member. While intimacy is an important quality of social support, it is not enough because the ecology of a given situation may limit individuals' access to intimates (see Hobfoll, 1985a). Support actually received is, therefore, an important component of social support, as it indicates the process of support that emerges in a given situation. So we studied actual support received, too.

We reasoned that when considering the time dimension of the model, mastery and self-esteem would be more effective resources than social support because they are immediately at the disposal of those who possess them, and in this stress situation everything was occurring very quickly. These resources are, let us say, part of the individual's personal baggage. Social support, on the other hand, is not as immediately obtainable.

Let us diverge for a moment to another study, in order to take a look at how the sequence of recruiting support may unfold. Based on interviews of women awaiting biopsy for suspected cancer (Hobfoll & Walfisch, 1984), a sequence of events was derived that was seen as consistent with the ecology of the social support process (Hobfoll, 1985b). First, persons must decide whether they, in fact, need help. If they decide they do, they must design and carry out efforts to obtain aid. Then supporters must decide whether they are willing and able to respond. The latter depends on their being able to break free of their own obligations and on the distance and expense involved in traveling. This is followed by a more intense phase of support, which requires that individuals make their needs clear and that they are capable of intimate contact. There are more stages to complete the sequence, but these first three must be accomplished in order to arrive at the point where the individual is receiving a full dose of social support. Applying this process to the study of women during the first week of war, we thought that the time constraint would limit achievement of the intense support phase. This, in turn, would favor the use of the quickly recruitable personal resources over the use of social support.

Values were also considered as to how they might influence a preference for one type of resource over another. Nothing had really "happened" as yet to these women. True, their loved ones were mobilized in the army, but they had not received a notice of their loved ones being injured or killed. Consequently, there is social pressure in a society in which "doing it alone" has been a symbol of its existence to do just that. Israelis have been found to be the most likely of seven national groups from the East and West to believe that their well-being could be controlled by their own actions, rather than by luck, fate, or powerful others (Parsons & Schneider, 1974). This tendency to see oneself in control, we believed, would also contribute to women's preference for personal rather than social resources.

Findings and discussion. When we debriefed the women, before we examined the data, we already saw that social support might actually have a negative effect, which we came to call the "pressure cooker" effect. Specifically, we found that the more intimate relationships women reported with friends, the greater their state anxiety ($r = .26$, $p < .05$). Also, the greater the actual support women reported as receiving during this period, the higher they were in state depression ($r = .22$, $p < .05$). Intimacy with a family member had almost no effect on either measure of emotional distress.

Personal resources were, however, related to less psychological distress. The higher women's self-esteem, the lower they were found to be in state depression ($r = -.30$, $p < .05$). Furthermore, the higher their mastery, the lower their state depression ($r = -.54$, $p < .001$), and the lower their state anxiety ($r = -.23$, $p < .01$). It may be noted that the measures of self-esteem and mastery had been found in previous research to be trait measures, so that there is some basis to believe that possessing these resources reduced state psychological distress, and not that increased psychological distress reduced sense of self-esteem and mastery.

It was seen of interest to ascertain how women who were high on personal resources compared to women who were low on personal resources in relation to how they were affected by social support. To this end, the self-esteem and mastery measures were converted to standard scores and combined to create a single measure, which we termed personal coping resources. A similar procedure was followed to combine the two measures of emotional distress, anxiety and depression, into a single outcome measure. The sample was then divided between those who were high and low on personal coping resources using a median split. When the high and low personal coping resource groups were compared, the negative effects of social support on emotional distress were found among the high personal resource women only. The results of this analysis are reported in Table 1.

Interpreting these results, it appears that those who had intimate relationships and active social support found themselves only able to talk about their common plight. In addition, they were privy to the rumor mills, which inevitably brought bad news. This tendency to become more emotionally distressed with greater interpersonal contact may be compared to the risky-shift phenomenon, whereby groups are known to take a more extreme stance than individual group members (Lamm & Myers, 1976). Consistent with our discussion of values, women might also have only sought support when they felt very distressed. In turn, such admission of weakness might have resulted in negative self-attributions.

Why, however, should the women who had strong personal coping resources be more susceptible to these negative self-attributions? Nadler & Mayseless (1983) argue that those who are high in self-esteem may find help threatening because it is inconsistent with their view of self. They wish to see themselves as independent and strong, and accepting help signifies for them that they are being weak. In contrast, those low in self-esteem can more easily accept aid because they do not view it as inconsistent with their self-image. So those who have strong personal coping resources may be seen as benefiting from mobilizing these personal resources, but they may actually be threatened by help if they interpret the situation as one in which they should be able to cope independently.

Study Two

Rationale and methodology. In the second study we went back one year later and studied 220 students, many of whom were involved or had a loved one involved in the fighting (Hobfoll, London, & Orr, 1985). Because this study is not yet published elsewhere, the findings will be presented in more detail than those of the first. As in study one, we

TABLE 1

Pearson Correlations between Social Support Variables and Emotional Strain for Women High and Low on Coping Traits

	High on coping traits (*n* = 24)	Low on coping traits (*n* = 24)
Intimacy with friends	.54**	−.17
Intimacy with family	−.03	−.01
Amount of support	.38*	−.01

*p < .05
**p < .01

were interested in how possessing intimate relationships and a sense of mastery might aid stress resistance during war. However, whereas in study one we expected mastery to be more ecologically congruent with situational demands, in this study we did not necessarily expect this to be so. This thinking stemmed from the argument that after a year there was ample time to seek and receive social support. On the other hand, there was some evidence that in uncontrollable situations, persons who see themselves in control do worse than those who do not expect to control their fate (Breznitz, 1983a; Lazarus, 1983). In such situations high-mastery persons might try to do something about the situation, which would only lead to greater frustration. This has typically been found in medical contexts, but the ecology of war and serious illness seemed to share the element of uncontrollability.

One year into the war, there was certainly enough cause for stress. A static, but steady, war of attrition had developed in Lebanon. Israeli troops were involved in the grueling task of policing urban areas and patrolling rural villages and pockets of potential terrorist strongholds. Such circumstances favor guerrilla warfare, not tactics of trained armies such as Israel's. Each day the death count increased, and the nightly news almost invariably screened another soldier's funeral. By the time of this study, over 500 Israelis had been killed. This number is proportionally equivalent to about 35,000 Americans, approximately 70 percent of all those killed in the decade-long Vietnam War.

Israeli students were very much involved in the war. Serving as reservists, many of the male students were in Lebanon two or three times during the academic year. Being students they had to simultaneously concentrate on their studies and make smooth entry and exit in and out of the army. This point accentuates their special status as civilian soldiers. Female students were often married to or romantically involved with combatants. In addition, many female students were related to regular soldiers or reservists.

The actual degree of war-related stressors was measured via a life events questionnaire consisting of war-related items (e.g., a close friend or relative was killed in battle, I [or my partner] served in Lebanon). The cumulative total of endorsed events was used as the indicator of the intensity of the war-related stressors that were confronted. Such an event scale is more consistent with the ecological congruence model than general life event scales. This follows from the supposition within the model that like events place similar demands and that resources need to be considered in light of defined demands, not general level of threat.

Mastery was measured using a scale that was designed for stress research (Pearlin & Schooler, 1978) and used in previous stress research in Hebrew, including the previously described study (Hobfoll & London, in press; Hobfoll & Walfisch, 1984). As intimacy has been seen as a key ingredient in effective social support (Brown et al., 1975), an intimacy scale used by Vanfossen (1981) in prior stress research was adapted for work in Hebrew (Hobfoll & London, in press). This adaptation included items referring to intimacy with spouse/partner, family, and friends. A total intimacy score, weighted equally for items representing these three types of relationships, was employed. Intimacy was defined as in the first war study.

Psychological reactions to stress have typically been evaluated using anxiety, depression, or psychiatric symptom measures. However, it seemed ecologically congruent with war-related stress reactions to go in two supplementary directions. So, in addition to measuring state anxiety, state anger and behavioral adjustment were also examined, all in terms of how individuals felt "lately." Anger was judged to be relevant because anger is a common reaction to an unmanageable stressor. Behavioral adjustment seemed important because the situation demanded adjustment between environments that impose conflicting demands. One day students would be fighting in Beirut or attending a funeral and the next day they would be preparing for an examination.

Standardized scales were available for measurement of state anxiety (Spielberger, Gorsuch, & Lushene, 1970) and state anger (Spielberger, 1980). However, since no suitable behavioral measure was available, a questionnaire was devised. Students were asked to rate on a four-point scale how well they felt themselves adjusting lately to work, family life, studies, and life with their spouse or partner. The scale had reasonable internal reliability ($\alpha = .76$). In addition, the scale was found to have a correlation approaching zero with the anger and anxiety measures, indicating it was not a mere reflection of emotionality or the product of a general response set (e.g., war is bad emotionally, behaviorally, etc.).

Findings. The means and standard deviations for the measures used are presented in Table 2. Because the variables were interrelated, multivariate statistics were employed. A series of regression analyses was performed for men and women separately. In each analysis, the stressor (war events), mastery, and intimacy were entered in the regression equation simultaneously. Following this, the interactions of (1) war events with mastery and (2) war events with intimacy were added. These interaction terms are conceptually similar to the interaction effect gained in analysis of variance (Cohen & Cohen, 1975).

TABLE 2
Means and Standard Deviations for Dependent and Predictor Variables

	Men (n = 72)		Women (n = 148)	
	X̄	SD	X̄	SD
State anger	27.28	10.28	27.59	9.56
State anxiety	39.84	11.09	42.27	11.62
Behavioral adjustment	9.12*	3.02	8.79	3.10
War events	1.69	1.74	1.14	1.28
Mastery	39.11	5.49	37.21	6.89
Intimacy	38.27	5.93	38.23	7.06

*Higher scores indicate poorer adjustment

Findings for men. The results of the regression analysis for men are presented in Table 3. Regressing on state anger, mastery significantly contributed to anger, such that greater mastery was related to less anger. But the lack of significant interaction between war events and mastery indicates that mastery does not limit any effect of war events on anger level. No other indicators significantly predicted to anger.

Regressing on state anxiety, greater mastery was significantly related to lower anxiety, but the war events × mastery interaction was not significant indicating that mastery does not limit any effect of war on state anxiety. The war events × intimacy interaction was significant and accounted for 4.6% of the explained variance. Other predictors did not significantly contribute to state anxiety.

Examination of the nature of the war events × intimacy interaction showed that men who were low in intimacy increased in anxiety the greater their exposure to war-related stressors. Those high in intimacy were actually somewhat lower in anxiety the greater their exposure to war-related stressors. Said another way, the advantage of possessing intimate ties increased, the greater the stress level. This interaction is consistent with the stress-buffering hypothesis, which states that social support aids stress resistance under high stress levels, but not under low stress levels.

Regressing on behavioral adjustment, greater exposure to war-related events was found to be related to poorer adjustment. The interaction of war events × intimacy was also significant and accounted for 6.5% of the explained variance. Other predictors were not significant.

TABLE 3

Multiple Regression Analyses of Emotional Reactions and Behavioral Adjustment on War Events, Mastery, and Intimacy and Related Interactions for Men ($n = 72$)

Dependent variable	Predictor variables	B	F	R^2
State anger	War events (A)	−2.33	.12	
	Mastery (B)	−.72	6.16*	
	Intimacy (C)	−.39	1.34	
	A × B	.24	3.23	
	A × C	−.18	1.38	.21
	Constant	66.32		
State anxiety	War events (A)	2.97	2.06	
	Mastery (B)	−1.17	16.82***	
	Intimacy (C)	−.08	.10	
	A × B	.23	3.01	
	A × C	.80	3.94*	.34
	Constant	88.04		
Behavioral adjustment	War events (A)	4.93	7.19**	
	Mastery (B)	.07	.80	
	Intimacy (C)	.01	.04	
	A × B	−.01	.07	
	A × C	−.10	5.24*	.29

*$p < .05$
**$p < .01$
***$p < .001$

Examination of the nature of the war events × intimacy interaction showed that men with low intimacy were more negatively affected, the greater their exposure to war events, but this trend was not found for men with high intimacy. As in the finding for anxiety, this interaction is consistent with the stress-buffering hypothesis.

Findings for women. The results of the aggression analysis for women are presented in Table 4. Regressing on anger and anxiety for women, only mastery independently contributed to the explained variance. In both cases greater mastery was related to lower anger and anxiety. When behavioral adjustment was regressed on the predictor variables, no significant main effects or interaction effects were found. Said another way,

TABLE 4

Multiple Regression Analyses of Emotional Reactions and Behavioral
Adjustment on War Events, Mastery, and Intimacy and Related
Interactions for Women ($n = 148$)

Dependent variable	Predictor variable	B	F	R^2
State anger	War events (A)	2.69	.30	
	Mastery (B)	−.56	13.25***	
	Intimacy (C)	−.02	.03	
	A × B	−.04	.14	
	A × C	−.03	.13	.20
	Constant	49.56		
State anxiety	War events (A)	9.45	3.05	
	Mastery (B)	−.73	18.41***	
	Intimacy (C)	−.07	.20	
	A × B	−.19	2.85	
	A × C	−.04	.17	.34
	Constant	71.61		
Behavioral adjustment	War events (A)	1.16	.44	
	Mastery (B)	.03	.24	
	Intimacy (C)	.03	.48	
	A × B	−.02	.22	
	A × C	−.01	.05	.02
	Constant	6.32		

***$p < .001$

women did not report being negatively affected by war-related stressors
at this time and so, in a sense, there was no stress to buffer.

Discussion. Why might war-related events affect women in study one
but not in study two? It may be that women in the second study were
not confronted with war-related stressors during the year. This is not
reflected in their reporting of war-related events, however, as most
women reported at least one major event of this kind. Another possibility
is that women were unlikely to be threatened by the war at the specific
time of filling out the questionnaires. This is quite possible as relatively
few reservists were mobilized at any point in time after the initial fighting. Consequently, it is likely that for them no loved one was a combatant
at the time of the study.

Why, then, would men be affected by the war and not women? It was also true that few men had a current involvement in the war. The answer may be found in the ecology of the event for men. Stressors for them could include the memory of battle, the images of death and destruction, and feelings of guilt. Noncombatants may have also felt survivor guilt. In addition, reservists might also be expected to be troubled by the fact that they could be called up again. An inability to avoid thinking about war and presence of intrusive noxious events are typical of returning soldiers (Horowitz & Solomon, 1975), and anticipatory anxiety has been suggested as playing a major role in stress reactions (Breznitz, 1983b). Therefore, for men, the stress of war might very well have been present, even if they were not currently involved directly.

General Discussion of Study One and Study Two

Final conclusions cannot be drawn from these two initial investigations of stress during war. Both have cross-sectional designs that do not allow for more than weak inferences as to causality. This may have been corrected by follow-up data or reliable information concerning subjects prior to the war. Unfortunately, financial resources and logistics did not allow for such preferred methods. The employment of only a superficially validated behavioral measure also limits the generalizations that can be made regarding behavioral reactions to war.

The model of ecological congruence might also have been more comprehensively applied if subjects had been evaluated longitudinally. In addition, in study two it would have been more consistent with the model to have measured values vis-à-vis the war, and not assume what they were. During the first week of the war there was a widespread positive consensus, but it was not so clear after one year how widespread agreement with the war was among students. Agreement with the war might have reduced stress, because people could have justified their involvement or loss by arguing that the war must be fought for a greater good (i.e., to wipe out terrorism, to protect the country).

SUMMARY AND CONCLUSIONS

Research on war-related stress among civilians is in its infancy. This chapter has emphasized how models of person-environment fit may be applied to the study of this special problem. It was argued that this issue is significant both because war is a widespread phenomenon affecting millions of civilians today and because international terrorism threatens civilians within borders that were not long ago considered impervious to foreign attack. In addition, war represents a general case for stress research in which the threat is objectively observable and in which individuals cannot be construed to have caused the event. Such conditions are important for carrying out good stress research, but have seldom been met (Dohrenwend, Dohrenwend, Dodson, & Shrout, 1984).

The almost singular emphasis on cognitions evidenced in much stress research was challenged in light of observations of war-related stress. In this regard, it was argued that personality traits play a larger role in stress resistance than some theories have acknowledged. A process of reverse negotiation was presented as occurring simultaneously with more independent perception and appraisal. This process involves individuals entering situations with trait beliefs that circumstances hardly alter. The individual goes through the motions of debating the balance between perceptions of threats and capability of meeting the resultant demands in order to arrive at what was almost a foregone conclusion. So depressed persons see themselves as overwhelmed and helpless, while hardy persons see few challenges as beyond their ultimate power to overcome. If the negotiation process can be called perception, then this is only a trivial case of semantics. However, if its product is a foregone conclusion, this seems to dilute the word "perception." If the negotiation process is just part of perception, then the term perception seems to be too broad to be meaningful.

The process characteristics that have been highlighted in person-environment fit theories were seen as especially germane to war-related stress. War, it can be seen, is not a single event, but a series of connected events. There is a common link to these events, but as pointed out in this chapter, the nature of this chain is quite dynamic.

Process theories also imply the importance of the concept of ecology. Thus, people do not live in static laboratory settings, but in rich, interactive environments. The model of ecological congruence was presented as one possible framework for describing this ecology as it applies to stress resistance. Like other models of person-environment fit, the model of ecological congruence attributes special significance to the interaction of persons to the demands relevant to specific events. However, this model emphasizes cognitions less than other models and places greater emphasis on a combination of situational and trait characteristics. Unlike other theories, in the model of ecological congruence, values were seen as an integral part of the stress-resistance process. Two research examples were described in an attempt to illustrate the adaptation of the model of ecological congruence to war-related stress resistance.

Future research should focus on longitudinal research of the effect of war on civilians. This is necessarily expensive research, and it will require both researchers and funding sources to make a significant commitment toward this end if progress is to be made. Seemingly limitless contributions of money and manpower are allotted for the purpose of war. Hopefully, a small fraction of that could be designated for remedying some of the resultant personal tragedy among civilians.

22

Generalizations from Theory and Practice in War-Related Stress

NORMAN MILGRAM and STEVAN HOBFOLL

This chapter is selective in focus, reviewing certain concepts and findings presented in this volume, providing a particular perspective and integration, and offering some recommendations for research, theory building, and therapeutic intervention. Notwithstanding its selective focus, the chapter is written to stand alone and may be read first or last as the reader prefers.

The chapter consists of four parts. First, some nonmilitary implications of Israeli research on war stress are examined. The topics include the confounding of stress stimuli and stress reactions and the merits of proposed solutions to unconfound the two; the application of principles derived from treating combat stress to stress reactions in civilian disasters; and the effect of personal and social support resources on coping with life-threatening and physically exhausting stress situations.

Second, the history of diagnosis, prevalence, and treatment of combat stress reactions and disorders from World War I on is presented. Distinctions between initial stress reactions and subsequent stress disorders are made, and corresponding differences in treatment principles and treatment efficacy are discussed.

Third, the American involvement in the Vietnam War and the Israeli involvement in the War in Lebanon are compared. Although the two conflicts are superficially similar, an in-depth analysis of the differences—in circumstances and conduct of the war, nature of military service, treatment of combat stress reactions, and public reaction—broadens our understanding of the high rates of post-traumatic stress disorder observed in Vietnam veterans and of the low rates in Israeli veterans of the conflict in Lebanon.

Fourth, treatment approaches for combat stress disorders currently being used in the United States are described and are compared with new approaches being developed in Israel. The adoption and adaptation of these latter approaches by the appropriate mental health and military authorities in the United States are discussed.

NONMILITARY IMPLICATIONS OF WAR-RELATED STRESS RESEARCH

The Problem of Confounding in Stress Research

The extreme stress of war and particular properties of war-related stress may provide some answers to a methodological problem that has plagued one area of stress research from the very beginning: the confounding of predictor and criterion variables. Brown (1974) cautioned that measures of stressful life events, the tool principally employed to provide an operational definition of the intensity level of stress confronting the individual, may be confounded with the psychological outcomes predicted from that stress level. Hudgens (1974) estimated that almost three-fourths of the items on the Holmes and Rahe Social Readjustment Scale, for instance, are themselves psychological symptoms, the consequences of psychological illness.

This assertion was confirmed in a recent study (Dohrenwend, Dohrenwend, Dodson, & Shrout, 1984). Clinicians were found to rate a large percentage of the items that constitute the typical stressful life event scales as themselves symptoms of psychological disturbance. The threat of confounding was especially powerful for two reasons: first, because the events with the strongest relationship with psychological distress were negative life events, the category of event most likely to be judged a symptom of psychological distress; second, because the conclusions of the study were based on the most widely used measures of life events. These findings are not a criticism of one stressful life measure or another, but are a challenge to the accepted research paradigm. This situation makes any statement of cause and effect based on a correlation between life event measures and outcomes extremely tenuous.

Several solutions have been proposed to handle this problem. One is to remove statistically the effect of psychological disturbance from measures of stressful life events at the onset. Changes in stressful life events from this initial assessment to some later time could then be assessed and correlated with subsequent physical and mental health outcomes. The assumption is that by removing the initial influence of symptoms, one has removed the confounding of the effect of symptoms on the occurrence of stressful events. In fact, this procedure only removes the *main effect* of initial symptoms on the stressful event-outcome relationship. It does not remove the *interaction* of stressful events and initial symptoms on outcome.

This statistical solution would be sound if after equating both groups, we assign their members randomly to experimentally manipulated high and low stress conditions and observe the subsequent effect of these stress conditions on depression level. Since it is both unethical and unfeasible to randomly expose people to stressful life events, we must rely instead on these events when they occur spontaneously in the lives of people. When they do, depression may cause stressful events as much as stressful events cause depression. So it can be seen that the statistical solution is at best a partial answer to the problem of confounding.

Another potential solution is theoretical. Many cognitive theories argue that the *objective* level of the stressors associated with outcomes is less important than the *subjective appraisal* of these events (Caplan, 1983; Lazarus & Folkman, 1984; McGrath, 1972). This thinking sidesteps the problem of the confounding of event and illness by arguing that what is meaningful is not whether certain events actually occurred and how stressful they "really" were, but that these events were perceived in a certain fashion. This approach assumes, for example, that depression will affect the reporting of previous life events, but focuses instead on how these perceptions affect the occurrence of future outcomes.

This theoretical solution does not answer, however, the question of the effect on people of *objective stress events* such as the death of a loved one, loss of job, failure in school, or many of the other events that commonly occur to people. Is the answer inextricably tied to wholly subjective perceptions? We acknowledge the contribution of perception to stress research, but this solution finesses the answer to the above question.

A more direct and satisfying solution to the problem of confounding is to select events that are clearly independent of the psychological or physical condition of the subject (Brown, 1981; Dohrenwend et al., 1984; Hobfoll & Walfisch, in press). By selecting such events for study, researchers can make clear theoretical connections between stressors and stress outcomes. Since the individual did not cause the event and since it did not happen because of some indirect connection with some characteristic of the person, events and symptomatic outcomes cannot be confounded. Such events are surprisingly rare, however. Loss of job, marital discord, and school failure all have symptom-related components in their etiology. Even cancer or becoming a victim of a criminal attack or a traffic accident may be related to negligence or some other symptom-related behavior of the victim.

War: An Unconfounded Stressor

War meets the definition of an event whose occurrence may be regarded as independent of illness outcomes (Dohrenwend et al., 1984). Nations, not individuals, cause war, but individuals are affected by war. The term "pawns in the game" derives from chess, a game of war. How people are affected by war gives researchers one avenue of unconfounded study of the effect of stressful life events on psychological and physical outcomes.

Israel meets this condition of independence better than many other countries because almost everyone serves in the military. Whereas in most countries the poor, the adventurous, the young, and inhabitants of rural areas are most likely to go to war, in Israel the people who serve in the military are a representative cross-section of the entire population. This follows from the fact that regular army duty is required of all young men and most (unmarried) young women, and that the active reserves cover so large a proportion of the population that virtually everyone has an extended, if not an immediate, family member serving in the army in time of war. Accountants, truck drivers, clerks, and college professors all serve in the reserves, which constitute a major segment of the combat troops during war.

These conflicts also affect Israeli civilians because of the small size of the country (about the size of New Jersey) and the geographical proximity of Israel to hostile neighbors. Israelis felt this sense of vulnerability less prior to the 1973 Yom Kippur War when confidence in the deterrent character of Israeli military might was high. The first push of Egyptian and Syrian forces well into Israeli territory in 1973 and the magnitude of the attack undermined this overconfidence and made it clear that the threat of invasion is always realistic.

The recurring wars, terrorist attacks within Israel, dramatic changes in ethnic demography and acculturation, and other trends occurring rapidly in this dynamic society have recommended Israel as a natural stress laboratory (Breznitz, 1983b; Lazarus, 1982; Milgram, 1982a, b).

Although this is a dubious distinction, it is one that holds some advantage for an understanding of the stress-and-coping process.

The Contribution of War-Related Stress Research to Crisis Theory and Crisis Intervention

Crisis theory and crisis intervention have been major topics in the community psychology and the community mental health movements. A major tenet of crisis theory is that situational factors affect behavior during crisis more than personal characteristics of the individuals caught up in the crisis (Miller & Iscoe, 1963). Little research, however, has actually been carried out on this thesis (Hobfoll & Walfisch, in press).

The research that has been done relies on self-report by people when they come to regard their reaction to a crisis situation as abnormal and then seek help (Calsyn, Pribyl, & Sunukjian, 1977; Langsley & Kaplan, 1968; Parad & Parad, 1968). Although this form of self-report and self-referral is an accepted definition of crisis, namely, a marked change perceived by the individual as constituting a threat to one's well-being, it is often distant in time and place from the crisis event. It is the personal side of the crisis and not the event side.

Recently some crisis theorists have called for putting the crisis back in crisis research. They recommend studying reactions to major stressor events from the time of their occurrence (Hobfoll & Walfisch, in press; Ruch, Chandler, & Harter, 1980). This is easier said than done, first because many crises are private events and it is difficult to locate the people in crisis quickly enough, and second because it is unethical to conduct research on people in the throes of a major life crisis. These two problems, however, may be resolved in a satisfactory manner when conducting research on war, first because war is a public event and victims are readily identifiable, and second because war concerns all members of society and all have a moral obligation to aid others in need. In order to do so, we need to understand what is happening to them. Hence, war offers the opportunity and the ethical justification for research and intervention in acute crisis situations.

One of the major targets of crisis intervention in war is combat stress conditions. The research and clinical treatment literature on this topic has been extensive in recent years (e.g., Figley, 1978a; Kelly, 1985). The treatment principles cited by Salmon (1919) in World War I—proximity, immediacy, and expectancy—are still regarded as valid in dealing with acute stress reactions and have been effective in reducing psychiatric casualties in World War II and in the Korean War (Coleman, Butcher,

& Carson, 1984). They have not been applied in an explicit manner to civilian crisis disasters.

Intervention in a Civilian Disaster

One application of these intervention principles recently occurred in Israel in the wake of the worst traffic accident in the country's history, in which 19 children and three adults died in a schoolbus-train collision and countless other children were seriously injured. As we shall see, teachers and children were helped to cope with the aftermath of this traumatic event by interventions based in part on these principles (Milgram & Toubiana, 1985).

The accident occurred at about 8:30 A.M., Wednesday, June 11, 1985 and involved children from a junior high school in Petach Tikwa, a small city very close to Tel-Aviv. Within an hour a psychologist in the Youth Department of the Municipality of Petach Tikva (Yosef Toubiana, coauthor of Chapters 11 and 20 in this volume) was at the school and served as a participant–observer and member of the mental health team involved in the week-long intervention. There were pressing matters on which teachers requested immediate consultation: how to inform the other children of the disaster; to decide whether school was to remain open or to close immediately; how to greet the returning teachers and children of the other 12 buses that had left on the ill-fated school outing; how to conduct school in the days ahead so as to facilitate coping by children and teachers and to minimize psychiatric fallout; how to organize sensitive and comprehensive treatment for families of injured or deceased children. These issues and other treatment issues that arose in the harrowing days that followed were dealt with by the mental health team on location in conjunction with professional and lay groups offering services to the stricken community.

All children in the school were assumed to be at risk for a post-traumatic stress reaction or disorder. Most children in the same age classes knew well the victims of the bus accident. Children in other grades were also assumed to be at risk, since this was their first concrete experience with the death of age peers. The application of each combat stress treatment principle to this high risk group is described below.

Proximity. Teachers were told to insist that all children attend school and that no one remain home for any reason. Truant officers followed up on all missing children and implemented this policy. Parents were called and told that if their children were upset by the tragedy, they would receive help when they came to school. Since the traumatic event occurred to their schoolmates and, in some instances, their classmates, the proper treatment setting was judged to be the school and not the home or a community clinic.

Immediacy. The intervention was immediate and schoolwide. The day after the accident, all teachers were given orientation sessions to clarify their role in developing memorial activities in their own classroom and in guiding their class in schoolwide memorial activities. There was no effort to ignore or gloss over the magnitude of the human tragedy. There were discussions in the classroom about the circumstances of the event and its behavioral and emotional implications for the children. All children were given numerous opportunities to pay their respects to their deceased or injured friend(s). They wrote poems and drew pictures, visited the families of deceased or injured children, and visited the bedside of injured schoolmates. They stood silently for a few moments of prayer by a temporary monument constructed on school premises.

Expectancy. The official theme, enunciated in a variety of ways by teachers and counselors alike, was that a terrible tragedy had happened. Such tragedies do happen at times, but fortunately they are rare events. It was emphasized that all would grieve and no one would ever forget what had happened. An additional underlying message was that some of their reactions to the loss of their friends might persist for a while, but that all of their reactions were normal and understandable. Finally, they were told with a tone of total conviction: All of the children would recover very soon, resume their daily school and home routines, and regain their capacity for joy and pleasure in life, because that was the wish of the children who had died.

Children were seen briefly at their own request in one or two individual sessions to help them in coping with their sorrow, fear, and, in some instances, anger about the loss of their friends. In a few cases there was exploration of prior losses or other events in their past considered relevant to their current severe stress reaction. These children were also subjected to similar strong expectancies about recovery.

Community. A less well-known principle cited by Salmon in treating combat stress reactions is *community*, the recognition that each combat soldier's stress reaction is not necessarily or solely his own personal problem but is also the concern of his comrades and officers (Salmon & Fenton, 1929). Two military interventions follow from this principle.

First, soldiers with stress reactions are organized formally to help one another in self-help groups. Second, intact soldiers are briefed informally to reassure and encourage their temporarily incapacitated comrades to return to their units and duties.

The same principle was applied to the schoolchildren. Since the traumatic event occurred to their schoolmates, the appropriate context for dealing with the tragedy was within the school framework. Children were told by their teachers or counselors that some children would take this tragedy harder than others. It was their job to help one another, to encourage and involve the others in the various memorializing activities and in returning to routine classroom instruction, but not to mollycoddle anyone.

Because the academic year was rapidly drawing to a close, mental health workers and school authorities were concerned that some children might still be harboring symptoms detrimental to their recovery. Accordingly, all children filled out a symptom checklist and were offered the opportunity to attend a week-long session of sport, recreational, and *other* activities after school officially closed for the summer. These activities were on the school grounds. Guidance counselors had access to these questionnaires and were able to contact selected children. Nearly all children who had expressed interest in this program enrolled. This amounted to well over half the age peers of the victims, and the program was later endorsed by these participants as successful on all accounts.

A month after the accident, children who had originally expressed interest in counseling were invited to participate in group sessions, but only 3 of the 101 children invited showed up for the session. In addition, as of this writing (Yosef Toubiana, personal communication, November 1985), injured survivors and siblings of deceased children were in ongoing treatment, but only three other children from the school and none from other city schools approached the three major mental health settings in the area because of problems connected with the bus accident. A systematic follow-up of these children is underway, but the initial follow-up is consistent with our expectation of a low level of psychiatric fallout from this stressful, tragic event.

The Effect of Personal and Social Support Resources on Coping with Life-Threatening and Physically Exhausting Situations

The magnitude of the relationship between stressful events and outcomes has been modest (Rabkin & Struening, 1976), thereby encouraging researchers to investigate mediating variables that enhance this relationship. These variables may be loosely called personal and social re-sources. The former category refers to such resources as self-esteem, hardiness, self-confidence, strong physical and psychological constitu-tion, and prior experience and training in dealing with crisis situations. The latter refers to helpful family members, friends, neighbors, and strangers experiencing the threatening situation. These internal personal resources and external social support systems lend themselves to in-vestigation in wartime and to application in peacetime. Numerous stud-ies have shown that access to and reliance on these resources lead to more effective performance in stressful situations (Lazarus & Folkman, 1984; Lieberman, 1982; Milgram & Zucker, 1986).

Biological stressors and biological fatigue reactions are frequently en-countered in wartime military service and are of considerable theoretical and practical interest. In many wartime situations enormous physical effort over long periods of time is required for effective functioning. These situations may also be characterized by lack of opportunity for sleep, food, and other amenities of normal living. Given these condi-tions, one finds large differences in biological fatigue, and in adaptive behavior despite fatigue, between soldiers in the same unit and between units exposed to exhausting situations of comparable intensity and du-ration.

The research on biological stressors and fatigue has been considerable. One direction has been laboratory and field studies on the effect of physical stressors on performance as a function of variations in the stressor themselves (e.g., hours of sleep deprivation). Another direction, represented by the five chapters in Section Four of this book, has been the study of the mediating or buffering effect of personal, motivational, and interpersonal variables on performance in physically taxing situa-tions in the field or the laboratory. The variables investigated were com-petition and coaction (Chapter 15), competition and feedback (Chapter 14), strategies of self-regulation (Chapter 16), styles of cognitive appraisal (Chapter 17), and personal characteristics (e.g., confidence expectancy, Chapter 13).

War offers an unusual opportunity to examine the buffering effect of still other personal and social variables on biological exertion in physi-cally threatening, if not life-threatening, situations. We shall examine four combat situations, the first in the Israeli Defense Forces and the other three in the American Army.

Consider the case of the Israeli Seventh Armored Brigade in the 1973 war against Syria and Egypt. On Yom Kippur, the holiest day of the Jewish year, October 6, 1973, Israel was attacked by Arab forces that were the equivalent of the combined NATO command (Herzog, 1984). When the Golan Heights were invaded by Syrian forces, there were only two armored brigades facing them. Because of Israel's lack of preparedness, the Seventh (led by Colonel Avigdor Ben Gal) had to bear the full brunt of the Syrian attack in the central sector. Experts estimate that at the onset of the battle there were 177 tanks in the brigade against 1,500 Syrian tanks of comparable quality (Herzog, 1984).

Three days later the brigade was still engaged in continuous battle, with little opportunity for sleep and limited food and water supplies. Some soldiers continued fighting although they were wounded. Two days later the brigade was still on the same line, but not a single Syrian tank remained in fighting condition within the original Israeli battle line. An experienced psychiatrist visited the brigade at this time, fully expecting the men to fall back for hospitalization and rest. To his experienced eye, they appeared to have persevered beyond physical endurance. But in fact, they were making preparations not to retire, but to mount a major counteroffensive against the Syrians. On October 11, the Seventh Armored Brigade led the Israeli advance into Syrian territory.

How did these men continue to fight at peak levels for such sustained periods? They had come directly from synagogues and homes and from the Yom Kippur fast itself. They were surprised and hopelessly outnumbered, yet they fought on. We can find answers to our questions in their training, their *esprit de corps*, their leadership, and the fact that they were fighting on their own native soil close to their loved ones. We can, in addition, move from the level of inspiring saga or anecdote to that of scientific data by interviewing men who participated in such battles some time later and by obtaining other data in their military files and in unit reports about the quality of their training, group cohesiveness, performance in previous combat encounters, and leadership.

Contrast this event with the wartime performance of two divisions in the Pacific who were never able to recover from the surprise attack on Pearl Harbor that brought the United States into World War II. The 24th Division, which had been responsible for the defense of Oahu (the island on which Pearl Harbor is located), and the 43rd, deployed in New Georgia, were plagued by poor leadership, poor morale, chronic organizational problems, high psychiatric casualty rates, and high rates of noncombat injuries (e.g., minor injuries and dehydration). In the latter, peer and officer support were so low that entire platoons broke down (Marlowe, 1979).

By contrast, the 442nd Regimental Combat Team, which was composed almost entirely of Nisei (native-born Americans of Japanese background) from Hawaii and from relocation centers in the United States, was the most highly decorated unit in the American army. This unit participated in some of the most intensive fighting in the Italian campaign. Despite, or more likely because of, the fact that their families were in relocation camps and their patriotism was questioned because of their race, this unit developed and sustained high morale and group cohesion.

These examples (Marlowe, 1979) illustrate that lack of a sense of mastery (one way to define poor morale), poor social support in the form of poor commanders, and adverse experiences, without a countervailing commitment to persevere in adversity, exercise an adverse effect on performance during life-threatening and physically exhausting situations and on subsequent health outcomes. In contrast, a commitment to persevere, high morale, and group cohesiveness lead not only to better coping, but to achievements beyond expectation.

Marlowe (1979) notes that over half of the cases of combat fatigue in World War II took place during the soldier's *first time in combat* and before he had the opportunity to establish cohesive group ties within his unit. The implications for nonwar stress situations are clear. Groups considered at high risk for breakdown in threatening and physically demanding situations must be given the incentive, the training experiences, and the opportunities for developing cohesive ties *before* they accept assignments that might bring about this exposure. This kind of thinking is relevant for the training of Americans working overseas for American government agencies, civilian airline personnel, and local officials and professional people residing in areas vulnerable to natural disasters (e.g., hurricanes, floods).

The answers to these questions are relevant to the functioning of everyday people in psychologically and physically draining experiences. Consider the mother at a sick child's bedside maintaining a vigil for long hours with little sleep and then having to make a rapid decision when the child appears to take a turn for the worse. Or the medical resident called upon to perform surgery after a diet on duty of coffee and doughnuts and after having been on call for 30 hours consecutively. Or the team of electrical linemen working in inclement conditions to repair a major power failure due to a windstorm. We can better understand how these people function and can better provide guidelines and training procedures for people in advance of their being called upon to function in such crises if we analyze the relevant data on mind-body interaction in war-related stressful situations.

COMBAT STRESS REACTIONS AND DISORDERS: DIAGNOSIS, PREVALENCE, AND TREATMENT

Reactions to combat stress take the form of disruptions in autonomic sensitivity (hypo- or hyper-), emotionality (anxiety, depression, or constricted affect), cognition and attention (confusion, distractibility, hypervigilance), and in purposive behavior. These reactions occur during or following exposure to extraordinary events that threaten life and/or one's beliefs about personal invulnerability and about the predictability of events. Whatever form these reactions take, the common denominator is behavior incompatible with sustained, effective functioning as a soldier.

Figley (1985, p. xix) draws a distinction within this phenomenon between *traumatic stress reaction* and *post-traumatic stress reaction*. The first refers to symptomatic behavior that occurs in response to, and in the continuing presence of, the *stressors* of the catastrophic event or that occur immediately afterward. The second refers to symptomatic behavior occurring later in response to the *memories* of these stressors, the original stressors no longer being present in the new setting in which the soldier finds himself (e.g., new terrain, a rear-echelon encampment, a hospital). We do not make this distinction, but agree with Figley in distinguishing these acute, fluid stress reactions from crystallized, persistent *post-traumatic stress disorders*. The latter are psychiatric conditions that are refractory to opportunities for rest and recovery and to routine front-echelon treatment, and may become chronic and irreversible.

Large numbers of combat soldiers display combat stress reactions: as many as 10% of the American soldiers engaged in combat in World War II (Bloch, 1969; Coleman, Butcher, & Carson, 1984). The actual incidence in that war or in any other war is not known, since many soldiers receive supportive therapy at their battalion aid stations and return to combat within a few hours without any record made of their transient reaction and brief treatment. Records are kept mainly on soldiers evacuated from the frontlines for more serious disturbances and treated for several days rather than for several hours.

These men are regarded as temporarily incapacitated and are typically provided with short-term treatment based on the traditional principles of crisis intervention in general and of early intervention in combat stress reaction in particular. This treatment emphasizes Salmon's well-known principles, which are elaborated below:

1. *Temporal immediacy,* as reflected in the brief passage of time from the appearance of symptomatic behavior to the removal of the soldier from the traumatizing setting and the initiation of treatment

2. *Physical proximity and ecological similarity* of the field treatment setting to the military setting in which the traumatic experience occurred

3. *Expectancy of recovery,* as reflected in the behavior of the mental health and other military personnel toward the incapacitated soldier, and in the demands and duties required of the soldier during his stay at the forward-echelon field station

4. *Community,* the recognition that the *individual's* behavioral problem arose within the context of a military *group* exposed to traumatic combat events and is more effectively resolved in another military group by members of the group. One's military identity was shattered by the combat experience and is best reconstituted in a group effort of combat veterans with similar problems (see the discussion on group therapy in Chapter 12D).

Front-echelon treatment of acute combat stress reaction provides respite from the rigors of combat (rest, relaxation, food, warmth), maintains military discipline, and requires the performance of drills and routines during the brief stay at the field station. It affords the opportunity for ventilation of feelings and abreaction of the unique experiences that the individual soldier underwent in combat.

This treatment does not examine the personal vulnerabilities or premorbid characteristics of the soldier that may have contributed to the breakdown in adaptive behavior. The reasons for avoiding these topics in front-echelon treatment are both practical and theoretical: first, because the brief nature of the front-echelon treatment precludes considering personal as well as situation factors; second, because even if there were opportunity for considering relevant material from the past, the rationale of the treatment precludes it. We are reluctant to raise the issue of personal factors contributing to symptom formation because it may encourage the soldier to regard himself as weak, ill, and responsible in some way for his condition. If front-echelon treatment proves unsuccessful in restoring the soldier to effective functioning, we then consider rear-echelon treatment for a post-traumatic stress disorder. The setting and the rationale of the latter treatment are appropriate for eliciting and dealing with psychodynamic material from one's past.

Efficacy of Front-Echelon Treatment for Combat Stress Reaction

This approach was found to be successful in returning the majority of soldiers to duty in World War II. Prior to its initiation, combat exhaustion was considered the greatest single cause of loss of manpower in the war; during certain periods early in the war one-third of all casualties and one-half of all medical discharges from service were for psychiatric reasons (Glass, 1971; Glass & Bernucci, 1966). When front-echelon treatment was instituted, however, recovery rates were very high. The Bartemeier Commission was able to conclude from its postwar review that combat stress reactions represented a temporary disorganization. They reported that in 95% of the cases, the acute reactions subsided after a brief period away from combat, with the soldiers returning to their units (Bartemeier, Kubie, Menninger, Romano, & Whitehorn, 1946). Other studies on the effectiveness of forward-echelon treatment in World War II yielded lower estimates of recovery, an 80 to 90% rate of return to duty for soldiers who had been in combat for a month or less, but a far lower recovery rate (30 to 35%) for soldiers who had been in intensive, continuous combat for many months (Ludwig & Ransom, 1947).

Comparable statistics were obtained for forward-echelon treatment in the Korean War, with 65 to 75% (Hausman & Rioch, 1967) returning to duty and functioning symptom-free for the duration of their military service. Even more favorable findings were reported during the early years of the Vietnam War (Allerton, 1970; Bourne, 1970), with claims that the psychiatric disability rate was far lower than in the Korean War or World War II.

These figures and comforting conclusions have since been challenged for many reasons:

1. The criteria for combat stress reactions were less well defined in previous wars and were sufficiently vague so that commanders and mental health officers might elect to ignore some mild cases altogether or, alternately, to assign severe cases to other diagnostic categories and dispositions (conduct or personality disturbance). The motivation for underreporting combat stress reaction may be found in the reluctance of some field commanders to report the prevalence of a psychiatric syndrome, however transient, that casts aspersions on the quality of leadership and cohesiveness of the military unit.

2. Findings were frequently based on clinical judgment or on impressions rather than on empirical data.

3. Some findings were based on heterogeneous and unrepresentative groups. Some stress reaction groups included soldiers whose disability was attributed to exposure to combat and soldiers whose functioning deteriorated for other reasons and without exposure to combat. Findings based on such heterogeneous groups compared to equally heterogeneous control groups can be very misleading.

4. Some studies based their generalizations on piecemeal criteria of initial disturbance and subsequent functioning rather than on a comprehensive assessment of the stress reaction, its consequences, and the extent of remission or recovery.

5. Few studies provided for comprehensive long-term follow-up. It is necessary to follow-up and compare the subsequent military performance of soldiers successfully treated for combat stress reactions and of soldiers symptom-free during combat, but at risk for delayed stress reactions. It is also necessary to follow up their civilian adjustment, especially if discharge from military service is soon after combat.

Given these limitations, we may draw a qualified conclusion about treatment efficacy for combat stress reaction: the majority of soldiers will return to their unit and acquit themselves well if certain favorable circumstances prevail. These include (1) optimal levels of the situational variables in the soldier's unit that inoculate against adverse stress reactions; (2) effective short-term, front-echelon treatment as described earlier; (3) low levels of combat stress intensity preceding the appearance of the combat stress reaction; (4) low level of combat stress intensity in the combat situation to which the soldier returns; and (4) the war is *conventional* in character. The actual size of this majority remains an open question. The data presented in Sections Two and Three of this volume provide some estimates of success rates in the Israeli Defense Forces in the early phase of the War in Lebanon.

Post-Traumatic Stress Disorders: Diagnosis and Treatment

Some soldiers who initially recover from combat stress reaction afterward succumb to a recurrence of crippling symptoms. They join others who did not respond to initial treatment and a third group displaying *delayed stress reaction* as much as six months after the stressful experience. These three groups constitute a new category, that of soldiers at high risk for a formal diagnosis of *post-traumatic combat stress disorder* (PTSD). This diagnosis is associated with extensive and severe maladjustment and a potentially chronic and irreversible disability. Lengthy treatment in VA hospitals and clinics follows. Negative consequences may arise from the iatrogenic character of treatment in these psychiatric settings and the system of veterans' disability compensation payments.

Generalizations about the efficacy of treatment of veterans with PTSD are as problematic as the diverse studies and research methodologies on which they are based. Suffice it to say that substantial numbers of World War II and Korean War veterans receive disability payments to this day because of psychiatric conditions that are regarded as combat-connected. Since this is the case, one may safely conclude that many veterans did not respond to treatment. Others experienced a recurrence of symptoms later in military service or after discharge, were found to be seriously disturbed, and receive veterans benefits for psychiatric disability. In addition, there are men not receiving veterans disability compensation who are symptom-ridden, unhappy, and incapacitated.

Waller's incisive indictment of American society for failing to redress the just grievances of its returning warriors describes some of the normative postwar residuals of traumatic stress disorder in World War II veterans after returning home. His descriptions suggests that large numbers of soldiers who may never have appeared on the PTSD rolls during the war were, indeed, afflicted, but were never afforded the opportunity to work through their residual symptoms. His book is as timely for Vietnam veterans today as it was for the World War II veterans in whose behalf it was written 42 years ago (Waller, 1944 in Figley, 1980a).

Post-Traumatic Stress Disorders in Vietnam Veterans

It is premature to draw conclusions about the incidence of PTSD in Vietnam veterans even a decade after the end of the war. In his comprehensive reviews of the studies extant, Figley (Figley, 1978b; Figley & Southerly, 1980) was very cautious in forming generalizations about the prevalence and severity of PTSD in these veterans.

The conventional wisdom during the war itself was that combat stress reactions and subsequent PTSD were remarkably low, as compared with earlier wars. These encouraging conclusions were attributed to the special circumstances of the conduct of this war, especially the rule that a soldier's term of duty was 12 months, and that his date of expected return from overseas (DEROS) dictated when he would depart from the war zone and immediately return to the United States. Since the soldier's tour of duty was relatively short and time limited and his return home at its end was assured, these circumstances were presumed to minimize the deleterious effects of combat stress.

Many years have passed since the veterans have returned home, and opinions about the short- and long-term effects of DEROS and about the form that PTSD took in the Vietnam War have changed drastically. We are now provided with a rich clinical literature and with new data asserting that Vietnam was not the best, but the worst, of wars with regard to the prevalence of PTSD (see the empirical investigations, surveys, and case studies reported in Figley, 1985; Figley & Leventman, 1980a; and Kelly, 1985).

Estimates of the prevalence of PTSD in veterans of the Vietnam War range upward from 25% of *all military personnel serving in the combat area* (Walker & Cavenar, 1982). Frye and Stockton (1982) report that 43% of officers in their sample reported moderate to severe symptoms of PTSD 10 years after returning from combat. Since officers tend to have lower incidence of post-traumatic stress disorders than enlisted men, we can assume that the percentages for enlisted men are even higher. Hendin and Haas (1984) cite a report of the Veterans Administration in 1980 estimating that about half of the combat veterans in Vietnam are afflicted with post-traumatic stress disorders.

Definitive generalizations about the incidence of PTSD in these veterans will depend in the final analysis on a number of factors: (1) the extent to which the follow-up is systematic and comprehensive; (2) whether there is strict adherence to current DSM-III criteria (APA, 1980) or a broadening of these criteria to cover new psychopathologies; and (3) the treatment and compensation policies adopted by government and mental health authorities with regard to service-connected psychiatric disabilities stemming from the Vietnam War.

The postwar adjustment of Vietnam veterans has been complicated and aggravated by a number of developments. Among these are the changing occupational patterns that produced unemployment in those occupations in which many of the veterans were seeking employment, and increased drug abuse in American society in general and adjustment complications due to drug use by returning veterans in particular. More important, however, were the unique features and societal implications of this particular war and its aftereffects. These features and their implications are dealt with in the next part of this chapter.

A COMPARISON OF THE AMERICAN INVOLVEMENT IN VIETNAM AND THE ISRAELI INVOLVEMENT IN LEBANON

Numerous observers in Israel and in the United States have drawn comparisons between the American involvement in Vietnam and Israel's involvement in Lebanon. We examine this issue here in terms of the psychological consequence of these involvements for combat soldiers. In doing this, we found it necessary to refer to historical, political, and ideological developments. We tried to be objective in these matters, but we recognize that biases affect everyone. A sincere effort was made, however, to stick to factual information and to draw balanced conclusions.

The Surface Similarities of the Vietnam and Lebanon Wars

The similarities between Lebanon and Vietnam are impressive:

1. Both were the longest wars ever fought by the respective countries, over 10 years for the United States and over three years for Israel.
2. The goals of both wars became unclear and unconvincing to many of their own citizens.
3. Both Vietnam and Lebanon were non-Western countries wracked by civil war and highly motivated to rid the region of Western presence and influence. This complex situation lent an unconventional character to each war (including guerrilla warfare and other unorthodox combat features).
4. The outcomes were unsatisfactory in both wars, more unsatisfactory than in any previous war fought by either country.
5. There was dissension in both countries during the war over objectives, proper conduct of the war, and the involvement of its soldiers in alleged atrocities against defenseless civilians. The magnitude of the dissent was greater than each country had known in its conduct of previous wars in this century.
6. The incidence of post-traumatic combat stress disorder was reported to be extraordinarily low in the initial stages of both wars.

We have seen that the initial American estimates missed the mark and that there are projections of Vietnam war-related stress disorders of endemic proportions (Fuller, 1985). Sections Two and Three of this volume present a picture of a low incidence of PTSD in Israeli combat soldiers, far lower than in the previous Yom Kippur War. Are these reports premature? Do the similarities between conflicts cited above portend a corresponding development in Israel, a rise in the incidence of PTSD in veterans of the War in Lebanon to endemic proportions? And if not, why not?

Vietnam: The Worst of American Wars

Circumstances of the war. When we look back on the Vietnam War, it is an easy matter to enumerate some of the factors in the war itself that contributed to poor psychiatric outcomes for combat soldiers.

1. *Vietnam was not a conventional war.* The United States intervened to bolster one side invaded by another in a civil and ideological war. It intervened to maintain Western influence in a region of the world that had been struggling to expel Western occupation, presence, and influence for most of the twentieth century. Given the unusual features of the war, American political and military leadership never clarified for itself, much less for the soldiers or for the society as a whole, realistic and convincing objectives (Leventman & Camacho, 1980; see preface in Figley & Leventman, 1980b).

As a consequence, American society became increasingly disenchanted with the war. Many young men who were to be drafted to fight in this war questioned its goals. Moreover, the official goals of the war for which soldiers in the field were asked to risk and sacrifice their lives became nebulous and unconvincing, and at times absurd. This was especially true of the goals of a particular military operation in the field where one seized territory at considerable loss of life one day only to relinquish it voluntarily the next. Ultimately the goal became to kill the enemy and to avoid getting killed oneself (Shatan, 1978).

2. *The identity of friend and foe in the native population became hopelessly blurred.* Since this was a civil war, one could be attacked and seriously harmed by civilian combatants, e.g., babies wired to explode, children concealing grenades, women armed and ready to kill. The ethnic identity of friend and foe alike encouraged the development of racist attitudes and hatred of the Vientamese people whether friends or foes (Wikler, 1980).

3. *Vietnam was a dirty war.* The war was conducted with a disregard for life and the suffering of civilians. Many Vietnamese, not unlike many Koreans and Campocheans, tortured and murdered their own people in an appalling manner to achieve their ends. Given the unusual character of a war in which civilians, including women and children, killed soldiers, the Americans retaliated in kind. In addition, they exploded in pointless violence against helpless civilians because of their inability to achieve tangible objectives in the war. Losing the distinction between soldiers and civilians, they became involved in atrocities that shocked the American people. Moreover, the atrocities that soldiers witnessed

or committed continued to haunt them when they returned home (Haley, 1985; Laufer, Frey-Wouters, & Gallops, 1985; Tanay, 1985).

Circumstances of military service in Vietnam. There were specific conditions of military service that contributed to adverse stress reactions in combat soldiers.

4. *Individual tours of duty.* Soldiers rotated in and out of Vietnam as individuals for a prescribed tour of duty. The stage of the war and the individual soldier's role in the campaign underway were irrelevant considerations. When one's date of return came up, he left for home.

This system had two negative consequences. First, combat soldiers did not feel that they were part of an ongoing campaign. Their participation was not important or necessary, and their own major goal was simply to bide time and to stay alive. Second, there was little opportunity to develop group cohesiveness. Men came and went on the basis of their individual date of return. Unit cohesiveness and the sense of mutual responsibility that function as stress-buffering factors in military service were largely absent (Kormos, 1978; Moskos, 1980).

5. *The ratio of combat to support troops in Vietnam.* Especially galling to combat troops was the realization that the vast majority of soldiers serving in Vietnam were noncombat. This silent majority served in support and logistic capacities in the large cities or in protected bases, and their lives were rarely in danger. Combat soldiers, by contrast, jeopardized life and limb whenever they went into the countryside, walked a jungle trail, or approached a Vietnam hamlet. Waller (in Figley & Leventman, 1980) documents the anger and resentment of combat troops against soldiers who sit out the war in safe billets.

6. *Drug addiction.* One way to handle the anguish of military service in Vietnam was to wipe it out with the use of drugs that were in ample supply and inexpensive. Although the majority of veterans did not persist in the same forms of drug addiction when they returned home, the long-term adjustment problems of many combat veterans were complicated by excessive use of alcohol and other substances (Nace et al., 1978; Stanton, 1980).

7. *Psychiatric treatment was inadequate in Vietnam.* During the war itself military psychiatrists reported very low figures for PTSD, failing to realize or refusing to acknowledge that the true figures were masked by extensive use of drugs in Vietnam and by false reports of troop efficiency in operations. Nor was Vietnam the proper setting for soldiers to abreact their feelings about witnessing or participating in atrocities of one kind

or another. These topics were taboo in the military unit and in the psychiatric setting (Panzarella, Mantell, & Bridenbaugh, 1978).

8. *The effect of the antiwar protest while overseas.* One cannot minimize or ignore the effect of antiwar protest on soldiers when serving in Vietnam or when preparing to return for a second tour of duty. Soldiers can be trained to ignore these forms of protest when conditions in the field justify in their eyes pursuing the goals of the war to a successful end. No amount of indoctrination could blind soldiers in Vietnam to the nature of the day-to-day conduct of the war, especially in the latter half of the war. The evidence from the field confirmed the doubts raised by the antiwar protest that they were serving in the wrong war, in the wrong place, at the wrong time (Silver, 1985; Smith, 1980).

Circumstances during and after discharge. The difficulties of soldiers were compounded when they were discharged from service.

9. *Transition.* The transition from combat to civilian life was very abrupt, a matter of days. There was no opportunity to undergo systematic or unsystematic desensitization before returning to a very different world (Borus, 1976; Smith, 1980). As a consequence, the unreality and horror of combat in Vietnam persisted in the form of respondent conditioned responses of terrifying import and impact.

10. *The bias in the antiwar protest movement after returning home.* This protest further demoralized combat soldiers once they returned home because it was wholly one-sided, focusing only on the inhumanity committed by American soldiers on the Vietnamese people and ignoring the character of this invasion–civil war and the atrocities perpetrated by Vietnamese, North and South, against one another. Combat soldiers who were struggling with their own conscience and sensibilities about atrocities they had witnessed or in which they had participated were further buffeted by accusations that they were killers of innocent people. They returned home not as heroes, but as fools at best and psychopathic killers at worst (Camacho, 1980; Schuetz, 1980; Silver, 1985; Tanay, 1985; Wilson, 1980).

11. *The conspiracy of silence.* There were no influential figures in political or cultural life who spoke up in the name of these confused and traumatized men at the time. No one really wanted to listen to them or to a recapitulation of what it was like. Family and friends were reluctant to listen to horror stories, the army itself preferred to ignore evidence of the true nature of the war in Vietnam, and the mental health establishment was ill equipped and attitudinally unsuited to deal with post-traumatic stress stemming from these hellish experiences.

Civilian psychiatry was unsympathetic, moreover, to the needs of returning veterans who tended to come from the less educated and less established segments of the community. In the view of many civilians in the mental health professions, the maladjustment of these veterans was either the cause of the atrocities they were accused of committing to begin with, or they were experiencing poetic justice, the punishment they deserved for serving in a terrible and evil war. These mental health professionals did not provide the setting in which veterans could unburden themselves of the sequelae of their experiences (Egendorf, 1978; Figley & Leventman, 1980b; Haley, 1978).

Coming home a second time. This conspiracy of silence or outright refusal to listen to this material reminds one of the plight of Holocaust survivors emerging from the death camps of Europe at the end of World War II. They had been the victims of hellish experiences and nobody wanted to listen, at least not for very long. They were to get about the business of rebuilding their lives and keep their nightmares and horror stories to themselves. No wonder that for many survivors, the material lay dormant, but intrusive, and would appear to torment them or to disrupt their behavior in the future. In the case of the Holocaust survivors, over 30 years passed before survivors, mental health practitioners, and the public were ready for an interchange (Danieli, 1985).

In the case of Vietnam combat veterans, the latency period was far shorter, about 10 years. Today in the mass media, in plays and novels, and in the halls of Congress, the current predicament of these combat survivors from the Vietnam War is being recognized and better appreciated (see postscript in Figley, 1980a; Fuller, 1985; Milano, 1980).

How to help extricate them from their predicament is a complex question. Restricting ourselves to a discussion of treatment, defined narrowly, we are heartened by recent innovative approaches. The chief one is readjustment counseling provided by storefront counseling centers for Vietnam veterans. The program, which became known as Operation Outreach, was initiated in 1979 and was placed outside the physical and administrative structure of the VA. Formal results are not yet in, but the program was praised by veterans who came to these Vet Centers and began to achieve better social and economic adjustment (Bitzer, 1980; Fuller, 1985). A second development is more empathic understanding of the veteran in the mental health professions treating former combat soldiers in hospitals, clinics, and storefront centers (Racek, 1985; Sax, 1985; Woods, Sherwood, & Thompson, 1985), and better training of personnel.

Was the War in Lebanon Regarded by Combat Soldiers as a Costly and Tragic Mistake?

The Israeli involvement in Lebanon was assessed according to the same features applied to American involvement in Vietnam.

1. Lebanon was an unconventional war and many of the goals set by the government and the military services were never realized. Nevertheless, many segments of Israeli society and many soldiers in regular service considered the war justified and believe that a number of its goals were realized.

2. Blurring of the identities of the various groups battling in Lebanon and hatred of one or all of them did not develop in Israeli combat soldiers for several reasons. Lebanon borders on Israel. Its internal politics, civil war, and internal ethnic animosities are common knowledge in Israel. Israeli soldiers and Lebanese civilians share at least two languages (Arabic and English) and communicate freely. There have been friendly ongoing contacts with the population of Southern Lebanon for many years. The Lebanese resemble Israelis, especially Israelis whose parents came from Arab-speaking countries. The identities of friends and foes changed during the war,* but there was no blurring of ethnic identities, and Israelis did not develop racist or dehumanizing attitudes toward the Lebanese people.

3. Israeli involvement in Lebanon was less gruesome, less cruel, and less traumatizing for combat soldiers than American involvement in Vietnam. There were massacres of ethnic groups in Lebanon by one another depending on a shift in power and opportunity. Notwithstanding the international furor over Israel's entry into Lebanon and the bombing of Beirut, Israeli soldiers never intentionally gunned down defenseless civilians, tortured or killed prisoners, or mutilated bodies. The death of innocent civilians was decried by Israel.† All battle orders were specific

---

*In the course of the conflict, the Maronite Christians in the North became increasingly unreliable friends, and the underprivileged Shiite Moslem population in the South, who first applauded the expulsion of the PLO (Palestine Liberation Organization), ultimately resorted to suicide and guerrilla attacks to accelerate Israel's withdrawal and to weaken Israel's support of the Christian South Lebanon militia. These developments were sources of frustration, but did not bring about hatred of these groups.

†The domestic reaction in Israel to the events of Sabra and Shatilla where Palestinian and non-Palestinian men, women, and children were killed by Maronite Christian militiamen was one of horror at the idea that Israel either knew of the impending action or stood by and permitted it to happen. If Israeli soldiers perpetrated such massacres during the conflict, it would have become common knowledge and the perpetrators would have been condemned and punished.

about this proscription. The vast majority of Israeli soldiers *shared the above perception*; they themselves had not witnessed or participated in massacres or other atrocities, and as a consequence, they were not haunted by mental intrusions about these themes. On occasion soldiers mistakenly harmed or killed civilians, and these events placed these men at high risk for combat stress reaction and later PTSD.

4. Reserve soldiers served several months in the early phase of the campaign and were discharged when certain objectives were attained. New reserve units were rotated in and out (for 60-day tours of duty), resulting in some reservists serving on two or three occasions up to six months in the first year, but usually less. The regular army served continuously with furloughs home as conditions permitted. During their service in Lebanon, the norm was for soldiers in the regular army to serve in units with their comrades in arms; this was somewhat less true for the reserves. Overall, one may conclude that if group cohesiveness was the exception in Vietnam, it was the rule in the conflict in Lebanon.

5. Israeli combat soldiers rarely have an occasion for directing resentment against others who either avoid the draft altogether or obtain safe and secure assignments far from the front. This may be related to a number of factors. First, there is universal conscription of Israeli males at age 18 and even men in their fifties are still serving in the reserves in wartime. Second, young women are drafted and handle many noncombat assignments, freeing a larger percentage of males for combat duty. Third, even men in noncombat roles serve in support roles that bring them up to the front lines and expose them to many hazards.

6. Drugs were easily available in Lebanon, but a number of circumstances worked against widespread use or addiction. There were frequent visits home even for the young men serving in the regular army. Second, there was a strong sentiment against drug use in the army. Third, continual contact between younger men in regular service and older family men in the reserves discouraged the use of drugs. Fourth, the only drug used was hashish. Overall, there is little evidence of addiction in Lebanon or when soldiers were discharged from military service.

7. Psychiatric treatment for combat stress reaction (described in Section Three of this volume) was successful in returning the majority of men to their units after a few days. The personnel were well trained and sympathetic.

8. The extent of the antiwar protest in Israel and its effect on the morale of Israeli troops has been exaggerated in the United States. There was protest, but it took the path of democratic dialogue and never re-

sulted in an us-them split. Antiwar sentiment in Israel never reached the dimensions it did in the United States where the party in power was driven out of office or thousands of young men fled the country to avoid military service.*

9. The transition from combat to noncombat activity and to home was more natural for Israeli soldiers. There were short furloughs during one's tour of regular duty and extended leave until the next tour of reserve duty. This transition is well practiced in Israel whose many wars have trained the entire populace to shift from war to no war and from firing guns to pulling plowshares as a matter of (unfortunate) routine.

10. There was a careful distinction in the mass media and in the most vitriolic of public attacks on the war between the ruling government figures who conducted the war and the armed forces who carried out the orders. Israeli soldiers were never called murderers by their own people. After all, they come from all walks of life and all ethnic groups and social classes, unlike American armed forces, heavily drawn from the less educated and underprivileged classes. Soldiers came home to a society that respected their courage, sympathized with their losses, and at worst indicted several political leaders for engaging in reckless adventurism.

11. There was no conspiracy of silence in Israel about the war. Soldiers could usually find ways to discuss their views, their grievances, and even their traumatic experiences. Pro- and antiwar sentiment coexisted and were debated within the society, but never at the expense of the soldiers themselves (Landes, *Yediot Ahronot*, 1982, July 11; Leor, *Yediot Ahronot*, 1983, July 26; Soldiers against silence, *Yediot Ahronot*, 1982, August 13).

Summary and Conclusions

On the basis of these considerations, we believe that a dramatic rise in PTSD among Israeli combat veterans is unlikely. We turned to Shabtai

---

*This conclusion is based on the following facts. First, the number of men who refused to serve in Lebanon was several hundred out of several hundred thousand or more. Second, a majority of soldiers in the regular army supported the war and voted in the 1984 elections for the party that initiated the war (the Likud Party) (Gal-Nur, *Haaretz*, September 2, 8, 1984). Third, public attitudes toward the war were so split that the leaders of the antiwar Labor Party decided not to attack the government on the war issue in the 1984 election campaign believing that criticism of the war would cost them more votes than it would gain. Fourth, despite a calamitous inflation caused by the prowar party in power, the antiwar Labor Party achieved only a razor-thin majority and had to form a coalition government with the prowar Likud Party, agreeing to a sharing of power and rotation of the office of Prime Minister.

Noy, a major researcher on PTSD in Israel (author of six chapters in Sections Two and Three of this volume) and Head of the Research Branch of the Mental Health Department of the Israel Defense Forces. We asked him if there was corroboration from his follow-up data of an increase in PTSD in the last year of the war as its character changed, casualties continued, and some of the earlier achievements turned to ashes: The Israeli-Lebanese Peace Treaty was unilaterally annulled by the Lebanon government and Israeli soldiers became *persona non grata* on Lebanese soil.

He stated that there was no evidence supporting a rise in combat stress disorders (Noy, personal communication, November 10, 1985). On the contrary, more than two-thirds of all cases of combat stress reaction occurred in the early and active phase of the war (June-September 1982) when the vast majority of the casualties (deaths and injuries) occurred. Furthermore, many of the cases presenting for treatment after cessation of intensive hostilities were diagnosed as late or delayed reactions and were attributed to the earlier intensive fighting. Subsequent combat stress reactions until the final withdrawal of Israeli soldiers from Lebanon were found to be specific to life-threatening situations personally experienced by those soldiers who were the object of suicide car bombings, sniper attack, or road mines. These life-threatening episodes occurred to a relatively small number of combat soldiers, and there was no evidence of spread of effect or increased psychiatric disturbance in soldiers who were not directly involved in these episodes. In his communication he reminded us that the major determinant, after all, of combat stress conditions is the objective stress level of victimizing circumstances, the number of direct casualties (deaths and injuries). These were relatively few in number and there was a correspondingly low level of indirect or psychiatric casualties.

The foregoing discussion and conclusion are not contradicted by the presence of significant numbers of former Israeli veterans with moderate to severe service-connected psychiatric disability. Milgram, Arad, Toubiana, and Falach (1984) interviewed a number of veterans with service-connected disability incurred between 1967 and 1981. These investigators found that some of the former veterans are characterized by chronic PTSD with severe maladjustment in both the occupational and interpersonal realm for a decade or more. In our opinion, many of these men were psychiatrically mismanaged when they first succumbed to combat stress reactions and afterward developed the chronic symptoms of PTSD. Efforts are being made in Israel today to avoid these mistakes and to emphasize, along with the short-term treatment of combat stress reactions, long-term treatment programs for chronic PTSD that are similar to the Combat Fitness Retraining Unit (described in Section Three of this volume).

TREATMENT FOR COMBAT STRESS DISORDERS: EVALUATIONS AND RECOMMENDATIONS

In the fourth and closing part of this chapter, outpatient and inpatient approaches currently used in the United States for treatment of chronic PTSD are examined. New treatment approaches being initiated in Israel are recommended for adoption and adaptation by other countries contending with these problems. Some features of military operations and military service that may affect the incidence of adverse combat stress conditions are identified, and recommendations are proposed.

Project Outreach

The success of the newest ambulatory outpatient treatment approach, Project Outreach, is based on the following features:

1. The Vet Centers provide combat veterans with an opportunity to ventilate feelings about the war, the reaction of society to that war and to them, and past and recent events in their lives.
2. The sharing with other veterans of grievances, shattered beliefs, and aspirations for something better helps to overcome a sense of isolation and alienation that has characterized these men from the onset of their symptoms to the present.
3. The group structure of the Vet Centers permits veterans to become a self-help group promoting their common interests and helping one another with emotional support, factual advice, and practical assistance. These centers may take on some of the features and goals of AA (Alcoholics Anonymous) in motivating members to achieve a better life by emphasizing common problems, common goals, and mutual help.
4. Project Outreach was set up as an autonomous program, separate from the medical establishment running the traditional VA hospitals and clinics. This is an advantage because the treatment approach used—group self-help, the mobilization of lay and nonprofessional support systems from the society, a pragmatic problem-solving approach toward one's symptoms and diffi-

culties—is more conducive to the perceived needs of these former combat veterans than conventional psychodynamic or behavioral treatments provided by civilian mental health professionals (Fuller, 1985).

There are enormous differences in assumptions about mental health, philosophy of life, cognitive style, manner, and preferred defense mechanisms between the kind of men who served in combat duty in Vietnam and the kind of men and women who offer mental health treatment in the hospitals and clinics, even in those institutions that are part of the Veterans Administration (Haley, 1974; Racek, 1985; Scurfield, 1985). We are convinced that both parties to the therapeutic contract, the veterans and the mental health practitioners, agree with this assertion, to their mutual frustration and discomfort (see discussions about therapist-client incompatibility in Acosta, Yamamoto, & Evans, 1982; Howard, 1976; Korman, 1973; Parson, 1985; Sue, 1981). On the basis of this clinical and research literature, we believe Project Outreach to be more effective with combat veterans than conventional therapeutic approaches precisely because its administrative and professional workers are closer to their clients in these respects than workers in traditional mental health settings.

Unfortunately, these centers cannot reach veterans living in sparsely populated parts of the country or small towns. Moreover, there are many veterans whose severe incapacitating symptoms and/or drug abuse do not permit them to participate in a part-time ambulatory program. Many are homebound, confined to psychiatric hospitals, or on lengthy waiting lists for psychiatric hospitalization.

The Rehabilitative Hospital

The other major development, psychiatric hospitalization designed to actively treat and rehabilitate the veteran, has been successful according to Sax (1985) and Racek (1985). In these settings there is an awareness that the professional staff should include people with military, even combat, experience, although such people in the mental health field are few and far between (see Racek, 1985, pp. 277, 281). Importance is placed on detailed reconstruction of the original traumatic combat experience(s) and appropriate abreaction with the aid of hypnosis (Brende, 1985; Silver & Kelly, 1985), and on the peer group and self-government by the patients on the ward. Occupational therapy is emphasized, but there is difficulty in motivating veterans to engage in the kinds of occupational therapy that are available in most hospitals (Racek, 1985; Sax, 1985). Physical activity is recommended for helping some men to discharge their aggressive impulses and for others to relax and sleep without medication. Systematic and individualized efforts are made to modify substance abuse by some patients. In summary, these program features reflect a conceptual grasp on the part of the directors of a multifaceted therapeutic milieu with a variety of therapeutic modalities.

Thus far, we have praised the light, but we are compelled to point out the dark or shadowy areas of these programs. Active rehabilitative effort in a hospital environment is expensive, and only limited numbers of veterans can be accommodated. Criteria for entering these programs are often stringent: an optimistic prognosis and a disorder occasioned by one or more psychiatric episodes associated with severe combat stress. Many people do not qualify for hospitalization according to these criteria, cannot use the ambulatory centers for reasons cited above, and are without professional treatment.

However, even if psychiatric hospitalization were available for all veterans and if the attending personnel were well trained and knowledgeable about PTSD, the Vietnam War, and the combat veteran, there are certain deficiencies in the best of these programs.

Ecological Consistency

The outpatient Vet Centers and inpatient rehabilitative hospitals appear to lack an important dimension necessary for optimal symptom reduction and rehabilitation. This dimension is the *ecological consistency of treatment and traumatic settings*. This is the conception that the optimal treatment setting is one that is ecologically similar, if not identical, to the setting in which the traumatic event occurred. By traumatic setting, we are not referring to the specific place in which the stressful events took place, but rather to the structural institution of which one was an accepted member before the trauma occurred and a rejected, disaffected outcast afterward. We have referred to this concept in earlier discussions in this chapter, but have never developed its treatment implications fully.

The programs described above, however well conceptualized and executed, lack ecological consistency. Their patients were once combat veterans, many highly motivated to serve in the armed forces and highly identified with its drills, skills, and goals. They were subsequently traumatized in two spheres of life, the military and the civilian. First, they became incapable of further functioning as combat soldiers and became alienated from, and disillusioned about, their former military identity. Second, they became traumatized when they failed to readjust to civilian life. The present programs seem addressed to the civilian trauma, but do not appear to be appropriate settings for dealing with the military one.

The principle of ecological consistency dictates that treatment of war-related trauma in combat veterans take place within a military setting, and that it resolve their ambivalence about the military, rebuild their shattered relationship toward the military, and restore their former valued military identity.

Basic Retraining

We propose for consideration a program that is radically different from other therapeutic and rehabilitative approaches in the field. This program has some basis in theory, but has never been tested in practice. Elements of the proposed program were explicit in the Combat Fitness Retraining Unit (CFRU) set up in Israel (and described in Section Three of this volume) and are included in new programs currently being considered in Israel. As of this writing, we have developed a general conception of this program of *basic retraining*, but do not know how it might be implemented in practice in Israel or in the United States. We will, nevertheless, make some general and some specific recommendations to initiate discussion on this proposal. This discussion may lead to the adoption, adaptation, and implementation of such a program, to the incorporation of part of it in existing programs, or, at the very least, to a deeper understanding of the limitations of current efforts.

This program is conceptualized as a multimodal residential treatment taking place within a military social structure on a military base. Former combat veterans with refractory PTSD would sign up for *basic retraining*, a program analogous to the *basic training* they went through many years ago. Under the terms of the retraining contract, they would commit themselves to a program of predetermined duration, one month or more.* The program would be restricted to these men, would draw from communities in the same part of the country, and would be implemented on an active army base with facilities currently not being used.

---

*The optimal duration of basic retraining is open to discussion and may be two or possibly three months maximum. The optimal size of a residential group is also open to discussion. A group of no fewer than 25 and no more than 50 would be manageable and not so large as to generate anonymity of recruits.

The men would live under military discipline and perform military drills and physical activities that are highly meaningful to men who have served in the armed forces. The appeal and import of the kind of activities inherent in basic retraining would be of a different order than the occupational therapy provided in a civilian psychiatric hospital from which many veterans currently recoil or which they reject out of hand. These new experiences are reminiscent of their original experiences in basic training many years ago, before they lost their innocence and their self-confidence. These experiences are designed to help restore some of the self-esteem and self-confidence that once characterized these men.

The military structure, content, and functioning of the basic retraining program would follow the format used in the CFRU and would include ongoing group and individual treatment, behavioral and/or psychodynamic. These treatments would be an integral part, but not the most important part, of the therapeutic milieu created by a team of mental health personnel and regular army personnel. These people would be familiar with, and sympathetic to, military service and to the psychic wounds of war experienced by veterans who were exposed to adverse conditions.

In this military milieu the previous military history of the recruits would be appreciated and understood. Efforts would be made to impart new skills and knowledge and to instill pride in the new army as the men settle into their daily routines. They would focus on how to meet the routine demands and challenges of the program and prepare for achieving the more difficult goals of basic retraining (maneuvers, marksmanship, first aid, endurance-and-survival treks). In addition, the program would require the inculcating of skills that would be genuinely useful in the National Guard or in civilian life in time of military or civil emergency. The physical and mental requirements of the program would be based on the highest level of stressful challenge that the men are capable of meeting, consistent with their age and condition.

All forms of psychotherapy used would be directed toward the solution of practical, current problems, talking and working together to meet the challenges of the program and of civilian life afterward: first, the problems of becoming a cohesive group of men trying to survive the rigors of basic retraining; second, the problems brought with them from civilian life; and third, the problems they will confront when they leave boot camp and return to civilian life.

The precipitating traumatic events in their prior military service, including atrocities witnessed or participated in, would be dealt with, to the extent that the men wish to bring them up. These veterans have presumably been exposed in the past decade to diverse forms of psy-chotherapy and have had opportunity for abreaction of ego-dystonic experiences. Abreaction may still be indicated, however, and would be brought about in a cautious and individualized manner (Silver & Kelly, 1985), but it would not be the major focus of therapeutic concern. Many experienced clinicians (e.g., Klein, 1945; Moses, Bargal, & Calev, 1975) have indicated that abreaction is a means to an end, but is not to be pursued as an end in and of itself. The importance of optimal abreaction today of the traumatic events that veterans experienced a decade or more ago may be somewhat exaggerated.

As the retraining program moves into high gear, and the veterans become more comfortable with their coping efforts, the focus of psy-chotherapy would shift to the future. What to do when they leave the base and return to civilian life? Will they be able to make it? What forms of continuing treatment will be offered them on the outside? Will they maintain contact with one another by ties of friendship and mutual aid? Will the group convene for annual weekend meetings on the base or elsewhere as befits survivors and graduates of a common experience?

We have described the framework for a new form of residential treat-ment. There are innumerable details to consider before such a program can be initiated: the legal status of the recruits in the program, its du-ration, the physical and psychiatric criteria for admission to the program and for termination (and referral elsewhere), the strictness of military discipline, the precise content of the program, the research design to evaluate the effectiveness of treatment in the groups to be admitted, etc. The experience acquired with the first few groups would shape the program offered to subsequent groups. If successful, basic retraining would eventually complement the outpatient Vet Centers and be avail-able nationwide on a number of military bases, offering the program to thousands.

Recommendations on Reducing Combat Stress Reactions

Certain features of the Vietnam and Lebanon conflicts, of the armed forces involved, and of the two societies, American and Israeli, provide generalizations for the reduction of combat stress reactions in future military involvements. Some of these recommendations are self-evident, and others may appear unrealistic. They are presented to generate dis-cussion in political, military, and public circles about how to implement them or how to handle the adverse consequences of our inability to do so. In presenting each recommendation, discussion is largely restricted to the implications for the combat soldier in the field, and little attention is given to the wider ramifications of these issues for the two societies that are party to the conflict.

The goals of military involvement. In a democratic society it is imperative to communicate in simple language the immediate goals of a particular military operation to ensure the support of the armed forces involved and of the homefront. These goals must be convincing both to soldiers who place their lives at risk and to their families and the general public. Otherwise, the morale of soldiers will be impaired *during* military service and they will be at high risk for post-traumatic stress disorders *after* military service.

The formulation of the goals of military involvement has become problematic for democratic societies. Both the United States and Israel have become extraordinarily sensitive to this issue. Both societies were involved in resource-exhausting military conflicts partly as a result of uncritically accepting vague or misleading statements about the goals of these involvements. As a consequence, people have become leery about vague references to national security, sentimental appeals to save freedom-loving governments or their people from foreign domination, or jingoist pronouncements. They also become resentful and mistrustful when they learn that outright falsehood (e.g., the Tonkin Bay incident) is employed to justify the initiation and/or expansion of military operations. These experiences may lead to an erosion of confidence in one's political and military leadership and mistrust of one's public spokespeople. Enlightened and successful national leaders avoid these errors by exercising judgment and caution both in selecting military options that are legitimate and moral to begin with, and by giving their citizens comprehensive and accurate briefings about their policies and objectives.

The morality of means as well as ends. Even with a national consensus for war, soldiers are at high risk for combat stress disorders if the *morality of the conduct of the war* is questioned. Soldiers must be convinced not only that they are engaged in military activities for moral ends, but that they are employing relatively moral means to achieve these ends. However legitimate their ends, wars that mandate the killing of noncombatants at close range or that permit or encourage the torture and killing of captured enemy soldiers or unarmed men, women, and children are illegitimate in means and cause incalculable damage to all parties. Soldiers who witness or participate in these atrocities are highly susceptible to pathological stress disorders and pay a very high personal price afterward.

Committing acts that are immoral and inimical to Western traditions causes demoralization on the battlefield and on the homefront. This means that military planning must take into consideration the potential loss of life and limb both of combatants and of civilians alike. A nation may win a Pyrrhic victory not only when it loses many of its own sons to achieve a military objective, but also when its sons commit acts of such infamy that the nation is repelled by the ends as well as by the means.

Dehumanization of the enemy. Efforts to dehumanize the enemy may raise death counts and legitimize, for a time, wartime behaviors inconsistent with one's ethical traditions, but in the long run these efforts are counterproductive and even self-destructive, since they increase the probability of chronic PTSD in combat soldiers. We should fight and, if necessary, kill enemy soldiers not because they are vicious, cruel, or subhuman, but because they are furthering the policies of leaders bent on undermining our vital interests and endangering our national security.

Group cohesiveness as stress buffer and stress intensifier. When soldiers go through basic training together or participate in other difficult or threatening military operations, they develop close personal ties based on mutual trust and friendship. These ties become a major source of support in subsequent life-threatening situations. Numerous studies have shown that these ties are a positive, stress-resistant factor that reduces the likelihood of succumbing to combat stress situations (Lieberman, 1982). In basic training and in subsequent training for combat duty, a certain degree of group cohesiveness develops without special efforts or arrangements by the training officers. Nevertheless, this is not always the case, and judicious, innovative thinking should be directed to enhancing group cohesiveness in the men and confidence in the competence and judgment of their officers. These techniques go well beyond the scope of this volume, but their effective implementation serves two major goals: (1) to buffer combat soldiers against disruptive stress reactions that would interfere with performing their combat assignments; and (2) to reduce the probability of combat stress reactions during or after the operation.

Group cohesiveness is, however, a double-edged sword that cuts in two directions. On the one hand, it facilitates performance under fire and reduces indirect casualties (see Chapter 5 in this volume). On the other, it increases the degree of victimization experienced by a soldier when one or more close friends are maimed or killed. Given the direct relationship between degree of victimization and severity of stress re-action, one could argue that group cohesiveness is a risk factor rather than a stress-resistant factor.

These two effects are not logically or empirically contradictory since they may be operating at different times and situations: Group cohe-siveness insulates the soldier against stress reactions to begin with, when the intact group is coping with a stressful combat situation. Later the group may suffer direct casualties and a low rate of indirect psychiatric casualties. With the cessation of life-threatening activities, survivors as-sess the toll enacted and experience a greater sense of loss and survivor guilt about the death of personal friends than of strangers. They may then succumb to post-traumatic stress reactions of high intensity, but prognosis for rapid recovery with treatment is good. The different effects of group cohesiveness must be taken into consideration in planning appropriate treatment for varying circumstances.

The support/combat troop ratio and its effect on combat troops. Men cope better with the stress of life-threatening combat when they believe that all are doing their share and that no one is shirking his duty. The per-ception that disproportionately large numbers of men are involved in noncombat assignments without risk to life and limb can be upsetting, if not demoralizing. It creates a sense of *us* and *them*, the few who are sent on life-threatening missions and may not return and the many who occupy desk jobs and send them. It is recommended that the number of support positions be reduced by more efficient utilization of support personnel, by replacing male with female soldiers, and by making efforts to guarantee that support and combat personnel are relatively similar in demographic variables (e.g., ethnic group membership, religion, so-cial class).

Respect for the armed forces. In many countries there is a tradition of respect for the armed forces, and in others there is poorly concealed contempt. Respect tends to be higher when the armed forces are re-cruited from men and women from all walks of life and are representative of the society as a whole. This is achieved in large-scale military con-scription of citizens, but not necessarily in a volunteer army that offers material (e.g., job training) and nonmaterial incentives (e.g., adventure and travel) appealing to different sectors of the population. Under these circumstances, it is important to minimize the stereotyping by outside groups of the volunteer army as currently composed (lower class, high-school education, black, rural or small town, conservative) and to establish communication and respect between the civilian and military sectors of society. Otherwise, alienation and mutual mistrust may develop between the two groups with each asserting a "we know better" attitude. Efforts should be made to bring intellectuals, liberals, and mass media workers in closer contact with the armed forces to bridge the gaps that frequently separate these groups and reduce animosity and misunderstanding.

Reduction of drug abuse in the military. There must be persistent efforts to keep drug abuse, including alcohol, at a low level during both peacetime and wartime operations. This is no easy task given the trends toward increased substance abuse in the society as a whole and the ease with which these substances are obtained around military bases. On the positive side, the hierarchical structure of the army facilitates the introduction of preventive educational programs, the detection of serious offenders, and the implementation of intensive group detoxification and rehabilitation programs.

Military and civilian psychiatry and counseling. The psychiatric treatment of members of the armed forces in peace and in dangerous military operations must achieve a better balance between many conflicting forces. One is the conflict between short-term and long-term needs of the military establishment. One short-term need is to present an image of a highly efficient, well-functioning, and well-adjusted army with no serious problems in morale, drug abuse, and psychiatric disorder, and when reality falls short of this image, to maintain this facade by neglecting serious problems that could and should be dealt with. The long-term needs of the army dictate open acknowledgment of current problems, with attempts to solve them in a variety of innovative ways.

A second source of conflict is between military and civilian orientations toward psychiatric treatment of members of the armed forces both during and after discharge from service. The former tends to focus on symptomatic treatment and administrative handling of personal or group problems and to emphasize the needs and goals of the service. The latter emphasizes in-depth understanding of personal problems and the needs of the individual. Whatever the orientation, professional mental health workers must develop respect for and appreciation of the armed services and intimate understanding of military identity, the character of military training, and combat. This appreciation and understanding will emerge if the professional workers have themselves been exposed to these military realities in some form.

The neutrality and personal integrity of the armed forces in public dissent.
There has been antiwar protest in every war ever fought by the United
States from the American Revolution on. The circumstances of American
participation in World War II were unusually favorable for national consensus and are not likely to recur. As a consequence, there is a high
probability of public dissent in a democracy when military operations
are launched under all but the most dire circumstances of national jeopardy. Whatever the extent and intensity of this dissent and debate, the
personal integrity of the armed forces should not be at issue. One may
castigate and even make personal attacks against political and military
leaders in the acrimony of public debate, but the character and conduct
of the men and women serving in the armed forces should not be maligned.

Closing Thoughts

We close this chapter and this volume with the observation that it is
unfortunate that humankind must devote precious energy and human
resources to plan for war and/or defend against the threat of war. To fail
to do so, however, is not to guarantee peace or to increase its likelihood.
On the contrary, history has shown that when one side appears unarmed
and defenseless, there is a strong temptation for the other side to resolve
grievances or to advance perceived interests by attacking and/or exploiting the unarmed group. We are fully aware that these very assertions
are self-fulfilling and that if other beliefs were widely held by the decision
makers of the world, armies would become unnecessary and untenable.

In the meantime, societies have an obligation to care for their physically and emotionally wounded. Soldiers and civilians need to be treated
by the best state-of-the-art techniques that psychology and psychiatry
can provide. It is unrealistic to think that the mental health professions
can directly limit or eliminate war. As a group, we are not all of one
political persuasion, party, or ideology, and would not cooperate as a
single-minded special interest group or lobby. We may work, however,
to treat war-related stress reactions and disorders more effectively. We
may also make efforts to enhance the quality of life in people affected
by life stressors in general and by war-related stress in particular. This
volume represents one effort to contribute toward these goals.

References

Ackerman, S. H., Manaker, S., & Cohen, M. I. (1981). Recent separation and the onset of peptic ulcer in older children and adolescents. *Psychosomatic Medicine, 43,* 305–310.

Acosta, F. X., Yamamoto, J., & Evans, L. (1982). *Effective psychotherapy for low-income and minority patients.* New York: Plenum Press.

Adler, T. S. (1975). Notes on shell shock in the wake of the Yom Kippur War. *Harefuah, 87* (Hebrew).

Adorno, T. W., Frenkel-Brunswik, E., Levinson, D. J., & Sanford, R. N. (1950). *The authoritarian personality.* New York: Harper.

Allerton, W. S. (1969). Army psychiatry in Vietnam. In P. C. Bourne (Ed.), *Psychology and physiology of stress.* New York: Academic Press.

Allerton, W. S. (1970). Psychiatric casualties in Vietnam. *Roche Medical Image and Commentary, 12,* 27.

Allport, F. H. (1924). *Social psychology.* Boston: Houghton Mifflin.

Allport, G. W. (1954). *The nature of prejudice.* Reading, MA: Addison-Wesley.

Alsop, S. (1971, July 12). The Masada complex. *Newsweek.*

Alsop, S. (1973, March 19). The Masada complex. *Newsweek.*

Alter, R. (1973, July). The Masada complex. *Commentary.*

American Psychiatric Association (1968). *Diagnostic and statistical manual of mental disorders* (2nd ed.). Washington: Author.

American Psychiatric Association (1980). *Diagnostic and statistical manual of mental disorders* (3rd ed.). Washington: Author.

Aneshensel, C. S., & Stone, J. D. (1982). Stress and depression: A test of the buffering model of social support. *Archives of General Psychiatry, 39,* 1392–1396.

Antonovsky, A. (1979). *Health, stress, and coping.* San Francisco: Jossey-Bass.

Antonovsky, A., Maoz, B., Dowty, N., & Wijsenbeek, H. (1971). Twenty-five years later: A limited study of the sequelae of the concentration camp experience. *Social Psychiatry, 6,* 186–193.

Archer, R. P. (1979). Relationships between locus of control and anxiety. *Journal of Personality Assessment, 43,* 617–626.

Archibald, H. C., Long, D. M., & Miller, C. (1962). Chronic stress reaction in combat: Fifteen year followup. *American Journal of Psychiatry, 119,* 317–322.

Archibald, H. C., & Tuddenham, R. D. (1965). Persistent stress reaction after combat: A twenty year followup. *Archives of General Psychiatry, 12,* 475–481.

Argyris, C. (1968). Conditions for competence acquisition and therapy. *Journal of Applied Behavioral Science, 4,* 147–179.

Arieli, A. (1974). Combat neurosis in an army field hospital. *Harefuah, 87,* 572–577 (Hebrew).

Arieti, S. (1970). Cognition and feeling. In M. Arnold (Ed.), *Feelings and emotions.* New York: Academic Press.

Artiss, K. (1963). Human behavior under stress from combat and social psychiatry. *Military Medicine, 128,* 1011–1019.

Ayalon, O. (1978). *Emergency kit: Rescue.* Haifa: Haifa University, School of Education.

Ayalon, O. (1979). Community oriented preparation for emergency: COPE. *Death Education, 3,* 227–245.

Ayalon, O. (1982a). Alternative strategies for coping with stress. *Journal of Social Medicine*, 22, 661–664.

Ayalon, O. (1982b). Children as hostages. *The Practitioner*, 226, 1773–1781.

Ayalon, O. (1983). Coping with terrorism: The Israeli case. In D. Meichenbaum & M. Jaremko (Eds.), *Stress reduction and prevention*. New York: Plenum Press.

Baade, E., Halse, K., Stenhammer, P. E., Ellertsen, B., Backer-Johnsen, T., Vollmer, F., & Ursin, H. (1978). Psychological tests. In H. Ursin, E. Baade, and S. Levine (Eds.), *Psychobiology of stress: A study of coping men*. London: Academic Press.

Baddeley, A. D. (1967). Diver performance and the interaction of stresses. *Underwater Association Report*, 10, 35–38.

Baker, S. L. (1980). Traumatic war disorders. In H. I. Kaplan, A. M. Freedman, & B. J. Sadock (Eds.), *Comprehensive textbook of psychiatry*, Vol. 2. London: Williams & Wilkins.

Bandura, A. (1977). Self-efficacy: Toward a unifying theory of behavioral change. *Psychological Review*, 84, 191–215.

Bandura, A., & Walters, R. H. (1963). *Social learning and personality development*. New York: Holt, Rinehart and Winston.

Barber, J. (1974). White rule and the outward policy. In A. Lefwich (Ed.), *South Africa: Economic growth and political change*. London: Allison & Busby.

Bard, M., & Sangrey, D. (1986). *The crime victim's book* (Second edition). New York: Brunner/Mazel.

Bar-On, O., Dotan, R., & Inbar, O. (1977). A 30 sec. all-out ergometric test, its reliability and validity for anaerobic capacity. *Israel Journal of Medical Science*, 13, 326.

Baron, R. A. (1977). *Human aggression*. New York: Plenum Press.

Bartemeier, L., Kubie, L., Menninger, K., Romano, J., & Whitehorn, J. (1946). Combat exhaustion. *Journal of Nervous and Mental Disease*, 104, 358–389, 489–525.

Beebe, G. W., & Apple, J. W. (1951). *Variations in psychological tolerance to ground combat in World War II. Final Report*. Washington, DC: National Academy of Science, National Research Council, Division of Medical Sciences, Followup Agency.

Bell, P. A. (1978). Effects of noise and heat stress on primary and subsidiary task performance. *Human Factors*, 20, 749–752.

Bell, P. A. (1981). Physiological comfort, performance, and social effects of heat stress. *Journal of Social Science*, 37, 71–94.

Bell, P. A., Loomins, R. J., & Cervone, J. C. (1982). Effects of heat, social facilitation, sex differences, and task difficulty on reaction time. *Human Factors*, 24, 19–24.

Benfari, R. C., Eaker, E. D., Ockene, J., & McIntyre, K. (1982). Hyperstress and outcome in a long-term smoking intervention program. *Psychosomatic Medicine*, 44, 227–235.

Benyakar, M., & Noy, S. (1975, January). *A suggestion for a therapeutic model for posttraumatic war neurosis*. Paper presented at the First International Conference on Psychological Stress and Adjustment in Time of War and Peace, Tel-Aviv.

Berger, P. L., Berger, B., & Kellner, H. (1973). *The homeless mind: Modernization and consciousness*. New York: Random House.

Bergin, A. E. (1980). Behavior therapy and ethical relativism: Time for clarity. *Journal of Consulting and Clinical Psychology*, 48, 11–13.

Bergum, B. O., & Lehr, D. J. (1962). Vigilance performance as a function of paired monitoring. *Journal of Applied Psychology*, 46, 341–343.

Berkowitz, L. (1969). *Aggression: A social psychological analysis*. New York: McGraw-Hill.

Biersner, R. J., Dembert, M. L., & Browning, M. D. (1980). Comparisons of performance effectiveness among divers. *Aviation, Space and Environmental Medicine*, 51, 151–179.

Bitzer, R. (1980). Caught in the middle: Mentally disabled Vietnam veterans and the Veterans Administration. In C. R. Figley & S. Leventman (Eds.), *Strangers at home: Vietnam veterans since the war*. New York: Praeger.

Blank, A. S. (1982). Stresses of war: The example of Viet Nam. In L. Goldberger & S. Breznitz (Eds.), *Handbook of stress: Theoretical and clinical aspects*. NY: The Free Press.

Blank, T. O., Staff, I., & Shaver, P. (1976). Social facilitation of word associations: Further questions. *Journal of Personality and Social Psychology, 34,* 725–733.

Blau, P. M. (1964). *Exchange and power in social life.* New York: John Wiley.

Bloch, H. S. (1969). Army clinical psychiatry in the combat zone. *American Journal of Psychiatry, 126,* 289–298.

Bolz, F. A. (1983). The hostage situation: Law enforcement options. In B. Eichelman, D. A. Soskis, & W. H. Reid (Eds.), *Terrorism: Interdisciplinary perspectives.* Washington, DC: American Psychiatric Association.

Bond, C. F., & Titus, L. J. (1983). Social facilitation: A meta-analysis of 241 studies. *Psychological Bulletin, 94,* 265–292.

Borus, J. F. (1976). The re-entry transition of the Vietnam veteran. In N. L. Goldman & D. R. Segal (Eds.), *The social psychology of military service.* Beverly Hills, CA: Sage.

Bosel, R., & Otto, J. (1981). Konnen diskrepanzwerte zwischen subjektiven and physiologischen belastungs indikatoren psychologischdiagnostische informationen liefern? *Schweizerische Zeitschrift fur Psychologie und ihre Anwendungen, 40,* 68–72 (German).

Bourne, P. G. (1970). Military psychiatry and the Vietnam experience. *American Journal of Psychiatry, 127,* 481–488.

Brecher, M. (1975). *Decisions in Israel's foreign policy.* New Haven, CT: Yale University Press.

Brehm, J. W. (1966). *A theory of psychological reactance.* New York: Academic Press.

Brende, J. O. (1985). The use of hypnosis in post-traumatic conditions. In W. E. Kelly (Ed.), *Post-traumatic stress disorder and the war veteran patient.* New York: Brunner/Mazel.

Breznitz, S. (1983a). Anticipatory stress reactions. In S. Breznitz (Ed.), *The denial of stress.* New York: International Universities Press.

Breznitz, S. (1983b). The noble challenge of stress. In S. Breznitz (Ed.), *Stress in Israel.* New York: Van Nostrand.

Breznitz, S. (Ed.). (1983c). *Stress in Israel.* New York: Van Nostrand.

Breznitz, S., & Eshel, Y. (1983). Life events: Stressful ordeal or valuable experience. In S. Breznitz (Ed.), *Stress in Israel.* New York: Van Nostrand.

Brickman, P., Rabinowitz, V. C., Karuza, J., Coates, D., Cohn, E., & Kidder, L. (1982). Models of helping and coping. *American Psychologist, 37,* 368–384.

Bronfenbrenner, U. (1964). Allowing for Soviet perceptions. In R. Fisher (Ed.), *International conflict and behavioral science.* New York: Basic Books.

Brown, D. (1966). *Against the world.* Garden City, NJ: Doubleday.

Brown, G. W. (1974). Meaning, measurement, and stressful life events. In B. S. Dohrenwend & B. P. Dohrenwend (Eds.), *Stressful life events: Their nature and effects.* New York: John Wiley.

Brown, G. W. (1981). Contextual measurement of life events. In B. S. Dohrenwend & B. P. Dohrenwend (Eds.), *Stressful life events and their contexts.* New Brunswick, NJ: Rutgers University Press (Prodist).

Brown, G. W., Bhrolchrain, M., & Harris, T. (1975). Social class and psychiatric disturbance among women in an urban population. *Sociology, 9,* 225–254.

Brull, F. (1974). *On the way to humanistic psychotherapy.* Tel-Aviv: Epstein Moden (Hebrew).

Bursill, A. E. (1958). The restrictions of peripheral vision during exposure to hot and humid conditions. *Quarterly Journal of Experimental Psychology, 10,* 113–129.

Butcher, J. N., & Gur, P. (1974). A Hebrew translation of the MMPI. *Journal of Cross-Cultural Psychology, 5,* 220–227.

Calsyn, R. J., Pribyl, J. F., & Sunukjian, H. (1977). Correlates of successful outcome in crisis intervention therapy. *American Journal of Community Psychology, 5,* 111–119.

Calvert-Boyanowsky, J., Boyanowsky, E. O., Atkinson, M., Gaduto, D., & Reeves, J. (1976). Patterns of passion: Temperature and human emotion. In D. Krebs (Ed.), *Readings in social psychology: Contemporary perspectives.* New York: Harper & Row.

Camacho, P. (1980). From war hero to criminal: The negative privilege of the Vietnam veteran. In C. R. Figley & S. Leventman (Eds.), *Strangers at home: Vietnam veterans since the war.* New York: Praeger.

Cantril, H. (1965). *The pattern of human concerns.* New Brunswick, NJ: Rutgers University Press.

Caplan, G. (1964). *Principles of preventive psychiatry.* New York: Basic Books.

Caplan, G. (1974). *Support systems and community mental health.* New York: Human Sciences.

Caplan, R. D. (1981). Mastery of stress: Psychosocial aspects. *American Journal of Psychiatry, 138,* 413–420.

Caplan, R. D. (1983). Person-environment fits: Past, present and future. In C. L. Cooper (Ed.), *Stress research: Where do we go from here?* New York: John Wiley.

Carlsmith, J. M., & Anderson, C. A. (1979). Ambient temperature and the occurrence of collective violence: A new analysis. *Journal of Personality and Social Psychology, 37,* 334–337.

Carr, R. A. (1973). *A comparison of self concept and expectation concerning control behavior between Vietnam-era veterans and nonveterans.* Unpublished doctoral dissertation, St. Louis University.

Chapman, A. J. (1973). An electromyographic study of apprehension about evaluation. *Psychological Reports, 33,* 811–814.

Chapman, A. J. (1974). An electromyographic study of social facilitation: A test of the "mere presence" hypothesis. *British Journal of Psychology, 65,* 123–128.

Clarke, J. H., MacPherson, B. V., & Holmes, D. R. (1982). Cigarette smoking and external locus of control among young adolescents. *Journal of Health and Social Behavior, 23,* 253–259.

Cobb, J. (1976). Social support as a moderator of life stress. *Psychosomatic Medicine, 38,* 300–314.

Coelho, G. V., Yuan, Y. T., & Ahmed, P. I. (1980). Contemporary uprooting and collaborative coping: Behavioral and societal responses. In G. V. Coelho and P. I. Ahmed (Eds.), *Uprooting and development: Dilemma of coping with modernization.* New York: Plenum Press.

Cohen, J., & Cohen, P. (1975). *Applied multiple regression/correlational analysis for the behavioral sciences.* Hillsdale, NJ: Lawrence Erlbaum.

Coleman, J. C., Butcher, J. N., & Carson, R. C. (1984). *Abnormal psychology and modern life.* Glenview, IL: Scott, Foresman and Company.

Collins, J. N. (1973). Foreign conflict behavior and domestic disorder in Africa. In J. Wikenfeld (Ed.), *Conflict behavior and linkage politics.* New York: David McKay.

Cooperman, H. (1973). *Adjustment to the military* (Technical Report). Tel Hashomer, Israel: Department of Behavioral Science, Israel Defense Forces.

Coser, L. A. (1956). *The functions of social conflict.* New York: Free Press.

Cottrell, N. B. (1968). Performance in the presence of other human beings: Mere presence, audience, and affiliation effects. In E. C. Simmel, R. A. Hoope, & G. A. Milton (Eds.), *Social facilitation and imitative behavior.* Boston: Allyn & Bacon.

Cottrell, N. B. (1972). Social facilitation. In C. G. McClintock (Ed.), *Experimental social psychology.* New York: Holt, Rinehart & Winston.

Cottrell, N. B., Rittle, R. H., & Wack, D. L. (1967). The presence of an audience and list type (competitional or noncompetitional) as joint determinants of performance in paired-associates learning. *Journal of Personality, 35,* 425–434.

Coyne, J. C., Aldwin, C., & Lazarus, R. S. (1981). Depression and coping in stressful episodes. *Journal of Abnormal Psychology, 90,* 439–447.

Crowley, J. B. (1966). *Japan's quest for autonomy.* Princeton, NJ: Princeton University Press.

Crowne, D. P., & Marlowe, D. A. (1960). A new scale of social desirability independent of psychopathology. *Journal of Consulting Psychology, 24,* 349–354.

Cunningham, M. R. (1979). Weather, mood, and helping behavior. *Journal of Personality and Social Psychology, 37,* 1947–1956.

Curreton, T. K. (1963). Improvement of psychological status by means of an exercise-fitness program. *Journal of the Association for Physical and Mental Rehabilitation, 17,* 14–17.

Dadson, L. C., & Mullens, W. R. (1969). Some effects of jogging on psychiatric hospital patients. *American Corrective Therapy Journal, 23,* 130–134.

Danieli, Y. (1985). The treatment and prevention of long-term effects and intergenerational transmission of victimization: A lesson from Holocaust survivors and their children. In C. G. Figley (Ed.), *Trauma and its wake: The study and treatment of post-traumatic stress disorder.* New York: Brunner/Mazel.

Dasberg, H. (1982). Belonging and loneliness in relation to mental breakdown in battle. In C. D. Spielberger, & I. G. Sarason (Eds.), & N. A. Milgram (Guest Ed.), *Stress and anxiety,* Vol. 8. Washington, DC: Hemisphere.

Datel, W. E. (1977). A summary of source data in military psychiatric epidemiology. *Military Medicine, 142,* 61.

Davis, J. E. (1947). Fundamental concepts of physical activity in rehabilitation. *Mental Hygiene, 31,* 630–635.

Dearborn, D. C., & Simon, H. A. (1958). Selective perception: A note on the departmental identification of executives. *Sociometry, 21,* 140–144.

de Rivera, J. H. (1968). *The psychological dimension of foreign policy.* Columbus, OH: Charles E. Merrill.

Derogatis, L. R., Lipman, R. S., Rickles, K., Uhlenhuth, E. H., & Covi, L. (1974). The Hopkins Symptom Checklist (HSCL): A measure of primary symptom dimensions. In P. Pichot (Ed.), *Psychological measurements in psychopharmacology.* Basel: Karger.

Dirks, J. F., Schraa, J. C., & Robinson, S. K. (1982). Patient mislabeling of symptoms: Implications for patient-physician communication and medical outcome. *International Journal of Psychiatry in Medicine, 12,* 15–27.

Dixon, D. J., Copeland, M. G., & Halcomb, C. G. (1980). *Psychomotor battery approaches to performance prediction and evaluation in hyperbaric, thermal and vibratory environments. Annotated bibliographies and integrative review.* San Diego, CA: Naval Biodynamics Laboratory NBDL-MOO2.

Dohrenwend, B. S., Dohrenwend, B. P., Dodson, M., & Shrout, P. E. (1984). Symptoms, hassles, social support, and life events: Problems of confounded measures. *Journal of Abnormal Psychology, 93,* 220–230.

Duval, S., & Wicklund, R. A. (1972). *A theory of objective self-awareness.* New York: Academic Press.

Egendorf, A. (1978). Psychotherapy with Vietnam veterans: Observations and suggestions. In C. R. Figley (Ed.), *Stress disorders among Vietnam veterans.* New York: Brunner/Mazel.

Eitinger, L. (1969). Psychosomatic problems in concentration camp survivors. *Journal of Psychosomatic Research, 13,* 183–189.

Eitinger, L. (1973). A followup study of Norwegian concentration camp survivors' mortality and morbidity. *Israel Annals of Psychiatry, 11,* 199–209.

Ellenberger, H. R. (1958). A clinical introduction to psychiatry, phenomenology, and existential analysis. In R. May, E. Angel, & H. R. Ellenberger. *Existence: A new dimension in psychiatry and psychology.* New York: Basic Books.

Endler, N. S., & Edwards, J. (1982). Stress and personality. In L. Goldberger & S. Breznitz (Eds.), *Handbook of stress: Theoretical and clinical aspects.* New York: Free Press.

Enoch, D., Bar-On, R., Barg, Y., Durst, N., Haran, G., Hovel, S., Israel, A., Reiter, M., Stern, M., & Toubiana, Y. (1983, January). *An indigenous military community as a psychotherapeutic agent: Specific application of forward treatment in combat.* Paper presented at the Third International Conference on Psychological Stress and Adjustment in Time of War and Peace, Tel-Aviv.

Enzie, R. F., Sawyer, R. N., & Montgomery, F. A. (1973). Manifest anxiety of Vietnam returnees and undergraduates. *Psychological Reports, 33,* 446.

Epley, S. W. (1974). Reduction of the behavioral effects of aversive stimulation by the presence of companions. *Psychological Bulletin, 81,* 271–283.

Epstein, Y., Keren, G., Moisseiev, J., Gasko, O., & Yachin, S. (1980). Psychomotor deterioration during exposure to heat. *Aviation, Space and Environmental Medicine, 51,* 607–610.

Evans, G. W. (1979). Behavioral and physiological effects of crowding in humans. *Journal of Applied Social Psychology, 2,* 27–46.

Fenz, W. W., & Epstein, S. (1967). Gradients of physiological arousal in parachutists as a function of an approaching jump. *Psychosomatic Medicine, 29,* 33–51.

Ferenczi, S., Abraham, K., Simmel, E., & Jones, E. (1921). *Psychoanalysis and the war neuroses.* New York: International Psychoanalytic Press.

Festinger, L., Riecken, H. W., & Shachter, S. (1956). *When prophesy fails.* Minneapolis: University of Minnesota Press.

Figley, C. R. (Ed.) (1978a). *Stress disorders among Vietnam veterans: Theory, research, and treatment.* New York: Brunner/Mazel.

Figley, C. R. (1978b). Psychosocial adjustment among Vietnam veterans: An overview of the research. In C. R. Figley (Ed.), *Stress disorders among Vietnam veterans.* New York: Brunner/Mazel.

Figley, C. R. (1980a). A postscript: Welcoming home the strangers. In C. R. Figley & S. Leventman (Eds.), *Strangers at home: Vietnam veterans since the war.* New York: Praeger.

Figley, C. R. (1980b). Preface. In C. R. Figley & S. Leventman (Eds.), *Strangers at home: Vietnam veterans since the war.* New York: Praeger.

Figley, C. R. (1985). Introduction. In C. R. Figley (Ed.), *Trauma and its wake: The study and treatment of post-traumatic stress disorder.* New York: Brunner/Mazel.

Figley, C. R., & Leventman, S. (Eds.) (1980a). *Strangers at home: Vietnam veterans since the war.* New York: Praeger.

Figley, C. R., & Leventman, S. (1980b). Introduction: Estrangement and victimization. In C. R. Figley & S. Leventman (Eds.), *Strangers at home: Vietnam veterans since the war.* New York: Praeger.

Figley, C. R., & Southerly, W. T. (1980). Psychosocial adjustment of recently returned veterans. In C. R. Figley & S. Leventman (Eds.), *Strangers at home: Vietnam veterans since the war.* New York: Praeger.

Fischer, L. (1951). *The Soviets in world affairs.* Princeton, NJ: Princeton University Press.

Flavius, J. (1928). *The Jewish war,* Vol. 3. Cambridge, MA: Harvard University Press.

Fly, C. L. (1973). *No hope but God.* New York: Hawthorn.

Folkman, S., & Lazarus, R. S. (1985). If it changes, it must be a process: Study of emotion and coping during three stages of a college examination. *Journal of Personality and Social Psychology, 48,* 150–170.

Folkman, S., Schaefer, C., & Lazarus, R. S. (1979). Cognitive processes as mediators of stress and coping. In V. Hamilton & Warburing, D. M. (Eds.), *Human stress and cognition.* Chichester, England: John Wiley.

Frankl, V. E. (1955). *The doctor and the soul: From psychotherapy to logotherapy.* New York: Alfred A. Knopf.

Frankl, V. E. (1962). *Man's search for meaning: An introduction to logotherapy.* Boston: Beacon Press.

Franklin, B. (1973). (Ed.), *The essential Stalin: Major theoretical writings 1905-1952.* London: Croom Helm.

Frenkel-Brunswik, E. (1949). Intolerance of ambiguity as an emotional and perceptual personality variable. *Journal of Personality, 18,* 108–143.

Freud, S. (1955). Introduction to psychoanalysis and the war neuroses. In *The complete psychological works of Sigmund Freud,* Vol. 17. London: Hogarth (published 1919).

Friedland, N. (1976). Social influence via threats. *Journal of Experimental Social Psychology, 12,* 552–563.

Frye, J. S., & Stockton, R. A. (1982). Discriminant analysis of posttraumatic stress disorder among a group of Vietnam veterans. *American Journal of Psychiatry, 139,* 52–56.

Fuller, R. B. (1985). War veterans' post-traumatic stress disorder and the U.S. Congress. In W. E. Kelly (Ed.), *Post-traumatic stress disorder and the war veteran patient.* New York: Brunner/Mazel.

Gal, R., & Lazarus, R. S. (1975). The role of activity in anticipating and confronting stressful situations. *Journal of Human Stress, 1*, 4–20.

Gardner, R. (1982). Attribution of control, essays and early medical school experience. *Psychosomatic Medicine, 44*, 93–108.

Gay, M. (1982). The adjustment of parents to wartime bereavement. In C. D. Spielberger, & I. G. Sarason (Eds.), & N. A. Milgram (Guest Ed.), *Stress and anxiety*, Vol. 8. New York: Hemisphere.

Geen, R. G. (1976a). The role of the social environment in the induction and reduction of anxiety. In C. D. Spielberger & I. G. Sarason (Eds.), *Stress and anxiety*, Vol. 3. Washington, DC: Hemisphere.

Geen, R. G. (1976b). Test anxiety, observation, and range of cue utilization. *British Journal of Social and Clinical Psychology, 15*, 253–259.

Geen, R. G., & Gange, J. J. (1977). Drive theory of social facilitation: Twelve years of theory and research. *Psychological Bulletin, 84*, 1267–1288.

Gentry, W. D., Chesney, A. P., Gary, H. E., Hall, R. P., & Harburg, E. (1982). Habitual anger-coping styles: I. Effect on mean blood pressure and risk for essential hypertension. *Psychosomatic Medicine, 44*, 195–202.

George, A. (1974). Adaptation to stress in political decision making: The individual, small group, and organizational contexts. In G. V. Coelho, D. A. Hamburg, & J. E. Adams (Eds.), *Coping and adaptation*. New York: Basic Books.

Geron, E., & Inbar, O. (1983, January). *Stress and motivation during maximal physical performance*. Paper presented at the Third International Conference on Psychological Stress and Adjustment in Time of War and Peace, Tel-Aviv.

Glass, A. J. (1949). An attempt to predict probable combat effectiveness by brief psychiatric examination. *American Journal of Psychiatry, 106*, 81.

Glass, A. J. (1955). Principles of combat psychiatry. *Military Medicine, 117*, 27–36.

Glass, A. J. (1957). *Observations upon the epidemiology of mental illness in troops during warfare*. Paper presented at Symposium on Preventive and Social Psychiatry, Walter Reed Army Institute of Research, Washington, DC.

Glass, A. J. (1959). Psychotherapy in the war zone. *American Journal of Psychiatry, 110*, 725–733.

Glass, A. J. (1971). Lessons learned. In *Neuropsychiatry in World War II*, Vol. 2. Washington, DC: Government Printing Office.

Glass, A. J., Artiss, K. L., Gibbs, J. J., & Sweeney, V. C. (1961). The current status of army psychiatry. *American Journal of Psychiatry, 117*, 673–683.

Glass, A. J., & Bernucci, R. J. (1966). *Zone of the interior, Neuropsychiatry in World War II*, Vol. 1. Washington, DC: Government Printing Office.

Goffman, E. (1961). *Asylums: Essays on the social situation of mental patients and other inmates*. New York: Anchor Books.

Goffman, E. (1963). *Stigma: Notes on identity*. Englewood Cliffs, NJ: Prentice-Hall.

Golan, N. (1978). *Treatment in crisis situations*. New York: Free Press.

Goldstein, K. (1939). *The organism*. New York: American Book Company.

Goodacre, D. M. (1953). Group characteristics of good and poor performing combat units. *Sociometry, 16*, 168–179.

Graves, P. L., & Thomas, C. B. (1981). Themes of interaction in medical students' Rorschach responses as predictors of midlife health or disease. *Psychosomatic Medicine, 43*, 215–225.

Greenberg, O. (1982). *Women in jail in Israel*. Tel-Aviv: Gomeh (Hebrew).

Greene, R. L. (1980). *The MMPI: An interpretive manual*. New York: Grune & Stratton.

Grinker, R. R., & Spiegel, J. P. (1945). *Men under stress*. Philadelphia: Blakiston.

Grosser, P. E., & Halperin, A. (1979). *Anti-semitism: The causes and effect of a prejudice*. Secaucus, NJ: Citadel Press.

Guttman, L. (1968). A general nonmetric technique for finding the smallest coordinate space for a configuration of points. *Psychometrika, 33*, 469–506.

Guttman, L., & Levy, S. (1974). The home front and the Yom Kippur War. *The 1974*

Yearbook of the Encyclopedia Judaica. Jerusalem: Keter.

Hacker, F. H. (1976). *Crusaders, criminals, crazies: Terror and terrorism in our time*. London: Norton.

Haley, S. A. (1974). When the patient reports atrocities. *Archives of General Psychiatry, 30*, 191–196.

Haley, S. A. (1978). Treatment implications of post-combat stress response syndromes for mental health professionals. In C. R. Figley (Ed.), *Stress disorders among Vietnam veterans*. New York: Brunner/Mazel.

Haley, S. A. (1985). Some of my best friends are dead: Treatment of the PTSD patient and his family. In W. E. Kelly (Ed.), *Post-traumatic stress disorder and the war veteran patient*. New York: Brunner/Mazel.

Hall, J. S., & Potte, J. W. (1960). Physiological index of strain and body heat storage in hyperthermia. *Journal of Applied Psychology, 15*, 1027–1030.

Hamburg, B. A., & Inoff, G. E. (1982). Relationship between behavioral factors and diabetic control in children and adolescents: A camp study. *Psychosomatic Medicine, 44*, 321–339.

Hancock, P. A. (1981). Heat stress impairment of mental performance: A revision of tolerance limits. *Aviation, Space, and Environmental Medicine, 52*, 177–180.

Hansell, S. (1982). Student, parent, and school effects on the stress of college application. *Journal of Health and Social Behavior, 23*, 38–51.

Hastorf, A. H., & Cantril, H. (1954). They saw a game: A case study. *Journal of Abnormal and Social Psychology, 49*, 129–134.

Hausman, W., & Rioch, D. M. (1967). Military psychiatry. *Archives of General Psychiatry, 16*, 727–739.

Hazan, H. (1980). Adjustment and control in an old age home. In E. Marx (Ed.), *A composite portrait of Israel*. New York: Academic Press.

Hazan, H. (1981). Totality as an adaptive strategy: Two case studies of the management of powerlessness. *Social Analysis, 9*, 63–76.

Healey, E. S., Kales, A., Monroe, L. J., Bixler, E. O., Chamberlin, K., & Soldatos, C. R. (1981). Onset of insomnia: Role of life-stress events. *Psychosomatic Medicine, 43*, 439–451.

Heaton, R. C., & Duerfeldt, P. H. (1973). The relationship between self esteem, self reinforcement, and internal-external personality dimension. *Journal of Genetic Psychology, 123*, 3–13.

Heider, F. (1958). *The psychology of interpersonal relations*. New York: John Wiley.

Hendin, H., & Haas, A. P. (1984). *Wounds of war: The psychological aftermath of combat in Vietnam*. New York: Basic Books.

Hendin, H., Haas, A. P., Singer, P., Houghton, W., Schwartz, M. F., & Wallen, V. (1985). The reliving experience in Vietnam veterans with post-traumatic stress disorders. In W. E. Kelly (Ed.), *Post-traumatic stress disorder and the war veteran patient*. New York: Brunner/Mazel.

Herman, S., Blumenthal, J. A., Black, G. M., & Chesney, M. A. (1981). Self-ratings of type A (coronary prone) adults: Do type A's know they are type A's? *Psychosomatic Medicine, 43*, 405–413.

Herz, M. I. (1979). Short-term hospitalization and the medical model. *Hospital and Community Psychiatry, 30*, 117–121.

Herzog, C. (1984). *The Arab-Israeli wars* (2nd ed.). London: Arms & Armour Press.

Hillman, R. G. (1981). The psychopathology of being held hostage. *American Journal of Psychiatry, 138*, 1193–1197.

Hobfoll, S. E. (1985a). The limitations of social support in the stress process. In I. G. Sarason & B. R. Sarason (Eds.), *Social support: Theory, research, and applications*. The Hague: Martinus Nijhoff.

Hobfoll, S. E. (1985b). Personal and social resources and the ecology of stress-resistance. In P. Shaver (Ed.), *Review of personality and social psychology*, Vol. 6. Beverly Hills, CA: Sage.

Hobfoll, S. E. (In press). The ecology of stress and social support among women. In S.

E. Hobfoll (Ed.), *Stress, social support and women*. Washington, DC: Hemisphere.

Hobfoll, S. E., & Leiberman, J. R. (In press). Personality and social resources in immediate and continued stress resistance among women. *Journal of Personality and Social Psychology.*

Hobfoll, S. E., & London, P. (In press). The relationship of self concept and social support to emotional distress among women during war. *Journal of Social and Clinical Psychology.*

Hobfoll, S. E., London, P., & Orr, E. (1985). *Mastery, intimacy, and stress-resistance during war.* Unpublished manuscript, Tel-Aviv University, Department of Psychology.

Hobfoll, S. E., & Walfisch, S. (1984). Coping with a threat to life: A longitudinal study of self concept, social support, and psychological distress. *American Journal of Community Psychology, 12,* 87–100.

Hobfoll, S. E., & Walfisch, S. (In press). Life events, mastery, and depression: An evaluation of crisis theory. *Journal of Community Psychology.*

Hockey, G. R. J. (1970). Signal probability and spatial location as possible bases for increased selectivity in noise. *Quarterly Journal of Experimental Psychology, 2,* 37–42.

Holsti, O. R. (1977). Foreign policy decision-makers viewed psychologically: Cognitive process approaches. In G. M. Bonham, & M. J. Shapiro (Eds.), *Thought and action in foreign policy.* Basel: Birkhauser Verlag.

Hornstein, H. A. (1976). *Cruelty and kindness: A new look at aggression and altruism.* Englewood Cliffs, NJ: Prentice-Hall.

Horowitz, M. (1976). *Stress response syndromes.* New York: Aronson.

Horowitz, M. J., & Solomon, G. F. (1975). Delayed stress response syndrome in Vietnam veterans. *Journal of Social Issues, 31,* 67–80.

Horshovsky, R., & Scheffer, G. (1983). *The evacuation of Sinai: Psychological processes within the community of the helping professions.* Papers presented at panel in annual meeting of the Israel Psychological Association, The Hebrew University, Jerusalem.

Howard, S. (1976). The Vietnam warrior: His experience and implications of psychotherapy. *American Journal of Psychotherapy, 31,* 121–135.

Hudgens, R. W. (1974). Personal catastrophe and depression: A consideration of the subject with respect to medically ill adolescents, and a requiem for retrospective life event studies. In B. S. Dohrenwend & B. P. Dohrenwend (Eds.), *Stressful life events: Their nature and effects.* New York: John Wiley.

Hunt, P. J., & Hillery, J. M. (1973). Social facilitation in a coacting setting: An examination of the effects over learning trials. *Journal of Experimental Social Psychology, 2,* 563–571.

Hunter, E. (1978). The Vietnam POW veteran: Immediate and long-term effects. In C. R. Figley (Ed.), *Stress disorders among Vietnam veterans: Theory, research, and treatment.* New York: Brunner/Mazel.

Inbar, O., Weingarten, G., & Bar-On, O. (1974). *The role of physical activity in the rehabilitation program for shell- and battle-shocked patients.* Unpublished report, Research Division, Wingate Institute for Physical Education and Sport, Netanya, Israel.

Jackson, G. (1973). *Surviving the long night.* New York: Vanguard.

Jacobson, N. S. (1975). Reduction of snake avoidance behavior using a symbolic coping model and verbal reinforcement. *Dissertation Abstracts International, 35,* 5114.

Jacobson, S. (1973). Individual and group responses to confinement in a skyjacked plane. *American Journal of Orthopsychiatry, 43,* 459–469.

Jaffe, D. T. (1975). The organization of treatment on a short-term psychiatric ward. *Psychiatry, 338,* 23–38.

Jaffe, Y., & Rosenfeld, H. (1982). Field dependence, handling of hostility, and sexual identification in posttraumatic Yom Kippur War veterans. In C. D. Spielberger, & I. G. Sarason (Eds.), & N. A. Milgram (Guest Ed.), *Stress and anxiety,* Vol. 8. Washington, DC: Hemisphere.

Janis, I. L. (1971). *Stress and frustration.* New York: Harcourt Brace Janovich.

Janis, I. L., & Feshbach, S. (1953). Effects of fear-arousing communications. *Journal of Abnormal and Social Psychology, 48,* 78–92.

Janis, I. L., & Mann, L. (1977). *Decision making*. New York: Free Press.

Janoff-Bulman, R. (1979). Characterological versus behavioral self-blame: Inquiries into depression and rape. *Journal of Personality and Social Psychology, 37*, 1789–1809.

Jenkins, B. M. (1982a). Statements about terrorism. *Annals of the American Academy of Political and Social Science, 463*, 11–23.

Jenkins, B. M. (1982b). Talking to terrorists. *The Rand Paper Series*. Santa Monica, CA: The Rand Corporation.

Jervis, R. (1976). *Perception and misperception in international politics*. Princeton, NJ: Princeton University Press.

Johnson, R. W. (1977). *How long will South Africa survive?* London: Macmillan.

Jones, A., Hornick, C. E., & Sells, S. (1972). *A social system analysis of the naval organization: Organizational characteristics and effectiveness of naval ships*. Fort Worth: Texas Christian University, Institute of Behavioral Research.

Kaplan, A. (1964). *The conduct of inquiry*. San Francisco: Chandler.

Kardiner, A. (1959). Traumatic neuroses of war. In S. Arieti (Ed.), *American handbook of psychiatry*, Vol. 1. New York: Basic Books.

Kedar, B. (1973, April 22). The Masada complex. *Haaretz* (Hebrew).

Kelly, J. G., Snowden, L. R., & Munoz, R. (1977). Social and community interventions. *Annual Review of Psychology, 28*, 323–361.

Kelly, W. E. (Ed.) (1985). *Post-traumatic stress disorder and the war veteran patient*. New York: Brunner/Mazel.

Kennan, G. (1947). The source of Soviet conduct. *Foreign Affairs, 25*, 566–582.

Kennan, G. F. (1960). *Russia and the West under Lenin and Stalin*. Boston: Little, Brown & Company.

Keren, A. B., Mester, R., Asphormas, Y., & Lerner, Y. (1983). Outcome of psychiatric hospitalization of Israeli soldiers in compulsory service. *Israel Annals of Psychiatry and Related Disciplines, 20*, 220–230.

Kerle, R. H., & Bialek, H. M. (1958). *The construction, validation, and application of the Subjective Stress Scale* (Staff Memorandum). Presidio of Monterey, CA: United States Army Leadership Research Unit.

Kern, R. P. (1966). *A conceptual model of behavior under stress with implications for combat training* (Technical Report 66-12). Washington, DC: HumRRO.

Kipper, D. A. (1977). Behavior therapy for fears brought on by war experiences. *Journal of Clinical and Consulting Psychology, 45*, 216–221.

Klein, E. (1945). Acute psychiatric war casualties. *Journal of Nervous and Mental Disease, 107*, 25–42.

Kobassa, S. C., Maddi, S. R., & Courington, S. (1981). Personality and constitution as mediators in the stress-illness relationship. *Journal of Health and Social Behavior, 22*, 368–378.

Kobassa, S. C., Maddi, S. R., & Kahn, S. (1982). Hardiness and health: A prospective study. *Journal of Personality and Social Psychology, 42*, 168–177.

Kobassa, S. C., & Puccetti, M. C. (1983). Personality and social resources in stress-resistance. *Journal of Personality and Social Psychology, 45*, 839–850.

Korman, N. (1973). National conference on levels and patterns of professional training in psychology. *American Psychologist, 29*, 441–449.

Kormos, H. R. (1978). The nature of combat stress. In C. R. Figley (Ed.), *Stress disorders among Vietnam veterans*. New York: Brunner/Mazel.

Kornitzer, M., Kittel, F., DeBacker, G., & Dramaix, M. (1981). The Belgian heart disease prevention project: Type A behavior pattern and the prevalence of coronary heart disease. *Psychosomatic Medicine, 43*, 133–145.

Kragh, U. (1960). The defense mechanism test: A new method for diagnosis and personnel selection. *Journal of Applied Psychology, 44*, 303–309.

Krech, D., Crutchfield, R. S., & Ballachey, E. L. (1962). *Individual in society*. New York: McGraw-Hill.

Kruglanski, A. W. (1980). Lay epistemological process and contents. *Psychological Review*, *87*, 70–87.

Kruglanski, A. W., & Ajzen, I. (1983). Bias and error in human judgment. *European Journal of Social Psychology*, *13*, 1–44.

Kruglanski, A. W., Baldwin, M. W., & Towson, R. (1986). The lay epistemological process in social cognition. In M. Hewstone (Ed.), *New directions in attribution theory*. Oxford: Blackwells.

Krystal, H. (Ed.) (1968). *Massive psychic trauma*. New York: International Universities Press.

Kuhn, T. S. (1962). *The structure of scientific revolutions*. Chicago: University of Chicago Press.

Kupperman, R. H. (1982). Terror, the strategic tool: Response and control. *Annals of the American Academy of Political and Social Science*, *463*, 24–38.

Kutash, I. L. (1980). Prevention and equilibrium-disequilibrium theory. In I. L. Kutash & L. B. Schlesinger (Eds.), *Handbook of stress and anxiety*. San Francisco: Jossey-Bass.

Lamm, H., & Myers, D. G. (1976). Machiavellianism, discussion time and group shift. *Social Behavior and Personality*, *4*, 41–48.

Langsley, D. G., & Kaplan, D. M. (1968). *The treatment of families in crisis*. New York: Grune & Stratton.

Laufer, R. S., Frey-Wouters, E., & Gallops, M. S. (1985). Traumatic stressors in the Vietnam War and post-traumatic stress disorder. In C. R. Figley (Ed.), *Trauma and its wake: The study and treatment of post-traumatic stress disorder*. New York: Brunner/Mazel.

Laufer, R. S., Gallops, M. S., & Frey-Wouters, E. (1984). War stress and trauma: The Vietnam veteran experience. *Journal of Health and Social Behavior*, *25*, 65–85.

Laughlin, P. R., & Jaccard, J. J. (1975). Social facilitation and observational learning of individuals and cooperative pairs. *Journal of Personality and Social Psychology*, *32*, 873–879.

Lazarus, R. S. (1966). *Psychological stress and the coping process*. New York: McGraw-Hill.

Lazarus, R. S. (1982). The psychology of stress and coping. In C. D. Spielberger, & I. G. Sarason (Eds.), & N. A. Milgram (Guest Ed.), *Stress and anxiety*, Vol. 8. Washington, DC: Hemisphere.

Lazarus, R. S. (1983). The costs and benefits of denial. In S. Breznitz (Ed.), *The denial of stress*. New York: Free Press.

Lazarus, R. S., & Folkman, S. (1984). *Stress, appraisal, and coping*. New York: Springer.

Lazarus, R. S., & Launier, R. (1978). Stress related transactions between person and environment. In L. A. Pervin & M. Lewis (Eds.), *Perspectives in interactional psychology*. New York: Plenum Press.

Lefcourt, H. M. (1966). Internal versus external control of reinforcement: A review. *Psychological Bulletin*, *65*, 206–220.

Lefcourt, H. M., Martin, R. A., & Selah, W. E. (1984). Locus of control and social support: Interactive moderators of stress. *Journal of Personality and Social Psychology*, *47*, 378–389.

Legum, C., & Legum, H. (1964). *South Africa-Crisis for the West*. London: Pall Mall Press.

Lehman, E. C. (1972). An empirical note on the transactional model of psychological stress. *Sociological Quarterly*, *13*, 484–495.

Lenin, V. I. (1943). *Selected works*, Vol. 8. London: Lawrence & Wishart.

Lenin, V. I. (1965). *Collected works*, Vols. 27 and 28. Moscow: Progress Publishers.

Lerner, M. J. (1970). Desire for justice and reaction to victims. In J. Macauley & L. Berkowitz (Eds.), *Altruism and helping behavior*. New York: Academic Press.

Lerner, M. (1977). Just world theory. In B. B. Wolman (Ed.), *International encyclopedia of psychiatry, psychology, psychoanalysis and neurology*. New York: Aesculapius.

Lerner, M. (1980). *The belief in a just world*. New York: Plenum Press.

Levav, I., Greenfeld, H., & Baruch, E. (1979). Psychiatric combat reactions during the Yom Kippur War. *American Journal of Psychiatry*, *136*, 637–641.

Leventhal, H. (1970). Findings and theory in the study of fear communications. In L. Berkowitz (Ed.), *Advances in experimental social psychology*, Vol. 5. New York: Academic Press.

Leventman, S., & Camacho, P. (1980). The "gook" syndrome: The Vietnam war as a racial encounter. In C. R. Figley & S. Leventman (Eds.), *Strangers at home: Vietnam veterans since the war*. New York: Praeger.

Levinson, H. (1979). *Television Series "Holocaust"* (Report [S] HL/127/H). Jerusalem: The Israel Institute of Applied Social Research (Hebrew).

Levy, S. (1980). *Partly-ordered social stratification* (Technical Report). Jerusalem: The Israel Institute of Applied Social Research.

Lewis, B. (1975). *History remembered, recovered, invented*. Princeton, NJ: Princeton University Press.

Lidz, T. (1948). Nightmares and combat neuroses. *Psychiatry, 8,* 193–213.

Lieberman, E. J. (1964). Threat and assurance in the conduct of conflict. In R. Fisher (Ed.), *International conflict and behavioral science*. New York: Basic Books.

Lieberman, M. (1982). The effect of social supports on response to stress. In L. Goldberger & S. Breznitz (Eds.), *Handbook of stress: Theoretical and clinical aspects*. New York: Free Press.

Liebman, C. (1978). Myth, tradition and values in Israeli society. *Midstream, 24,* 44–53.

Liebman, C., & Don-Yehiya, E. (1986). *Civil religion in Israel*. Berkeley, CA: University of California Press.

Lifton, R. J. (1973). *Home from the war*. New York: Simon and Schuster.

Lifton, R. J. (1978). Advocacy and corruption in the helping professions. In C. R. Figley (Ed.), *Stress disorders among Vietnam veterans*. New York: Brunner/Mazel.

Ludwig, A. O., & Ransom, S. W. (1947). A statistical followup of treatment of combat-induced psychiatric casualties. I and II. *Military Surgeon, 100,* 51–62, 169–175.

Lundberg, U. (1982). Psychological aspects of performance and adjustment to stress. In H. W. Krohne & L. Laux (Eds.), *Achievement, stress and anxiety*. Washington, DC: Hemisphere.

Lundberg, U., & Frankenhauser, M. (1978). Psychophysiological reactions to noise as modified by personal control over stimulus intensity. *Biological Psychology, 6,* 51–59.

Mackworth, N. H. (1946). Effects of heat on wireless operators hearing and recording Morse messages. *British Journal of Industrial Medicine, 3,* 143–158.

Marafiote, E. (1980). In T. Williams (Ed.), *Post traumatic stress disorders of the Vietnam veteran*. Washington, DC: Disabled American Veterans.

Marlowe, D. H. (1979). *Cohesion, anticipated breakdown, and endurance in battle: Considerations for severe and high intensity combat*. Unpublished manuscript. Division of Neuropsychiatry, Walter Reed Army Institute of Research, Washington, DC.

Marmullaku, R. (1975). *Albania and the Albanians*. London: Hurst.

Marrs, R. (1985). Why the pain won't stop and what the family can do to help. In W. E. Kelly (Ed.), *Post-traumatic stress disorder and the war veteran patient*. New York: Brunner/Mazel.

Marshall, N. S. (1976). The efficacy of vicarious extinction as a treatment for sex anxiety in women. *Dissertation Abstracts International, 37,* 2513.

Martens, R., & Landers, D. M. (1969). Coaction effects on a muscular endurance task. *Research Quarterly, 40,* 733–737.

Matlin, M. M., & Zajonc, R. B. (1968). Social facilitation of word associations. *Journal of Personality and Social Psychology, 10,* 435–460.

McEwen, C. A. (1980). Continuities in the study of total and nontotal institutions. *Annual Review of Sociology, 9,* 143–185.

McGrath, J. E. (Ed.) (1972). *Social and psychological factors in stress*. New York: Holt, Rinehart & Winston.

Mears, J. D., & Clearly, P. J. (1980). Anxiety as a factor in underwater performance. *Ergonomics, 23,* 549–557.

Meir, E., & Vardi, M. (1972). *Reliability and validity of ability tasks* (Technical Report). Jerusalem: Hadassah Institute (Hebrew).

Menninger, K. (1977). Regulatory devices of the ego under major stress. In A. Monat & R. S. La (Eds.), *Stress and coping*. New York: Columbia University Press.

Menninger, W. C. (1948). *Psychiatry in a troubled world: Yesterday's war and today's challenge.* New York: Macmillan.

Merari, A. (1983). *PLO: Core of world terror.* Jerusalem: Carta.

Merbaum, M., & Hefez, A. (1976). Some personality characteristics of soldiers exposed to extreme war stress. *Journal of Consulting and Clinical Psychology, 44,* 1–6.

Mewborn, C. R., & Rogers, R. W. (1979). Effects of threatening and reassuring components of fear appeals on physiological and verbal measures of emotion and attitudes. *Journal of Experimental Social Psychology, 15,* 242–253.

Mickolus, E. F. (1977). Statistical approaches to the study of terrorism. In Y. Alexander & M. Finger (Eds.), *Terrorism: Interdisciplinary perspectives.* New York: John Jay.

Milano, F. (1980). The politicization of the "Deer Hunters": Power and authority perspectives of the Vietnam veterans. In C. R. Figley & S. Leventman (Eds.), *Strangers at home: Vietnam veterans since the war.* New York: Praeger.

Milgram N. A. (1978). Psychological stress and adjustment in time of war and peace: The Israeli experience as presented in two conferences. *Israel Annals of Psychiatry, 16,* 327–338.

Milgram, N. A. (1982a). A general introduction. In C. D. Spielberger, & I. G. Sarason (Eds.), & N. A. Milgram (Guest Ed.), *Stress and anxiety,* Vol. 8. Washington, DC: Hemisphere.

Milgram, N. A. (1982b). The effect of war-related stress on Israeli children and youth. In L. Goldberger & S. Breznitz (Eds.), *Handbook of stress: Theoretical and clinical aspects.* New York: Free Press.

Milgram, N. A., Arad, R., Toubiana, Y., & Falach, H. (1984). *Followup of psychiatrically disturbed veterans: The results of treatment and their implications* (Final Report to Rehabilitation Branch of the Ministry of Defense). Tel-Aviv University, Department of Psychology. (Hebrew).

Milgram, N., & Toubiana, Y. (1985, September). *A major schoolbus disaster in Israel: Secondary and tertiary treatment.* Paper presented at Founding Meeting of the Society of Traumatic Stress Studies, Atlanta.

Milgram N. A., & Zucker, M. (1986). Stress-resistant factors and anxiety in a long-term stress situation. *Journal of Human Stress, 11,* 184–189.

Miller, J. G. (1953). *The development of experimental stress sensitive tests for prediction of performance in military tasks* (PRB Technical Report 1079). Washington, DC: Psychological Research Associates.

Miller, K., & Iscoe, I. (1963). The concept of crisis: Current status and mental health. *Human Organization, 22,* 195–201.

Mills, W. K., & Farrow, J. T. (1981). The transcendental meditation technique and acute experimental pain. *Psychosomatic Medicine, 43,* 157–164.

Minkowski, E. (1958). Findings in a case of schizophrenic depression. In R. May, E. Angel, & H. R. Ellenberger (Eds.), *Existence: A new dimension in psychiatry and psychology.* New York: Basic Books.

Moor, M. (1945). Recurrent nightmares: A simple procedure for psychotherapy. *Military Surgery, 97,* 282–285.

Moos, R. H. (1979). Sociol-ecological perspectives on health. In G. Stone, F. Cohen, & N. E. Adler (Eds.), *Health psychology.* San Francisco: Jossey-Bass.

Morgan, W. P. (1969). A pilot investigation of physical working capacity in depressed and non depressed psychiatric males. *Psychiatric Research Quarterly, 40,* 859–861.

Morley, J. W. (1974). *Japan's foreign policy 1868–1941.* New York: Columbia University Press.

Morrisette, J. O., Hornseth, J. P., & Shellar, K. (1975). Team organization and monitoring performance. *Human Factors, 17,* 296–300.

Moses, R., Bargal, D., & Calev, J. (1975). A rear unit for the treatment of combat reaction in the wake of the Yom Kippur War. *Psychiatry, 39,* 153–162.

Moskos, C. (1980). Surviving the war in Vietnam. In C. R. Figley & S. Leventman (Eds.), *Strangers at home: Vietnam veterans since the war.* New York: Praeger.

Mullins, W. S., & Glass, A. J. (1973). *Neuropsychiatry in World War II,* Vol. 2. *Overseas theaters*. Washington, DC: Medical Department, United States Army.

Nace, E. P., O'Brien, C. P., Mintz, J., Ream, N., and Meyers, A. L. (1978). Adjustment among Vietnam veteran drug users two years post-service. In C. R. Figley (Ed.), *Stress disorders among Vietnam veterans*. New York: Brunner/Mazel.

Nadler, A., & Mayseless, O. (1983). Recipient self-esteem and reaction to help. In J. D. Fisher, A. Nadler, & B. M. DePaulo (Eds.), *New directions in helping*, Vol. 1. New York: Academic Press.

Nehemkis, A. M., Charter, R. A., Stampp, M. S., & Gerber, K. E. (1982). Reattribution of cancer pain. *International Journal of Psychiatry in Medicine, 12*, 213–228.

Neumann, M. (1974). Combat syndrome and its treatment. *Harefuah, 87*, 566–568 (in Hebrew).

Nowicki, S. (1972). *Difficulty levels of locus of control scales*. Unpublished manuscript, Emory University, Atlanta.

Noy, S. (1978, June). *Stress and personality factors in the causation and prognosis of combat reaction*. Paper delivered at the Second International Conference on Psychological Stress and Adjustment in Time of War and Peace, Jerusalem.

Noy, S. (1979). *Division psychiatry in an intensive battle situation: Suggestions for improvement*. Paper presented at Walter Reed Institute of Army Research, Washington, DC.

Noy, S. (1980). *Israeli and American research in military psychiatry*. Paper delivered at the Annual Anglo-American Military Psychiatry Conference, London.

Noy, S. (1982). *Combat reactions: Etiology, overt appearance, prevention and treatment* (Report). Tel Hashomer, Israel: Israel Defense Forces, Medical Corps, Mental Health Department Research Branch (Hebrew).

Noy, S. (1984). *Battle reactions: Diagnosis, evaluation and treatment* (Report). Tel Hashomer, Israel: Israel Defense Forces, Medical Corps, Mental Health Department Research Branch (Hebrew).

Ochberg, F. M. (1982). A case study: Gerard Vaders. In F. M. Ochberg & D. A. Soskis (Eds.), *Victims of terrorism*. Boulder, CO: Westview.

Ochberg, F. M., & Soskis, D. A. (1982). Planning for the future: Means and ends. In F. M. Ochberg & D. A. Soskis (Eds.), *Victims of terrorism*. Boulder, CO: Westview.

Oxley, G. (1971). A life-model approach to change. *Social Casework, 52*, 627–633.

Panzarella, R. F., Mantell, D. M., & Bridenbaugh, R. H. (1978). Psychiatric symptoms, self-concepts, and Vietnam veterans. In C. R. Figley (Ed.), *Stress disorders among Vietnam veterans*. New York: Brunner/Mazel.

Parad, L. G., & Parad, H. J. (1968). A study of crisis-oriented planned short-term treatment: Part II. *Social Caseworker, 49*, 418–426.

Parson, E. R. (1985). Ethnicity and traumatic stress: The intersecting point in psychotherapy. In C. R. Figley (Ed.), *Trauma and its wake: The study and treatment of post-traumatic stress disorder*. New York: Brunner/Mazel.

Parsons, O. A., & Schneider, J. M. (1974). Locus of control in university students from Eastern and Western societies. *Journal of Consulting and Clinical Psychology, 42*, 456–461.

Pearlin, L. I., & Schooler, C. (1978). The structure of coping. *Journal of Health and Social Behavior, 19*, 2–22.

Pepitone, A. (1950). Motivational effects in social perceptions. *Human Relations, 3*, 57–76.

Phillips W. R. (1973). The conflict environment of nations: A study of conflict inputs in 1963. In J. Wikenfeld (Ed.), *Conflict behavior and linkage politics*. New York: David McKay.

Pilowsky, I., Basett, D. L., Begg, M. W., & Thomas, P. G. (1982). Childhood hospitalization and chronic intractable pain in adults: A controlled retrospective study. *International Journal of Psychiatry in Medicine, 12*, 75–84.

Plesset, D. (1946). Psychoneurotics in combat. *American Journal of Psychiatry, 103*, 87–90.

Poliakov, L. (1974). *The history of anti-semitism*, Vols. 1 and 2. London: Routledge & Kegan Paul.

Pollo, S., & Puto, A. (1981). *The history of Albania*. London: Routledge & Kegan Paul.

Pollock, J. C., White, D., & Gold, F. (1975). When soldiers return: Combat and political alienation among White Vietnam veterans. In D. Schwartz and S. Schwartz (Eds.), *New directions in political socialization*. New York: Free Press.

Ponomaryov, B., Gromyko, A., Uhvostov, N. (1969). *History of Soviet foreign policy 1917–1945*. Moscow: Progress Publishers.

Postman, L., & Brown, D. R. (1952). The perceptual consequences of success and failure. *Journal of Abnormal and Social Psychology, 47*, 213–221.

Poulton, E. C. (1970). *Environment and human efficiency*. Springfield, IL: Thomas.

Provins, K. A. (1966). Environmental heat, body temperature and behavior: A hypothesis. *Australian Journal of Psychology, 18*, 118–129.

Pruitt, D. (1965). Definition of the situation as a determinant of international action. In H. C. Kelman (Ed.), *International behavior*. New York: Holt, Rinehart and Winston.

Pruitt, D. G., & Snyder, R. C. (1963). *Theory and research on the causes of war*. Englewood Cliffs, NJ: Prentice-Hall.

Quarantelli, E. L., & Dynes, R. R. (1977). Response to social crises and disaster. *Annual Review of Sociology, 3*, 23–49.

Rabkin, J. G., & Struening, E. L. (1976). Life events, stress, and illness. *Science, 194*, 1013–1020.

Racek, W. D. (1985). An approach to treatment of post-traumatic stress disorder. In W. E. Kelly (Ed.), *Post-traumatic stress disorder and the war veteran patient*. New York: Brunner/Mazel.

Rapaport, L. (1970). Crisis intervention as a mode of brief treatment. In R. W. Roberts & R. H. Nee (Eds.), *Theories of social casework*. Chicago: University of Chicago Press.

Rogers, R. W. (1975). A projection motivation theory of fear appeals and attitude change. *Journal of Psychology, 91*, 93–114.

Rogers, R. W., & Mewborn, C. R. (1976). Fear appeals and attitude change: Effects of a threat's noxiousness, probability of occurrence, and the efficacy of coping responses. *Journal of Personality and Social Psychology, 34*, 54–61.

Rosenbaum, M. (1983). Learned resourcefulness as a behavioral repertoire for the self-regulation of internal events: Issues and speculations. In M. Rosenbaum, C. M. Franks, & Y. Jaffe (Eds.), *Perspectives on behavior therapy in the eighties*. New York: Springer.

Rosenheim, E., & Elizur, A. (1977). Group therapy for traumatic neurosis. *Current Psychiatric Therapies, 17*, 17–24.

Rotter, J. B. (1954). *Social learning and clinical psychology*. Englewood Cliffs, NJ: Prentice-Hall.

Rotter, J. B. (1966). Generalized expectancies for internal versus external control of reinforcement. *Psychological Monographs: General and Applied, 80* (Whole No. 609), 1–28.

Rotter, J. B. (1975). Some problems and misconceptions related to the construct of internal versus external control of reinforcement. *Journal of Consulting and Clinical Psychology, 43*, 56–67.

Ruch, L. O., Chandler, S. M., & Harter, R. A. (1980). Life change and rape impact. *Journal of Health and Social Behavior, 21*, 248–260.

Russell, J. A., & Ward, L. M. (1982). Environmental psychology. *Annual Review of Psychology, 33*, 651–688.

Salmon, T. (1919). The war neuroses and their lesson. *New York State Journal of Medicine, 59*, 933–944.

Salmon, T. W., & Fenton, N. (1929). The American expeditionary forces. In *Neuropsychiatry in the World War*, Vol. 10. Washington, DC: US Army Medical Corps.

Sanders, G. S., & Baron, R. S. (1975). The motivating effects of distraction on task performance. *Journal of Personality and Social Psychology, 32*, 956–963.

Sank, J., & Shaffer, C. S. (1979). Clinical findings while treating the Bnai Brith hostages. *Psychiatric Forum, 8*, 66–73.

Saul, L., Howard, R., & Denser, E. (1946). Desensitization of combat fatigue patients. *American Journal of Psychiatry, 102*, 476–478.

Sax, W. P. (1985). Establishing a post-traumatic stress disorder inpatient program. In W. E. Kelly (Ed.), *Post-traumatic stress disorder and the war veteran patient*. New York: Brunner/Mazel.

Schachter, S. (1959). *The psychology of affiliation*. Stanford, CA: Stanford University Press.

Schlegel, R. E. (1980). Application of a predictive core temperature model to heat stress experimentation. *Proceedings of the Human Factors Society 24th Annual Meeting*, 372–381.

Schmale, A. H., Morrow, G. R., Davis, A., Illies, E., McNally, J., Wright, G., & Crayton, J. K. (1982). Pretreatment behavioral profiles associated with subsequent psychosocial adjustment in radiation therapy patients: A prospective study. *International Journal of Psychiatry in Medicine, 12*, 187–195.

Schuetz, A. (1980). The homecomer. In C. R. Figley & S. Leventman (Eds.), *Strangers at home: Vietnam veterans since the war*. New York: Praeger.

Schwartz, R. A., & Schwartz, I. K. (1982). Psychiatric disorders associated with Crohn's disease. *International Journal of Psychiatry in Medicine, 12*, 67–73.

Scott, M. B., & Lyman, M. (1968). Accounts. *American Sociological Review, 33*, 46–62.

Scurfield, R. M. (1985). Post-trauma stress assessment and treatment: Overview and formulations. In C. R. Figley (Ed.), *Trauma and its wake: The study and treatment of post-traumatic stress disorder*. New York: Brunner/Mazel.

Segal, J. (1974). Long-term psychological and physical effects of the POW experience: A review of the literature. *Naval Health Research Center Publication* (No. 74-2). Washington, DC: Naval Health Research Center, Department of the Navy.

Seligman, M. E. P. (1975). *Helplessness: On depression, development and death*. San Francisco: Freeman.

Selye, H. (1975). Confusion and controversy in the stress field. *Journal of Human Stress, 1*, 37–44.

Shalit, B. (1978). *Perceptual organization and reduction questionnaire—Administration and scoring* (FOA Technical Report C 55021-H6). Stockholm: National Defence Research Institute.

Shalit, B. (1982). Perceived perceptual organization and coping with military demands. In C. D. Spielberger, & I. G. Sarason (Eds.), & N. A. Milgram (Guest Ed.), *Stress and anxiety*, Vol. 8. New York: Hemisphere.

Shalit, B., Carlstedt, L., Stahlberg Carlstedt, B., & Taljedal Shalit, I-L. (1982). *The theoretical formulation and construction of a checklist for perceived behavior for characterization of military groups* (FOA Technical Report C 55053-H3). Stockholm: National Defence Research Institute.

Shalit, B., Carlstedt, L., Stahlberg Carlstedt, B. & Taljedal Shalit, I-L. (1983, January). *Coherence of appraisal and coping: Parachute jumping effectiveness*. Paper presented at the Third International Conference on Psychological Stress and Adjustment in Time of War and Peace, Tel-Aviv.

Shapira, A. (1967). *The seventh day*. New York: Scribners.

Shapiro, M. J., & Bonham, G. M. (1973). Cognitive process and foreign policy decision-making. *International Studies Quarterly, 17*, 147–174.

Shatan, C. F. (1973). The grief of soldiers: Vietnam combat veterans self-help movement. *American Journal of Orthopsychiatry, 43*, 640–646.

Shatan, C. F. (1978). Stress disorders among Vietnam veterans: The emotional content of combat continues. In C. R. Figley (Ed.), *Stress disorders among Vietnam veterans*. New York: Brunner/Mazel.

Shatan, C. F. (1985). Have you hugged a Vietnam veteran today? The basic wound of catastrophic stress. In W. E. Kelly (Ed.), *Post-traumatic stress disorder and the war veteran patient*. New York: Brunner/Mazel.

Sheehan, D. V., O'Donnell, J., Fitzgerald, A., Hervig, L., & Ward, H. (1981). Psychosocial predictors of accident/error rates in nursing students. *International Journal of Psychiatry in Medicine, 11*, 125–136.

Shekelle, R. B., Raynor, W. J., Ostfeld, A. M., Garron, D. C., Bieliauskas, L. A., Liu, S. C., Maliza, C., & Oglesby, P. (1981). Psychological depression and 17-year risk of death from cancer. *Psychosomatic Medicine, 43*, 117–125.

Shweitzer, A. (1982, December 6). To Masada in the soul. *Haaretz* (Hebrew).

Shye, S. (1978). Partial order scalogram analysis. In S. Shye (Ed.), *Theory construction and data analysis in the behavioral sciences*. London: Jossey-Bass.

Silver, R. L., & Wortman, C. B. (1980). Coping with undesirable life events. In J. Garber & M. E. P. Seligman (Eds.), *Human helplessness*. New York: Academic Press.

Silver, S. M. (1985). Post-traumatic stress and the death imprint: The search for a new mythos. In W. E. Kelly (Ed.), *Post-traumatic stress disorder and the war veteran patient*. New York: Brunner/Mazel.

Silver, S. M., & Kelly, W. E. (1985). Hypnotherapy of post-traumatic stress disorder in combat veterans from World War II and Vietnam. In W. E. Kelly (Ed.), *Post-traumatic stress disorder and the war veteran patient*. New York: Brunner/Mazel.

Simmel, G. (1955). *Conflicts*. Glencoe, IL: Free Press.

Sledge, W. H., Boydstun, J. A., & Rabe, A. J. (1980). Self-concept changes related to war captivity. *Archives of General Psychiatry, 37*, 430–443.

Smith, C. (1980). Oral history as "therapy": Combatants' accounts of the Vietnam war. In C. R. Figley & S. Leventman (Eds.), *Strangers at home: Vietnam veterans since the war*. New York: Praeger.

Sohlberg, S. (1975). *Battle stress and fatigue during the Yom Kippur War*. Paper presented at the Mental Health Conference of the Israel Defense Force, Tel Hashomer.

Soskis, D. A. (1983). Behavioral scientists and law enforcement personnel: Working together on the problems of terrorism. *Behavioral Sciences and the Law, 1*, 47–58.

Soskis, D. A., & Ochberg, F. M. (1982). Concepts of terrorist victimization. In F. M. Ochberg & D. A. Soskis (Eds.), *Victims of terrorism*. Boulder, CO: Westview.

Spiegel, J. P. (1944). Psychiatric observations in the Tunisian campaign. *American Journal of Orthopsychiatry, 14*, 381–385.

Spielberger, C. D. (1966). Theory and research on anxiety. In C. D. Spielberger (Ed.), *Anxiety and behavior*. New York: Academic Press.

Spielberger, C. D. (1972). Anxiety as an emotional state. In C. D. Spielberger (Ed.), *Anxiety: Current trends in theory and research*, Vol. 1. New York: Academic Press.

Spielberger, C. D. (1980). *Preliminary manual for the state-trait anger scale (STAS)*. Tampa: University of South Florida, Human Resources Institute.

Spielberger, C. D. (1982). Stress and anxiety in sports. In E. Geron & A. Mashiach (Eds.), *Proceedings of the First National Conference on Psychology and Sociology of Sports and Physical Education*. Wingate Institute, Israel.

Spielberger, C. D., Gorsuch, R. L., & Lushene, R. E. (1970). *STAI Manual for the State Trait Anxiety Inventory*. Palo Alto, CA: Consulting Psychological Press.

Spielberger, C. D., & Sarason , I. G. (Eds.), & Milgram, N. A. (Guest Ed.) (1982). *Stress and anxiety*, Vol. 8. New York: Hemisphere.

Stagner, R. (1967). *Psychological aspects of international conflict*. Belmont, CA: Brooks/Cole.

Stanton, M. D. (1980). The hooked serviceman: Drug use in and after Vietnam. In C. R. Figley & S. Leventman (Eds.), *Strangers at home: Vietnam veterans since the war*. New York: Praeger.

Stayer, R., & Ellenhorn, L. (1975). Vietnam veterans: A study exploring adjustment patterns and attitudes. *Journal of Social Issues, 31*, 81–94.

Stein, H. (1978). Judaism and the group-fantasy of martyrdom: The psychodynamic paradox of survival through persecution. *Journal of Psychohistory, 6*, 151–210.

Steiner, M., & Neumann, M. (1978). Traumatic neurosis and social support in the Yom Kippur war returnees. *Military Medicine, 143*, 866–868.

Steiner, M., & Neumann, M. (1982). War neuroses and social support. In C. D. Spielberger, & I. G. Sarason (Eds.), & N. A. Milgram (Guest Ed.), *Stress and anxiety*, Vol. 8. Washington, DC: Hemisphere.

Stern, M., Bar-On, R., Barg, Y., Durst, N., Enoch, D., Haran, G., Hovel, S., Israeli, A., Reiter, M., & Toubiana, Y. (1983, January). *How to make treatment work when all odds predict failure*. Paper presented at Third International Conference on Psychological Stress and Adjustment in Time of War and Peace, Tel-Aviv.

Stockdale, J. B. (1978). The world of Epictetus: Reflections on survival and leadership. *The Atlantic, 241 (4)*, 98–106.

Stöfsel, W. (1982). Psychological sequelae in hostages and their aftercare. In D. Freedman,

L. C. Kolb, R. S. Lourie, H. Y. Meltzer, J. C. Nemiah, & J. Romano (Eds.), *The yearbook of psychiatry and applied mental health*. New York: Yearbook Medical Publishers.

Stouffer, S. A., Lumsdaine, A. A., Lumsdaine, M. H., Williams, R. M., Jr., Smith, M. B., Janis, I. L., Star, S. A., & Cottrell, L. S., Jr. (1949). *The American soldier: Combat and its aftermath*, Vol. 2. Princeton, NJ: Princeton University Press.

Strange, R. E., & Arthur, R. J. (1967). Hospital ship psychiatry in a war-zone. *American Journal of Psychiatry, 124*, 281–286.

Strentz, T. (1982). The Stockholm syndrome: Law enforcement policy and hostage behavior. In F. M. Ochberg & D. A. Soskis (Eds.), *Victims of terrorism*. Boulder, CO: Westview.

Stretch, J. J. (1967). Existentialism: A proposed philosophical orientation for social work. *Social Work, 12*, 997–102.

Stuart, R. B. (1980). *Helping couples change*. New York: Guilford.

Stuen, M. R., & Solberg, B. (1972). The Vietnam veteran characteristics and needs. In L. J. Sherman & E. M. Caffey (Eds.), *The Vietnam veteran in contemporary society*. Washington, DC: The Veterans Administration.

Sue, D. W. (1981). *Counseling the culturally different*. New York: John Wiley.

Sykes, G. M. (1970). *The society of captives: A study of maximum security prison*. Princeton, NJ: Princeton University Press.

Symonds, M. (1975). Victims of violence: Psychological effects and aftereffects. *American Journal of Psychoanalysis, 35*, 19–26.

Symonds, M. (1980). The "second injury" to victims. *Evaluation and Change (Special issue)*, 36–38. Minneapolis: Medical Research Foundation.

Tajfel, H. (1982). Social psychology of intergroup relations. *Annual Review of Psychology, 23*, 1–36.

Tanay, E. (1985). The Vietnam veteran-victim of war. In W. E. Kelly (Ed.), *Post-traumatic stress disorder and the war veteran patient*. New York: Brunner/Mazel.

Tausig, M. (1982). Measuring life events. *Journal of Health and Social Behavior, 23*, 52–64.

Teichman, Y. (1975). The stress of coping with the unknown regarding a significant family member. In I. G. Sarason & C. D. Spielberger (Eds.), *Stress and anxiety*, Vol. 2. New York: Wiley.

Tiryakian, E. A. (1980). Sociological dimensions of uprootedness. In G. V. Coelho & P. I. Ahmed (Eds.), *Uprooting and development: Dilemma of coping with modernization*. New York: Plenum Press.

Toubiana, Y., Milgram, N. A., & Falach, H. (1983, January). *The adjustment of Yamit settlers during and after the uprooting process*. Paper given at Third International Conference on Psychological Stress and Adjustment in Time of War and Peace, Tel-Aviv.

Trieschman, A. E., Whittaker, J., & Brendfro, J. K. (1969). *The other 23 hours: Child-care with emotionally disturbed children in a therapeutic milieu*. Chicago: Aldine.

Tsunoda, R., de Barry, T., & Kenne, D. (1958). *Sources of Japanese tradition*. New York: Columbia University Press.

Turner, V. (1974). *Dramas, fields and metaphors*. Ithaca, NY: Cornell University Press.

Ursano, R. J., Boydstun, J. A., & Wheatley, R. D. (1981). Psychiatric illness in U.S. Air Force Vietnam prisoners of war: A five year followup. *American Journal of Psychiatry, 138*, 310–314.

Ursin, H., Baade, A., & Levine, S. (1978). *Psychobiology of stress: A study of coping men*. New York: Academic Press.

Vachon, M. L., Lyall, W. A., Rogers, J., Cochrane, J., & Freeman, S. J. (1982). The effectiveness of psychosocial support during post surgical treatment of breast cancer. *International Journal of Psychiatry in Medicine, 11*, 365–372.

Vaernes, R. J. (1982). The Defence Mechanism Test predicts inadequate performance under stress. *Scandinavian Journal of Psychology, 23*, 37–43.

Vaihinger, H. (1924). *The philosophy of as-if*. New York: Scribners.

Vanfossen, B. L. (1981). Sex differences in the mental health effects of spouse support and equity. *Journal of Health and Social Support, 22,* 130–143.

Van Gennep, A. (1908). *Les rites de passage.* Paris: A. Picard & J. Picard.

Viteles, H. S., & Smith, K. R. (1946). An experimental investigation of the effects of change in atmospheric conditions and noise upon performance. *Heating, Piping and Air Conditioning, 18,* 107–112.

Walker, J. I., & Cavenar, J. O. (1982). Vietnam veterans: Their problems continue. *Journal of Nervous and Mental Disease, 170,* 174–180.

Walker, J. I., & Nash, J. L. (1981). Group therapy in the treatment of Vietnam combat veterans. *International Journal of Group Psychotherapy, 31,* 379–389.

Wallace, E. (1971). On the totality of total institutions. In E. Wallace (Ed.), *Total institutions.* Chicago: Aldine.

Waller, W. (1980). The victors and the vanquished, In C. R. Figley & S. Leventman (Eds.), *Strangers at home: Vietnam veterans since the war.* New York: Praeger (Abstracted from *The veteran comes back.* New York: Dryden, 1944, pp. 93–110, 180–182).

Warth, R. D. (1963). *Soviet Russia in world politics.* New York: Twayne Publishers.

Weisman, G. (1982). Wartime guilt feelings and their precursors. In C. D. Spielberger, & I. G. Sarason (Eds.), & N. A. Milgram (Guest Ed.), *Stress and anxiety,* Vol. 8. Washington, DC: Hemisphere.

Weisz, J. R., Rothbaum, F. M., & Blackburn, T. C. (1984a). Standing out and standing in: The psychology of control in America and Japan. *American Psychologist, 39,* 955–969.

Weisz, J. R., Rothbaum, F. M., & Blackburn, T. C. (1984b). Swapping recipes for control. *American Psychologist, 39,* 974–975.

Weltman, G., & Egstrom, G. H. (1967). Perceptual narrowing in novice divers. *Human Factors, 8,* 599–606.

Wikler, N. (1980). Hidden injuries of war. In C. R. Figley & S. Leventman (Eds.), *Strangers at home: Vietnam veterans since the war.* New York: Praeger.

Williams, T. (1980). *Posttraumatic stress disorders of the Vietnam Veteran.* Washington, DC: Disabled American Veterans.

Wilson, J. P. (1979). *Identity and crisis: The Vietnam veterans in transition.* Cincinnati: Disabled American Veterans.

Wilson, J. P. (1980). Conflict, stress and growth: The effects of war on psychosocial development among Vietnam veterans. In C. R. Figley & S. Leventman (Eds.), *Strangers at home: Vietnam veterans since the war.* New York: Praeger.

Winefield, H., & Martin, C. J. (1981). Measurement and prediction of recovery after myocardial infarction. *International Journal of Psychiatry in Medicine, 11,* 145–154.

Wing, J. F. (1965). Upper thermal tolerance limits for unimpaired mental performance. *Aerospace Medicine, 36,* 960–964.

Wolcott, D. L., Wellisch, D. K., Robertson, C. R., & Arthur, R. J. (1981). Serum gastrin and the family environment in duodenal ulcer disease. *Psychosomatic Medicine, 43,* 501–507.

Wolins, M., & Wozner, Y. (1982). *Revitalizing residential settings.* San Francisco: Jossey-Bass.

Woods, G. C., Sherwood, T. A., & Thompson, R. M. (1985). Management and implementation of nursing care for the post-traumatic stress disorder patient. In W. E. Kelly (Ed.), *Post-traumatic stress disorder and the war veteran patient.* New York: Brunner/Mazel.

Worthington, E. R. (1977). The Vietnam-era veteran, anomie and adjustment. *Military Medicine, 142,* 79–89.

Wrightsman, L. F. (1960). Effect of waiting with others on changes in level of felt anxiety. *Journal of Abnormal and Social Psychology, 61,* 216–222.

Yadin, Y. (1966). *Masada: Herod's fortress and the Zealots' last stand.* New York: Random House.

Yanagida, E. H., Streltzer, J., & Siemsen, A. (1981). Denial in dialysis patients: Relationship to compliance and other variables. *Psychosomatic Medicine, 43,* 271–280.

Zajonc, R. B. (1965). Social facilitation. *Science, 149,* 269–274.

Zander, A. F. (1975). Motivation and performance of sports groups. In D. M. Landers (Ed.), *Psychology of sport and motor behavior II*. University Park: The Pennsylvania State University Press.

Zimmerman, M. K., & Hartley, W. S. (1982). High blood pressure among employed women: A multi-factor discriminant analysis. *Journal of Health and Social Behavior, 23*, 205–220.

Author Index

Abraham, K., 155
Ackerman, S.H., 58
Acosta, F.X., 343
Adler, T.S., 104
Adorno, T.W., 43
Ahmed, P.I., 275, 278
Ajzen, I., 36, 44, 47, 51
Aldwin,, C., 298
Allerton, W.S., 130, 329
Allport, F.H., 207
Allport, G.W., 43, 216
Alsop, S., 33, 42
Alter, R., 33
Anderson,, C.A., 206
Aneshensel, C.S., 273
Antonovsky, A., 7, 8, 52, 53, 62, 65, 298
Apple, J. W., 73, 78, 82, 89
Arad, R., 90, 341
Archer, R.P., 300
Archibald, H.C., 85
Argyris, C., 31
Arieli, A., 104, 155
Arieti, S., 298
Arthur, R.J., 59, 130
Artiss, K., 110, 119
Asphormas, Y., 55
Atkinson, M., 206
Ayalon, O., 258, 260, 270

Baade, E., 214, 230
Baddeley, A.D., 214
Backer-Johnsen, T., 230
Baker, S.L., 130
Baldwin, M.W., 36
Ballachey, E.L., 36
Bandura, A., xxxiv, 77
Barber, J., 37
Bard, M., 258, 268
Barg, Y., 118
Bargal, D., 347
Bar-On, O., 168, 197
Bar-On, R., 118
Bar-Tal, D., 6, 7
Baron, R.A., 46

Baron, R.S., 208
Bartemeier, L., 329
Baruch, E., 55, 73, 82
Basett, D.L., 59
Beebe, G.W., 73, 78, 82, 89
Begg, M.W., 59
Bell, P.A., 206, 208, 213
Benfari, R.C., 63
Benyakar, M., 155
Berger, B., 218
Berger, P.L., 218
Bergin, A.E., 25
Bergum, B.O., 207
Berkowitz, L., 46
Bernstein, J., 7, 8
Bernucci, R.J., 329
Bholchrain, M., 304, 309
Bialek, H.M., 190
Bieliauskas, L.A., 57
Biersner, R.J., 214
Bitzer, R., 337
Bixler, E.O., 61
Black, G.M., 63
Blackburn, T.C., xxx
Blank, A.S., 10
Blank, T.O., 207
Blau, P.M., 46
Bloch, H.S., 327
Blumenthal, J.A., 63
Bolz, F.A., 257
Bond, C.F., 207
Bonham, G.M., 36
Borus, J.F., 336
Bosel, R., 203
Bourne, P.C., 130, 329
Boyanowski, E.O., 206
Boydstun, J.A., 258, 267
Brecher, M., 42
Brehm, J.W., 252
Brende, J.O., 343
Brendfro, J.K., 140
Breznitz, S., 29, 308, 313, 319
Brickman, P., 4, 18
Bridenbaugh, R.H., 336

Bronfenbrenner, U., 42
Brown, D., 37
Brown, D.R., 48
Brown, G.W., 304, 309, 317, 318
Browning, M.D., 214
Brull, F., 166
Bursill, A.E., 195
Butcher, J.M., 92, 320, 327

Calev, J., 347
Calsyn, R.J., 320
Calvert-Boyanowsky, J., 206
Camacho, P., 334, 336
Cantril, H., 48, 279, 280
Caplan, G., 22, 28, 257, 304
Caplan, R.D., 273, 299, 318
Carlsmith, J.M., 206
Carlstedt, L., 234
Carr, R.A., 85
Carson, R.C., 321, 327
Cavenar, J.O., 332
Cervone, J.C., 208, 213
Chamberlin, K., 61
Chandler, S.M., 320
Chapman, A.J., 207
Charter, R.A., 59
Chesney, A.P., 57
Chesney, M.A., 63
Clarke, J.H., 63
Clearly, P.J., 214
Coates, D., 4, 18
Cobb, J., 304
Cochrane, J., 61
Coelho, G.V., 275, 278
Cohen, J., 309
Cohen, M.I., 58
Cohen, P., 309
Cohn, E., 4, 18
Coleman, J.C., 320, 327
Collins, J.N., 46
Cooperman, H., 78
Copeland, M.G., 206
Coser, L.A., 44, 45, 48
Cottrell, L.S., 74, 104, 143
Cottrell, N.B., 207, 208
Courington, S., 65, 298
Covi, L., 279, 281
Coyne, J.C., 298
Crayton, J.K., 60
Crowley, J.B., 38
Crowne, D.P., 188
Crutchfield, R.S., 36
Cunningham, M.R., 206

Curreton, T.K., 168

Dadson, L.C., 168
Danieli, Y., 337
Dasberg, H., 55, 149, 155
Datel, W.E., 73
Davis, A., 60
Davis, J.E., 168
Dearborn, D.C., 48
DeBacker, G., 57
de Rivera, J.H., 36
de Barry, T., 38
Dembert, M.L., 214
Denser, E., 142
Derogatis, L.R., 279, 281
Dirks, J.F., 58
Dixon, D.J., 206
Dodson, M., 314, 317, 318
Dohrenwend, B.P., 314, 317, 318
Dohrenwend, B.S., 314, 317, 318
Don-Yehiya, E., 42
Dotan, R., 197
Dowty, N., 52
Dramaix, M., 57
Duerfeldt, P.H., 183
Durst, N., 118
Duval, S., 208, 215
Dynes, R.R., 85

Eaker, E.D., 63
Edwards, J., 183
Egendorf, A., 155, 337
Egstrom, G.H., 195
Eitinger, L., 85
Elizur, A., 148
Ellenberger, H.R., 28, 29
Ellenhorn, L., 85
Ellertsen, B., 230
Endler, N.S., 183
Enoch, D., 118
Enzie, R.F., 85
Epley, S.W., 215
Epstein, S., 230
Epstein, Y., 206
Eshel, Y., 29
Evans, G.W., 214
Evans, L., 343

Falach, H., 90, 275, 341
Farrow, J.T., 63
Fenton, N., 106, 322
Fenz, W.W., 230
Ferenczi, S., 155

Feshbach, S., 251
Festinger, L., 287
Figley, C.R., 104, 155, 294, 320, 327, 331, 332, 334, 335, 337
Fischer, L., 38
Fitzgerald, A., 62
Flavius, J., 34
Fly, C.L., 258
Folkman, S., 181, 232, 296, 300, 318, 324
Frankl, V.E., xxv, 180, 216, 219, 267
Franklin,, B., 39
Frankenhauser, M., 197
Freeman, S.J., 61
Frenkel-Brunswik, E., 43, 44
Frey-Wouters, E., 56, 335
Friedland, N., 252
Freud, S., 155
Frye, J.S., 332
Fuller, R.B., 333, 337, 343

Gaduto, D., 206
Gal, R., 16
Gallops, M.S., 56, 335
Gange, J.J., 207, 208, 215
Gardner, R., 62
Garron, D.C., 57
Gary, H.E., 57
Gasko, O., 206
Gay, M., 24
Geen, R.G., 207, 208, 215
Gentry, W.D., 57
Gerber, K.E., 59
George, A., 275
Geron, E., 209, 215
Gibbs, J.J, 119
Glass, A.J., 73, 78, 92, 104, 110, 111, 119, 130, 329
Goffman, E., 82, 140, 217, 218, 228
Golan, N., 27, 28
Gold, F., 85
Goldstein, K., xxxiv
Goodacre, D.M., 143
Gorsuch, R.L., 309
Graves, P.L., 58
Greenberg, O., 219, 227
Greene, R.L., 94
Greenfeld, H., 55, 73, 82
Grinker, R.R., 78, 104, 148, 155
Gromyko, A., 38
Grosser, P.E., 41
Gur, P., 92
Guttman, L., 233, 299

Haas, A.P., 15, 332
Hacker, F.H., 257
Halcomb, C.G., 206
Haley, S.A., 292, 335, 337, 343
Hall, J.S., 210
Hall, R.P., 57
Halperin, A., 41
Halse, K., 230
Hamburg, B.A., 61
Hancock, P.A., 206
Hansell, S., 61
Harris, T., 304, 309
Haran, G., 118
Harburg, E., 57
Harter, R.A., 320
Hartley, W.S., 56
Hastorf, A.H., 48
Hausman, W., 329
Hazan, H., 217, 218, 219, 227, 228
Healey, E.S., 61
Heaton, R.C., 193
Hefez, A., 92
Heider, F., 46
Hendin, H., 15, 332
Herman, S., 63
Hervig, L., 62
Herz, M.I., 132
Herzog, C., 295, 325
Hillery, J.M., 207
Hillman, R.G., 258
Hobfoll, S.E., 301, 303, 304, 305, 307, 309, 318, 320
Hockey, G.R.J., 195
Holmes, D.R., 63
Holsti, O.R., 36
Hornick, C.E., 143
Hornseth, J.P., 207
Hornstein, H.A., 44
Horowitz, M., 166, 313
Horshovsky, R., 292
Houghton, W., 15
Hovel, S., 118
Howard, R., 142
Howard, S., 155, 343
Hudgens, R.W., 317
Hunt, P.J., 207
Hunter, E., 179

Illies, E., 60
Inbar, O., 168, 197, 203, 215
Inoff, G.E., 61
Iscoe, I., 320
Israel, A., 118

Jaccard, J.J., 209
Jacobson, N.S., 120
Jacobson, S., 258
Jaffe, D.T., 132
Jaffe, Y., 54
Janis, I.L., xxviii, xxx, 74, 104, 143, 251
Janoff-Bulman, R., 298
Jenkins, B.M., 243, 257
Jervis, R., 36
Johnson, R.W., 37
Jones, A., 143
Jones, E., 155

Kahn, S., 65
Kales, A., 61
Kaplan, A., 33
Kaplan, D.M., 320
Kardiner, A., 92, 130
Karuza, J., 4, 18
Kedar, B., 33
Kellner, H., 218
Kelly, J.G., 301
Kelly, W.E., 320, 332, 343, 347
Kennan, G.F., 42, 47
Kenne, D., 38
Keren, A.B., 55
Keren, G., 206
Kerle, R.H., 190
Kern, R.P., 184
Kidder, L., 4, 18
Kipper, D.A., 142
Kittel, F., 57
Klein, E., 347
Kobassa, S.C., 65, 298, 303
Kormos, H.R., 335
Korman, N., 343
Kornitzer, M., 57
Kragh, U., 231
Krystal, H., 41
Krech, D., 36
Kruglanski, A.W., xxxiv, 36, 44, 47, 51
Kubie, L., 329
Kuhn, T.S., 26
Kupperman, R.H., 243
Kutash, I.L., 275

Lamm, H., 307
Landers, D.M., 209
Langsley, D.J., 320
Laufer, R.S., 56, 335
Laughlin, P.R., 209
Launier, R., 183
Lazarus, R.S., xxv, 15, 16, 181, 183, 231,
    232, 296, 297, 298, 300, 301, 308, 318,
    319, 324

Lefcourt, H.M., 193, 303
Legum, C., 37
Legum,, M., 37
Lehman, E.C., 183
Lehr, D.J., 207
Leiberman, J.R., 301, 303
Lenin, V.I., 38, 39, 48, 50
Lerner, M.J., xxxiv, 268, 273
Lerner, Y., 55
Levav, I., 55, 73, 82
Leventhal, H., 251
Leventman, S., 332, 334, 335, 337
Levine, S., 214, 230
Levinson, D.J., 43
Levinson, H., 42
Levy, S., 235, 299
Lewis, B., 33, 34
Lidz, T., 155
Lieberman, E.J., 46, 49
Lieberman, M., 279, 281, 324, 349
Liebman, C., 41, 42, 45
Lifton, R.J., 155, 292
Lipman, R.S., 279, 281
Liu, S.C., 57
London, P., 301, 304, 307, 309
Long, D.M., 85
Loomins, R.J., 208, 213
Ludwig, A.O., 329
Lumsdaine, A.A., 74, 104, 143
Lumsdaine, M.H., 74, 104, 143
Lundberg, U., 197
Lushene, R.E., 309
Lyall, W.A., 61
Lyman, M., 29

Mackworth, N.H., 205
MacPherson, B.V., 63
Maddi, S.R., 65, 298
Malizza, C., 57
Manaker, S., 58
Mann, L., xxx
Mantell, D.M., 336
Maoz, B., 52
Marafiote, E., 142
Marlowe, D.A., 188
Marlowe, D.H., 73, 104, 120, 123, 325, 326
Marmullaku, R., 37
Marrs, R., 15
Marshall, N.S., 120
Martens, R., 209
Martin, C.J., 58
Martin, R.A., 303
Matlin, M.M., 207
Mayseless, O., 307

McEwen, C.A., 217
McGrath, J.E., 183, 203, 296, 301, 318
McIntyre, K., 63
McNally, J., 60
Mears, J.D., 214
Meir, E., 211
Menninger, K., 166, 329
Menninger, W.C., 104
Merari, A., 244
Merbaum, M., 92
Mester, R., 55
Meyers, A.L., 335
Mewborn, C.R., 251
Mickolus, E.F., 243
Milano, F., 337
Milgram, N., xxiii, 3, 4, 5, 9, 90, 275, 319, 321, 324, 341
Miller, C., 85
Miller, J.G., 183
Miller, K., 320
Mills, W.K., 63
Minkowski, E., 28
Mintz, J., 335
Moisseiv, J., 206
Monroe, L.J., 61
Montgomery, F.A., 85
Morgan, W.P., 168
Morley, J.W., 38
Moor, M., 142
Moos, R.H., 65
Morrisette, J.O., 207
Morrow, G.R., 60
Moses, R., 347
Moskos, C., 335
Mullens, W.R., 168
Mullins, W.S., 73, 78, 104, 110, 111, 119, 130
Munoz, R., 301
Myers, D.G., 307

Nace, E.P., 335
Nadler, A., 307
Nash, J.L., 148
Nehemkis, A.M., 59
Neumann, M., 55, 120, 123
Nowicki, S., 193
Noy, S., 73, 74, 92, 104, 119, 143, 155

O'Brien, C.P., 335
Ochberg, F.M., 238, 258, 267, 270
Ockene, J., 63
O'Donnell, J., 62
Oglesby, P., 57
Orr, E., 307

Ostfeld, A.M., 57
Otto, J., 203
Oxley, G., 31

Panzarella, R.F., 336
Parad, H.G., 320
Parad, L.G., 320
Parson, E.R., 343
Parsons, O.A., 306
Pearlin, L.I., 301, 304, 309
Pepitone, A., 48
Phillips, W.R., 46
Pilowsky, I., 59
Plesset, D., 155
Poliakov, L., 41
Pollo, S., 37, 47
Pollock, J.C., 85
Potte, J.W., 210
Poulton, E.C., 206
Ponomaryov, B., 38
Postman, L., 48
Pribyl, J.F., 320
Provins, K.A., 206
Pruitt, D., 43, 49
Puccetti, M.C., 65, 298, 303
Puto, A., 37, 47

Quarantelli, E.L., 85

Rabe, A.J., 267
Rabinowitz, V.C., 4, 18
Rabkin, J.G., 323
Racek, W.D., 337, 343, 344
Ransom, S.W., 329
Rapaport, L., 27
Raynor, W.J., 57
Ream, N., 335
Reeves, J., 206
Reiter, M., 118
Rickles, K., 279, 281
Riecken, H.W., 287
Rioch, D.M., 329
Rittle, R.H., 207
Robertson, C.R., 59
Robinson, S.K., 58
Rogers, J., 61
Rogers, R.W., 251
Romano, J., 329
Rosenbaum, M., xxxiv
Rosenfeld, H., 54
Rosenheim, E., 148
Rothbaum, F.M., xxx
Rotter, J.B., 178, 184
Ruch, L.O., 320

Russell, J.A., 206

Salmon, T., xxxiv, 20, 97, 106, 110, 130,
    320, 322
Sanders, G.S., 208
Sanford, R.N., 43
Sangrey, D., 258, 268
Sank, J., 258
Sarason, I.G., xxiii
Saul, L., 142
Sawyer, R.N., 85
Sax, W.F., 337, 343, 344
Schachter, S., 215, 287
Schaefer, C., 232
Scheffer, G., 292
Schlegel, R.E., 205
Schmale, A.H., 60
Schneider, J.M., 306
Schooler, C., 301, 304, 309
Schraa, J.C., 58
Schuetz, A., 336
Schwartz, I.K., 60
Schwartz, M.F., 15
Schwartz, R.A., 60
Scott, M.B., 29
Scurfield, R.M., 343
Segal, J., 179, 258
Selah, W.E., 303
Seligman, M.E.P., xxxiv, 11
Sells, S., 143
Selye, H., 65
Shaffer, C.S., 258
Shalit, B., 232, 233, 234
Shapira, A., 155
Shapiro, M.J., 36
Shatan, C.F., 15, 155, 334
Shaver, P., 207
Sheehan, D.V., 62
Shekelle, R.B., 57
Shellar, K., 207
Sherwood, T.A., 337
Shrout, P.E., 314, 317, 318
Shweitzer, A., 33
Shye, S., 235
Siemsen, A., 63
Silver, R.L., 22, 65
Silver, S.M., 15, 336, 343, 347
Simmel, E., 155
Simmel, G., 45
Simon, H.A., 48
Singer, P., 15
Sledge, W.H., 267
Smith, C., 336
Smith, K.R., 205

Smith, M.B., 74, 104, 143
Snowden, L.R., 301
Snyder, R.C., 49
Sohlberg, S., 104
Solberg, B., 85
Soldatos, C.R., 61
Solomon, G.F., 313
Soskis, D.A., 238, 258, 261, 267, 270
Southerly, W.T., 331
Spiegel, J.P., 78, 104, 111, 120, 148, 155
Spielberger, C.D., xxxiii, 205, 215, 280,
    309
Stagner, R., 36
Staff, I., 207
Stahlberg-Carlstedt, B., 234
Stampp, M.S., 59
Stanton, M.D., 335
Star, S.A., 74, 104, 143
Stayer, R., 85
Stein, H., 41
Steiner, M., 55, 120, 123
Stenhammer, P.E., 230
Stern, M., 118
Stockdale, J.B., 267
Stockton, R.A., 332
Stofsel, W., 258
Stone, J.D., 273
Stouffer, S., 74, 104, 143
Strange, R.E., 130
Streltzer, J., 63
Strentz, T., 258, 267, 271
Stretch, J.J., 31
Struening, E.L., 323
Stuart, R.B., 141
Stuen, M.R., 85
Sue, D.W., 343
Sunukjian, H., 320
Symonds, M., 258, 268
Sweeney, V.C., 119
Sykes, G.M., 219

Tajfel, H., 254
Taljedal-Shalit, I-L., 234
Tanay, E., 335, 336
Tausig, M., 61
Teichman, Y., 292
Thomas, C.B., 58
Thomas, P.G., 59
Thompson, R.M., 337
Tiryakian, E.A., 275
Titus, L.J., 207
Towson, R., 36
Toubiana, Y., 90, 118, 275, 321, 341
Trieschman, A.E., 140

Tsunoda, R., 38
Tuddenham, R.D., 85
Turner, V., 29

Uhlenhuth, E.H., 279, 281
Uhvostov, N., 38
Ursano, R.J., 258
Ursin, H., 214, 230

Vachon, M.L., 61
Vaernes, R.J., 230
Vaihinger, H., 140
Vanfossen, B.L., 309
Van Gennep, A., 31
Vardi, M., 211
Viteles, H.S., 205
Vollmer, F., 230

Wack, D.L., 207
Walfisch, S., 304, 305, 309, 318, 320
Walker, J.I., 148, 332
Wallace, E., 217
Wallen, V., 15
Waller, W., 331, 335
Walters, R.H., xxxiv
Ward, H., 62
Ward, L.M., 206
Warth, R.D., 42
Weingarten, G., 168
Weisman, G., 155
Weisz, J.R., xxx
Wellisch, D.K., 59

Weltman, G., 195
Wheatley, R.D., 258
White, D., 85
Whitehorn, J., 329
Whittaker, J., 140
Wijsenbeek, H., 52
Wicklund, R.A., 208, 215
Wikler, N., 334
Williams, R.M., 74, 104, 143
Williams, T., 155
Wilson, J.P., 336
Winefield, H., 58
Wing, J.F., 206
Wolcott, D.L., 59
Wolins, M., 140, 174
Woods, G.C., 337
Worthington, E.R., 85
Wortman, C.B., 22, 65
Wozner, Y., 140, 174
Wright, G., 60
Wrightsman, L.F., 215

Yachin, S., 206
Yadin, Y., 34
Yamamoto, J., 343
Yanagida, E.H., 63
Yuan, Y.T., 275, 278

Zajonc, R.B., 207, 208
Zander, A.F., 198
Zimmerman, M.K., 56
Zucker, M., 324

Subject Index

Anxiety, 93, 105, 190, 214, 239, 244, 280, 306

Attribution, xxxiv, 4, 15, 29

Beliefs
central, 6, 32
effects of, 6, 46, 297
origins of, 6, 40
recommendations, 50
threat to, xxviii, 4, 12

Cognitive appraisal, 3, 181, 231, 296, 318
Control
effectiveness, 16
over external events and self, 11, 62, 219
primary and secondary, xxx
threat to, xxviii, 4
Coping
and helping models, 4, 16
effectiveness of, 15
palliation and problem-solving, xxix, 15, 261
primary and secondary, xxx
Countertransference, 17, 113, 121, 165, 337
Crisis
intervention, 5, 30, 257, 291, 321
theory, 5, 26, 320

Drug use, 154, 170, 335, 351

Ecological congruence, 242, 301
Expectancy, xxxiv, 28, 43, 116, 119, 177, 184, 322

Generalizations from Israeli data, xxxv,

23, 50, 68, 76, 82, 89, 95, 97, 107, 113, 127, 154, 166, 171, 204, 227, 238, 255, 270, 292, 306, 347
Grief, 21
Group psychotherapy, 120, 142, 147

Individual psychotherapy, 148, 155

Performance under stress
extreme exertion, 178, 197, 325
heat, 178, 205
situational variables, 192, 203, 212, 325
solitary confinement, 179, 216
threat to life and limb, 177, 183, 325
Personal resources, xxix, 79, 89, 91, 115, 131, 192, 212, 241, 296, 304, 323
Post-traumatic combat stress
forward echelon treatment, xxxiv, 97, 99, 106, 110, 117, 328
efficacy, 97, 111, 166
followup, 55, 70, 84, 100, 114, 124, 134, 330
premorbid adjustment, 71, 79, 85, 91, 130, 161
reactions and syndromes, xxxiv, 5, 17, 54, 67, 78, 327
rear echelon treatment, 71, 91, 99, 129, 136, 142, 147, 155, 168, 172, 342
efficacy, 111, 134, 330
followup, 100, 134, 341
recommendations, 345
situational factors, 69, 74, 85, 91, 115, 120
symptomatology, 85, 98, 107, 130
Post-traumatic non-combat stress, 5, 18, 241, 268, 281, 294, 321
Prisoners of war, xxxiii 179, 216

The first page reference for a given subject in a given chapter or introduction is cited in this index. The reader will find additional references to the subject in subsequent pages of the chapter in many instances.

Psychological warfare, 4, 12, 243

Sex differences, 242, 313
Social supports, 76, 241, 271, 288, 298, 323
Stress research
  methodology, 313, 317
  pathogenic versus salutogenic model, 7,
    52

Terrorism
  effectiveness of, 251, 299
  rationale, xxxi, 238, 243
  recommendations, xxxii
  societal impact, xxxi, 238, 245, 299
  treatment, 268
  victim symptomatology, 180, 238, 257

Uprooting and consequences, 241, 275
  recommendations, 291

Values and stress reactions, xxvii, 24, 219,
  303, 348

War
  Korean War, 17, 179, 329
  Lebanon War, 17, 40, 79, 84, 89, 98,
    103, 117, 129, 242, 308, 338
  Six-Day War, 54, 85, 104, 276, 299
  Vietnam War, xxvi, 23, 166, 179, 294,
    316, 329
  World War I, xxxiv, 97, 104, 110, 129,
    166
  World War II, 17, 20, 73, 89, 97, 104,
    110, 130, 166, 325
  Yom Kippur War, 17, 39, 54, 84, 89, 92,
    97, 108
War stress
  consensus, 22
  context, xxv
  moral issues, 14, 348
  research
    paucity of research, xxiv
    recommendations, xxxvi
    topics, xxxiii
  stressors, xxvi, 3, 10, 75, 319